P9-EDI-274

LEGO® MINIFIGURE
A Visual History
NEW EDITION

Written by
Simon Hugo and Gregory Farshtey with Daniel Lipkowitz

Updated edition

Senior Editor Ruth Amos
Senior Designers Anna Formanek, Lisa Sodeau
Editorial Assistant Nicole Reynolds
Additional Editors Tori Kosara, Julia March,
Helen Murray, Rosie Peet
Americanization Editor Kayla Dugger
Jacket Designer James McKeag
Production Editor Marc Staples
Senior Production Controller Lloyd Robertson
Managing Editor Paula Regan
Managing Art Editor Jo Connor
Publisher Julie Ferris
Art Director Lisa Lanzarini
Publishing Director Mark Searle

Additional photography Gary Ombler
Index Vanessa Bird

Original edition

Senior Editor Helen Murray
Senior Designer Lisa Sodeau
Project Art Editor Owen Bennett
Pre-Production Producer Siu Yin Chan
Producer Louise Daly
Managing Editor Elizabeth Dowsett
Design Manager Nathan Martin
Publishing Manager Julie Ferris
Art Director Ron Stobbart
Publishing Director Simon Beecroft

Consultant Giles Kemp
Additional writing Catherine Saunders,
Jo Casey, Julia March, Lindsay Kent
Additional photography Gary Ombler,
Thomas Baunsgaard Pedersen, Tim Trøjborg

This American Edition, 2020
First American Edition, 2013
Published in the United States by DK Publishing
1450 Broadway, Suite 801, New York, New York 10018

Page design copyright © 2013, 2020 Dorling Kindersley Limited
DK, a Division of Penguin Random House LLC
20 21 22 23 24 10 9 8 7 6 5 4 3
006–316423–Oct/2020

LEGO, the LEGO logo, the Minifigure, the Brick and Knob configurations, the DUPLO,
BELVILLE, EXO-FORCE, FRIENDS, and HIDDEN SIDE logos, BIONICLE, MINDSTORMS,
LEGENDS OF CHIMA, NINJAGO, NEXO KNIGHTS, and LEGOLAND are trademarks
and/or copyrights of the LEGO Group. ©2013, 2020 The LEGO Group. All rights reserved.

Manufactured by Dorling Kindersley, One Embassy Gardens, 8 Viaduct Gardens,
London SW11 7BW under license from the LEGO Group.

All rights reserved. Without limiting the rights under the copyright reserved above,
no part of this publication may be reproduced, stored in, or introduced into
a retrieval system, or transmitted, in any form, or by any means (electronic,
mechanical, photocopying, recording, or otherwise), without the
prior written permission of the copyright owner.
Published in Great Britain by Dorling Kindersley Limited.

A catalog record for this book is available from the Library of Congress.
ISBN: 978-1-4654-9789-5
978-0-7440-2373-2 (library edition)

DK books are available at special discounts when purchased in bulk for sales
promotions, premiums, fund-raising, or educational use. For details, contact:
DK Publishing Special Markets, 1450 Broadway, Suite 801, New York, New York 10018
SpecialSales@dk.com

Printed and bound in China

For the curious

www.dk.com
www.LEGO.com

LEGO® MINIFIGURE
A Visual History

NEW EDITION

DK

CONTENTS

1970s

16

1980s

22

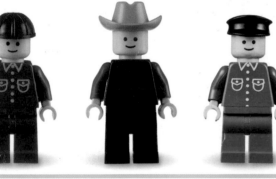

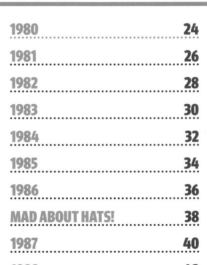

1990s

46

2000s

 80

2010s

 146

2020s

 244

BRINGING LEGO® PLAY TO LIFE

IN THE 1960s and early 1970s, the focus in LEGO® building was on constructing models like houses, cars, and trains. But something important was missing: people to live in the houses, drive the cars, and run the trains! If children wanted characters to play in their LEGO creations, they had to make them out of bricks themselves. To address this need for role-play and storytelling, the company first created large, buildable family figures, and later shrunk them down to a size that would fit in better with smaller LEGO models. In 1975, a figure was launched with a blank yellow head, a torso with arm-shaped bumps, and a single solid leg. In 1978, this forerunner to the minifigure was updated with moving arms and legs, hands that could hold accessories, and a face painted with two dots for eyes and a friendly smile. The famous LEGO minifigure was ready to play!

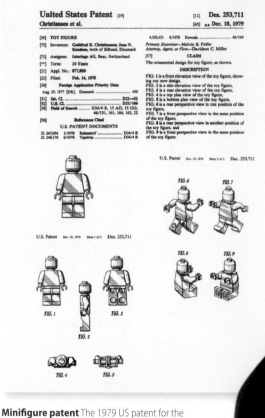

Minifigure patent The 1979 US patent for the LEGO minifigure design demonstrated its iconic shape, the brick-compatible holes on its feet and legs, and the way its limbs could move.

Girl power The female minifigure went through many concept stages before it was decided that it would share the same standard legs as male minifigures.

BIRTH OF A LEGEND

To create the prototype for the first minifigure, designer Jens Nygård Knudsen and a team of colleagues sawed and filed LEGO bricks into a miniature human form. Three years and 50 additional prototypes carved in plastic and cast in tin later, he produced the updated modern-style minifigure. Among the sets it debuted in was set 600, featuring a policeman and a buildable brick patrol car.

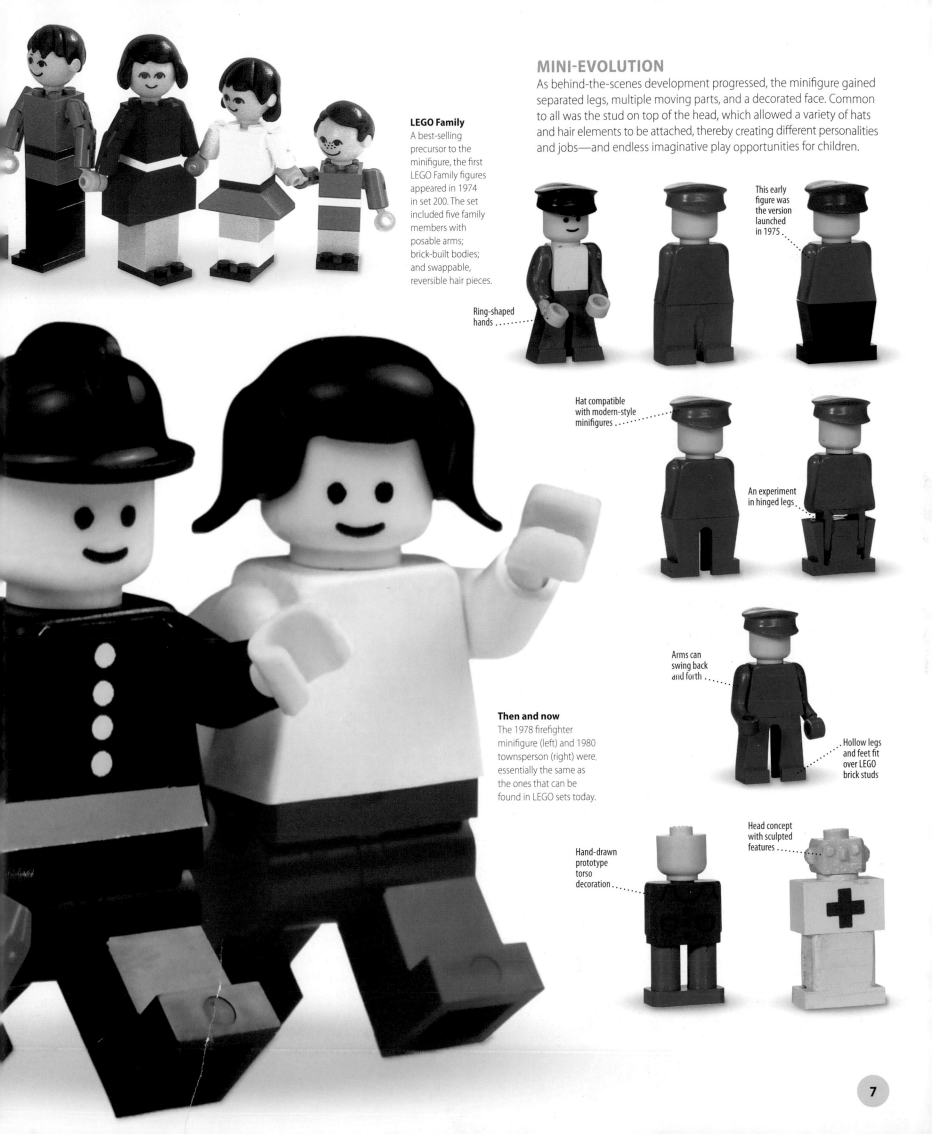

LEGO Family
A best-selling precursor to the minifigure, the first LEGO Family figures appeared in 1974 in set 200. The set included five family members with posable arms; brick-built bodies; and swappable, reversible hair pieces.

MINI-EVOLUTION

As behind-the-scenes development progressed, the minifigure gained separated legs, multiple moving parts, and a decorated face. Common to all was the stud on top of the head, which allowed a variety of hats and hair elements to be attached, thereby creating different personalities and jobs—and endless imaginative play opportunities for children.

This early figure was the version launched in 1975

Ring-shaped hands

Hat compatible with modern-style minifigures

An experiment in hinged legs

Arms can swing back and forth

Then and now
The 1978 firefighter minifigure (left) and 1980 townsperson (right) were. essentially the same as the ones that can be found in LEGO sets today.

Hollow legs and feet fit over LEGO brick studs

Head concept with sculpted features

Hand-drawn prototype torso decoration

WHAT'S A MINIFIGURE?

A LEGO® MINIFIGURE is a small, posable figure of a person or being. Most minifigures have rotating arms, legs, hands, and heads. They have connectors on their bodies that are compatible with LEGO bricks and other elements. They often represent famous archetypes, such as firefighters, astronauts, and knights. A minifigure can be disassembled and combined with parts from other minifigures to create an entirely new character. The faces of many minifigures carry a friendly smile, but some have other expressions—even multiple ones! Minifigures drive cars, live in castles, fly spaceships, and fill the world of construction with endless possibilities for fun, role-play, and imagination.

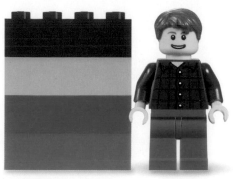

Size matters Without a hat or hair piece, a minifigure stands exactly four LEGO bricks high. This precise measurement makes it easy to construct LEGO buildings and vehicles that can fit minifigures inside.

Stud on top of head can connect to headgear and other LEGO pieces

Build a minifigure
A standard LEGO minifigure comes in three sections when you open a new LEGO set: the head, the torso with arms and hands, and the waist and legs.

Arm rotates 360 degrees at the shoulder

Hand swivels at the wrist

MINIFIGURES AT WORK

LEGO minifigures hail from many different places and times, including the past, present, and future, as well as worlds of fantasy and science fiction. You can tell where a minifigure comes from and what kind of job it has by looking at the details of its printed clothing and its accessories.

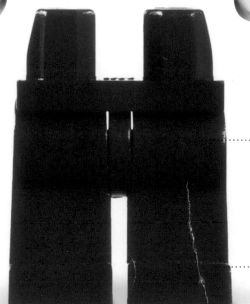

Legs swing back and forth for sitting and walking poses

Holes on backs of legs and bottoms of feet attach to LEGO brick studs

A uniform with reflective stripes and a special helmet makes it clear that this is a firefighter.

With his overalls, cap, and shovel, what else could this hardworking fellow be but a farmer?

An ancient gladiator carries a sword and shield and wears a protective helmet and leather armor.

MEET THE MINIFIGURES …

A minifigure must have a number of essential key minifigure characteristics in order to be considered a true LEGO minifigure. Although all of the characters shown here have different faces, clothes, accessories, and even some body parts, each one is still a minifigure because it is based around the same basic LEGO minifigure design.

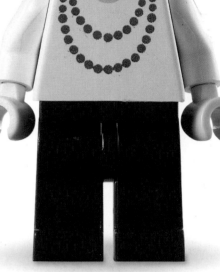

The pirate has a hook hand, a peg leg, and a printed eyepatch and beard.

This retro robot has a mechanical arm with a claw, a helmet with a visor, and bolts printed on his body and legs.

This mermaid stands on a single-piece fish tail instead of legs.

A queen from LEGO® Castle wears a dress made from a printed sloped piece.

A beastly warrior has an animal head with a reversible minifigure face underneath.

This cheerleader has legs that are printed to look like a skirt and socks.

Some minifigures have short legs to make them appear smaller.

The EXO-FORCE™ heroes are based on the look of Japanese animation.

Minifigures can represent anybody from any country or culture.

Handy A zookeeper holds a banana in one hand and a hungry baby chimpanzee in the other.

MEET THE NON-MINIFIGURES …

Not every LEGO figure is a minifigure! Many other colorful characters inhabit the universe of LEGO building. The LEGO® *Star Wars*™ droid and the LEGO® Friends mini doll are not minifigures because they are not made up of any standard minifigure parts. The skeleton does not have enough standard parts to count as a true minifigure.

LEGO skeleton

LEGO *Star Wars* Battle Droid

LEGO Friends mini doll

HAIR, HATS, AND GEAR

The minifigure's head stud lets you attach and swap hundreds of different hair pieces, hats, and helmets. Their hands can hold a wide variety of accessories, and backpacks and armor can be attached to their bodies.

Armor This knight wears a helmet and an armor piece fitted over his torso.

HOW TO USE THIS BOOK

Some themes have a style of figure that is all their own, such as LEGO® DUPLO® figures and LEGO Friends mini dolls. These non-minifigure themes appear in gray boxes throughout the book.

Some non-minifigures are designed to fit in and interact with minifigures in their themes, such as LEGO *Star Wars* droids, LEGO Castle skeletons, and LEGO Space aliens. These appear in the book in boxes with a dotted key line

HOW IS A MINIFIGURE MADE?

Many minifigures start out as a rough concept sketch that shows how the character might appear when it's created.

CREATING A NEW MINIFIGURE isn't a quick process. It can take more than a year from the time an idea is first sketched out on paper to the moment a brand-new plastic character is picked off the LEGO® production line to be packed up and shipped to shops all around the world. Many individuals contribute to the creation of a minifigure, from sculptors to graphic artists, as well as the machines that make sure each one is perfectly molded and ready for play. Here's how it's done.

The LEGO Minifigures team hold brainstorming sessions at the LEGO offices in Billund, Denmark.

BRAINSTORMING

When it's time to start work on new sets for a LEGO play theme, the whole design team sit down for a "Design Boost" brainstorming session. They share their ideas to come up with the best concepts for new models and the minifigures that will populate them. If a new set will need one or more new minifigures to be created, then the character design process begins.

DESIGNING

The design team make sketches and decide what new accessories or body-part elements are needed. For research, they might visit a fire station or study historical armor at a library. Element designers hand-sculpt organic-looking pieces such as hair at a 3:1 scale out of clay, while more regularly shaped parts are designed via a computer using a 3D program. Meanwhile, graphic designers create a map of face and body details that will be applied to the minifigure. Minifigures are chosen to be included in a set based on how well they help tell that set's story. If it is a licensed character from a movie or comic book, then the team collaborates with licensing partners until both are totally satisfied with the design. Finally, a Model Committee checks that everything fits and works properly, and the completed design is approved for production.

Design work begins on a blank minifigure template, bare of any colors, personality, or details.

A graphic designer comes up with a design for the face and costume of the new minifigure and adds color.

The approved design is refined and finalized on a computer as a 2D version of what the minifigure will look like when it is produced in plastic.

Most minifigures are manufactured at the LEGO Group headquarters in Billund, Denmark. Others come from factories in Hungary, the Czech Republic, China, and Mexico.

MANUFACTURING

Just like LEGO bricks, minifigures start out as piles of tiny, colorful plastic granules made out of acrylonitrile butadiene styrene (ABS), each one about the size of a grain of rice. These granules are mixed together and heated until they melt and become a plastic goo, which is pressed into shape inside metal molding machines. Automated assembly machines attach legs to waists, hands to arms, and arms to torsos. Decorating machines then use special inks to print faces and clothing decorations directly onto the assembled parts. At last, the new minifigure is complete and ready to be purchased, shipped, and sold.

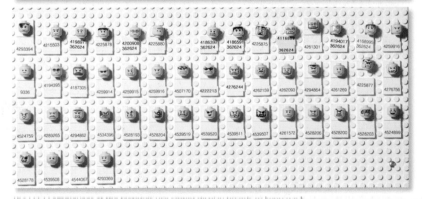

The LEGO employees at the factories use coded display boards to keep track of the many different minifigure faces that are currently in production.

TIMELINE

EVEN THOUGH their fundamental design has remained the same for 42 years (and counting), minifigures have gone through many changes over the decades. This timeline chronicles some of the most important events in minifigure history, including the first new facial expressions and new body parts and the first licensed characters from the big screen, as well as the debuts of classic minifigure elements, accessories, and other LEGO® figures.

LEGO Family figures

1974
- The first LEGO figures—LEGO Family building figures—have round heads with painted expressions, posable arms, and bodies built out of LEGO bricks.

Freddy Fox LEGO FABULAND figure

1979
- First yellow Space minifigure.
- First female Castle character.
- First male hair piece. ● First chef's hat.
- Animal-headed LEGO® FABULAND™ figures.

1980
- First top hat.

1985
- Record number of new Town minifigures are released.
- New Space jet pack with stud on the front accessory.

1990
- The first LEGO ghost minifigure has a glow-in-the-dark shroud element.
- First time a slope is used instead of legs for a minifigure's dress.

1992
- First minifigure head with freckles.
- New surfboard accessory.

1993
- First female LEGO Space minifigure.
- First separate beard piece. ● First minifigure headgear with printing. ● First LEGO Town crook.
- First fabric minifigure cape.

Early three-piece figure with
red hat

LEGO DUPLO figures

1975
● Small and simple three-piece LEGO figures
are released, with an unpainted face and
no separate limbs. ● First minifigure-
compatible headgear.

1976
● LEGO® DUPLO® figures
are launched.

1978
● The first true LEGO minifigure, with posable arms and
legs and the classic smile expression. ● The LEGOLAND®
subthemes Town, Castle, and Space launch with new
minifigure accessories and wearable gear.

LEGO
Technic
figure

Monkey
figure with
curly tail

1986
● LEGO® Technic figure is launched.
● New Castle maiden hat.

1987
● New Forestman cap.

1989
● LEGO® Pirates introduces the first minifigures
with different facial expressions and body parts,
such as peg legs and hook hands.
● Monkey uses minifigure arms for all four limbs.

LEGO BELVILLE figures

LEGO *Island* video
game

1994
● First printed minifigure legs.
● First robot minifigure head.
● LEGO® BELVILLE™ figures
are launched.

1995
● First skeleton figure has new body
and limb components. ● New diver
accessories: helmet, visor, and flippers.
● First minifigure crown.

1996
● First minifigure nose.

1997
● First minifigure with a printed sloped
skirt piece. ● LEGO *Island* is the first
video game to star (digital) minifigures.
● LEGO® SCALA™ figures are launched.

1998

● LEGO® Adventurers introduces new headgear: wide-brimmed hat, pith helmet, and aviator cap with goggles. ● LEGO Castle's Ninja subtheme launches samurai and ninja gear.
● First mummy minifigure.

1999

● LEGO® *Star Wars*™ minifigures introduce many new parts and accessories.
● First minifigure head to be sculpted into a different (nonstandard) shape.

2000

● LEGO® Studios Director minifigure.
● An 1,849-piece minifigure sculpture is released as set 3723.

2001

● First minifigure with a two-sided face print.
● First glow-in-the-dark minifigure head.

Skeleton figure with sword

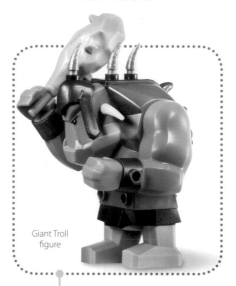

Giant Troll figure

2007

● For the 30th anniversary of *Star Wars*, 10,000 gold chrome C-3PO minifigures are randomly packed into LEGO *Star Wars* sets, and five 14-carat gold versions are given away. ● Skeleton minifigure body is updated so its arms can move.
● LEGO® Mars Mission features aliens with transparent glow-in-the-dark bodies.
● First minifigures with soft plastic heads.

2008

● "Go Miniman Go!" event celebrates the 30th anniversary of the LEGO minifigure.
● LEGO® Agents introduces a new robotic minifigure arm.
● The Castle theme introduces the Giant Troll figure.

2009

● Tiny microfigures appear in LEGO Games sets.
● LEGO® Space Police features new modified alien heads. ● First hair piece with a hole for accessories.

The first US President minifigure, Abraham Lincoln, from THE LEGO MOVIE.

2013

● First minifigure with chicken wings.
● New animal minifigure elements in LEGO® Legends of Chima™.
● New heads and turtle shells for the LEGO® Teenage Mutant Ninja Turtles™.

2014

● THE LEGO® MOVIE™ brings minifigures to the big screen.
● The first LEGO® Minecraft™ minifigures come with new block-shaped heads. ● LEGO® The Simpsons™ introduces new molded heads for Bart and co. ● LEGO® *Disney Princess*™ launches as the second mini doll theme.

2015

● Minifigures from different fictional worlds join forces in the innovative LEGO® DIMENSIONS video game and its associated play sets.
● The third mini doll theme, LEGO® Elves, launches alongside its own TV show.

2016

● A LEGO CITY People Pack is the first to include a baby figure and a minifigure wheelchair piece. ● LEGO® NEXO KNIGHTS™ introduces new minifigure armor.
● LEGO® Disney minifigures including Mickey Mouse and Donald Duck feature new molded parts.

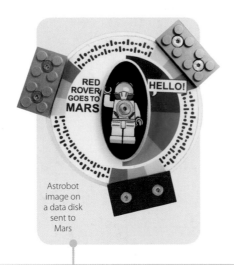

2002

- First minifigures to feature new short LEGO leg piece. ● First Super Hero minifigure.
- LEGO® Studios werewolf mask transforms an ordinary minifigure into a howling beast.
- Neck bracket element allows objects to be attached to a minifigure's back.

2003

- Minifigures with special arms and spring-loaded legs for holding and throwing basketballs. ● First minifigures based on actual people—with realistic skin tones. ● First minifigure with arm printing. ● The first minifigures on Mars—illustrations of astrobots Biff Starling and Sandy Moondust land on the Red Planet aboard the NASA rovers *Spirit* and *Opportunity*.

2005

- Minifigures with built-in batteries let Jedi lightsabers and police flashlights light up when the heads are pushed down. ● Hand-held magnetic accessory lets Harry Potter™ grab a golden dragon egg. ● First minifigure mermaid tail. ● First Viking helmet.

2006

- LEGO® EXO-FORCE™ features minifigures with faces and hair pieces designed after Japanese animation, as well as robot villains with new body, arm, and leg pieces. ● First printed hair piece.

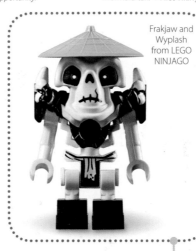

Frakjaw and Wyplash from LEGO NINJAGO

Meet mini doll Nicole from LEGO Friends

2010

- LEGO® *Toy Story*™ sets introduce minifigures with extra-long arms and legs.
- A new tentacle-legs element first appears in LEGO® Atlantis.
- Han Solo (from LEGO *Star Wars*) is the first minifigure to be frozen in carbonite. ● The collectible LEGO® Minifigures line adds many new body parts and accessories. ● First minifigure legs with side printing. ● *The Adventures of Clutch Powers* is the first feature-length movie starring minifigures.

2011

- Aluminum minifigures of the Roman gods Jupiter and Juno and the astronomer Galileo are launched aboard the Juno space probe. ● A new leg piece gives boots to LEGO® NINJAGO® skeleton figures. ● First hair piece with ears.

2012

- LEGO NINJAGO introduces snake head and tail pieces and a torso extender with extra arms.
- LEGO® Friends debuts the mini doll.
- LEGO® Monster Fighters features new bat-winged arms and steampunk mechanical leg pieces.

Sweet Mayhem from THE LEGO MOVIE 2

2017

- Sets based on THE LEGO® BATMAN MOVIE include a new Utility Belt piece. ● The six LEGO ninja get new looks in THE LEGO® NINJAGO® MOVIE™ and its associated sets. ● Mini dolls flex their muscles in a new LEGO® DC Super Heroes Girls theme.

2018

- Seventeen collectible Minifigures in party costumes mark the 40th anniversary of the LEGO minifigure. ● LEGO® Wizarding World™ sets see the return of Harry Potter and his pals with new medium-length leg pieces.

2019

- THE LEGO® MOVIE 2™ is the first theme to include both minifigures and mini dolls in the same sets.
- Anniversary minifigures mark 20 years of LEGO *Star Wars*. ● LEGO® Hidden Side sets include minifigures with interchangeable normal and haunted heads.

2020

- LEGO Hidden Side unleashes the first two-headed minifigure. ● Minifigures in LEGO® Trolls World Tour sets have oversized Troll heads with studs for connecting hats and hair. ● Micro dolls make their debut in LEGO Disney storybook sets.

1970s

The 1970s were when it all began. First, there were big, buildable people with round yellow heads. Then came mini-sized, solid-bodied figures with swappable hats and expressionless faces. Finally, in 1978, the best parts of both were combined to create a smiling little character with movable arms and legs. The LEGO® minifigure was born, and with it came three new lines—Town, Castle, and Space—creating an entire world of constructible buildings, vehicles, and accessories to bring it to life.

Air tank piece attaches with a neck bracket

Black torso with fire uniform sticker was last worn by LEGO firemen in 1981

Fireman Two parts of this minifigure's firefighting equipment—his fireproof helmet and air tank—are still used by the firefighters of LEGO CITY today.

1978

THE MODERN MINIFIGURE as we know it was born in 1978, making it one of the biggest years ever for LEGO® building. The new LEGO characters were vastly different from their precursors released in 1974, which were static, unprinted, and made from bricks. Made up of nine separate pieces (a head, a torso, hips, two arms, two hands, and two legs), minifigures now had cheery printed faces and arms and legs that moved to make them posable for play. You might think that that would be enough excitement for one year, but there was more! Three new subthemes were introduced—Town, Castle, and Space—as part of the LEGOLAND® play theme.

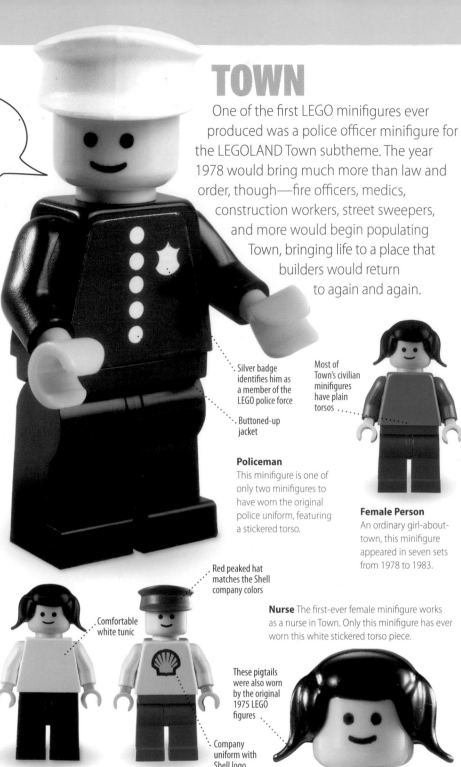

I'M THE LAW IN THIS TOWN!

TOWN

One of the first LEGO minifigures ever produced was a police officer minifigure for the LEGOLAND Town subtheme. The year 1978 would bring much more than law and order, though—fire officers, medics, construction workers, street sweepers, and more would begin populating Town, bringing life to a place that builders would return to again and again.

Silver badge identifies him as a member of the LEGO police force

Buttoned-up jacket

Policeman This minifigure is one of only two minifigures to have worn the original police uniform, featuring a stickered torso.

Most of Town's civilian minifigures have plain torsos

Female Person An ordinary girl-about-town, this minifigure appeared in seven sets from 1978 to 1983.

Red peaked hat matches the Shell company colors

Comfortable white tunic

Nurse The first-ever female minifigure works as a nurse in Town. Only this minifigure has ever worn this white stickered torso piece.

These pigtails were also worn by the original 1975 LEGO figures

Company uniform with Shell logo

Passenger This minifigure is dressed in plain traveling clothes for her debut on the Passenger Coach (164).

Shell Employee This oil company worker keeps the citizens of Town on the move.

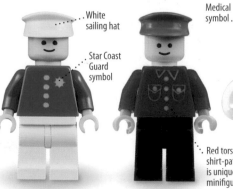

White sailing hat

Star Coast Guard symbol

Medical symbol

Red torso with shirt-pattern sticker is unique to this minifigure

Coast Guard Captain The head of sea security only appears at the Coast Guard Station (575).

Street Sweeper Town is kept pristine by this busy minifigure in Town Square (1589).

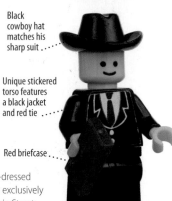

· Workman's cap protects his head

· Red hat makes him visible on the tracks

· Plain clothes for heavy manual work

Town House with Garden (376) Two minifigures live in this delightful house, complete with flowers and sun lounger.

· Black cowboy hat matches his sharp suit

· Unique stickered torso features a black jacket and red tie

· Red briefcase

DID YOU KNOW?
All male minifigures wore hats until male hair pieces appeared in 1979.

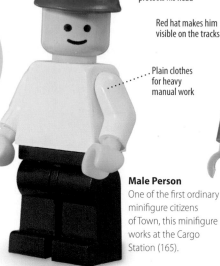

Male Person One of the first ordinary minifigure citizens of Town, this minifigure works at the Cargo Station (165).

· Dressed professionally in a jacket over a shirt and tie

Train Conductor This minifigure was the first to feature a torso that was printed instead of stickered.

Patron This well-dressed man-about-town exclusively appears in the Main Street set (1589). He must have lots of important errands to run!

· Helmet with chinstrap

Red Spaceman This trailblazing minifigure was first into LEGO Space and first to wear his helmet, which was in sets until 1988.

· Printed torso features the LEGO Space logo

· Classic, all-white space suit

· Protective space suit covers the hands, too

White Spaceman Ready for an out-of-this-world adventure! This excited astronaut appeared in 37 sets from 1978 to 1987.

SPACE

It was time for minifigures to blast off into Space in 1978, when the subtheme's first three sets were launched. The Rocket Launcher (462), Space Cruiser (487), and Space Command Center (493) all featured astronaut minifigures. Each intrepid space adventurer wore a full-body space suit in white or red—with the classic yellow face peering out from the helmet.

LEGO® DUPLO®

The earliest DUPLO figures predate the modern minifigure, having first appeared in 1976. They had a head and a one-piece body, with no arms or legs—a design that would change in the years that followed.

· Blue sailor hat identifies him as a seafaring figure

DUPLO Sailor With a wide smile and a freckly face, this happy sailor popped up in five nautical-themed DUPLO sets from 1978 to 1990.

· Only this knight has ever worn this visor in light gray

CASTLE

The very first Castle set charged onto the LEGO building scene in 1978. It would go on to become a best-seller for the next six years. Castle (375)—nicknamed the "Yellow Castle"—featured a working, crank-raised drawbridge and contained 14 knight minifigures and four brick-built horses, making it great for endless play.

· Defending soldiers wear a purple tabard with a crown

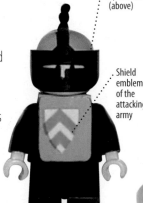

· Visor with plume fits over the classic LEGO helmet worn by the astronauts (above)

· Shield emblem of the attacking army

I LOVE THE YELLOW CASTLE. THE KNIGHT LIFE IS GREAT!

· Helmet with neck guard was first worn by this knight

· Stickered tabard with neck bracket fits over the knight's torso

Plume Helmet Knight Part of the blue cavalry that protects the Yellow Castle, only one Knight of this kind appears in the set.

Black Cavalry Knight Dressed in black and ready to attack, this Black Cavalry Knight has a foreboding appearance.

Blue Knight An army of seven of these minifigures defends the Yellow Castle from the invading army.

Helmet for protection against flying arrows

Torso with a royal crest

YOU RANG, SIR?

Knight Modeling a new helmet for the Castle theme, this minifigure appears in Knight's Procession (677).

1979

THE MINIFIGURE CELEBRATED

its first birthday in grand style in 1979, with new sets for LEGOLAND® Castle, Space, and Town. In other non-minifigure news: SCALA, a jewelry and accessories line for girls, was introduced; LEGO® DUPLO® expanded with two new subthemes, Playhouse and Farm; and LEGO® FABULAND™ was launched, which was seen as a bridge theme for children growing out of LEGO DUPLO. But for many fans, this was the year that showed the minifigure was here to stay.

CASTLE

The second and third Castle sets in history came out in 1979: Knights' Tournament (383) and Knight's Procession (677). They were both released in Europe this year, but would not reach US shelves until 1981. Knights' Tournament came with six minifigures but no horse figures as we know them today—the horses had to be built using bricks.

Helmet in light gray

Red torso with crest

Procession Knight This Knight has a helmet with neck and nose guards for maximum protection.

CAN YOU ATTACH A HAIR DRYER TO MY THRONE?

Red, short hair piece

Gold necklace

Male hair piece new to this year

Tricolor crest

Prince This regal Prince sports a new hair piece, which has since become an iconic LEGO element.

Princess With her bright red hair, this is the first female minifigure in the Castle theme, paving the way for many more.

DID YOU KNOW?
The Prince's brown hair piece has been used in more than 130 sets.

A yellow helmet matches his head color

SPACE

The year 1979 was a huge one for Space, with a dozen sets released, plus building plates resembling a lunar landscape and minifigure packs. Unlike later Space subthemes, these sets were free of any kind of conflict or aliens. Astronaut minifigures explored the galaxy with smiles on their faces in spaceships and are still remembered with fondness by many adult fans.

Landing Plates (454) This set comes with a circular landing pad and a section of spaceport roadway.

Gold space logo

Yellow Spaceman This minifigure is bright yellow—a new color for an astronaut in the Space theme.

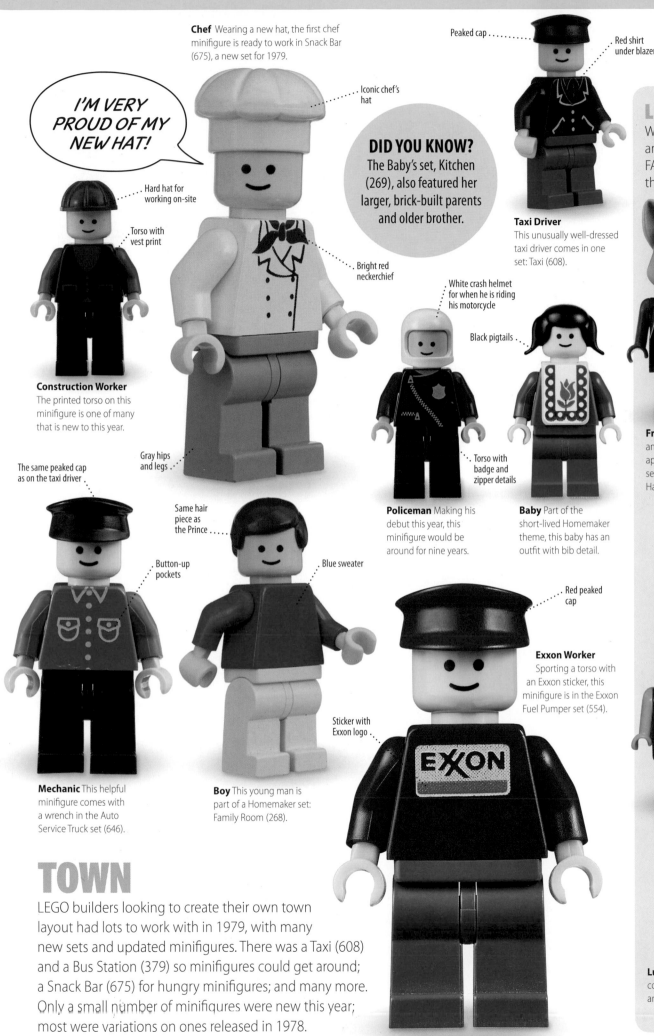

Chef Wearing a new hat, the first chef minifigure is ready to work in Snack Bar (675), a new set for 1979.

Iconic chef's hat

I'M VERY PROUD OF MY NEW HAT!

Hard hat for working on-site

Torso with vest print

DID YOU KNOW?
The Baby's set, Kitchen (269), also featured her larger, brick-built parents and older brother.

Bright red neckerchief

Construction Worker The printed torso on this minifigure is one of many that is new to this year.

Gray hips and legs

Peaked cap

Red shirt under blazer

Taxi Driver This unusually well-dressed taxi driver comes in one set: Taxi (608).

White crash helmet for when he is riding his motorcycle

Black pigtails

Torso with badge and zipper details

Policeman Making his debut this year, this minifigure would be around for nine years.

Baby Part of the short-lived Homemaker theme, this baby has an outfit with bib detail.

LEGO FABULAND
With colorful, easy-to-build models and fun animal characters, LEGO FABULAND was introduced to fill the niche between DUPLO and LEGO System models. The popular play theme would last until 1989.

Oversized molded fox head

Red, chunky legs

Freddy Fox Bright-eyed and bushy-tailed, this fox appears in six FABULAND sets, including Town Hall (140).

The same peaked cap as on the taxi driver

Same hair piece as the Prince

Button-up pockets

Blue sweater

Mechanic This helpful minifigure comes with a wrench in the Auto Service Truck set (646).

Boy This young man is part of a Homemaker set: Family Room (268).

Red peaked cap

Exxon Worker Sporting a torso with an Exxon sticker, this minifigure is in the Exxon Fuel Pumper set (554).

Sticker with Exxon logo

Bear face with printed snout

Bernard Bear This friendly bear comes with his own pick-up truck in one set (329).

Distinctive feline features

Charlie Cat This smiling cat works at FABULAND's Doc David's Hospital (34 and 137).

Head molded to look woolly

Torso with yellow top

Lucy Lamb This lamb comes with long ears and printed eyelashes.

TOWN

LEGO builders looking to create their own town layout had lots to work with in 1979, with many new sets and updated minifigures. There was a Taxi (608) and a Bus Station (379) so minifigures could get around; a Snack Bar (675) for hungry minifigures; and many more. Only a small number of minifigures were new this year; most were variations on ones released in 1978.

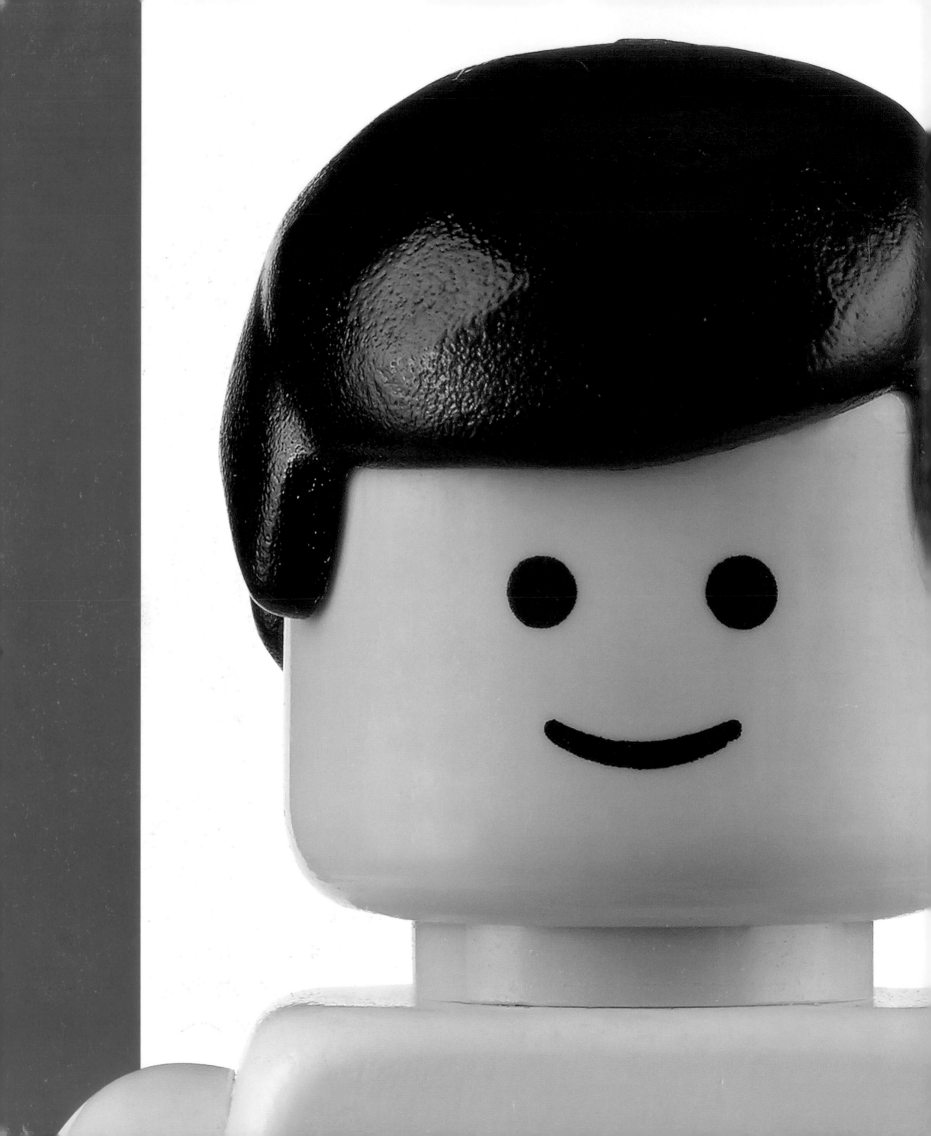

1980s

The 1980s were a golden age for LEGO® minifigures, as many young builders were discovering them for the first time. Although the beloved minifigure's clothes and headgear might be switched around from set to set, the basic style remained the same—until 1989, when the arrival of the swashbuckling new LEGO® Pirates theme changed everything. Suddenly, minifigures could have eyepatches, mustaches, stubble, or lipstick, not to mention hook hands and peg legs. The possibilities were endless!

HEY, I'VE GOT AN IDEA!

Striped blue T-shirt

Bill This clever minifigure came with the *LEGOLAND Idea Book*, which followed the adventures of Bill and Mary.

1980

THIS YEAR SAW the LEGO Group continuing to expand, with new factories being built and the brick establishing itself in more and more homes. No new themes were introduced this year, but the LEGOLAND® Town subtheme saw significant expansion. The latest in a line of LEGO Ideas Books would also come out, with a story centered on Bill and Mary, the two minifigures packaged with it. But inventive LEGO fans were already coming up with great ideas of their own and experimenting with their new sets and minifigures!

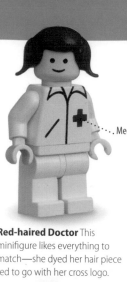

Medical symbol

Glamorous Lady Wearing a gold necklace that was first seen on a princess in the Castle theme in 1979, this lady appropriately features in Town Square—Castle Scene (1592).

Red-haired Doctor This minifigure likes everything to match—she dyed her hair piece red to go with her cross logo.

Pen for scribbling medical notes

Black-haired Doctor This doctor is ready for any medical emergency—as long as it can be solved with a stethoscope …

I HOPE IT'S BETTER THAN YOUR LAST ONE!

Glamorous gold necklace

DID YOU KNOW? The pigtails hair piece has appeared in three colors—red, black, and white.

TOWN

The Town subtheme kept growing in 1980, with the addition of a Main Street (6390), an Auto Repair Shop (6363), a Gas Station (6375), and a number of new vehicles cruising the streets. Some minifigures were used in multiple sets or multiple times in the same set, often with only minor variations.

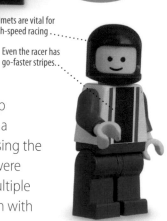

Helmets are vital for high-speed racing

Even the racer has go-faster stripes

Race Car Driver Dressed up in racing gear, this driver loves to zoom around in his car.

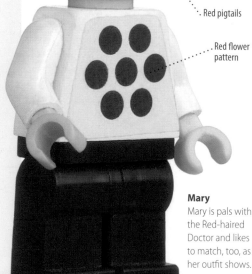

Red pigtails

Red flower pattern

Mary Mary is pals with the Red-haired Doctor and likes to match, too, as her outfit shows.

Top hat

GOT MY TOP HAT This black figure represents a statue in the Town Square (1592). Nobody seems to know just who it is supposed to be a statue of, but he had a very nice hat!

Statue This mysterious figure is wearing the top hat accessory for the first time.

Builder Introduced this year, the Builder minifigure was last seen residing in one of the houses he helped build on Main Street (10041).

Torso with shirt detail

Exxon Worker Run out of gas? This helpful lady will be at your service in Exxon Gas Station (6375).

Exxon logo

Red hard hat

Construction Worker Appearing in more than 20 sets, this minifigure has been catching up on his sleep for the past 10 years.

Blue button-down shirt

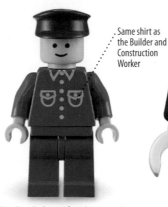

Same shirt as the Builder and Construction Worker

Engine Driver After driving trains in more than 12 sets, he ran out of steam in 1985... until he came roaring back down the tracks in 2020!

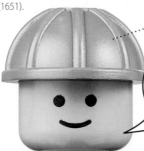

Mærsk Line Worker This minifigure works for container shipping company Mærsk. He appears in the promotional set Mærsk Line Container Truck (1651).

Sky-blue hard hat

I'M SO EXCITED, I JUST CAN'T CONTAIN MYSELF.

Black fire helmet

Fire Chief The Fire Chief is the first minifigure to wear the fire uniform. But he isn't the last—it is seen on more than five other minifigures.

Rare white pigtails piece

Police badge

Inspector This law-enforcing minifigure makes sure Town is a safe and peaceful place to be.

CASTLE GUARD

This guard minifigure does not come from an official Castle set. He was part of two identical sets, both called Town Square, which came out in the Netherlands and United Kingdom. Although dressed in medieval garb, this cheery minifigure is actually wearing a costume and "guarding" a castle in a modern town.

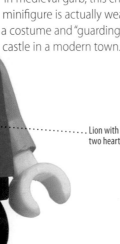

Domed medieval-style helmet

Lion with two hearts

Castle Guard This minifigure has a distinctive design on his torso, possibly inspired by English King Richard the Lionheart.

Town Square—Castle Scene (1592) This set comes with a book store, castle, and fish-and-chips kiosk, plus 11 minifigures, including castle guards and villagers.

Blue vest with shirt underneath

Fancy top hat

DID YOU KNOW?
The LEGO top hat piece has been worn by around 20 minifigures.

Shop Patron The Shop Patron seems to have based his style on the Statue; both wear the same new top hat piece.

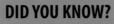

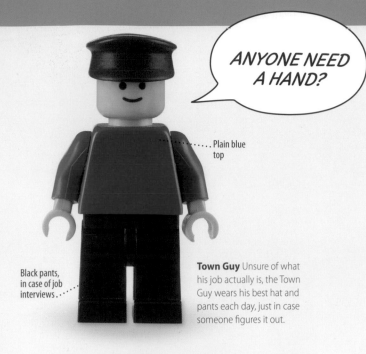

ANYONE NEED A HAND?

Plain blue top

Black pants, in case of job interviews

Town Guy Unsure of what his job actually is, the Town Guy wears his best hat and pants each day, just in case someone figures it out.

1981

THE JOURNEY OF the minifigure soared onward and upward this year. The LEGOLAND® Town and Space subthemes continued to expand, bringing with them new and exciting places for LEGO fans to build and play. New police, fire, and medical minifigures joined the ever-growing cast of LEGO characters as Town continued to base imaginative play on real-world places and the heroes who work in them.

MY FACE HURTS FROM SMILING SO MUCH.

TOWN

You never know what may happen in Town. You could be relaxing in a Summer Cottage (6365) while firefighters race from the Fire Station (6382) to save the day. Got a medical emergency? The LEGO ambulance or the minifigures from the Red Cross Helicopter (6691) may help out. Real life was the key theme this year, and this would continue for years to come.

Policeman's hat

All-weather jacket

Precinct badge

Pigtails are very popular in Town sets

Casual clothing

Police Officer It's quite safe in Town, so the Police Officer spends his time greeting visitors, directing traffic, and eating donuts.

Red Top Woman There's plenty to see from her front garden, so the Red Top Woman spends her time sipping tea and watching her neighbors.

Neatly combed hair

6365 LEGO

Summer Cottage (6365) The Red Top Woman has spent a lot of time perfecting the Summer Cottage's front garden so she can entertain her guests.

DID YOU KNOW?
The Red Cross Helicopter (6691) was the first minifigure-compatible helicopter to be released.

Always smiling

Red Top Man This minifigure can always be found in some kind of scrape, waiting to be rescued. But he seems pretty cheerful about it!

White Top Guy No one knows where this minifigure comes from or why he's in Town, but he helps out whenever there's trouble.

Hard hat protects from falling debris...

Neat overalls...

Firewoman Dressed in a basic station uniform, this Firefighter also maintains the fire engines.

Fireman's uniform...

Fireman This Firefighter's torso printed with gold buttons is featured on six minifigures in 1981.

Fire Station (6382) This station is very busy. There is always something to do, whether it is polishing the engine or manning the radios.

Gas Worker When this minifigure signed up for her job, she thought the Shell symbol on her uniform meant she'd be working at the beach ....

Shell logo...

Blue overalls are perfect for any task...

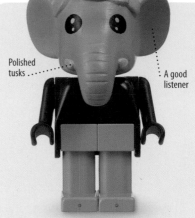

Polished tusks...

A good listener...

Elton Elephant Everyone is friendly in FABULAND, but Elton is also known for his stylish outfits and polite nature. He appears in three sets.

LEGO® FABULAND™

The gentle fun of FABULAND continued this year, with the introduction of cute new characters Elton Elephant, Bonnie Bunny, Boris Bulldog, and Barney Bear, who all showed up to play.

DID YOU KNOW?
The first LEGO firefighter to wear a white hat was introduced this year.

Warm pants for working outdoors...

Blue Top Woman Changing tires or fighting fires, this minifigure lends a hand wherever she is needed.

Red hat stands out in a crowd...

Medic
When there is not an emergency, the Medic drives his ambulance around the town, greeting people and offering lifts.

I THINK YOUR HEAD NEEDS TO BE REPLACED.

Pocket holds bandages and treats...

Symbol indicates he works at the hospital...

Bright red pants match red emblem on torso...

LEGO® BASIC

LEGO Basic introduced figures this year—these colorful finger puppet figures would be a part of LEGO Basic Building sets for decades. These sets were designed to promote creative play and focused solely on building rather than a specific model.

Doctor This torso, with broad collars and a medical symbol, has featured in 13 sets.

Female Finger Puppet This figure has appeared in 21 sets. She just loves overseeing building construction.

Made from one piece...

Even her pigtails are pristine!...

Pilot's helmet...

Standard white medical uniform...

A keen eye for detail...

Male Finger Puppet After appearing in 24 sets, this finger puppet is also an expert in LEGO architecture.

Surgeon The Surgeon is always spotless—she hates getting anything on her crisp white uniform.

Helicopter Pilot The Pilot always has his helmet on in case he has to fly at short notice.

I LOOK LIKE A DANDY NEXT TO MY BIKER PALS!

· · · · Classic helmet in red

· · · · Red torso with zipper details

Red-suited Biker This minifigure won't ever get lonely—he featured in Little People with Accessories (1066) with 35 other minifigure friends!

1982

TOWN AND SPACE were the big stories this year. Three new Space sets rocketed into the universe in 1982, bringing with them four astronaut minifigures. Meanwhile, Town fans could explore everywhere from the local post office to the highways and byways of the city. Also released this year was a set featuring an amazing 36 minifigures, including a chef, a doctor, a firefighter, and a police officer.

MINIFIGURES SURE GET LOTS OF FAN MAIL!

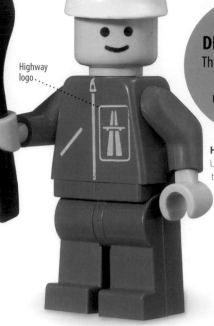

Black wrench for breakdown emergencies · · · ·

White police hat · · · ·

Highway logo · · · ·

Black shirt with pockets · · · ·

Breakdown Repair Man Coming to the rescue of minifigures in broken-down cars is this helpful repair man in Breakdown Assistance (1590).

DID YOU KNOW? The first postal worker minifigures were released this year.

Highway Patrol Usually seen patrolling the highway in his emergency truck, this minifigure is debuting a new torso with a highway design.

Torso also seen on Lord Sam Sinister from the Adventurers theme in 1998 · · · ·

Driver On his way to the office, this minifigure's car breaks down. Luckily, Breakdown Repair Man is on the case in Breakdown Assistance (1590).

TOWN

Town went postal this year! Although there had been other sets in the past with the word "Mail" on a brick, 1982's Mail Truck (6651) and Post Office (6362) models were the first ones to really focus on the postal delivery service. This would later be expanded into the Cargo subtheme.

Postman Proudly wearing a new shirt with the post office logo, this minifigure always delivers the mail with a smile.

Post office logo · · · ·

Postal Worker This postman looks happy, but really he wishes his shirt had the post office logo on it, too.

Blue shirt with pocket detail · · · ·

Mail Van (6651) This set features a truck, a mailbox, and a postal worker minifigure.

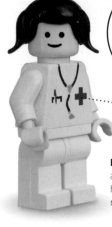

I CAN FACE ANY PERIL DRESSED IN MY FANCY UNIFORM.

Medical red cross logo

Doctor With a stethoscope around her neck and a pen in her top pocket, this doctor is ready to take someone's vitals.

All-black uniform is set off by gold details and red belt

White pigtails

Oversized molded bear head

Billy Bear This bear works at the service station in FABULAND and comes in three sets.

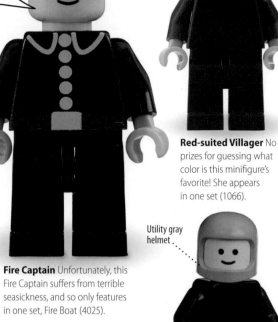

Firefighter This firefighter gets to the scene of a fire in super-fast time in his helicopter, featured in Fire Patrol Copter (6657).

White helmet with chin guard

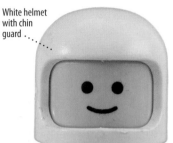

Red-suited Villager No prizes for guessing what color is this minifigure's favorite! She appears in one set (1066).

Gold lapel detail on torso

Fire Captain Unfortunately, this Fire Captain suffers from terrible seasickness, and so only features in one set, Fire Boat (4025).

Big, yellow beak for gnawing

Patrick Parrot Say cheese! This colorful parrot prefers to be behind the camera in Photographer Patrick Parrot (3782).

Utility gray helmet

DID YOU KNOW? Yellow was chosen for minifigures from the original LEGO color palette as an ethnically neutral color—to represent all races and ethnicities.

Monochrome Man This minifigure likes to blend in, hence his plain black-and-white outfit.

LEGO® FABULAND™

FABULAND roared ahead in 1982, releasing 24 figures, more than any other theme. Eleven new sets were added, including a FABULAND House complete with a car.

Red belt with gold buckle

Striped Lady This lady is extremely proud of her home—in fact, she loves her Town House (6372) so much, she never leaves it.

DON'T I LOOK GREAT IN STRIPES? BE HONEST.

Daredevil Pilot Complete with an aviator-style hat and an impressive mustache, this pilot is ready to take to the skies.

Fearless expression

White peaked hat

Blue jacket with white shirt

Striped sweater

Firefighter hat

Firefighter These DUPLO figures have much more detailed faces than early minifigures and include eyebrows, detailed eyes, and a nose.

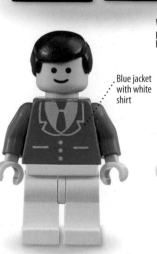

Businessman This minifigure thought that his business suit was unique and was upset to discover that it's been worn by dozens of other minifigures.

Multicolor Man Hanging out with his minifigure friends makes this guy smile in Little People with Accessories (1066).

LEGO® DUPLO®

Little builders got the chance to have some adventures of their own as a fire engine and a plane joined the assortment, complete with Firefighter and Daredevil Pilot figures.

Helmet also seen on the Space astronauts from 1978 . . . .

I'M SURE MY RED STRIPE MAKES ME GO FASTER!

. . . Striped torso popular with both male and female minifigures

Motorcycle Dude
This minifigure is usually seen with a wrench in his hand—his motorcycle breaks down often.

1983

THIS YEAR, TOWN provided a lot of action and fun with new sets and minifigures, while Space hit the stratosphere with five exciting sets. Castle released only one set, but it was a minifigure collection, so that was definitely worth getting excited about. It all added up to new police, fire, and knight minifigures, plus some new townspeople to populate a playscape. Many of these minifigures became highly collectible in later years.

TOWN

Town offered a varied mix of sets this year, including a new Police Station (6384) and Police Car (6623); two construction-themed sets; and a forerunner of the Cargo subtheme, the Delivery Van (6624). There was a new Railway Station (7824), complete with nine new minifigures, and four firefighters appeared in a minifigure-only set.

Firefighter
Classic firefighter to the rescue! This torso was first seen in 1980, and it still looks pristine!

. . . Plain white torso has been worn by more than 100 other minifigures

Motorcycle Rider
Uh oh! This guy's motorcycle has broken down. Luckily, he has a trailer to take it to the mechanic in Motorcycle Transport (6654).

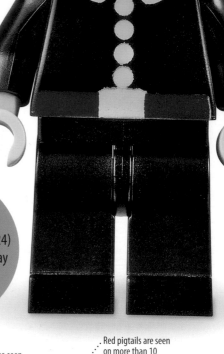

Air tank is full of oxygen

DID YOU KNOW?
The Railway Station (7824) would be the last Railway Station released for eight years.

. . Classic cowboy hat worn by more than 30 other minifigures

Torso seen on more than 10 other minifigures

. . Red pigtails are seen on more than 10 other minifigures

Gold necklace . . .

Dapper Passenger
This minifigure's hat may look like a classic policeman's hat, but he's just a train passenger.

Train Station Worker
The passengers better have their train tickets ready—this worker is just about to inspect them.

Train Passenger
This passenger feels like a princess—her torso was also seen on a Classic Castle Princess in 1979.

Patient Cowboy
This cowboy will be waiting a long time for a train to arrive in Railway Station (7824)—the set doesn't come with a train!

7824

Railway Station (7824)
Nine minifigures, a ticket booth, and a food stand for hungry commuters are included in this set.

HEY, CENTER PARTS ARE JUST SO COOL RIGHT NOW.

Similar torso also seen on the Motorcycle Dude

Parted hair piece

Striped torso is new this year.

Vacationer This tourist is staying at her new Holiday Home (6374). She is most excited about her sliding patio roof.

DID YOU KNOW?
From their launch in 1978 until the end of 2019, 8.3 billion minifigures have been produced.

Striped Top Lady
The first to wear a parted hair piece (a minifigure style that has endured for years), this minifigure is a trend-setter.

Service Station Attendant
This helpful attendant is debuting the new style cap, which has since been worn by more than 400 other minifigures.

Company logo

There are no ketchup stains on this chef's whites!

Zip-up jacket in torso is identical to Service Station Customer and Freight Operator

Chef Serving the hungry townspeople hamburgers always puts a smile on this chef's face.

Hungry Lady This minifigure wants a hamburger, and she wants it *now*, in Burger Stand (6683).

Helmet has protected more than 30 other minifigure heads

Visor with grille clips onto helmet

Standard black hair piece

Red police hat

Service Station Customer
This customer always gets a speedy service at the Service Station (6371).

Red Top Guy First seen in this year's Police Station (6384), this colorful character joined a TV Camera Crew in 1986.

Freight Operator A job at the Freight Loading Depot (7838) keeps this minifigure smiling.

Freight Train Operator
Wearing his blue uniform and yellow cap, this figure keeps all the DUPLO trains running smoothly.

Blue train uniform

Classic Castle shield emblem

CASTLE

Only one Castle set was released in 1983—Castle Minifigures (6002)— a collection of four Knight minifigures. The two pairs of Knights had different helmets and torso designs, marking them as belonging to different royal factions.

LEGO® DUPLO®

This DUPLO figure appeared in two DUPLO Train sets this year, Freight Train (2700) and Passenger Train (2705). He also made an appearance in later years in DUPLO Gas Station (2639) and DUPLO Farm sets.

Black Knight
This brave Knight's torso was first worn by a knight in 1978, and has only been seen on five other Knight minifigures.

YAY! SOMEONE TO JOUST AGAINST!

···· Fixed face grille helmet

···· Armored breastplate is new this year

Yellow Plume Knight
This brave Knight helps protect the King's castle with his lance and shield.

1984

IN THE EARLY YEARS, LEGO® minifigures rarely ran into conflict or encountered anything that would wipe the big grins off their faces. Space explorers didn't clash with aliens, everything ran smoothly in Town, and the Castle knights only had gentle adventures. However, the peace was disrupted in 1984, as Castle introduced two new opposing groups—the Crusaders and the Black Falcons—complete with their own castles, catapults, and siege towers.

CASTLE

The Crusaders and the Black Falcons were the first of several groups that would make up the Castle mythos. They arrived with two fortresses, the Knight's Castle (6073) and King's Castle (6080), plus an impressive Siege Tower (6061).

Black plume ····

Blue Knight The Blue Knight takes his job very seriously, but unfortunately for him, he features in only one set, Knight's Castle (6073).

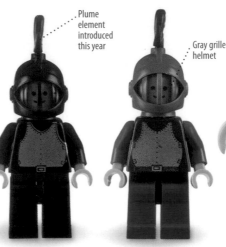

···· Plume element introduced this year

···· Gray grille helmet

Black Knight
An accomplished horseman, this Knight shows off his skills in Knight's Challenge (1584).

Red Knight This Knight looks friendly, but just try escaping from the Siege Tower (6061), and he quickly turns fierce!

Black Falcon Soldier
Proudly wearing the new Falcon crest on his torso, this Soldier is ready to defeat the Crusaders!

···· The Black Falcons typically wear black helmets with chinstraps

New cowl element keeps minifigure's head warm ····

··· Tie shirt also comes in blue and green in later years

Peasant This Peasant is debuting a new torso with printed pouch and a farmer's cowl.

Brown apron exclusive to this minifigure ···

Helmet with neck protector ····

Blacksmith Being a Blacksmith is a messy job. Luckily, this minifigure wears an apron to keep his yellow torso clean.

Black Falcon with Nose Guard This soldier loves a brutal battle—he appears in no less than seven sets.

DID YOU KNOW?
The Blacksmith's apron piece is also worn by knights as a cape in red, blue, and black.

Catapult (6030) This set features a catapult with flags and two minifigures to operate it.

Crusader with Nose Guard
This Crusader guards the Blacksmith Shop (6040). In 1987, he reappears with a spear in Battering Ram (6062).

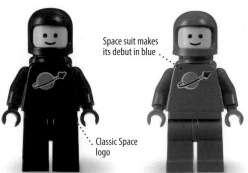

Crusader crest

Crusader with Quiver This Knight prefers to ride his horse and cart than do battle in Horse Cart (6022).

Quiver of arrows is a new element this year

> **WHO'S GONNA ATTACK A BLACKSMITH'S SHOP?**

Helmet with chin guard

DID YOU KNOW?
Horses became sturdier this year—now made of one piece instead of being brick-built.

Fisherman
The last time this figure went to sea, all he caught was a cold. He hopes to be more successful on his next trip.

Life jacket

Diver This deep sea diver is determined not to get stranded at sea, so he is attached to a safety reel.

Diving helmet

LEGO® DUPLO®

LEGO DUPLO sailed the ocean blue this year with sets including Deep Sea Diver (2618) and Sea Explorer (2649). New figures sported diving gear and life jackets as they adventured on and beneath the waves.

Bow and arrow piece is new this year

Lion Crusader
This Crusader is debuting the alternative Crusader coat of arms—the upright lion.

Ax Crusader If this Crusader knew his archenemies were on the opposite page, he wouldn't look so happy!

SPACE

Space returned with eight new sets in 1984, including the Intergalactic Command Base (6971) and the Robot Command Center (6951). Astronaut minifigures appeared in two new colors, as they explored the universe and searched for precious uranium.

Cool leather jacket

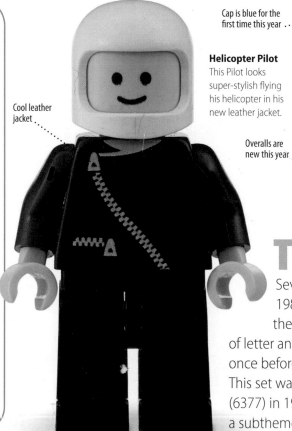

Space suit makes its debut in blue

Classic Space logo

Black Spaceman
Black is a new color for the Space astronauts this year.

Blue Spaceman
This astronaut is about to set off on his first mission into space in Space Dart-I (6824).

Cap is blue for the first time this year

Helmet and torso combination exclusive to this minifigure

Helicopter Pilot
This Pilot looks super-stylish flying his helicopter in his new leather jacket.

Overalls are new this year

Repair Man This handyman can repair anything, from tires and trucks to trains and tractors.

Postman The Town mail is never delivered late thanks to this postman.

TOWN

Seventeen new sets hit the shelves in 1984, with the most significant being the first Cargo Center (6391). The subject of letter and package delivery had only been seen once before, in a 1982 Post Office set (6362). This set was followed up with a Delivery Center (6377) in 1985. Cargo later appeared as a subtheme of its own in 2007.

Helmet with chin guard

Crusader Knight with Quiver
This minifigure is identical to his Crusader Knight friend, apart from a quiver accessory, which makes him feel special.

1985

THE LEGO® SYSTEM in play with its endless possibilities celebrated its 30th birthday in 1985, with a record number of new minifigures released and the launch of Airport as part of the Town subtheme. Both Town and Space saw strong assortments this year, while Castle took a bit of a back seat before making a comeback in 1986. This year offered further proof that the dynamic world of LEGO building and LEGO minifigures would continue to change and grow every year.

CASTLE

This year, Castle only released two sets and a minifigure collection. These added to the Black Falcon and Crusader factions but were smaller models. Prisoner Convoy (6055) featured five horses and four minifigures and was the only Castle carriage to be drawn by four horses. Black Knight's Treasure (6011) featured only one Black Falcon knight minifigure.

Black Falcon emblem

Crusaders lion emblem

Crusader Knight
Not having a quiver accessory is fine by this Knight—he prefers using a spear, anyway.

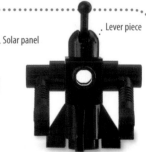

Black Falcon This knight doesn't feature in any action sets this year, which makes him sad, but he doesn't show it.

DID YOU KNOW?
The 1985 Castle sets were released in Europe and other parts of the world, but not the United States.

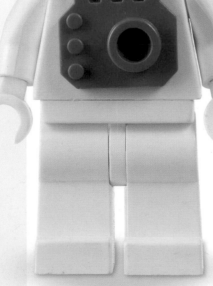

Jet pack also seen in gray in 1986 and black in 1990

White Spaceman The Space astronauts breathed a sigh of relief this year—they finally received a jet pack element.

Solar panel

Lever piece

Blue Droid This Droid accompanies the astronauts on their Solar Power Transporter (6952). Which is good, as he's running out of solar power.

Black Droid This rookie Droid is about to travel into space for the first time in Space Scooter with Robot (6807).

ROBOTS ROCK
These two robots appeared in Space sets this year. Although neither is officially classed as a minifigure, they represent some of the earlier robots and androids in a LEGO theme.

SPACE

Thirteen new Space sets were released in 1985, most of them consisting of a small vehicle with one astronaut minifigure. The larger sets, including the Solar Power Transporter (6952) and FX-Star Patroller (6931), continued the tradition of Space models being modular, with features such as detachable cockpits.

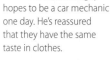

Forklift Driver This guy hopes to be a car mechanic one day. He's reassured that they have the same taste in clothes.

Overalls with a handy pocket

Car Mechanic This minifigure makes his debut this year. He's handy with a wrench, which is why he works in the Car Repair Shop (1966).

Overalls are black for the first time

Caring face

Bright red hair

Community Worker Caring for citizens is this minifigure's specialty in Community Workers (1063).

Blue helmet also seen on the Classic Spacemen in 1984

DO I GET FREQUENT BUILDER MILES?

Same zipper detail as Helicopter Pilot

Biker This Biker's torso is new this year—it probably won't stay pristine white for long!

Hat worn by more than 200 minifigures

Horn emblem

Postman This minifigure's first career choice was a pilot, but he only got as far as buying the hat.

TOWN

Town set a record this year, with an impressive 49 new minifigures released. The big story, however, was the chance to fly the buildable skies of LEGO Air as the first ever Airport set (6392) made its appearance.

Torso with airplane detail introduced this year

Ground Crew Directing all the minifigure vacationers to the planes is a hard job—this guy wishes he was taking off, too.

Gold buttons

Airplane logo

Pressed black pants

Pilot The frequent flyer is about to take to the skies wearing the Pilot's uniform, introduced this year.

Standard LEGO hair piece

Cargo Trailer Driver Heavy LEGO luggage is no problem for this minifigure. He just carts it to the airplane in his trailer.

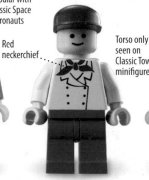

Red helmet is also popular with Classic Space astronauts

Helicopter Pilot The Pilot takes to the skies, looking stylish in his new zip-up jacket.

Red neckerchief

Ice-Cream Server This guy keeps the Town minifigures refreshed with ice cream from his cart.

Gray cowboy hat

Torso only seen on Classic Town minifigures

Container Truck Driver Despite appearances, this guy doesn't ride a horse. He actually drives a truck.

Airport Tower Operator Responsible for directing all the LEGO airplanes, this minifigure is always calm—apart from when she sees another minifigure wearing her hair piece.

6392

Airport (6392) LEGO building finally took to the skies from this airport, which included eight minifigures, a control tower, a plane, a helicopter, and even a restaurant for hungry passengers.

Hair piece seen on more than 100 minifigures

Color scheme on torso same as old LEGO logo from 1968

35

THIS CAP GIVES ME HAT HAIR.

· Plain white cap

Plain red torso also used on Classic Castle Knights between 1978 and 1981 (underneath their breastplates) ·

Speedboat Driver Exclusive to set RV with Speedboat (6698), this minifigure can't wait to get out on the water.

1986

ANOTHER BRILLIANT YEAR for fun and imagination, 1986 saw a wide variety of Town sets, new Crusader and Black Falcon sets in Castle, and more classic Space sets. Town and Space also got the first Light and Sound kits, an electronic system that used light and sound bricks powered by a 9V battery box, bringing even more excitement to the LEGO® play experience. Minifigures were joined by new LEGO® Basic, LEGO® DUPLO®, and LEGO® Technic figures as the world of LEGO building continued to expand.

Young Man This minifigure is new this year but is wearing a striped T-shirt, first introduced in 1985.

Torso used only on Town minifigures ·

I HAVE NO HAIR TO GET HAT HAIR.

Perhaps the "S" logo stands for speed? ·

Motorcycle Racer This speedster comes in Motocross Racing (6677) and is wearing a new torso this year.

Hair piece later used in 2001 for Professor Snape from the Harry Potter™ theme

Blue undershirt ·

TOWN

Twenty-eight sets appeared in 1986, including the first police station in three years, Police Command Base (6386); a new RV with a Speedboat (6698); and a detailed Riding Stable (6379).

Townsperson She lives in the Town, not Castle, but this minifigure has the same torso as the maiden minifigures from the Castle theme, also first seen in 1986.

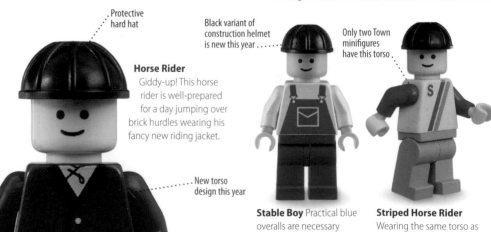

Protective hard hat ·

Horse Rider Giddy-up! This horse rider is well-prepared for a day jumping over brick hurdles wearing his fancy new riding jacket.

Black variant of construction helmet is new this year ·

Only two Town minifigures have this torso ·

New torso design this year ·

White-gloved hands ·

Stable Boy Practical blue overalls are necessary when mucking out stables and cleaning horses all day.

Striped Horse Rider Wearing the same torso as the motorcycle racer, but in yellow, this horse rider isn't as well dressed as the other horse rider.

Riding Stable (6379) Two horses have plenty of exercise and a luxurious stable in this set, which also comes with a horse rider, stable boy, and hay cart.

CASTLE

Only five Castle sets were released this year, but they included the impressive Black Falcon's Fortress (6074) and the Guarded Inn (6067), which was rereleased in 2001 as part of the LEGO Legends series. Two maiden minifigures—with different-colored hats—appeared this year, along with new Crusader and Black Falcon soldiers.

DID YOU KNOW?
The Black Falcons were the longest-lived Castle faction, appearing for eight years.

Hat piece also seen in black on Queen Leonora from the Castle theme in 2000

Maiden This merry Maiden's cone-shaped hat is new this year.

Helmets are either gray or black

Helmet with neck guard

Showing off his armor wares

Crusader Ax
This Crusader has the important job of guarding the maiden in set 6067.

Crusader Lion
The Crusaders' traditional coat of arms is an upright lion.

Weapons Trader
This is the first male minifigure to wear this hair piece.

Blue plastic cape is attached between neck and torso at the back

Maiden with Cape
This Maiden likes to show off her new cone hat to visitors of the Guarded Inn (6067).

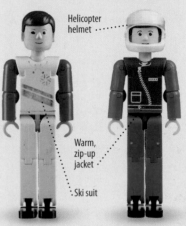
Huge smile

Boy This may be the first Basic figure to have legs, but he decides to sit down and fly a Helicopter (390).

LEGO BASIC
This figure was one of the few to appear in LEGO Basic sets, the predecessor to today's Classic theme.

Helicopter helmet

Warm, zip-up jacket

Ski suit

Skier One minute this figure is having fun on the slopes on his Snow Scooter (8620), the next he is being rescued by the Air Rescue Unit (8660).

Pilot This figure pilots his Polar Copter (8640) and Prop Plane (8855), making sure the Skier figures stay safe on the slopes.

LEGO TECHNIC
Figures were introduced in 1986 in the new LEGO Technic Arctic Action subtheme, which also featured vehicles and structures designed for an arctic environment. Arctic Action only lasted one year.

Red fire helmet

Firefighter
This figure has fought many fires—all with a smile on his face.

DROIDS
These two robots were included in a Space Minifigures set (6702). Droids like these were a popular addition to Space in the 1980s.

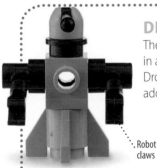
Robot claws

Short Space Droid
The Short Space Droid may not have a computer on its front, but it does have a flashing red light!

Lever piece commonly used on droids and robots

Tall Space Droid
This Space Droid is a bit more technologically advanced than its short friend, with the addition of a computer tile on its front.

SPACE

Time for lift-off! Sixteen Classic Space sets were released this year, featuring the traditional modular space vehicles and astronauts in primary colors. Major sets this year included Alien Moon Stalker (6940) and Cosmic Fleet Voyager (6985).

Jet pack

Black Spaceman
The Spaceman's jet pack was introduced in 1985, but the gray variant is new this year.

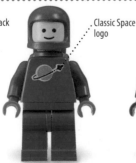
Classic Space logo

Blue Spaceman
Wearing a blue space suit, helmet, and air tank, this astronaut isn't feeling blue—he's off to explore space!

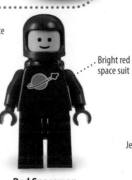
Bright red space suit

Red Spaceman
This red Spaceman is the most common Spaceman minifigure featuring in 46 sets.

Helmet first released in 1978

Jet pack

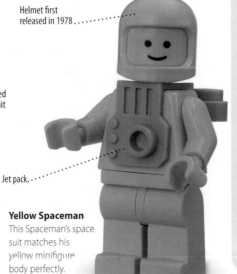

Yellow Spaceman
This Spaceman's space suit matches his yellow minifigure body perfectly.

LEGO® DUPLO®
This figure first appeared in his fire engine in 1985 in the DUPLO Town set (2611). He continued to help citizens in 1986, appearing in Community People (1042) and Community Vehicles (1044).

Classic astronaut helmet · 1978
· Red Spaceman · LEGOLAND Space

Peaked cap · 1978 · Coast Guard
Captain · LEGOLAND Town

Black fire helmet · 1978 · Fireman
· LEGOLAND Town

Black stetson · 1978 · Patron
· LEGOLAND Town

Norman helmet with neck guard
· 1978 · Blue Cavalry Knight
· LEGOLAND Castle

**Yellow helmet with blue
visor** · 1987 · Yellow Futuron
· LEGOLAND Space

**Pointed hat with brim and
yellow feather** · 1987 · Forestman
with Pouch · LEGOLAND Castle

Bicorne with crossbones · 1989
· Captain Redbeard · LEGO Pirates

Red bandanna · 1989 · Blue Pirate
· LEGO Pirates

Tricorne · 1989 · Pirate Blue Shirt
· LEGO Pirates

Fluorescent bubble helmet
· 1998 · Gypsy Moth · LEGO Space

Nemes headdress · 1998 · Pharaoh
Skeleton · LEGO Adventurers

Pith helmet · 1998 · Baron Von
Barron · LEGO Adventurers

Eagle ceremonial headdress
· 1999 · Achu · LEGO Adventurers

Ninja mask · 2000 · Ninja Princess
· LEGO Castle

Beret · 2010 · Mime
· LEGO Minifigures

Bearskin · 2011 · Royal Guard
· LEGO Minifigures

Domed sailor's hat · 2011 · Sailor
· LEGO Minifigures

Asian conical hat · 2011
· Master Wu · LEGO NINJAGO

Santa hat · 2012
· Santa Claus · LEGO Minifigures

Winter hood · 2014
· Arctic Explorer · LEGO CITY

Crooked witch hat · 2015
· Wacky Witch · LEGO Minifigures

Hard hat with ear defenders · 2015
· Construction Worker · LEGO CITY

Bandages · 2016
· Clumsy Guy · LEGO Minifigures

Hard hat with lamp · 2018
· Miner · LEGO CITY

Hard hat · 1979
· Construction Worker
· LEGOLAND Town

Chef's hat · 1979 · Chef
· LEGOLAND Town

Top hat · 1980 · Shop Patron
· LEGOLAND Town

Grille helmet with black plume · 1984 · Blue Knight
· LEGOLAND Castle

Hennin · 1986 · Maiden with Cape
· LEGOLAND Castle

Fusilier hat · 1989 · Imperial Soldier
· LEGO Pirates

Cone-shaped wizard's hat · 1993
· Majisto Wizard · LEGO Castle

Islander mask and feathered headdress · 1994 · King Kahuka
· LEGO Pirates

Gold crown with white plume
· 1995 · The King · LEGO Castle

Helmet with nose guard and bat wings · 1997 · Basil the Bat Lord
· LEGO Castle

Jester's hat · 2008 · Jester
· LEGO Castle

Gold crown tiara · 2009
· Crown Queen · LEGO Castle

MAD ABOUT HATS!

Red crested helmet
· 2013 · Roman Commander
· LEGO Minifigures

Elf hat with ears · 2013
· Holiday Elf · LEGO Minifigures

LEGO® HEADGEAR has been around longer than the modern minifigure. The precursors to the LEGO minifigure, released in 1975, may have had blank faces, but they were also wearing hats! LEGO hats fit onto a stud on the top of the standard minifigure head. They not only look stylish, but also help establish a minifigure's identity and suggest story ideas during play. Some hats (and helmets) are common, while others are made especially for just one character. All of them, of course, are endlessly interchangeable, so there is no limit to the different hats a standard minifigure can wear!

Hoodie over baseball cap · 2019
· Jack Davids · LEGO Hidden Side

Sou'wester · 2019
· Captain Jonas · LEGO Hidden Side

Helmet with blue visor element is new this year

BOLDLY GOING WHERE NO MINIFIGURE HAS GONE BEFORE!

Gold zipper

Red Futuron Moving on from the Classic Spacemen from 1986, the Futuron astronauts have a new, flashy torso design with gold zipper detail.

1987

NO MATTER WHERE a minifigure went in 1987, he or she was sure to run into adventure. Deep in the woods of Castle, Forestmen minifigures made an appearance for the first time. Beyond the stars, the forces of Futuron and Blacktron were about to have a galaxy-shaking clash. Closer to home, a new LEGO® Club was founded in this year and would eventually bring minifigure fun into the homes of millions of LEGO fans. Buckle up your rocket belt and get ready to blast off into 1987!

FUTURON
Premiering with six sets, Futuron centers on peaceful minifigures based on Earth's moon. They have fun exploring the galaxy, but they have to constantly contend with the wicked Blacktron Astronauts.

Air tank

DID YOU KNOW?
Faces are printed onto LEGO minifigures using a mechanized process called Tampo printing.

Blue Futuron
The Futurons all wear a new helmet design, since worn by more than 1,000 other minifigures.

Classic Space logo

Yellow Futuron
The busiest astronaut out of his space pals, this Futuron has featured in 12 sets. He retired in 1990.

Monorail Transport System (6990) This set features a battery-operated monorail plus five Futuron minifigures.

SPACE
Space introduced its first two competing factions in 1987, the Futuron explorers and the fiendish Blacktron Astronauts. Design of the minifigures, particularly on Blacktron, was a huge advance from Classic Space and helped cement Space as a much-loved LEGO line.

DARK DROID
The Blacktron Astronauts don't carry out all their missions alone—they need the help of this droid figure. The Blacktron Droid was only available in one set, Invader (6894).

Robot arm

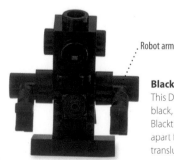

Blacktron Droid
This Droid is all in black, just like the Blacktron Astronauts, apart from a red translucent piece.

Air tank is attached with neck bracket

Torso also seen on the Blacktron Racer minifigure from the 1992 Classic Town theme

BLACKTRON
The Blacktron Astronauts made their debut in three sets, including their starship, Renegade (6954). These minifigures are in space for profit and aren't going to let the peaceful Futuron explorers get in their way.

Blacktron Astronaut
Wearing a new torso with a silver power pack design, the Blacktron Astronaut looks sleek and striking.

Black Falcon Knight
A grilled helmet and armored breastplate should be enough to protect this Knight in battle!

Fixed grille helmet

Silver armor

Blue plume

Green hat matches tunic and pants

FORESTMEN
The Forestmen minifigures made their first appearance in the Camouflaged Outpost set (6066), identifiable by their distinctive hats.

New basket element also seen on the Hunchback from the Studios theme in 2002

KNIGHT CLASH
The Crusader and Black Falcon minifigures squared off in sets including Battering Ram (6062) this year, with the Crusaders laying siege to Black Falcon strong points. The "Black Falcon" name came from one of their sets.

Blue Forestman
Wearing his new forestman hat, this skilled archer gets to work, sharpening his arrows.

Red Forestman
This Forestman likes hanging out with his Forestmen friends deep in the woods in set 6066.

Helmet with chin guard

Crusaders gold lion symbol

Crusader
This courageous Crusader is on the lookout for Black Falcon knights—their Battering Ram doesn't scare him!

CASTLE
New characters joined the medieval scene in 1987, as the Forestmen minifigures joined the Castle cast. They appeared in only one set this year, but their arrows would continue to fly until 1990. Elsewhere, the Crusaders battled the Black Falcons and would clash with the Forestmen, too, in future sets.

Tie shirt

Red plume

Black Forestman Carrying a heavy basket on his shoulders is hard work, but this Forestman seems happy enough.

Brown-hatted Forestman
His brown hat distinguishes this Forestman from his Red Forestman friend.

Forestman with Pouch
This Forestman looks after the precious gold pieces he "collects" from the rich in his waist pouch.

White hat is usually seen on Police minifigures

LOW BRIDGE! EVERYONE TAKE OFF THEIR HEADS!

Double-breasted suit jacket

Boat Admiral As Captain of the Cargo Carrier (4030), this Admiral wears a new suit, with shiny gold buttons and a gold anchor logo.

TOWN
Cargo had to be transported, and the Town minifigures were on the job! The Cargo Carrier (4030) appeared this year, complete with a captain and crew. But it wasn't all work in Town—the 4-Wheelin' Truck (6641) tore up the roads, looking for adventure!

Fire helmet

Zip-up jacket

Truck Driver This minifigure drives a truck and he's wearing a truck on his vest—he's probably thinking about trucks, too. He just loves trucks, okay?

Red cap

Firefighter This minifigure might not look like a classic Firefighter—his zip-up torso commonly appears on bike racers—but he's just as brave.

Construction hard hat is white for the first time

Truck logo on vest

Cargo Worker Sporting a new top with anchor logo, this Cargo Worker is ready for his first day hauling cargo at the dock.

Standard black male hair piece ·····

·····Pocket for essential tools

WE ONLY TAKE PLASTIC.

Mechanic This Mechanic's new red overalls are only seen on Classic Town minifigures, both male and female.

1988

IT WAS ANOTHER exciting year for LEGO® builders. Town was back with the biggest race-themed set produced to date. Castle introduced the brutish Black Knights, and Futuron and Blacktron continued to clash in the far reaches of the Space subtheme. No matter what the situation, though, minifigures were always smiling. The minifigures from the three LEGOLAND® subthemes (Town, Castle, and Space) seemed content to carry on as they were. However, little did they know that this time next year, what it meant to be a minifigure would change forever ....

TOWN

It was all about cars and keeping them well-serviced and on the LEGO roads in Town this year. Victory Lap Raceway (6395), with a whopping 13 minifigures—including mechanics, spectators, and four racers—left the starting line, as did the Metro Park & Service Tower (6394).

DID YOU KNOW?
Metro Park & Service Tower (6394) is the first set to feature car wash brushes.

Metro Park & Service Tower (6394) Keeping all the Town cars running, this set includes a service station, multistory car park, and six minifigures.

Service Station Worker
Servicing the cars of Town must be a great job—this worker can't wipe the smile from her face.

Striped T-shirt ·

·Standard helmet with visor

WHY AM I SMILING? I LOST!

Baton for signaling to pilots ·

Blue cap matches pants

Airplane logo ·

Motorcycle Driver
This Motorcycle Driver has the same torso as the Horse Rider from 1986.

Aircraft Controller
If the Aircraft Controller ever forgets where he works, he just looks at his torso for a reminder.

· Torso also seen on the Trucker from 1987

Spectator A huge race car fan, this guy supports LEGO race car drivers at all of their races.

Red Forestman
The Forestmen are skilled with a bow and arrow, thanks to hours of target practice in sets like the Forestman's Hideout (6054).

·····Red collar

FORESTMEN
Only one set, Forestmen's Hideout (6054), marked the second year of the Forestmen faction. With vines to climb up and targets to shoot at, the Forestmen would be ready to take on any naughty Knights.

Pouch is full to bursting

Green Forestman hat

The Forestman's spear always hits its target·····

CASTLE
The Black Knights arrived this year with their powerful fortress, the Black Monarch's Castle (6085). Guarded by 12 Knight minifigures, it was the first of two castles for this popular Castle faction. Beyond the gates, the Black Knights and the Crusaders would oppose each other in the Knight's Challenge joust before the eyes of two spectator minifigures.

Forestman with White Plume
This Forestman is a variant of the Forestman with Pouch, seen in 1987, but this minifigure's plume is white instead of yellow.

Circus Ringmaster
Keeping the Circus Clowns in line, as well as making sure his mustache is neatly trimmed, is no laughing matter for the Ringmaster.

·····Bow tie

Aviator helmet ·····

Blue Clown This Clown has guts—he is blasted out of a cannon every night, much to the DUPLO audience's amusement.

Big bow tie

Red Clown Luckily for this Clown, he just has to ride an elephant while carrying an umbrella in the DUPLO Town Circus Caravan (2652).

LEGO® DUPLO®
LEGO DUPLO was off to see a show with the Circus Caravan set, one of seven sets released this year. This was the first appearance of the Circus Ringmaster figure.

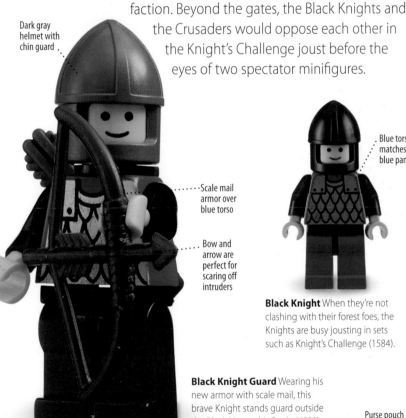

Dark gray helmet with chin guard

····Scale mail armor over blue torso

···· Bow and arrow are perfect for scaring off intruders

Black Knight Guard Wearing his new armor with scale mail, this brave Knight stands guard outside the Black Monarch's Castle (6085).

Blue torso matches blue pants

Black Knight When they're not clashing with their forest foes, the Knights are busy jousting in sets such as Knight's Challenge (1584).

The Crusaders' crossed halberts emblem

Crusader Squire This Crusader Knight is standing next to his archenemies. Luckily for them, he doesn't realize this.

Dragon Shield Black Knight The red torso with scale mail pattern that adorns this Knight is new this year.

Long pole with ax attachment

Helmet is seen on many LEGO Knights ·····

Knight's Challenge (1584)
Let the games begin! Depicting a jousting tournament, this set includes an audience stand, a weapons rack, and a tapped keg, as well as eight minifigures.

1584

Purse pouch

Peasant The humble Peasant is attending a jousting tournament—just as a spectator, however.

Black helmet with neck protector ·····

Black Knight The Black Knight's armor was first seen in 1984, but it still looks just as shiny this year.

SHIVER ME LEGO BRICK TIMBERS!

- Eyepatch seen for the first time
- Striped top underneath jacket

Blue Jacket Pirate This Pirate is proud to be the first of his pals to wear the new Pirate torso and tricorne hat.

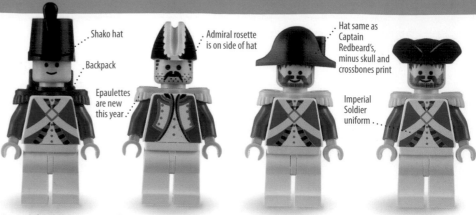

- Shako hat
- Backpack
- Epaulettes are new this year

Imperial Soldier This Soldier likes his home comforts—he keeps his bedding in his backpack.

- Admiral rosette is on side of hat

Governor Broadside With his fancy hat and blue coat, there's no doubting that this Soldier is in charge.

Lt. de Martinet The courageous Lieutenant often leads the charge into battle— and he never loses his head.

- Hat same as Captain Redbeard's, minus skull and crossbones print
- Imperial Soldier uniform

Imperial Officer The Officer has the same head as the Lieutenant but a different hat.

1989

NOT SINCE 1978 had there been such an exciting year for the LEGO® minifigure. LEGO® Pirates was launched, and it was an immediate hit. Suddenly, minifigures had moved on from the traditional simple smile to having multiple facial expressions. Many new elements also arrived as the minifigure took a quantum leap toward the minifigure of today. Meanwhile, on the other side of the law-and-order fence, the Space Police arrived to whip Blacktron into shape and bring peace to the galaxy … and a lot of new fans to Space!

This is the first time a minifigure has worn lipstick!

- New red corset matches ruby necklace

Female Pirate This Pirate risks her life every day sailing the seas—she is always looking for a new adventure.

PIRATES

No one had ever seen anything like it before: a bunch of minifigures with scruffy beards and thick mustaches, with peg legs and hook hands, and carrying flintlock pistols and muskets. The Pirates had arrived in a big way, sailing the Black Seas Barracuda (6285) against the forces of the Imperials. The seas—and the world of LEGO minifigures—would never be the same again.

DID YOU KNOW? A comic book called "The Golden Medallion" was released in 1989 to promote the LEGO Pirates theme.

Captain Redbeard Ahoy, me hearties! With all new elements, Captain Redbeard is ready to sail the seas on the lookout for treasure.

- New bandanna protects minifigure head from bracing sea winds

Young Pirate Striped vests are a favorite with Pirates. This sea dog's red bandanna matches perfectly.

- Ominous skull and bones bicorne hat

- Blue-and-white striped vest

Blue Pirate This rascally fellow's stubbly face with its droopy mustache is new this year.

Blue Bandanna Pirate This Pirate is sporting the same vest as his pal, but he has chosen white pants instead.

- Red-and-white striped vest
- Peg leg
- Hook hand

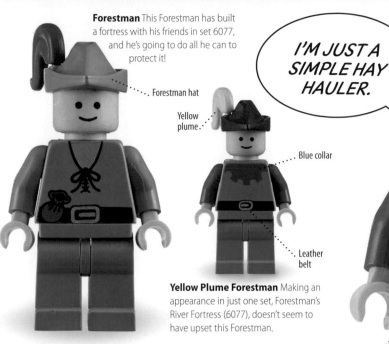

Forestman This Forestman has built a fortress with his friends in set 6077, and he's going to do all he can to protect it!

· · · Forestman hat

Yellow plume · · ·

Yellow Plume Forestman Making an appearance in just one set, Forestman's River Fortress (6077), doesn't seem to have upset this Forestman.

I'M JUST A SIMPLE HAY HAULER.

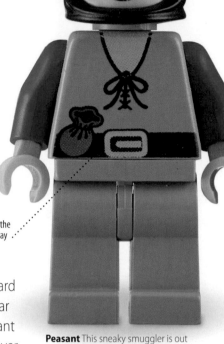

Farmer's cowl also seen on the LEGO Castle Wolfpack gang in 1992 · · ·

Blue collar · · ·

Leather belt · · ·

Torso is the same as the Forestman, but in gray · · ·

Peasant This sneaky smuggler is out to steal what he can—today, it's pieces of gold and some hay to bed down on.

CASTLE

The Forestmen were back with their largest set to date, the Forestmen's River Fortress (6077), which they fought hard to protect from the Crusaders. Another set released this year was the Smuggler's Hayride (1974), which featured a peasant smuggler and a wagon with gold bars hidden away. However, the Forestmen subtheme had only one more year to be merry.

LEGO® DUPLO®

These two LEGO DUPLO figures were part of an 18-figure set intended to represent people from all over the globe.

Tie matches pants

Red necklace

Man with Tie This figure makes an appearance in the DUPLO Figures International set (9159), and he's dressed for the occasion!

Woman with Beads From the same set, this figure is dressed more casually in a yellow top and red pants.

Black torso with bare arms is new this year

Accident Victim Unfortunately, this man has had an accident. Fortunately, the Minifigure Doctor comes to his rescue in the Rescue Helicopter (6482).

Company sticker is on the front and back of torso

Dairy Driver This dairy truck driver came with a promotional set, Dairy Tanker (1952).

Yellow legs with black hips make their debut this year

TOWN

Town was at sea this year with a new Coast Guard Base (6387) and a Rescue Helicopter (6482). This was the first time a new LEGO Coast Guard logo was used in a set and the last Coast Guard base produced until 1995. This year's Rescue Helicopter was the largest LEGO System chopper to date. The year 1989 also saw the release of a Dairy Tanker (1952) promotional set, featuring a friendly minifigure driver.

SPACE

The Space Police, one of the most-loved Space lines, arrived this year to serve and protect the civilians of Futuron from the evil forces of Blacktron. This was the first of three Space subthemes based around intergalactic law enforcement.

Visor is red for the first time · · ·

Gold logo · · ·

Lever · · ·

FUTURON FRIEND

Appearing exclusively in the Lunar MPV Vehicle set (1621), this figure accompanied the Futurons on their space mission. The Futurons needed all the help they could get against the Blacktrons!

Futuron Droid The Droid has a hinged base, allowing it to bend forward.

Torso design is the same as the Futuron astronauts from 1987 · · ·

Space Policeman Whenever this Space Policeman witnesses Blacktrons misbehaving, he sees red—literally.

1990s

LEGO® mania! The '90s saw an explosion of wild new LEGO play themes, and with them came an even wilder array of new minifigures. Ghosts, cowboys, robots, aliens, witches, and wizards abounded. Minifigures traveled through time, blasted off to futuristic frozen planets, explored ancient pyramids, and went diving to the bottom of the sea. Capping it all off at the decade's end was the biggest news in minifigure history: a famous licensed theme of truly galactic proportions!

TIME TO BLAST OFF INTO THE '90S!

Helmet with visor is vital for space walks

NASA sticker on torso

Shuttle Astronaut This NASA minifigure appears in only one set: Space Launch Shuttle (1682).

1990

AS A NEW DECADE began, LEGO® Town, LEGO® Space, and LEGO® Castle became play themes in their own right, and their minifigures were getting ready for many new adventures. Far up in LEGO Space, M:Tron joined the lineup, while the Forestmen said farewell in LEGO Castle. Over in LEGO Town, everyone was getting ready to travel on a jet plane to visit far-off lands. LEGO® DUPLO® also continued to grow, adding new subthemes this year. With new minifigures in space, on land, and even a new minifigure haunting a medieval castle, it was a year of action and adventure for builders, young and old.

LEGO TOWN

Builders visiting LEGO Town in 1990 had lots to choose from. They could take off from the airport, visit the Breezeway Café (6376) for lunch, or ride with the police from the Pursuit Squad (6354). LEGO Town continued its tradition of presenting a fun variety of places to play.

Classic female hair piece

Showjumper With a sharp-suited torso and white gloves, this minifigure is competition-ready!

Red neckerchief offsets the chef's whites

Not a hair out of place

New torso with vest and bow tie

Chef This minifigure works at the Breezeway Café, where he serves delicious food to all the minifigure patrons.

Waiter Sporting formal attire and a slick hairdo, this waiter works in a classy establishment.

Helmet protects head in rough seas

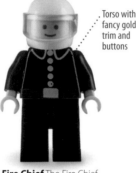

Torso with fancy gold trim and buttons

Bright yellow life jacket makes Coast Guard visible at sea

Fire Chief The Fire Chief came to the rescue in only one set, the Fire Control Center (6389).

Coast Guard Wearing a new life jacket accessory, this minifigure is ready for action.

M:Tron With a new torso and visor color, this minifigure is ready to blast off into space.

LEGO SPACE

The M:Tron subtheme introduced a new innovation to LEGO building: the use of magnets to hold parts together. It was the first major Space theme to feature only vehicles—and not bases—in its seven sets. The Futuron subtheme came to an end this year, after four years in Space.

Air tanks for a space walk

M:Tron logo

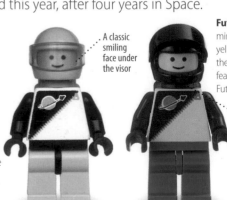

A classic smiling face under the visor

Futuron This minifigure and his yellow friend were the last figures to feature in the Futuron subtheme.

Air tank attaches to back with neck bracket

Yellow Futuron Four of these minifigures appeared in set 9355.

Ghost
Underneath the Ghost's new shroud piece is a white torso and a plain black head.

Ghoulish face, but still smiling

White minifigure arms

BOO!
The first LEGO ghost minifigure mysteriously appeared this year, glowing in the dark in the King's Mountain Fortress (6081). This smiling spirit would be around for the next five years.

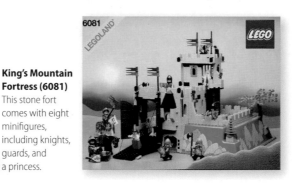

King's Mountain Fortress (6081)
This stone fort comes with eight minifigures, including knights, guards, and a princess.

Female Zookeeper
This figure came in two DUPLO Zoo sets (2669, 2666) and a DUPLO People set (9979).

Green zookeeper's uniform

Red Knight
The Black Falcons had better watch out—this Knight is armored and ready for battle.

Scale mail torso provides protection

Helmet with covered visor and red plume

Breastplate armor

Blue Knight
This minifigure likes his new visor—he is just finding it a bit hard to breathe.

LEGO CASTLE
There was plenty of excitement in the world of LEGO Castle in 1990, with the introduction of the first skirted female minifigure and the finale of the Forestmen subtheme. This year also saw the first castle built on a raised baseplate. It was a merry medieval time for all!

Traditional forestman hat

Quiver full of arrows

Red Forestman
This Forestman looks happy—he has smuggled goodies from the Crusaders in Crusader's Cart (1680).

Yellow hat to keep the elements off

Zoo logo on torso

Male Zookeeper
This figure is seen in many locations, from safaris to zoo trains—he's a busy guy.

LEGO DUPLO
Preschool toys were made even more fun this year with the introduction of sets based on Zoo and Race. Little builders had plenty to see and do with these new worlds!

IS IT A HAT OR A ROCKET NOSE CONE? YOU DECIDE!

Red cone hat worn by four other minifigures

Red feather plume

Visor to protect face

New torso with necklace detail

Belt with money pouch

Motorcycle Racer
This figure appeared in Racer (2609) with a blue DUPLO car.

Number helps identify racer on the course

Black Knight
Underneath his new breastplate, this minifigure is trembling—he's just seen a spook in Black Monarch's Ghost (6034).

Maiden
This medieval Maiden has a sloped piece instead of legs—the first time it has been seen.

Green Forestman
None of the parts are new, but this minifigure features a new combination of pieces.

Red hat matches tie

Railway logo

TICKETS, PLEASE!

Station Manager
The Station Manager is happy with his new torso—it makes him look and feel important.

.White hard hat

.Chevron-style design on torso

Hair piece seen on more than 125 other minifigures

Trackside Staff
The trackside worker is glad he can't see his new torso with chevron design—it makes his minifigure eyes go funny!

Onboard Staff
This minifigure is most impressed with the new railway uniform, especially the bright red neckerchief.

Same torso as Railway Worker.

Maintenance Man The railway tracks don't repair themselves—this guy fixes them in Road and Rail Maintenance (4546).

1991

THE BIGGEST NEWS of 1991 came from the high seas. After the massive success of LEGO® Pirates in 1989, the line had effectively taken a year off in 1990. It came back with the roar of cannon fire this year and with sets that are still fondly remembered to this day. An old LEGO® Space friend returned, too, as Blacktron was updated and turned into Blacktron II. In LEGO® Town, the Firefighters dispatched a new unit— RSQ911—to save the day.

Same red hat as the Station Manager's

Railway logo printed on torso

I NEED A TIMETABLE ACCESSORY!

LEGO® TRAIN

LEGO Train entered a new era in 1991, as 9V train sets took over from 12V and 4.5V. Six new sets appeared this year, including the Metroliner (4558) and the Metro Station (4554), with 19 minifigures between them. These included conductors, railway workers, and passengers. 9V dominated LEGO Train until 2006.

Railway Worker Whether at the Metro Station (4554) or aboard the Metroliner (4558), this minifigure is always ready to help passengers!

LEGO PIRATES

The second major wave of Pirates sets came out this year, including Rock Island Refuge (6273) and Lagoon Lock-Up (6267). Five sets sailed the Spanish Main, featuring Pirate and Imperial Soldier minifigures and the second female Pirate ever released. Hoist the sails!

.Red bandanna

.Orange belt

Gray Pirate This scruffy guy wears gray pants instead of blue—the only difference between him and his 1989 variant.

New torso with lime green logo

Jet pack for freestyle flying

Blacktron II Spaceman
This minifigure spaceman thinks the new Blacktron logo is simply out of this world.

M:Tron Spaceman
With his new jet pack, this M:Tron minifigure can finally breathe easily in space.

DID YOU KNOW?
So far, more than 500 minifigures have worn the standard helmet since its redesign in 1987.

Blacktron II Commander
Wearing new bodywear, the jet pack with twin handles, this minifigure is ready for a mission.

Lime green visor to protect his grin

Jet pack with twin handles

Blacktron II logo

LEGO SPACE

Blacktron II rocketed into the stratosphere in 1991, with a dozen sets. This was a remake of the original Blacktron from 1987, and many of the sets were similar to those released previously. The major change was in the look of the minifigures, who all received new uniforms with a black octagon logo. An M:Tron minifigure was also released—the first minifigure from the M:Tron subtheme to feature a jet pack.

LEGO® DUPLO®

Police became a part of DUPLO Town in 1991, with the release of a new Police Station (2672) and a Police Emergency Unit (2654). New figures included police officers and a prisoner.

Prisoner number matches set number

Silver police badge

Jailbreak Joe
This stubbly-faced figure came in one set: Police Set (2672).

Policeman
Part of six sets, this figure was a familiar face on the beat in 1991.

Black cap

Police Chief
If there was a minifigure emergency this guy would be there, in Emergency Unit (2654).

Knight There are no new parts on this minifigure, but it is a new combination of parts.

Scale mail decoration on torso

LEGO TOWN

RSQ911, part of the Fire subtheme, came out this year, along with some new nautical-themed sets like Cabin Cruiser (4011) and Coastal Cutter (6353). Minifigures learned to love the life jacket, as a total of 10 minifigures wore this accessory in 1991.

Cap to combat glare from water

Boater Part of the Cabin Cruiser set (4011), this minifigure came with a new accessory: a fishing rod.

LEGO® CASTLE

Only one new Castle set was released this year: King's Catapult (1480). Launched as part of the Crusaders subtheme, it featured pieces to build a catapult and one new Crusader soldier minifigure. It was a lonely year for this fellow, but Castle would return in 1992.

Yellow life jacket

I NEED COFFEE, NOW!

Classic hair piece

Airplane design on torso

Business suit

Policeman The life jacket had only been worn by one minifigure in 1990. The Policeman thinks that safety is always in fashion!

Commuter
This minifigure is always rushing to work, complete with a suitcase accessory.

Airport Fireman
This is the first fireman to be featured in the Airport subtheme.

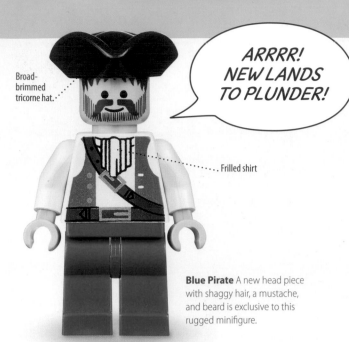

Broad-brimmed tricorne hat

> *ARRRR! NEW LANDS TO PLUNDER!*

Frilled shirt

Blue Pirate A new head piece with shaggy hair, a mustache, and beard is exclusive to this rugged minifigure.

1992

THIS YEAR SAW SOME new faces and the return of some old ones. Both LEGO® Space and LEGO® Castle followed the lead of LEGO® Pirates and upgraded their minifigure heads to the more modern look that is visible today. The Space Police subtheme returned (nicknamed Space Police II), while Castle got a brand-new bunch of bad guys, and Pirates faced a new military foe. For those minifigures who just wanted to get away from it all, new theme LEGO® Paradisa offered up a variety of tropical delights.

LEGO PIRATES

The Pirates got a new enemy this year, the Imperial Guard, as nine new sets appeared. The Imperial Guard minifigures were very similar to Imperial Soldiers, which featured from 1989 to 1991, with only a change of uniform. They would battle the Pirates for four years before being replaced by the Imperial Armada in 1997.

Brimmed hat keeps rainwater at bay

New torso with striped vest

Striped Pirate Protocol requires this pirate to maintain a rugged appearance.

Imperial Trading Post (6277) This is one of the largest Imperial Guard sets. It comes with a merchant ship, rowboat, and cannons.

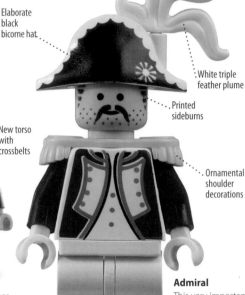

Elaborate black bicorne hat

White triple feather plume

Printed sideburns

Ornamental shoulder decorations

Shaggy beard

New torso with crossbelts

Gray hook replaces hand

Black Pirate A new torso for this minifigure has a black knife tucked into his crossbelt—so the Pirate's one hand can be free.

Officer A new head piece with an unkempt hairstyle shows this Imperial Guard focuses on keeping his robes neat, rather than his hair.

Admiral This very important Imperial Guard minifigure has a dashing new head piece and torso.

LEGO SPACE

It was Space Police's turn to get revamped in 1992, with new uniforms and new ships—but no permanent base. Pitted against their enemies, Blacktron II, Space Police II would protect civilian space explorers for the next year.

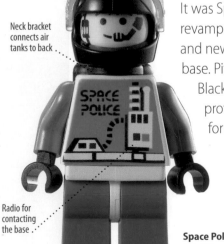

Neck bracket connects air tanks to back

SPACE POLICE

Radio for contacting the base

Space Police Officer This Officer proudly bears the Space Police logo on his brand-new torso.

DID YOU KNOW?
Space Police II was the first Space subtheme to replace the classic minifigure head with a more detailed one.

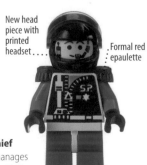

New head piece with printed headset

Formal red epaulette

Space Police Chief This minifigure manages a police station and jail aboard a spaceship.

LEGO CASTLE

LEGO Castle was inspired by Pirates this year, premiering the same kind of printed head pieces as Pirates debuted in 1989. The Wolfpack, robbers, and renegades who appeared in two sets in 1992, also featured this year. One Wolfpack minifigure appeared in 1993, before the subtheme came to an end.

A farmer's cowl covers unkempt hair

Wolfpack motif

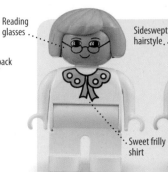

Reading glasses

Sideswept hairstyle

Sweet frilly shirt

DUPLO Grandma This bespectacled veteran appears only in Grandma's Kitchen (2551).

DUPLO Grandpa This figure is featured in two sets: DUPLO Supermarket (9167) and Grandma's Kitchen (2551).

LEGO® DUPLO®

These two figures were cooking up something good in the DUPLO Playhouse Grandma's Kitchen set (2551). Although LEGO DUPLO had no new themes this year, it continued to provide plenty of fun for young builders.

Dragon-shaped plume

Shaggy appearance

Strong breastplate armor

Red belt to hold up pants

Knight The biggest challenge for this armored minifigure is getting around without making too much noise.

Eyepatch Bandit The new brown torso worn by this minifigure helps him hide among the trees in the forest.

Mustachioed Bandit For a fierce bandit, he has a cheerful expression! This new rugged minifigure was introduced this year.

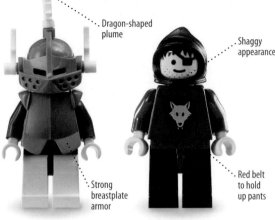

Poolside Paradise (6416) This vacation dream house has a waiter to serve drinks and a mailbox to send letters back home.

Unique base plate with built-in pool

Rare convex, transparent panels

Open-top sports car

The sunglasses print was new this year

Pool Guy Sleeveless vests and white pants are perfect attire for a casual sun-lover.

THIS PLACE IS A MINIFIGURE'S PARADISE ...

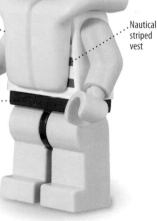

Life jacket

Nautical striped vest

Black swimming trunks

Speedboat Driver Nothing pleases this minifigure more than feeling the wind in his hair piece as he sails.

Hard riding hat

Vest for hot days

Stable Hand This minifigure's head piece and torso were introduced this year.

Swimmer This minifigure has a pretty new torso and appears in Poolside Paradise (6416).

Polka-dot swimming costume

Palm tree motif on new torso

Vendor This is the first minifigure to feature freckles. He wears a cap to shield his face from the sun.

LEGO PARADISA

Bright and breezy new theme Paradisa launched with four sets in 1992. Aimed primarily at young girls, it focused on tropical destinations and used plenty of pink bricks. A number of new female minifigures were produced for the line, featuring a new facial design and new hair pieces. The Paradisa theme would continue for five years.

New pointed hat piece

ADMIT IT, YOU LOVE THE HAT.

Pouch for carrying potions

Majisto As the first wizard minifigure, Majisto is as proud of his wizard's hat as he is of his brand-new separate beard piece.

Helmet with chin guard

Brave Knight A new head piece and torso were introduced this year for this minifigure.

Dragon emblem on chest

DID YOU KNOW?
Majisto was the first Castle minifigure to be given an official name.

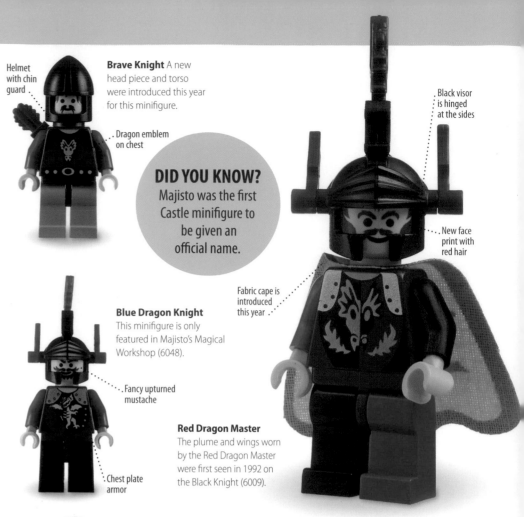

Black visor is hinged at the sides

New face print with red hair

Fabric cape is introduced this year

Blue Dragon Knight This minifigure is only featured in Majisto's Magical Workshop (6048).

Fancy upturned mustache

Chest plate armor

Red Dragon Master The plume and wings worn by the Red Dragon Master were first seen in 1992 on the Black Knight (6009).

1993

THE STRENGTH OF LEGO® minifigures as a concept rested on the idea that each minifigure could be customized and used in a variety of settings. The ability to add to new and old sets would help keep long-standing themes looking fresh and current. Both the LEGO® Castle and LEGO® Space themes got new factions and new places to explore this year. From the scorched plains ruled by the Dragon Masters to the frigid wasteland of the Ice Planet, LEGO fans and their minifigures were given plenty of exciting and innovative ways to stir their imagination in 1993.

Dragon-shaped plume

LEGO CASTLE

The beat of huge, leathery wings announced the arrival of Dragon Masters, the newest Castle subtheme. The wizard Majisto sent his dragons into battle in a line that introduced several new minifigures, cloth pieces, and the now-famous flame piece to LEGO building. The dragons roared only until 1995.

HA! NOW THIS IS WHAT I CALL A HAT!

New shoulder armor printing

Fire Breathing Fortress (6082) Featuring six minifigures, this set has a trap door that dumps intruders into a pit.

Blue Dragon Master Almost identical to the Red Dragon Master, this minifigure also has a red hip piece mismatched with blue and black legs—new for this year.

Large dragon figures were new this year

LEGO® TOWN

The year 1993 proved to be a big one for LEGO Town, starting with the move of all Police and Fire sets to a new subtheme, Rescue. Airport and Race both had new sets, but the highlight had to be the new Central Precinct HQ (6398), the first police station in two years, following Pier Police in 1991 (6540).

Helmet protects in high-speed pursuits · · · · Thick, weatherproof jacket

Patrol Officer Found in two sets this year, this minifigure has a new torso and helmet.

Prison number

Jailbreak Joe The printed torso on this crook has been featured on four minifigures in total.

DID YOU KNOW?
Central Police HQ (6398) was the first set to have a prisoner minifigure—Jailbreak Joe.

Helmet is essential
Stubbled cheeks and chin
Fur collar for warmth

Red Stunt Pilot The new flight jacket torso print on this minifigure appears for the first time this year.

Peaked cap is official Police uniform

Policeman This new torso with a single-breasted suit print was introduced this year.

Helmet printed with stripes.
Green vest

Stunt Pilot This is the first year in which printing is featured on a minifigure's helmet.

Standard ponytail hair piece
Jogging suit

Spectator A new torso with all-weather gear shows this minifigure is ready to watch the pilots' air show.

New police baseball cap.
Police Sheriff The sheriff only appears in Central Precinct HQ (6398) and is the first minifigure to feature this new torso.
ID card clipped to chest

New movable visor with antenna
Breathing apparatus
Heavy-duty space boots

Ice Planet Man Clearly pleased to be heading into space, this minifigure has the first face print with a messy white-blond fringe.

Ice Planet Woman Wearing a focused expression, this minifigure checks that her breathing apparatus is secure.

Ice Planet Chief The Chief features a new torso with a formal jacket print—fitting for a high-ranking minifigure.

IT'S SO COLD, MY MUSTACHE HAS FROZEN!

Shaggy eyebrows

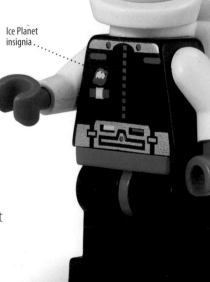

Ice Planet insignia

LEGO SPACE

Another new faction joined the LEGO Space saga with Ice Planet 2002. Civilian scientists conducting top-secret research on a frozen world found themselves the target of villains Blacktron (and later Spyrius). Six sets were released in 1993, and then more at irregular intervals through to 1999.

Peaked pilot's hat
Airline logo

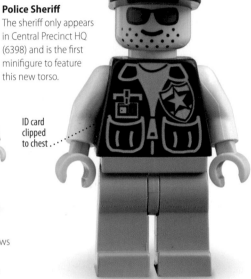

Jetliner Pilot This pilot only appears this year and is seen in three sets. His eager expression and wide eyes show that he is ready to take to the air.

Pilot with Helmet The pilot is seen in two sets alongside the Jetliner Pilot: Airport (2679) and DUPLO Airport (9163). He has a headset to listen to ground control.

LEGO® DUPLO®
For the first time in eight years, DUPLO figures took to the air with the release of the DUPLO Airport sets. The Airport subtheme would be up and away until 2005.

Head can also be seen in 1996 on a droid in the Time Cruisers theme ....

Standard LEGO helmet is totally clear for the first time

HI, I'M RUSTY ... WHAT'S SO FUNNY?

Exclusive blue-and-silver Spyrius printing on helmet ......

Breathing tubes printed on torso ....

Spyrius Droid
The Spyrius Droid minifigure is all new, with exclusive torso and legs. This is also the first time a minifigure has printed legs!

Spyrius Chief
The leader of this year's Space villains has a unique rugged head piece and printed helmet.

LEGO SPACE

Good fought against evil beyond the stars in 1994, as two new subthemes of LEGO Space were launched. Unitron took over from Space Police II as the heroes of LEGO Space, battling the villains of Spyrius. From their Lunar Launch site, this team of spies carried out their devious plans in five sets this year.

Dark gray uniform is a new LEGO color in the Space theme ....

Unitron Chief
Although the head piece, helmet, and torso are new for this year, only the helmet is exclusive to the Unitron Chief.

DID YOU KNOW?
Spyrius was the first LEGO subtheme to feature robot minifigures.

1994

THIS YEAR SAW a combination of venturing into new areas and building on what already worked. LEGO® Pirates and LEGO® Space were both back with new subthemes, while LEGO® BELVILLE™, a non-minifigure line aimed primarily at girl builders, started what would become a 15-year run. LEGO® Town was in the air with a new aircraft and stunt chopper, on land with new Fire and Police sets, and at sea with the Coastal Patrol. There were many adventures to be had for LEGO minifigure fans in 1994.

Detachable plume .....

Removable mask with painted face underneath

Torso is exclusive to the two King Kahuka variants

King Kahuka The leader of the islanders features a new head print and a new and exclusive head piece, mask, and torso.

LEGO PIRATES

LEGO Pirates returned for its fifth year. This time, the fierce pirate minifigures journeyed to faraway islands and met the natives. But were King Kahuka and his tribe friends or enemies? Another exciting Pirates adventure was about to begin.

Pirate hat has space for a feather.

Knife held in crossbelt ......

Captain Ironhook
This salty sea dog has a gray hook in place of a hand and wears a torn red top.

Construction helmet ....

LEGO® TRAIN

In 1994, Freight Rail Runner (4564) was the largest of the three LEGO Train sets released. The set included three minifigures, a Conductor, and two railway workers.

Torso exclusive to this conductor and the 1991 variant

Conductor
This minifigure is a variant of a 1991 Conductor with black pants.

Construction worker
This minifigure is exclusive to set 4564, but the torso can be see on five others.

LEGO TOWN

LEGO Town had something for everyone this year: five sets were released in the Rescue subtheme, including Flame Fighters (6571), which featured a fire station, fire engine, and helicopter. Car fans had three Race sets to build, while those in need of a vacation could take a jet plane from the busy Century Skyway airport (6597).

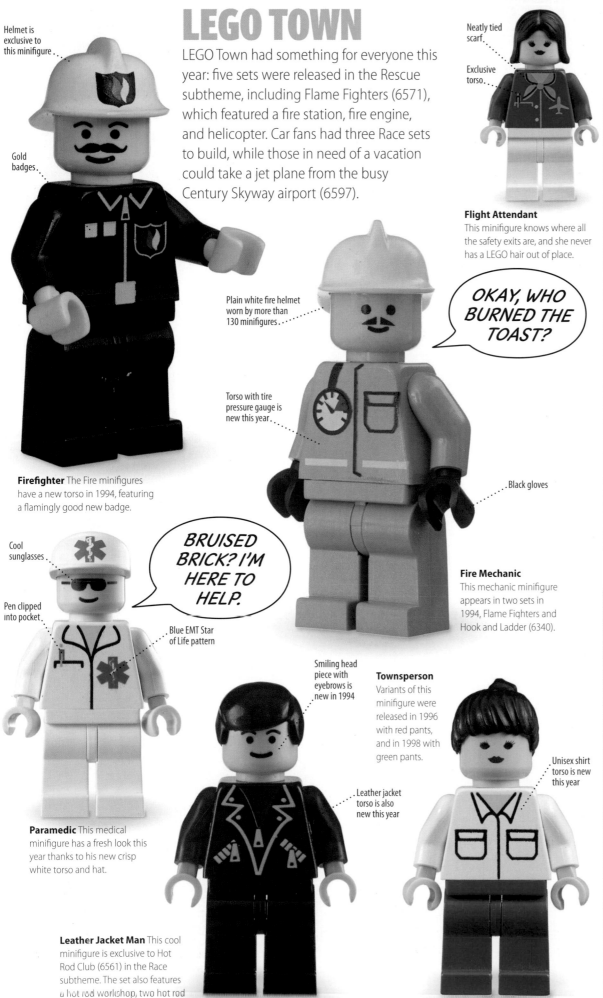

Helmet is exclusive to this minifigure

Gold badges

Firefighter The Fire minifigures have a new torso in 1994, featuring a flamingly good new badge.

Plain white fire helmet worn by more than 130 minifigures

OKAY, WHO BURNED THE TOAST?

Torso with tire pressure gauge is new this year

Black gloves

Fire Mechanic
This mechanic minifigure appears in two sets in 1994, Flame Fighters and Hook and Ladder (6340).

Neatly tied scarf

Exclusive torso

Flight Attendant
This minifigure knows where all the safety exits are, and she never has a LEGO hair out of place.

Cool sunglasses

Pen clipped into pocket

Blue EMT Star of Life pattern

BRUISED BRICK? I'M HERE TO HELP.

Paramedic This medical minifigure has a fresh look this year thanks to his new crisp white torso and hat.

Smiling head piece with eyebrows is new in 1994

Leather jacket torso is also new this year

Leather Jacket Man This cool minifigure is exclusive to Hot Rod Club (6561) in the Race subtheme. The set also features a hot rod workshop, two hot rod cars, and a motorcycle.

Townsperson
Variants of this minifigure were released in 1996 with red pants, and in 1998 with green pants.

Unisex shirt torso is new this year

Adult Man
This posable male appeared in Pretty Wishes Playhouse (5890) with a woman, a girl, and a baby boy.

Young Girl
Three variants of this figure were released between 1994 and 1996, wearing pink shorts (above), a pink skirt, and a yellow skirt.

LEGO BELVILLE

A combination of traditional LEGO bricks and new pink and purple elements, BELVILLE also featured larger, doll-like figures with more joints for greater posability. Early sets were themed around everyday family life.

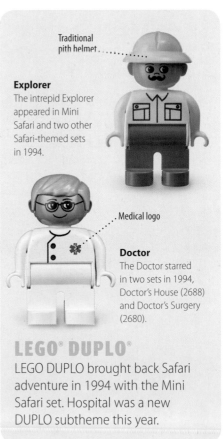

Traditional pith helmet

Explorer
The intrepid Explorer appeared in Mini Safari and two other Safari-themed sets in 1994.

Medical logo

Doctor
The Doctor starred in two sets in 1994, Doctor's House (2688) and Doctor's Surgery (2680).

LEGO® DUPLO®

LEGO DUPLO brought back Safari adventure in 1994 with the Mini Safari set. Hospital was a new DUPLO subtheme this year.

Blue visor

White helmet piece covers the shoulders

I THOUGHT THIS WAS GOING TO BE A POOL PARTY ...

All the Aquanauts wear the same blue suits

Aquanaut Commander
This minifigure's job is to drive the submarine. His head with freckles and a red headband with a "C" in the middle is new this year.

LEGO® AQUAZONE

Adventure lurked beneath the waves in Aquazone, a new play theme set in the depths of the ocean. The Aquanauts were undersea miners searching for crystals. However, the villainous Aquashark miners were out to steal whatever the Aquanauts dug up!

DID YOU KNOW?
Aquazone lasted for four exciting years, until it was discontinued in 1998.

Aquashark This villain's black diving suit is decorated with a grinning shark logo. The black helmet with shoulder protection is new this year.

Torso is exclusive to the 1995 Aquasharks

Black-gloved hands

Head piece was first seen on the Space Police Chief in 1992

Black visor

Aquanaut diving suit

Jock Clouseau
Radio expert Jock Clouseau has two variants in 1995—one with flippers and one without.

1995

ANOTHER LANDMARK year, 1995 saw the 40th anniversary of LEGO® System building sets. To celebrate, the next big play theme was introduced: Aquazone, along with a new version of Castle. Over in LEGO® Space, Unitron was discontinued after only one year and two sets. However, 1995 was a year with far-ranging effects, sparking a trend for underwater play themes and introducing one iconic bony figure who would appear in almost 50 sets over the next 18 years. Can you guess who he is?

5...4...3...2...1... GET READY FOR BLAST-OFF!

LAUNCH COMMAND
Five sets blasted off this year as LEGO® Town explored space in a big way. Unlike LEGO Space, Launch Command focused on real-world space exploration, including space shuttles and moon walkers.

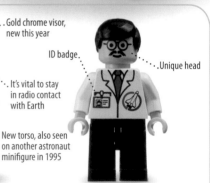

Gold chrome visor, new this year

It's vital to stay in radio contact with Earth

New torso, also seen on another astronaut minifigure in 1995

ID badge

Unique head

Astronaut Thanks to the hard work of the minifigures on the ground, the Astronaut makes it to space in Moon Walker (6516).

Scientist
Exclusive to Shuttle Launch Pad (6339), the brainy Scientist has two unique parts—his head and his torso.

Mærsk logo

LEGO® TOWN

It was a year of excitement and variety for LEGO Town. Hurricane Harbor (6338), the first Coast Guard base set in six years, kept watch over the waves. Two special Mærsk cargo truck sets appeared, but were sold only in Denmark. LEGO Town even went into space with the new Launch Command models.

Mærsk Truck Driver
Mærsk is a real-world company based in Copenhagen, Denmark. This minifigure is exclusive to the two 1995 sets.

LEGO® CASTLE

The Royal Knights arrived this year in five sets, including a castle of their own. This Castle subtheme is best known for introducing the skeleton figure and the first king minifigure to wear an actual crown. The Royal Knights would reign supreme through 1995 and 1996.

Royal Bowman
A variant without a quiver was released in 1996.

Helmet with chin guard

Lion's head shield is exclusive to this minifigure

HELLO BONES

The skeleton figure made his first appearance in 1995 in three sets—two from LEGO® Castle and one from LEGO® Pirates. Including variants with hats, he has appeared in more than 50 sets.

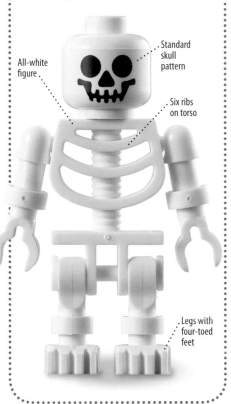

All-white figure

Standard skull pattern

Six ribs on torso

Legs with four-toed feet

The King
Three variants of the King were released in 1995, each with a new torso featuring a lion's head design.

Detachable plume of white feathers

The gold crown makes its debut in 1995.

New torso with fearsome lion crest

THIS CROWN IS REALLY HEAVY!

Two variants have blue pants, one has white.

Cape

Gray helmet with neck and nose protectors

Mustache Knight
This noble Knight is distinguished by his impressive mustache.

Dungarees Boy
This figure of a young boy appears in 12 LEGO Primo sets between 1995 and 2001.

Dark brown hair

Red shirt with blue dungarees

LEGO® PRIMO™

Aimed at the youngest builders, PRIMO replaced LEGO Baby in 1995. It featured colorful toys intended for children from 6 to 24 months and single-piece figures that were perfect for little hands.

I'M THE COOLEST CRANE OPERATOR YOU'LL SEE.

Torso with red safety bib print is new this year

Crane Operator
It takes a steady hand to operate a huge cargo crane, but this calm minifigure is up to the job in Cargo Crane (4552).

LEGO® TRAIN

Two new sets roared down the tracks in 1995, all of them dealing with cargo hauling. Five minifigures worked the rails, making sure that LEGO freight got where it needed to go. The new Cargo Station (4555) was the first one produced since 1978, and the first Cargo set using the battery-operated 9V power system.

Torso with a sunset and dolphin print vest is new this year

Dolphin Fan
Set 6414 featured a dolphin and a female minifigure who was eager to swim with it.

Dolphin Point (6414)
Hungry minifigures can climb the pink stairs to the ice-cream parlor for a treat in this Paradisa set.

DID YOU KNOW?
Paradisa sets were the first to feature pink, dark pink, and lime green colors.

LEGO® PARADISA

Once again, Paradisa was the place to be with the new Dolphin Point set (6414) featuring four minifigures. This elaborate model included a two-story lighthouse complete with lantern and an ice-cream shop.

This head is also used on a LEGO® Aqua Raiders minifigure in 1997.

SOME PRETTY RARE FINDS HERE!

Headset to call crew during missions

Exploriens logo

Nova Hunter
Chief Explorien Nova Hunter leads the team on missions. This minifigure features a torso with the Exploriens logo.

1996

PERHAPS THE BIGGEST news for LEGO® minifigures this year was the introduction of LEGO.com. For the first time, fans could go online to access information, games, and activities and also to shop for their favorite minifigures and sets. And there was plenty for LEGO fans to see online this year, as new themes LEGO® Western and LEGO® Time Cruisers were introduced, along with the Castle Dark Forest and Space Exploriens subthemes. From the distant past to the far future, LEGO building was everywhere in 1996!

WHERE TO GO NEXT ... WHO FANCIES A TRIP TO ANCIENT EGYPT?

LEGO® SPACE

The Exploriens were new space travelers introduced in nine sets in 1996. They searched the galaxy for fossils, accompanied by their robot Ann Droid—the second robot in the history of LEGO Space. Operating out of Android Base (6958), as well as the smaller Nebula Outpost (6899), the Exploriens hung up their space helmets in 1996.

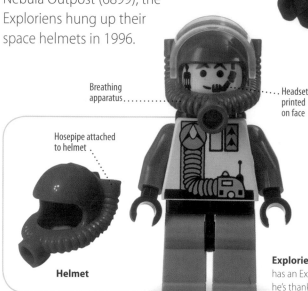

Transparent green light stud

Android face print

Armor protects internal mechanics

Breathing apparatus

Headset printed on face

Hosepipe attached to helmet

Helmet

Ann Droid The LEGO Exploriens team's robot features a unique transparent head piece. Her name is a play on the word "android."

Explorien This minifigure has an Explorien torso—he's thankful that it has oxygen controls.

LEGO TIME CRUISERS

The first and so far only LEGO theme focused on time travel featured a team—Dr. Cyber, Tim (his assistant), a robot, and a monkey—that traveled back in time on various missions. It lasted two years.

Head piece also seen on Spyrius Droid from LEGO Space in 1994.

Wacco This robot is designed and built by inventive Dr. Cyber.

Freckles on face

Nose print debuted this year, but it is rarely used as a feature

"T" print on torso for Tim

Tim Dr. Cyber's assistant, Tim, travels with him on all trips back in time.

Cross-eyed expression is unique

Pencil tied to bow tie

Pocket watch

Dr. Cyber Traveling in time has made Dr. Cyber cross-eyed. Well, he's seen some crazy things!

· Plume
fits into
helmet hole

LEGO® PIRATES

LEGO Pirates underwent a major redesign in 1996, as the Pirates and Islanders were joined by a new faction. The Imperial Armada was out to hunt down the pesky Pirates, but even their Flagship (6280) was no match for the Pirates' dreaded Skull's Eye Schooner (6286).

Pirate hat ···

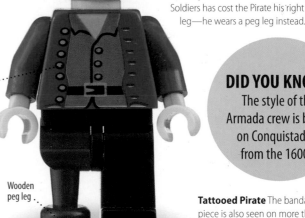

Pirate Captain A clash with the Soldiers has cost the Pirate his right leg—he wears a peg leg instead.

Admiral Head of the Armada flagship, the Admiral minifigure is always seen with his armor plate on—hunting Pirates is a risky business.

Officer This elaborately dressed minifigure wears a triple plume piece, which fits into his hat.

Silver button print on jacket ···

DID YOU KNOW?
The style of the Armada crew is based on Conquistadors from the 1600s.

· Silver breastplate guards against attacks

Decorative gold medal ···

Wooden peg leg ···

Tattooed Pirate The bandanna piece is also seen on more than 80 minifigures, including the 2009 Hondo Ohnaka minifigure from the LEGO® Star Wars™ theme.

Shirt collar print ····

White Shirt Pirate No Pirate would be complete without a bandanna accessory. This minifigure's bandanna is hiding a bald patch on his head!

Green vest ···

Anchor tattoo ···

····· Striped uniform design

Leather belt print ···

Red Soldier Clad in red, this Soldier is the most common minifigure in the sets from the Imperial Armada theme.

Armada Flagship (6280) This set comes with a twin-mast ship and three Imperial Armada minifigures.

LEGO® CASTLE

DID YOU KNOW?
LEGO designers rarely add printed noses to minifigures to keep the graphics as neat and simple as possible.

Blue Forestman This Forestman doesn't follow the minifigure crowd—unlike his friends, he has a blue-and-brown color scheme.

HAND OVER YOUR GOLD BRICKS!

Scraggly hair visible under cowl ···

Castle fans ventured into the Dark Forest this year, with three sets produced for this short-lived subtheme. In a reimagining of the Forestmen subtheme from the late 1980s, green-clad bandits hid in the hollow trees of the woods, clashing with Royal Knights, Black Knights, and Dragon Masters. Led by Rob N. Hood, they stole from the rich, but who they gave the treasure to was never clear.

Studded shirt pattern on torso ···

Fringed hair pattern ···

Drooping mustache ···

··· Stylized mustache and goatee

Pouch to carry supplies ···

Rob N. Hood Rob's plume accessory also came in black, yellow, blue, and white.

Red leather belt ···

Forest Archer This cheery Archer has a new head with a choppy fringe, and he can't stop smiling about it.

Forest Swordsman Working in the forest can be dangerous. This Forestman wears a brown cowl to try and blend in.

1996

LEGO WESTERN

It was all about lawmen and outlaws in 1996, with plenty of new pieces and fun for young cowpokes. It was the first LEGO play theme to focus on the Wild West, and it lasted into 1997. In 2013, The LEGO Group returned to the Wild West with LEGO® *The Lone Ranger*™, based on the Disney movie.

Pencil for quick calculations

NEW TO THESE PARTS, STRANGER?

Unique detailed torso

Banker Carrying a stash of $100 bills, pocket watch, and gold-rimmed glasses, this banker minifigure is asking for trouble ....

HOWDY! ANYBODY KNOW WHERE I CAN GET A HAIRCUT?

Messy blond hair partially covers eyes

Sheriff is smiling— for now.

Sheriff's badge

Zack Dandy cowboy Zack dons a fringed vest over a red shirt to stand out from the cowboy crowd.

Emblem of two crossed sabers

Stars indicate rank

Cavalry Colonel The printed cowboy hat is new and the Western Cavalry torso is exclusive to this minifigure.

Gold tooth

Playing cards pattern on vest

Gold chain

Watch fob

Missing teeth

Removable neckerchief

Belt carries bullets

Flatfoot Thompson This nasty outlaw minifigure features a unique realistic nose and scowling eyes pattern.

Sheriff The brave sheriff looks good, with a unique torso and new star-painted cowboy hat.

Belt has "US" initials

Pouch for storage

Cavalry Lieutenant The Lieutenant's neckerchief accessory is a new element introduced this year.

Imperial Soldiers from the LEGO Pirates theme and knights from the LEGO Castle theme also have this head.

Cavalry Soldier The Calvary Soldier is debuting a new cap design for this year.

Dewey Cheatum Cheatum is his name, and cheating is his game. Although judging from his angry expression, he must have just lost a card game!

Gun tucked into belt for easy access

Black Bart Armed with a gun, Bart is always ready to blow things up at the drop of a hat.

Reversed neckerchief piece

Sheriff's Lock-up (6755) Accessories in this set include a wanted poster, printed dynamite, and seven guns, as well as four minifigures.

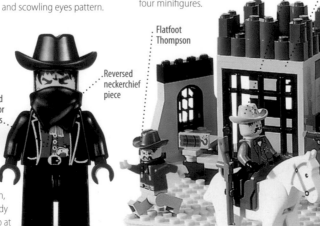

Flatfoot Thompson

Sheriff

Jail cell

Zack's up to no good again

Sheriff station

Dewey Cheatum

LEGO® TOWN

It was back to the racetrack with awesome sets like Indy Transport (6335), complete with three new minifigures, a truck, and three race cars. The truck carried the cars to the track, where the mechanics readied them for the race. Several new airplanes were also released this year.

VELUX PROMOTION

This minifigure was included in the promotional set House with Roof-Windows (1854). The house featured a dining area and a bedroom on the top floor.

Velux sticker on torso

Handyman This minifigure is all set to install windows onto the LEGO house. He comes with a sticker to place on his torso.

As well as this cap, the driver came with a racing helmet

Black sunglasses

Zipped jumpsuit

Jet Pilot This pilot minifigure is ready for some thrills in his star-patterned jumpsuit and helmet.

Turbo Charger
This race car driver minifigure is wearing a new torso, printed with the Octan logo.

Red belt

Indy Transport (6335) Three race track minifigures are included in this set, ready to battle it out on the race track.

Pointed mustache print

NOW BOARDING FOR LEGO TOWN AND DARK FOREST.

Ponytail hair piece

Railway logo

Torso with palm tree and horse detail is new for this year

Passenger Although this minifigure is wearing clothes from the LEGO® Paradisa theme, she actually appears in the LEGO Train set Cargo Railway (4559).

DID YOU KNOW?
The Train Station set (2150) was largely based on 1991's Metro Station (4554).

Train Engineer
This important-looking train engineer maintains the tracks for the LEGO DUPLO trains.

Curly mustache

Railway Employee
This minifigure's head is also used on the LEGO® Star Wars™ Biggs Darklighter minifigure released in 1999.

LEGO® TRAIN

Passengers were ready to board the LEGO Train, thanks to a new Train Station set (2150) featuring eight minifigures. The station was complete with a waiting room, a snack bar, and a platform for boarding. This was the first train station set in five years and the last until 1999.

LEGO® DUPLO®

This engineer was ready to take little builders on new adventures! After a two-year absence, DUPLO Train returned with six sets this year. Both battery-operated trains and push-along trains were available.

A CUT ABOVE

Pigtails · 1978 · Doctor · LEGOLAND Town

Short back and sides · 1979 · Boy · LEGOLAND Town

THE FIRST MINIFIGURES had very simple hairstyles, but as time has passed, hair pieces have got more varied and downright crazy! As with hats and other headgear, hair pieces attach to the stud on top of the head piece. Hair can help to identify a character—for example, hair can also reflect the style of a theme, such as the LEGO® EXO-FORCE™ anime-inspired hair pieces. Some hair pieces include facial hair, such as the Caveman's bushy beard, while others, such as Grandpa's comb-over, feature very little hair at all! From pigtails to quiffs and even mohawks—minifigures have had them all.

Floppy hair in angular sections · 2006 · Takeshi · LEGO EXO-FORCE

Flowing, swept-back long hair · 2007 · Crown Princess · LEGO Castle

Slick bob with gold headband · 2011 · Egyptian Queen · LEGO Minifigures

Smooth bun · 2011 · Kimono Girl · LEGO Minifigures

High ponytail with pink stripe · 2012 · Skater Girl · LEGO Minifigures

Long, layered bob · 2012 · Rocker Girl · LEGO Minifigures

Extra-long, straight hair with headband · 2012 · Hippie · LEGO Minifigures

Messed-up bed hair · 2012 · Sleepyhead · LEGO Minifigures

Swept fringe with headphones · 2012 · DJ · LEGO Minifigures

Tangled snakes · 2013 · Medusa · LEGO Minifigures

Sleek, layered hair · 2013 · Trendsetter · LEGO Minifigures

Long hair and bushy beard · 2015 · Classic King · LEGO Minifigures

Mullet · 2016 · Wrestling Champion · LEGO Minifigures

Bald with handlebar mustache · 2017 · Circus Strong Man · LEGO Minifigures

Short bob cut with a swept fringe · 1983 · Striped Lady · LEGOLAND Town

Ponytail · 1992 · Horse Rider · LEGO Town

Crew cut · 2001 · Dash Justice · LEGO Alpha Team

Combed widow's peak · 2002 · Vampire · LEGO Studios

Futuristic hair with spikes to the side · 2006 · Hikaru · LEGO EXO-FORCE

Severe bob with a straight fringe · 2008 · Claw-Dette · LEGO Agents

Striped spikes · 2008 · Dr. Inferno · LEGO Agents

Tousled hair and stubble · 2010 · Surfer · LEGO Minifigures

Bubble perm · 2010 · Circus Clown · LEGO Minifigures

Shoulder-length, tousled · 2010 · Caveman · LEGO Minifigures

Messy updo with bone headband · 2011 · Cave Woman · LEGO Minifigures

Upswept hair with bun · 2011 · Ice Skater · LEGO Minifigures

Mohawk · 2011 · Punk Rocker · LEGO Minifigures

Long hair with flower · 2011 · Hula Dancer · LEGO Minifigures

Swept-back hair with attached pointy ears · 2011 · Elf · LEGO Minifigures

Judge's wig · 2013 · Judge · LEGO Minifigures

Combed short hair with gold leaves · 2013 · Roman Emperor · LEGO Minifigures

Hair braided with strips of bark · 2013 · Forest Maiden · LEGO Minifigures

Wavy retro bob · 2013 · Hollywood Starlet · LEGO Minifigures

Comb-over · 2013 · Grandpa · LEGO Minifigures

Undercut · 2018 · Nails · LEGO NINJAGO

Topknot · 2018 · Cole · LEGO NINJAGO

1950s quiff · 2018 · Rock Star · LEGO Creator Expert

Messy bun · 2019 · Programmer · LEGO Minifigures

Beehive · 2019 · Gardener · LEGO Minifigures

Quiver holds arrows

Drooping mustache print

Fleur-de-lis pattern on torso

DON'T CALL ME CONE HEAD!

Helmet Knight A new torso design adorns this minifigure. His conical helmet also has a chin guard.

Single tooth printed on mouth

Cape has a spider printed on the back

Spider emblem

Willa the Witch
This is the first (but not the last) witch minifigure. The sloped skirt piece is printed for the first time.

LEGO CASTLE

Things took a spooky turn with the introduction of Fright Knights, a new Castle subtheme featuring creepy knights led by Basil the Bat Lord. Black dragons, witches, crystal balls, and flying broomsticks figured in the 10 seriously supernatural sets. Fright Knights lasted for two years before disappearing into the shadows.

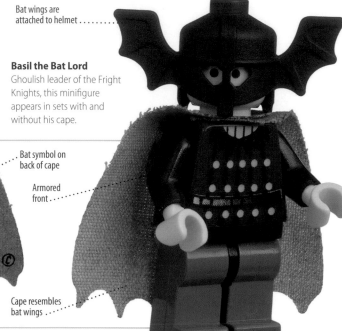

Bat wings are attached to helmet

Basil the Bat Lord
Ghoulish leader of the Fright Knights, this minifigure appears in sets with and without his cape.

Bat symbol on back of cape

Armored front

Cape resembles bat wings

Basil's cape

1997

IT WAS ALL ABOUT weird and wild villains this year. Witches, bats, and evil dragons appeared in Fright Knights, the new LEGO® Castle subtheme, while the heroic LEGO® Time Cruisers met their match in the fiendish Time Twisters. Meanwhile, in LEGO® Space, strange aliens from the UFO subtheme battled the robots of Roboforce. For those who preferred more peaceful play, LEGO® Town offered Australian exploration in the Outback subtheme or a trip beneath the sea with the Divers.

Knight's plume on helmet

Oxygen tubes on helmet

Red Plume Fright Knight
This Knight is clad in a new armored torso, also seen on Professor Millennium in 1997, from the LEGO® Time Cruisers theme.

Halberd

Helmet with neck protector

Bushy beard

I'M ACTUALLY REALLY SCARED OF BATS.

Studded armor printed torso

Armored Knight
This minifigure is proudly wearing an armored torso introduced this year.

Shield with bat print

Suit mechanics printed on torso

Aquaraider with Hook
With a green hook to aid him, this Aquaraider is sure to find some precious minerals on the sea floor.

Green hook replaces left hand

LEGO® AQUAZONE

The Aquaraiders appeared in 1997, with three ships and plans to mine valuable minerals from the sea floor. Although they were part of the Aquazone universe, no Aquanauts or Aquasharks appeared in their sets. This was to be their only year beneath the sea.

LEGO SPACE

Up to 1997, LEGO Space focused primarily on human astronauts, with a few robots thrown in. This year, aliens showed up in a big way in the UFO subtheme, the first characters in what was a long and colorful line-up of LEGO extraterrestrials.

Wire pattern on helmet

Red Alien This alien might look like he's smiling, but he definitely doesn't come in peace.

Trans-orange head piece

Large blue eye shield

Blue Droid The concept of walking is alien to this droid minifigure—he can usually be seen on his Cyber Blaster (6818).

Golden circuitry on torso.

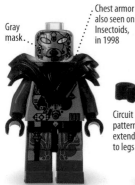

Gray mask.

Chest armor also seen on Insectoids, in 1998

Rectangular visor serves as eyes

Circuit pattern extends to legs.

Unique torso with intricate circuit detail

Blue Alien Traveling in the Cyber Saucer (6999) makes this alien minifigure green around the gills.

Andy Droid When this droid minifigure malfunctions, it takes a space age to figure out which circuit has broken.

Golden wires on legs.

Head piece also worn by Unitron Chief from the Unitron subtheme in 1994

ROBOFORCE

Fighting for justice in the galaxy, the astronauts of Roboforce pilot big robots equipped for battle or to rescue space explorers.

Roboforce logo.

Chip Nebula As leader of Roboforce, Chip feels it's only right that he gets to wear super-cool silver shades.

Printed red bandanna

Roboforce Astronaut Nothing makes this astronaut happier than controlling his Robo Stalker (2153).

Alpha Draconis This alien leader is terrified of his own reflection, so he wears his helmet at all times.

UFO

The first UFO minifigure was released as a keychain in 1996, serving as the advance guard for this year's full alien fleet. Thirteen sets included all-alien characters, with no human friends or foes.

LEGO TIME CRUISERS

The second year of Time Cruisers introduced the evil Time Twisters. Professor Millennium and his twin brother, Tony, traveled to the past to loot ancient treasures, pursued by the Time Cruisers. A ghost and a skeleton also came along for the ride as the Time Twisters meddled with history.

I'M STEALING THE PYRAMIDS NEXT!

DID YOU KNOW? This precise ghost shroud piece appears in more than a dozen sets.

Top hat

Skeleton From the Time Cruisers board game, this is the first time a skull head was featured on a regular torso.

Biker-style leather jacket

Black cap worn by more than 80 other minifigures

Epaulette

Silver striped armor

Tony Twister This evil-looking minifigure features removable yellow epaulettes worn over the torso.

Professor Millennium The evil Professor's torso is also seen on the Fright Knight minifigures in 1997.

White minifigure legs are new for the ghost this year

Blank head piece

Beneath the Ghost

Ghost A long, glow-in-the-dark shroud piece covers a standard LEGO minifigure to create the updated iconic ghost

Cameraman
This Cameraman captures all the off-road racing action in the outback—he would actually prefer to be in front of the camera.

Cap to shield face from sun

LEGO TOWN

Town traveled from the arid desert to the depths of the ocean in 1997, launching two new subthemes: Divers and Outback. The Race subtheme entered its final year, but there was still lots of action with exciting sets such as Crisis News Crew (6553). This year also saw the launch of Town Jr., which had simpler sets for younger builders.

Camera-ready face

News channel logo

News Anchor Unfortunately, this News Anchor had a short-lived career, appearing in only one set: Crisis News Crew (6553).

CLASSIC

A total of 48 new Town sets came out this year, as Town minifigures explored the Australian wilderness and traveled the sea, looking for adventure wherever they went.

LEGO® SCALA™

The SCALA name returned after 17 years, launching figures for the first time. SCALA figures wore real clothing and had hair made from strands instead of molded plastic. The new SCALA came to an end in 2001.

"i" for Infomaniac

LEGO® ISLAND

This promotional minifigure came with the LEGO *Island* video game— the first to feature minifigures. The game was released only in the United States.

Infomaniac The Infomaniac's head is full to bursting with all sorts of information about LEGO Island—well, he did create it!

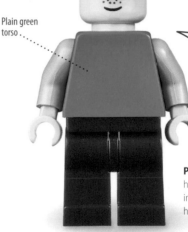

Plain green torso

YET ANOTHER FEATHER IN MY CAP!

Pilot When this guy heard he was going to be included in the Flying Duck (1824), he went quackers!

Voluminous blonde hair

Kate This SCALA figure appears only once, in Nursery (3241), where she looks after the baby.

Posable arms

Shoe pieces are separate

Happy but hungry

Baby
This happy, red-hatted toddler is waiting for her feed.

White lace top

Blue floral skirt

Emma This doll has every beauty product at her disposal in Beauty Studio (3200).

Only four police minifigures have worn this police hat ever

TOWN JR.

The sirens were blaring as Town Jr. launched with new Fire sets, including the Blaze Brigade (6554) and a Fire Engine (6486). The Town also got a new bank to keep their LEGO money safe (6566), and the police were in hot pursuit of a robber in Roadblock Runners (6549).

THAT'S SOME BIG POLICEMAN!

Police badge

Policeman The robber's definitely not going to get away with this police minifigure in pursuit in Roadblock Runners (6549).

Bank uniform torso is exclusive to this minifigure

Guard The townspeople trust this man with their hard-earned dollars in Bank (6566).

Gray bank uniform

ID card

Bank Driver Looking cool in shades, this minifigure drives an armored car full of cash in Bank (6566).

Diving mask element is new this year

Sunglasses

DIVER? NO, I ALWAYS DRESS LIKE THIS.

Diving suit

Diver Equipped with a scuba tank and flippers, this Diver is all geared up to explore life under the sea.

Sleeveless top

Boat Man This minifigure assists the divers in their underwater explorations, and he is determined to look cool doing it!

DIVERS

A brand-new LEGO Town subtheme, Divers made a splash this year with 12 sets. Unlike Aquazone, Divers was a realistic line focusing on real-world undersea exploration.

Deep Reef Refuge (6441) This underwater lab comes with sea animals and five diver minifigures who long to explore the mysteries of the deep blue sea.

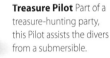

Headset for communicating with divers

Treasure Pilot Part of a treasure-hunting party, this Pilot assists the divers from a submersible.

DID YOU KNOW?

This is the only underwater subtheme to include real-world diver down flags (flags placed on the water to indicate that there is a diver below).

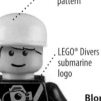

Cap covers blond hair pattern

Printed headset for communicating with crew

LEGO® Divers submarine logo

Hair peeks out from under cap

Blond Diver This minifigure works on a research ship, but he dreams of becoming a diver one day.

Air gauge on diving suit

Chopper Pilot Four diver minifigures have the same head piece with headset and shaggy brown hair.

DIVER AND SHARK

This happy explorer might not be happy for much longer—he encounters a nasty shark in a promotional set (2871). This minifigure was also used for a restaurant promotion in 1998.

Diver (black flippers) Nothing will distract this Diver on his hunt for sea treasure—not even a scary shark.

Red diving helmet

Black scuba glove

LEGO® DUPLO® DINO

DUPLO Dino combined DUPLO cave people with dinosaurs for junior-aged fun. The dinosaurs and figures roamed the Earth for three years before the subtheme went extinct.

Caveman This figure is wearing a hide top; they were all the rage back in the day.

Nose printed on head piece

Same head piece as Blond Diver

Treasure Hunter This Diver discovers treasure in Sea Hunter (6555). He still hasn't told his fellow divers ....

Red flippers

LEGO® PARADISA

Pretty lace collar

Paradisa ended its five-year run this year with the release of four sets, bringing the island vacation to a close. The figures and ponies have not reappeared (so far), and many of the building pieces are rare.

Paradisa Girl There's never a dull day for this girl—she works at the Fun Fair (6547).

·····Wool lining to keep warm

·····Bomber jacket torso is exclusive to Harry Cane

Harry Cane The brave pilot dons an aviator cap and goggles, both new elements this year.

Egyptian nemes headdress······

Red eyes of the undead·····

Sewn-up mouth·····

Pharaoh breastplate·····

Pharaoh Hotep This is the first mummy minifigure. It features exclusive head, legs, and torso.

1998

IT WAS A BUSY and rewarding year for LEGO® minifigure fans. LEGO® Space fans ran into a swarm of Insectoids, while Ninja snuck into the LEGO® Castle theme. The LEGO® Adventurers headed for Egypt to battle a nasty mummy, the Hydronauts challenged the Stingrays beneath the waves, and LEGO® Technic launched CyberSlam, which featured more LEGO Technic figures. This was the final year in which a licensed play theme was not part of the assortment. Times were about to change ….

LEGO ADVENTURERS

New this year, Adventurers launched with 21 sets, centered on the search for the Re-Gou Ruby by a group of daring heroes. The ruby was guarded by undead Pharaoh Hotep and pursued by wicked treasure hunters like Baron Von Barron. Johnny Thunder, Pippin Reed, and Professor Lightning were the theme's heroes, appearing repeatedly in its five-year run under various names in various countries.

Monocle·····

·····Scarred face

·····Hook hand

Holster to keep pistol·····

Baron Von Barron Johnny Thunder's main enemy, the Baron sports a unique torso and head piece.

Pith helmet·····

Backpack

Helmet identical to Charles Lightning's·····

Bow tie·····

·····Backpack element is new this year

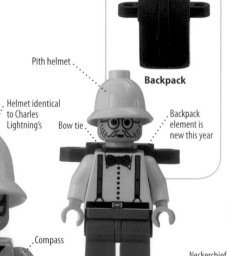

·····Compass

Charles Lightning The archaeologist minifigure is wearing a pith helmet, a new element this year.

Pinned-up slouch hat·····

Accessories can be slotted into the sides of the backpack·····

Neckerchief knotted around neck·····

Pen for jotting down notes·····

Pippin Reed Traveling the world with her friend Johnny Thunder, reporter Pippin takes her trusty compass everywhere.

Johnny Thunder The fearless adventurer minifigure makes his debut in a desert safari jacket and brand-new slouch hat.

LEGO® AQUAZONE

Deep beneath the sea, the Hydronaut miners were locked in battle with the aquatic mutant Stingrays, in what was to be the final Aquazone subtheme. This was the last year of underwater adventures until Alpha Team's Mission Deep Sea in 2002.

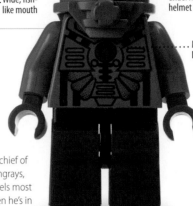

Intense red eyes

Head piece

- Gills for breathing underwater
- Wide, fish-like mouth

Helmet is unique to the Stingrays

Power supply

Protective underwater helmet

Mutant, fish-like armor

Visor also seen on Aquaraiders from LEGO® Aquazone in 1997

Captain Hank Hydro
Leader of the Hydronaut missions, Hank is well respected by the other Hydronauts.

Chrome rebreather

Diving instrument

Red diving gloves

Raven Ray Despite his high-tech suit and wicked mind, the evil Raven Ray is often captured by the Hydronauts.

Manta Ray The chief of the villainous Stingrays, this minifigure feels most comfortable when he's in charge of the Stingray Stormer (6198).

Bulbous alien design

Helmet

Tough armor protects torso

Armor

Cyborg eye print

PHEW! THIS ARMOR IS HEAVY!

Cybernetic power circuits

Gypsy Moth The Queen of the Zotaxians, Gypsy Moth commands mining operations on Holox—their home in exile.

LEGO SPACE

Fleeing their home planet, the Zotaxians crash-landed on a planet populated by large insects in this new Insectoid subtheme. They disguised their armor and vehicles to look insectlike to try to fool the hostile wildlife (not altogether successfully). The Insectoid minifigures were designed to look like cyborgs, with lots of circuitry printing on their legs and torsos.

DID YOU KNOW?
This was the last Space subtheme to have only one faction.

Trans-clear helmet

Data storage unit in head

Emblem shows Insectoid affiliation

Instrument panel

Transparent helmet

Power connector lines on torso

Danny Longlegs A communications expert and leader of the Arachnoid Star Base, this minifigure appears in Cosmic Creeper (6837) only.

Armor protects from bug attacks

Circuit pattern on leg

Dark Zotaxian
This Zotaxian hunts for crystals in Arachnoid Star Base (6977).

Trans-neon green helmet

Zotaxian This alien minifigure is seen only once, in Celestial Stinger (6969).

Power gauge

Green Alien Unluckily for this Green Alien minifigure, he seems to have misplaced his insectlike armor and helmet ....

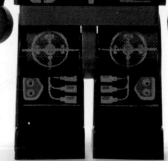

Gigabot This droid minifigure is made of a bronze-printed head, torso, and legs—all exclusive to the helpful Gigabot.

LEGO CASTLE

LEGO Castle took inspiration from the Far East in 1998 and launched a Ninja subtheme set in feudal Japan. Shogun Gi-Dan and his friend Ito, the gray ninja, battled the bandit Kendo, his henchmen, and the black ninja Bonsai for an ancient treasure. The ninja were in action until 2000.

Sharp eyes on the lookout for trouble

I WEAR THIS TO COCKTAIL PARTIES.

Head wrap hides identity

Protective scale mail armor underneath wrap

Ninja throwing star

Ito The only ninja to wear a gray ninja wrap, Ito makes his debut in the Flying Ninja Fortress (6093).

LEGO TECHNIC

LEGO Technic released more figures in 1998, with the Cyber Strikers (8257)—twin combat vehicles, each with a figure— and CyberMaster (8483), which included a model with a programmable brick that worked with a software program.

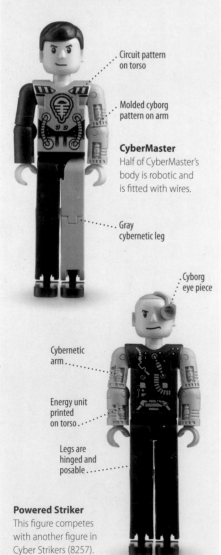

Circuit pattern on torso

Molded cyborg pattern on arm

CyberMaster
Half of CyberMaster's body is robotic and is fitted with wires.

Gray cybernetic leg

Cyborg eye piece

Cybernetic arm

Energy unit printed on torso

Legs are hinged and posable

Powered Striker
This figure competes with another figure in Cyber Strikers (8257).

Shogun-style crest fits into helmet slot

White sideburns

Armor piece worn over torso

Golden armor printed on legs

Gi-Dan Shogun Gi-Dan wears a protective armor piece and guards the ninja treasures.

Ragged head wrap

Slanted eyepatch

Tattered armor

Kendo The robber chief has an exclusive face and torso print.

Thin mustache

Patchwork on vest

Robber With his tattered vest, it looks like this robber has encountered the ninja warriors recently!

Knife tucked under belt

Bonsai This stealthy ninja wears an all-black ninja wrap so he can hide in the shadows undetected.

Flying Ninja Fortress (6093) With 687 pieces and nine minifigures, this set has three ninja treasures, as well as a number of traps to be discovered.

DID YOU KNOW?
The Ninja subtheme introduced the samurai helmet, ninja hood, and katana sword elements.

Samurai-style helmet with clip for crest

Strapped-on armor

Dojo is not afraid to use his musket

Dojo Underneath his helmet, this samurai wears a red bandanna— being a warrior can be sweaty work!

LEGO® TOWN

Two new subthemes were introduced in 1998—Res-Q and Extreme Team. Res-Q in particular made an impact on future themes, and emergency vehicles are still a popular part of the LEGO CITY assortment. Classic Town was also well represented, including a new Truck Stop (6329). An exciting new Cargo Center (6330) arrived, including a forklift and a helicopter!

> **UM, HELLO? I CAN'T SEE!**

Movable visor

Extreme Racer
An action junkie, this minifigure flies a plane in the Daredevil Flight Squad (6582).

> **ROGER AND OUT? BUT I'M BOB!**

EXTREME TEAM

Town went extreme with this subtheme, which focused on wild sports such as hang gliding, drag racing, and whitewater rafting. The Extreme Team screeched to a halt after 1999.

Printed air gauge

Gray crew uniform

Ground Crew
Assistant for Team Extreme, this guy prefers to keep his minifigure feet firmly on the ground.

Double pockets

RES-Q

Res-Q launched as a new Town subtheme in 1998 with eight sets, the largest being the Emergency Response Center (6479). The line ended in 1999, but the organization continued to come to the rescue in the Studios, Soccer, and Jack Stone themes.

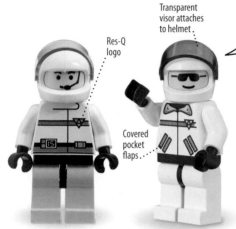

Res-Q logo

Transparent visor attaches to helmet

Covered pocket flaps

Lifeguard Featuring only in the Res-Q Lifeguard (2962), this helmeted lifeguard keeps minifigures safe at the beach.

Chopper Rescuer
This Res-Q team pilot minifigure often gets hot under his collared jacket.

The Postal Worker's favorite color is red.

Striped shirt under jacket

Thick zipper pattern

Reflective silver shades

Cargo logo

Pants match tie

LEGO® LOCO

One of the highlights of 1998 was the release of LEGO Loco, a town-building video game with an emphasis on trains. These two minifigures were from a promotional Handcar set (2585) given out with the CD-ROM.

Rare nose printing

Cool Kid Exclusive to the Handcar set (2585), this minifigure has a unique white torso with a LEGO brick design on it.

2x4 LEGO brick element printed on torso

Red mask hides identity

Plastic cape fits over neck

LEGO Train logo

Super Station Master
Looking more super hero than station master, this minifigure's masked head piece is unique.

Mechanic Seen only once in Truck Stop (6329), this minifigure is an expert in vehicle repair.

Postal Worker A newly designed LEGO Post logo adorns this minifigure's torso.

Biker Bob The head and torso pieces of this speed-loving minifigure are unique—and cool dude Bob knows it!

Cargo Staff An expert in handling cargo, this staffer is exclusive to the Cargo Center set (6330).

LEGO® SEASONAL

This festive Santa Claus appeared in the 1998 and 1999 Advent Calendars, and then reappeared in 2010 as part of the Vintage Minifigure Collection.

Molded beard piece

The 1995 Santa variant has red hips

Santa Claus Despite wearing a bandanna commonly seen on Pirate minifigures, Santa still prefers sleighing to sailing.

THIS COULD BE THE START OF SOMETHING EPIC!

Head also used on Luke Skywalker minifigures

Padawan robes

Padawan Obi-Wan Kenobi This is the first of more than 30 Obi-Wan minifigures. It shows him as a young Jedi apprentice in Episode I.

Later variants have tan legs

LEGO *STAR WARS*

It was a great experiment—could sets based on the classic *Star Wars* films and the newest movie, Episode I *The Phantom Menace*, be a hit? Could a licensed play theme bring in legions of new fans for LEGO building? The answer to both was a resounding yes, producing one of the greatest success stories in the LEGO Group's history. And it's still going strong over 20 years later!

Pulled-back hair piece and head piece are exclusive to Qui-Gon

Qui-Gon Jinn Appearing in four sets in 1999 alone, the LEGO version of the doomed Jedi Master has lasted much longer than the movie version!

1999

THE WORLD OF LEGO® minifigures changed forever in 1999, with the release of the first LEGO® *Star Wars*™ sets. It was the first licensed minifigure theme ever produced by the LEGO Group and would prove to be a massive success, spawning LEGO video games, animated shorts, books, and more in years to come. Other big news this year included the opening of LEGOLAND® California in Carlsbad, CA, and the release of the LEGO® Rock Raiders, LEGO® Adventurers: Jungle, and LEGO® DUPLO® Winnie the Pooh™ themes.

Long hair piece with top braid also seen on Padmé's daughter Princess Leia

Torso is unique to this variant

Standard black pants

Padmé Naberrie The Queen of Naboo is in disguise as a handmaiden. Padmé wasn't seen in her royal robes until 2012.

Head piece also used on a female soccer player in the Soccer theme in 2001

Boy Anakin Skywalker This young minifigure saves the galaxy in one set— Naboo Fighter (7141).

This variant appears in two sets in 1999—Anakin's Podracer (7131) and Mos Espa (7171)

Gray helmet and matching goggles

Boy Anakin Skywalker variant The only difference between the two 1999 Anakin variants is the helmet color.

EPISODE I

The first LEGO *Star Wars* subtheme was *Star Wars*: Episode I *The Phantom Menace*, with eight sets and all-new minifigures. Many of the models and minifigures would be revised and updated in later years.

Jar Jar's clothing is simple

Head piece also used on a Gungan soldier in 2001

Dark gray legs can be seen on more than 45 minifigures

Jar Jar Binks This Gungan was the first minifigure not to have a round head piece. His untidy torso is also unique.

Maul's Zabrak horns are missing from this version

Unique torso

Darth Maul The Sith apprentice featured a regular head piece with unique facial tattoos.

Sith Infiltrator (7151) Darth Maul's Sith Infiltrator stealth ship, known as the *Scimitar*, was released in 1999, and then updated in 2007, 2011, and 2015.

DROIDS AND PODRACERS

The famous Boonta Eve Classic podracing scene came to life with figures of Anakin's rival drivers and a Pit Droid. The first Battle Droid also debuted this year.

Gasgano wears the same helmet and goggles as Anakin Skywalker

Gasgano Only appearing in one set, this rare podracing figure has unique head and torso pieces.

Sebulba This unusual figure is made of a single LEGO piece and is only found in Mos Espa Podrace (7171).

Later versions had more detail and colors

Yellow photoreceptor

Pit Droid Three Pit Droid variants were released in 1999, ready to fix any malfunctions. This version belongs to Anakin Skywalker.

Head piece specially created for the Battle Droids

Later versions do not have a backpack

Battle Droid The first version of the Battle Droid is easy to defeat—it can't even hold a blaster properly!

Hair piece also seen on Draco Malfoy from the LEGO® Harry Potter™ theme

Unique torso with simple white tunic

Young Luke Skywalker The future Jedi's early life as a Tatooine farmboy is the inspiration for his first LEGO minifigure.

Tan leg wraps

EPISODES IV, V, AND VI

The first five classic LEGO *Star Wars* sets also came out this year, with minifigures of favorite characters such as Luke Skywalker, Darth Vader, and Obi-Wan Kenobi and models of the X-wing and TIE fighter.

Head piece also seen on more than 15 pirate minifigures

Rebel Technician The tan uniform is worn only by this hardworking minifigure and a Rebel Engineer in 2000.

Obi-Wan "Ben" Kenobi This older version of the exiled Jedi Knight has a unique head and torso and is exclusive to Landspeeder (7110).

2011 version has a buckle detail on the belt

Brown visor

Torso is unique to this variant

Hoth Rebel Trooper Warmly dressed for the ice planet Hoth, this rebel minifigure appears in Snowspeeder (7130).

Rebel pilot helmet

Dak Ralter Also in set 7130, this rebel pilot mans the snowspeeder's guns for Luke Skywalker, who flies the craft.

Rebel g-suit worn by 12 minifigures

Helmet is exclusive to four Luke pilot variants

Luke Skywalker Pilot Tatooine is a distant memory for this minifigure as he makes his debut as a rebel pilot in two sets this year.

Unique torso— the back is plain khaki

Camouflage Luke This minifigure is designed to blend in on the forest moon of Endor, but his chin dimple and cybernetic hand reveal his identity.

ASTROMECH DROIDS

The most famous astromech droid of all is R2-D2. The first LEGO version of this iconic character was released this year, and at least one version of him has been produced every year since.

R2-D2 Each of R2-D2's three parts were created specially for his figure and then refined on later versions.

R2-D2's legs are joined to his body with LEGO Technic pins

Head piece pattern is slightly different from R2's

R5-D4 This red astromech droid uses the same torso design as R2 but has red printing instead of blue.

Helmet is exclusive to Biggs

Biggs Darklighter This minifigure did not survive the rebels' attack on the first Death Star. He appears in the X-Wing Fighter set (7140).

Biggs wears the same suit as his friend Luke Skywalker

Imperial Scout Trooper Wearing lighter armor than a normal stormtrooper, this minifigure often undertakes dangerous solo missions.

Unique torso

G-suit is worn by X- and Y-wing pilots

Dutch Vander This brave rebel minifigure flies a Y-wing fighter in set 7150, but he perishes in the Battle of Yavin.

Darth Vader The Sith warrior's minifigure debut is just as menacing as his on-screen counterpart.

Vader has a scarred gray head piece underneath his helmet

Standard LEGO cloak completes the Sith lord's look

Scout helmet fits over head so that only the black visor shows.

AAARRRGH— WHERE'S THE BRAKE?!!!

Scout Trooper in Action The Scout Trooper usually comes with a specialist helmet and rides a speeder bike.

LEGO® TOWN

LEGO Town continued to push the boundaries in 1999, flying high with Space Port and diving deep with the Coast Guard. The former was a subtheme in its own right, building on the success of earlier Launch Command sets. The latter was part of the new City Center line, which was geared toward 5- to 10-year-olds.

Popular head piece, seen on more than 20 minifigures

Pristine white lab coat

Scientist Featuring an updated torso, this variant of the Scientist is exclusive to a single 1999 set—Test Shuttle (3067).

Space Port logo

Same head, hat, and torso as other variant

Scientist Variant Wearing black pants instead of white, this Scientist variant appears in three sets in 1999.

Shuttle Security Guard
This serious minifigure patrols the Space Port in his helicopter, checking that everything is in order.

Head piece seen on more than 10 other minifigures

Exclusive torso with ID badge, Space Port logo, and Security insignia

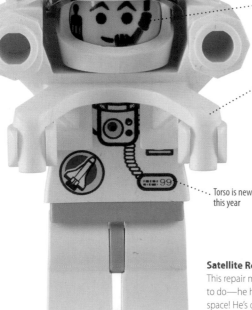

The first variant has a construction helmet, the second a white cap, and a third has a red cap

Torso is exclusive to three Ground Controller variants

Ground Controller
Exclusive to Mission Control (6456), this minifigure is the vital link between Earth and the astronauts out in space.

Ground Controller Variant Three very similar variants of the Ground Controller minifigure are released in 1999. The only differences are their hats!

Standard red pants

Black visor is attached to breathing gear

Air pressure gauge

Fireman with Breathing Apparatus This Fireman has an identical head, torso, and legs to the Fire Mechanic released in 1994, but he has a specialist helmet, breathing apparatus, and air tanks.

SPACE PORT

Space Port was the successor to 1995's Launch Command, and it featured more sets and a greater variety of vehicles and minifigures than the previous theme. Minifigures included astronauts, scientists, and ground crew.

Head piece also used on the Aquanaut Jock Clouseau in 1995

Jet pack previously seen in the 1991 Blacktron II space theme

Torso is new this year

Satellite Repair Guy
This repair man has a tough job to do—he has to fix a satellite in space! He's got his space suit and jet pack on, but where has his wrench floated off to?

Gold visor is down to protect the Moon Explorer's eyes from the sun's rays

Female Astronaut
The only female astronaut in the line-up has a unique new torso featuring the Space Port logo and breathing pipes.

Helmet first seen on the Aquazone Hydronauts in 1998

Same head and torso as the Satellite Repair Guy

Moon Explorer This intrepid minifigure travels all the way to the moon and explores it in his Lunar Rover (6463).

Female head piece with radio set is new this year

White helmet is also used on the Moon Explorer

LEGO® TOWN JR. AND CITY CENTER

LEGO Town Jr. was phased out in 1999 and was replaced by City Center. The sets continued to feature more simplified building for younger fans and included Coast Guard, Fire, and Police models.

It's a good thing my mustache is waterproof!

Detachable life jacket

Another variant has a ponytail instead of a cap

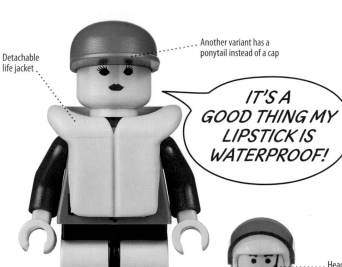

It's a good thing my lipstick is waterproof!

New torso is unique to this minifigure

Coast Guard logo

ID badge

Coast Guard HQ (6435) This set includes six minifigures, a speedboat, small boat, helicopter, beach buggy, and trike.

Female Coast Guard
One of two female minifigures in Coast Guard HQ (6435), this variant does her job at sea while the other variant rides to the rescue on land using an all-terrain trike.

Headset ensures that the Coast Guard can radio for backup if he needs it

Rapid Response If the Coast Guard needs to travel a short distance fast, this Rapid Response minifigure uses a small motor-powered inflatable boat.

Head piece with blue sunglasses is new this year

Coast Guard Chief The Chief is in charge of all the Coast Guard minifigures. During a mission, he has to think quickly and tell everyone else what to do.

Standard Coast Guard torso with white arms

CLASSIC

Special licensed minifigures also appeared this year, including a Shell Oil worker and a Boston Red Sox baseball player, which was available only through a promotion at Fenway Park (the Red Sox's home stadium).

Red helmet with black visor

Standard LEGO baseball cap.

The torso is the only new element

Exclusive Shell logo

Shell Oil Worker
This minifigure appears in two sets this year—one from Town, Dragster (1250) and one from City Center, Shell Service Station (1256).

Beach Patrol Appearing in his own set, Beach Buggy (6437), this Coast Guard patrols the beach checking for sharks or swimmers in distress.

DID YOU KNOW?
LEGO Town's first and only Milk Delivery Truck (1029) was released in 1999— available exclusively in Norway!

RED SOX

All-white uniform with Red Sox logo

Red Sox Baseball Player
This promotional minifigure has a unique torso in white with the official Red Sox logo on the front.

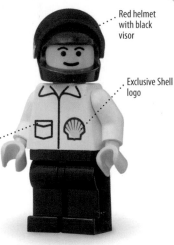

Mechanic One of five minifigures in Roadside Repair (6434), the Mechanic can fix any vehicle in record time.

Torso used on four Mechanic minifigure variants

McDonald's Worker
LEGO McDonald's Restaurant (3438) was only available in the United States via the LEGO online store.

Standard red LEGO cap

Unique torso with the McDonald's logo

Matching red pants complete the uniform

"NO SLIMY SPACE SLUG IS GOING TO STOP ME!"

Axel Appearing in four sets in 1999, Axel has a new head piece that is exclusive to his two variants and a 2001 Boat Driver in the Studios theme.

Underwater helmet first seen on the Explorien Chief in 1996.

· Trans-neon green visor

Torso is new and unique to Jet

In 2000, Axel wears a black visor instead

New torso with overalls and goggles printing

Jet The only female Rock Raider has a new head piece with red lips, blonde hair, and a headset. It is exclusive to the 1999 and 2000 variants of Jet.

LEGO ROCK RAIDERS

In 1999, a crack team of space miner minifigures found themselves trapped on an alien world. The good news was that there were energy crystals to mine, but the bad news was that there were some pretty nasty monsters there, too. This first visit to the LEGO underground had an impressive multimedia life with a video game and in-box comics, as well as traditional sets.

DID YOU KNOW?
The construction helmet has been worn by around 170 minifigures since 1978.

Printed bandanna keeps sweat out of Bandit's eyes when he's mining

Torso with red sweater and overalls is unique to this minifigure

Head piece is new this year

Torso is exclusive to three variants of Docs

Rock Raiders (4930) This set features Axel, Sparks, Docs, Bandit, and Jet, plus a rock for them to raid for crystals.

Goggles were first introduced in 1998

Docs This miner minifigure has an unusual look—he wears his glasses on his forehead and a black neckerchief knotted around his neck.

Sparks is the miners' mechanic, so he always keeps a wrench handy

Head piece is new this year

Standard issue blue pants

Bandit This tough minifigure has a unique head with angry brown eyebrows, a bushy beard and mustache, and a cool blue bandanna. Don't mess with him!

FIRST LEGO® LEAGUE

Every year since 1998, the LEGO Group and the nonprofit organization *FIRST* have held the *FIRST* LEGO League global tournament. In it, teams of elementary and middle school students use LEGO® MINDSTORMS® technology to build a working robot and solve a problem involving minifigures in a real-world situation. This minifigure was a giveaway to school teams of up to 10 children, participating in the 1999 season.

Head piece is new this year, but not exclusive

Exclusive torso

***FIRST* LEGO League Minifigure**
Given to each team member, the minifigure features the name and location of the participating school on the back of the torso.

LEGO® SCALA™

This year the SCALA line continued its focus on the SCALA dolls, which were larger than minifigures with many accessories. Eight were released in 1999.

Polka-dot halter top with jeans and extra accessories

Marie
Vivacious Marie appears in four sets between 1998 and 2001. This casually dressed version is from Marie in her Studio (3142).

Sparks Unlike his mining colleagues, Sparks' torso is not exclusive to him. In fact, his torso can also be seen on a 2001 female minifigure from the Town theme.

LEGO ADVENTURERS

Johnny Thunder and the Adventurers team were back for their second year. This time, they were heading to the South American jungle in search of the mysterious sundisk, and many new minifigures and new pieces took part in this quest. The Adventurers were determined to obtain the artifact from the powerful Achu before villains Señor Palomar and Rudo Villano. Of course, Johnny won in the end!

New, unique head piece

Gabarros A new character this year, the South American sailor uses his local knowledge to help both Señor Palomar and Johnny Thunder find the sundisk.

Villano wears a black version of Johnny Thunder's hat

Backpack

Villano has two pistols tucked into his belt

Rudo Villano Another new arrival for this year, Rudo (also known as Max in the UK) has a new, exclusive scruffy torso and scarred head. He also has a variant without a backpack.

Elaborate feathered headdress is detachable

Head piece has two gray stripes printed on it

Cape has tribal pattern printed on the back

Unique tribal markings on torso and legs

Achu This mystical minifigure guards an ancient treasure, and he's not about to give it up! Every piece is new and unique to Achu.

New head piece also used on a 2003 LEGO Sports NBA player

Classic white LEGO cowboy hat

Backpack clips around neck

> CURSES! I FORGOT MY SUNSCREEN!

Torso with white jacket and brown vest is unique to Señor Palomar

Señor Palomar New for this year, Señor Palomar appears in Spider's Secret (5936). In this set he has a backpack, but in two others released this year, he does not.

Jungle Surprise (1271) Inside a small Jungle temple lies a sundisk waiting to be discovered by a minifigure.

Backpack is worn by several minifigures in this theme

Pippin Reed Keen journalist and partner to Johnny Thunder, Pippin (sometimes known as Gail Storm) is ready for anything with her jungle gear.

Female head piece is seen on more than 10 other minifigures

Compass detail print on torso is exclusive to Pippin Reed

Pith helmet was first produced in 1998

LEGO® DUPLO®

LEGO DUPLO continued to entertain in 1999. DUPLO Dino entered what seemed to be its final year, until a revival in 2007 brought it back. DUPLO Construction was also big this year.

Smiling face with stubble detail

Construction Worker This figure was hard at work in 1999, appearing 10 times in five sets. He seems pretty happy though.

Fur bib printed on torso

Cave Baby This cute prehistoric baby appears with three other figures in Dinosaurs Fun Forest (2821).

2000s

LEGO® *Star Wars*™ was just the start of licensed play themes. Other film-based characters soon followed, from student wizard Harry Potter to the web-slinging Spider-Man. New design revolutions led to the advent of realistic skin tones for licensed LEGO themes. The minifigures of the new millennium grew extra faces on the backs of their heads, threw basketballs, shrank down on shorter legs, landed on Mars, and even dabbled in some movie-making of their own!

SAVE! AND A BEAUTY, IF I SAY SO MYSELF!

Different national flag stickers are supplied. This minifigure wears the German flag

Black gloves—the ball won't slip through his fingers

Black Team Goalkeeper
This black-capped minifigure is the goalkeeper from the Black Team Bus (3404). Like all team bus goalies, he has a plain green torso.

2000

PICKING THE BIGGEST LEGO® event of 2000 is no easy task. Was it the release of some of the most iconic LEGO® *Star Wars*™ sets ever? How about exciting new subthemes for LEGO® Adventurers and LEGO® Castle? Or the snowy action of the LEGO® Arctic subtheme? Could it be the amazing success of LEGO® Soccer (known as LEGO® Football in the UK), which went on to launch dozens more LEGO® Sports sets? One thing is beyond any doubt: 2000 was a year when excitement and sheer fun ruled—and what's more, it held the promise of an incredible decade to come!

LEGO SOCCER

Hair piece introduced in 1979 is still in style for many LEGO soccer players!

German flag sticker on front torso

The LEGO Group scored in the world of sports in 2000 with the launch of the first LEGO Soccer sets. (The LEGO Sports brand would not be used until 2003.) These were a surprise hit, spawning future sets for basketball, hockey, and extreme sports. Soccer player minifigures were designed to be personalized so that they could play for different teams and countries.

TEAM BUS SETS
To play, teams must first get to the stadium! Five team bus sets were brought out in 2000, including an Americas Team transport and buses for Red, Blue, and Black teams. Each included six minifigures and a soccer ball.

Black Team Player With a change of sticker, this minifigure could play for any one of five teams in the Black Team Bus (3404).

Blank torso ready for team sticker to be applied

Spectator
A mega soccer fan, this minifigure can be found supporting his team in Grandstand with Scoreboard (3403).

Head pieces from Blue Team Bus set (3405)

Personalized Player Each team bus set includes a goalkeeper and five outfield players in team colors, such as this Blue team minifigure. Players have different heads and can be personalized with flag and number stickers to play for several countries and in a variety of positions.

This is the last time this head print was used, after first appearing in a 1992 Pirates set

Blue Team Bus (3405) This set contains the bus elements, six minifigures, and sticker sheets with a choice of national flags for their front torsos and numbers for their backs.

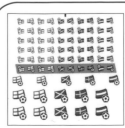

Flag stickers (above)
Number stickers (right)

SOCCER SETS

The most popular Soccer set was the Championship Challenge (3409), which featured 10 outfield players, two goalkeepers, and a field of play. Mounted on flexible stands, minifigures could flick the ball. The set was such a hit that it inspired a sequel, Championship Challenge II (3420), in 2002.

Green and White Team Player In the Field Expander set (3410), players wear the same shirt but have different numbers on their backs.

He shoots, he scores— and he looks pretty pleased with himself!

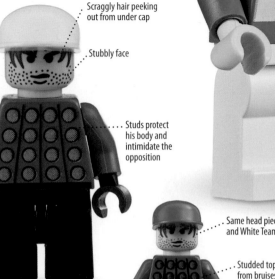

Scraggly hair peeking out from under cap

Stubbly face

Studs protect his body and intimidate the opposition

Angry Goalie
This assertive-looking goalie appears only in the Championship Challenge set (3409).

Same head piece as Green and White Team Goalie

Studded top saves him from bruises when he's saving goals

Blue Goalie The Goal Keeper set (3413) comes with a blue variant of the angry goalie. A stick and turntable arrangement allows him to move around the goal to make some agile saves.

SHOOT 'N' SCORE

This small set featured two minifigures— a soccer player and a goalie. It was ideal for young builders who wanted to practice shots on goal before moving on to actual competition.

New head with intense, smoldering expression

Soccer Legend
French soccer superstar Zinedine Zidane got his own minifigure in the Shoot 'n' Score with Zidane set (3401). Magnifique!

Sideburns are printed on head and hair piece is separate

Adidas sponsor logo printed on legs.

LEGO ADVENTURERS

The Adventurers faced prehistoric peril this year in LEGO® Dino Island, the third subtheme in the series. Fourteen sets were released, but most contained fewer than 100 pieces, making this the second-smallest subtheme in Adventurers history—but not in popularity!

DID YOU KNOW?
LEGOLAND® California features a land based on the LEGO Adventurers theme.

Aviator helmet and goggles

Shady, wide-brimmed hat

Another variant has brown hips instead of black

Pippin Reed Also known as Gail Storm, this fearless minifigure hunts down flying reptiles in her Island Chopper (3933). She carries a rifle and a shovel!

Mr. Cunningham
He may be a minifigure master of disguise, but Mr. Cunningham can't hide the pot belly printed on his new torso.

All-Terrain Trapper (5955) The three minifigures in this set include the evil villains' leader, Baron Von Barron.

Hair piece worn by around 100 minifigures in black

Pursed lips—she's concentrating!

Belt has lots of pouches to hide things in

Alexia Sinister
The sister of Baron Von Barron, Alexia is always scheming to steal treasure. The Baron himself used the name "Sam Sinister" in some sets this year.

Mike This minifigure likes to partner with other Dino Island heroes. He's a mean shot with his trusty slingshot!

Brown cavalry cap

The Dino Island sun has given him freckles

Exclusive torso design

Slingshot tucked away in belt

Horns clip to helmet via a dragon's mouth crest

Unique head has angry, scowling face

Red gloves make him stand out from his men

Cheek guards protect his face (and hide his unkempt hair)

Brown leather scale mail torso pattern

Cedric the Bull Like his namesake animal, this minifigure is always ready to charge! He leads his band of robbers in their constant attacks on King Leo's castle.

Gilbert the Bad
Gilbert has an eye (just the one) for designing foul war machines, like the giant catapult in the Catapult Crusher set (6032).

Broad-brimmed archer's helmet with chin guard

Detachable breastplate over scale mail torso

John of Mayne Richard's partner wears unique metallic armor in the Dungeon set (4817).

Red plume fits into hole on visor

Richard the Strong
Richard is the best and bravest among King Leo's knights. He features in the Royal Joust set (6095).

Knights' Kingdom plate armor printed on legs

NINJA

Only three LEGO Ninja sets were released this year, none of them building sets. Instead, they were known as Mini Heroes Collections (3344, 3345, and 3346) and contained just minifigures, display bases, and collector cards.

DID YOU KNOW?
Female ninja, such as the LEGO Ninja Princess, were known as *kunoichi* in ancient Japan.

WATCH US DISAPPEAR BEFORE YOUR EYES!

Ninja Princess
Only the second female to appear in the LEGO Ninja subtheme, this warrior is dressed for stealth in her robe and head wrap.

Ninja hides a shuriken and dagger in her robes

Ninja crest appears on three minifigures' helmets

Red bandanna printed on head under helmet

White Ninja Shogun This fierce ancient warrior minifigure is equipped with metallic leg armor and golden antlerlike helmet crest in set 3346.

LEGO CASTLE

This year saw the end of the LEGO® Ninja subtheme. The ninja would slip quietly into the shadows until 2011, when the concept would return with LEGO® NINJAGO® (although one Ninja would briefly sneak back in 2009 as a Vintage Minifigure). Elsewhere, LEGO Castle continued, returning to medieval Europe with the first Knights' Kingdom subtheme. This line focused on the battle between King Leo's knights and Cedric the Bull's raiders. The two kings were locked in a ferocious feud over the future of the minifigure kingdom.

LEGO® KNIGHTS' KINGDOM

King Leo lived in the first medieval-style LEGO castle made since 1995, which was also the first to come with a complete royal family. Cedric had no castle, so he and his Bulls made it their mission to knock down Leo's using ax carts, catapults, cannons, and battering rams.

Crown and helmet are one piece

Aged, lined face—he has reigned for a long time

Torso features King Leo's lion head shield

King Leo This regal minifigure of King Leo is the central character in Knights' Kingdom and appears in all five sets.

Hinged visor can be raised and lowered

Elegant, close-fitting armor in gold and silver

Princess Storm
King Leo's brave daughter is the first female knight minifigure in the LEGO Castle theme.

King Leo's Castle (6098) This set comes with seven minifigures, including King Leo, Queen Leonora, and Princess Storm—and a creepy skeleton figure, too.

Queen Leonora
This majestic minifigure of King Leo's wife has a printed sloped piece instead of legs. She is part of King Leo's Castle (6098).

Headdress based on medieval hennin

Outer red robe printed across torso and skirt

Keys to the castle safely attached to chain belt

LEGO® TOWN

LEGO Town headed due north in 2000, with the Arctic subtheme creating a short, sharp blizzard of activity. But while things were ice cold in some places, they were red hot in others. LEGO Race burned up the race track, Space Port headed for the Red Planet, and there were new Fire Fighters sets. A year of variety indeed!

Crystal Aput Rescue helicopter pilot Crystal makes sure the Red Medic always drops in where he's needed. Like him, she wears a red snow suit.

- Transparent blue visor on helmet
- Polar bear image for Arctic theme

Flat beaked blue cap

Captain Ross
The minifigure Captain wears a plain blue cap when he's chilling out in Mobile Outpost (6520).

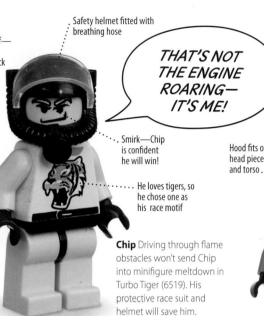

- Safety helmet fitted with breathing hose
- Crocodile motif—she's snappy around the track
- Gloves help her keep a firm grip on the wheel

Lucky Clad in her favorite color, Lucky is all set to try her racing luck in Green Buggy (1284).

THAT'S NOT THE ENGINE ROARING—IT'S ME!

- Smirk—Chip is confident he will win!
- He loves tigers, so he chose one as his race motif

Chip Driving through flame obstacles won't send Chip into minifigure meltdown in Turbo Tiger (6519). His protective race suit and helmet will save him.

RACE

The Race subtheme made its final pitstop this year, with 13 sets that included new driver and pit crew minifigures and vehicles such as buggies, dragsters, and monster trucks. A new line, Racers, would begin revving up in 2001.

ARCTIC

Brrrrr! Brave explorers headed to the freezing Arctic in this Town subtheme, which lasted for a year. They were hunting for meteorites that had fallen to Earth with alien life trapped inside. Ten sets came out, featuring realistic snow vehicles and the first ever polar bear figures to appear in a LEGO set.

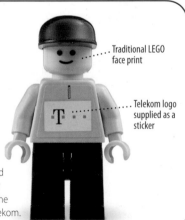

- Hood fits over head piece and torso

Red Medic Dealing with colds, frostbite, and polar bear bites are all part of this minifigure's job. He appears only in the Polar Base set (6575).

- Gray beard and eyebrows suggest age

Scooter Scooter is ready to face chillier challenges in his snug hoodie. The subtheme was the first to feature fur-lined hood pieces.

- "Star of life" is symbol of emergency medical services

FIRST LEGO® LEAGUE

In its second year, *FIRST* LEGO League challenged its teams and their robots to complete tasks such as rescuing a trapped scientist and retrieving crates of rock before a volcano erupted. It was the final year in which no actual set was produced for FLL tournaments.

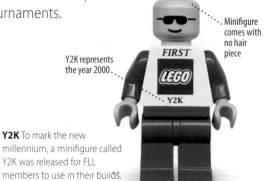

- Minifigure comes with no hair piece
- Y2K represents the year 2000

Y2K To mark the new millennium, a minifigure called Y2K was released for FLL members to use in their builds.

CLASSIC

In spite of a trend toward detail, the pre-1989 classic minifigure still made an appearance now and then. This happy fellow remains, to many, the iconic symbol of the LEGO minifigure.

- Traditional LEGO face print
- Telekom logo supplied as a sticker

Telekom Cyclist This minifigure is included in set 1199—a promotional set for the Tour de France cycle race. He bears the logo of the German telecommunications company Telekom.

CITY CENTER

The largest City Center set this year was Highway Construction (6600), with five minifigures. Fire Fighters' HQ (6478) was in second place, featuring a hose-bearing helicopter, motorcycle with trailer, and four minifigures.

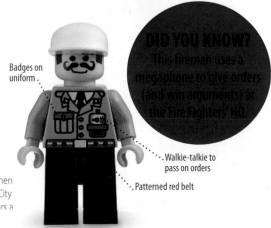

- Badges on uniform
- Walkie-talkie to pass on orders
- Patterned red belt

Fireman Like all Firemen released in 2000, this City Center minifigure wears a new gray uniform.

DID YOU KNOW? This fireman uses a megaphone to give orders (and win arguments) at the Fire Fighters' HQ.

LEGO STAR WARS

The Force was strong with LEGO *Star Wars* fans this year, as some of the most famous characters in the epic saga—Han Solo, Princess Leia, Emperor Palpatine, Boba Fett, C-3PO, and Chewbacca—became minifigures for the first time. A total of 19 sets were released in 2000, including the first *Millennium Falcon* starship.

I'VE ALWAYS BEEN A BIT OF A REBEL.

Specially created braided buns hair piece

Flowing senatorial gown printed on torso

Silver belt symbolizes Alderaan royalty

Princess Leia The first minifigure of Princess Leia Organa is dressed in her senatorial robes and features her famous bun hairstyle.

Trademark lopsided grin on head piece

"Han style" black vest and light shirt

Legs printed with gun belt holster pattern

Han Solo This is one of three minifigure variants of lovable pilot Han Solo released in 2000. He wears the casual, open-necked shirt and vest *Star Wars* fans know so well.

Unique head piece has hair that flows down his chest and back

Audio sensors on either side of head

Bowcaster ammunition bandolier

C-3PO A new head mold was cast for C-3PO's minifigure, which debuted in the *Millennium Falcon* set (7190).

Plain pearl gold legs unique to C-3PO

Chewbacca
This Wookiee hero is taller than humans, so his special head piece is designed to add height. It sits on a torso also used for two Ewok minifigures.

TIME FOR A FACIAL.

Angry, distorted face print unique to this minifigure

Sith robes printed on torso

Black cloth cape

DID YOU KNOW?
Three of this year's LEGO *Star Wars* sets were LEGO® Technic models.

Helmet covers black head piece with no face

Rocket power for quick getaways

All in One
Boba's detailed helmet and jet pack are one piece.

Mandalorian body armor printed on gray torso

Boba Fett This is the original minifigure of the Mandalorian bounty hunter.

Uniform printed on torso is unique to the Security Officer

Cap has been worn by many minifigures, such as Stan Shunpike with his purple version in LEGO® Harry Potter™

Naboo Security Officer
The smiling Security Officer minifigure keeps the peace on Naboo, aided by his green Flash Speeder craft from set 7124.

Emperor Palpatine The evil Lord of the Sith has a suitably scary, wrinkled face for his first appearance in the LEGO *Star Wars* theme. His minifigure features the same hood piece as the Darth Maul minifigure from 1999.

LEGO® STUDIOS

Fans got a chance to make their own movies this year with the LEGO Studios Steven Spielberg MovieMaker set (1349). This innovative item came with a stop-motion camera and editing software and included a recreation of a scene from *The Lost World: Jurassic Park*.

Pen for jotting down notes

Stylish white bandanna

Assistant The cameraman's assistant uses her wireless headset to keep tabs on the shoot at all times.

Like all crew members, she wears an ID badge

Shades protect his eyes from the glare of studio lights

Grip This guy brings a bit of bare-armed muscle to the set. He'll lift or shift anything the film crew needs him to.

Padded gloves for carrying heavy equipment

Utility belt holds screwdriver for dismantling props

Practical orange vest

Same face design as Docs from the Rock Raiders theme

Beard and glasses like those worn by Steven Spielberg

Director
Looks familiar? This minifigure is based on filmmaker Steven Spielberg. He features in 11 sets, including Explosion Studio (1352).

CREW

Along with the director and cameraman, the LEGO Studios set featured a grip, an assistant, a stunt man, and a fireman in case things got a bit heated on the movie lot. A camera track with camera provided more realistic fun.

Cameraman's emblem

Cameraman
The Cameraman is always right at the center of the on-set action, tracking, panning, and zooming. That's how he rolls!

CAST

The actors in this set played Adventurers Johnny Thunder and Pippin Reed in an exciting scene where they flee from a rampaging dinosaur. They were the first of a number of actors to grace the LEGO Studios' big screen.

Tumbling tresses

Crop top under open jacket

Compass for checking directions

Actress This glammed-up minifigure is the star in the Steven Spielberg MovieMaker set (1349).

Red bandanna protects against harsh winds

Playing Pippin Our leading lady is playing adventurer Pippin Reed in the Dino Head Attack (1354). She's changed her clothes, but not her makeup!

Stuntman When there are dangerous stunts to be done, this highly trained (and highly insured) minifigure steps in.

Protective gloves also provide grip

Same legs, torso, and head as the Pilot

Pilot The wily Pilot is part of a single set (1349) this year. This minifigure plays the part of an extra.

LEGO® ROCK RAIDERS

The Rock Raiders' adventures came to an end this year. The four sets produced were all promotional models. Some Rock Raider minifigures were also released as part of a LEGO Mini Heroes Collection set (3347).

Chief The Commander of the LMS Explorer is a unique minifigure with two different-colored arms.

Power box and power cables for plasma cannon

Utility pouch and high-visibility jacket detail

67

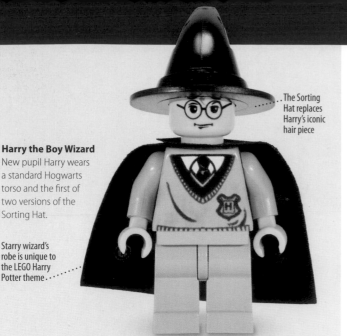

Harry the Boy Wizard
New pupil Harry wears a standard Hogwarts torso and the first of two versions of the Sorting Hat.

The Sorting Hat replaces Harry's iconic hair piece

Starry wizard's robe is unique to the LEGO Harry Potter theme

2001

SUPER-SPIES, SORCERERS, and space aliens helped to make 2001 a magical year for LEGO® fans! Two major themes—LEGO® Harry Potter™ and the non-minifigure based BIONICLE®—launched in 2001, but that was only the beginning. Exciting LEGO System themes such as LEGO® Alpha Team and LEGO® Life on Mars also joined the line-up. Aspiring movie-makers had a lot of LEGO® Studios sets to choose from, while younger builders could enjoy the new LEGO® Jack Stone models. LEGO building was bigger and better than ever in 2001!

LEGO HARRY POTTER

Gryffindor uniform

Trademark lightning-shaped scar

LEGO Harry Potter was the second major licensed theme after LEGO® *Star Wars*®, premiering with 11 sets and 30 new minifigures based on the *Harry Potter and the Sorcerer's Stone* movie.
Also appearing were the first sets of Hogwarts Castle (4709) and Hogwarts Express (4708), which would both prove so popular that several updates would be issued over the next few years.

THE WIZARD AND HIS FRIENDS
Fans just couldn't get enough of Harry and his friends. The theme's first year saw no less than four variants of Harry, three of Hermione Granger, and three of Ron Weasley.

Harry Potter™ A new, violet variant of the cloth robe was introduced specially for the theme. Harry wears the colorful robe in three sets.

Gryffindor crest

Hogwarts school crest

Hermione Granger™ All Gryffindor minifigures, including Hermione, wear the scarlet-and-gold uniform in years one and two. Their torsos and legs are identical.

Hogwarts Witch
This Hermione minifigure is not yet in Gryffindor, so she wears a school crest on her torso piece instead of a Gryffindor one.

Draco Malfoy™ This is the first of 10 Draco Malfoy minifigures. As a member of Slytherin, his uniform bears the green-and-silver snake crest of his house.

Bowl-shaped hair piece in Earth orange

Face printed with arrogant sneer

Ron Weasley™ The first 18 Ron minifigures feature this quirky, grinning face, with eyebrows colored to match his hair piece.

Casual Harry This is one of more than 40 different Harry minifigures. He wears these casual clothes to board Hogwarts Express (4708).

Yellow hands and face were used for all Harry minifigures until 2004

Unique knitted sweater pattern

Casual Hermione Hermione has changed into a casual but stylish blue sweater and jeans for Diagon Alley Shops (4723).

Redhead Ron's face has exclusive freckle pattern

Standard Hogwarts robe

Casual Ron Ron's robe keeps him warm when he's relaxing in the common room in Gryffindor House (4722).

Shaggy beard and hair are one piece

Super-sized legs are unposable

Extra-long torso piece gives Hagrid his half-giant height

Rubeus Hagrid™ There are five variants of Hogwarts' half-giant gamekeeper. Each one stands a whole head taller than his minifigure friends.

CASTLE RESIDENTS

Not all LEGO Harry Potter minifigures are human—or even alive! Peeves was the first LEGO ghost to be built from standard minifigure parts, the Silver Knight was a statue in Hogwarts castle, and the Chess Queen was a minifigure-sized chess piece guarding the Sorcerer's Stone.

Face printed onto a light gray standard LEGO head

Ghostly markings of jacket and shirt

Peeves the Poltergeist This gray-bodied minifigure appears in two LEGO sets (4705 and 4709).

Shiny silver crown

Faceless head is a cylindrical LEGO brick

Chess Queen Harry and Ron come up against this ghastly game piece in The Chamber of the Winged Keys (4704).

A spooky gray face lurks under the two-piece helmet

Silver Knight The warrior statue minifigure holds a large LEGO sword and stands guard at Hogwarts Castle (4709).

HOGWARTS PROFESSORS

It wasn't just about the students! Professors Dumbledore, Snape, and Quirrell joined in the fun this year. Quirrell was the first of several Defense Against the Dark Arts teacher minifigures and has appeared in only one more set since.

DID YOU KNOW? There have been six versions of the Hogwarts Express so far, including a promotional mini one in 2011.

Face printed with sarcastically raised eyebrow

Glowing complexion

Professor Snape™ The Potions Master is the first minifigure to have a glow-in-the-dark head.

Long, purple frock coat

Plain black cloth robe

Albus Dumbledore™ The first minifigure of the Hogwarts headmaster has detailed purple robes and a purple wizarding cloak.

Ornate details on robes can be seen if beard is removed

Hair and beard are two separate removable pieces

Legs printed with wizarding gadgets

Evil face Voldemort's features are printed on the reverse of the head.

Unique purple turban hides a hideous secret

Purple jacket and scarf match color of turban

Professor Quirrell The Professor Quirrell minifigure is the first to have a special double-sided head. Turn it around and Lord Voldemort's face is revealed!

LEGO® SPACE

LEGO Space traveled to the Red Planet for the first time with the Life on Mars subtheme, which focused on astronauts exploring Mars and encountering a friendly species of alien. Adventures revolved around the humans helping the good Martians stop a planned rebellion by a bad Martian. Life on Mars lasted for only one year, and its sets would be the last in the Space theme until 2007.

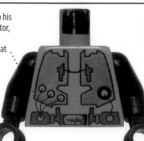
Chrome visor

Wired up to his heart monitor, Mac never misses a beat

Special unit Mac's exclusive torso is printed with the heart-monitoring unit he has to wear in space.

Doc Ailing astronauts can rely on this dedicated doctor to fix them up. His minifigure appears in two sets (7315 and 7312).

Gray beard and eyebrows show he is a mature medic

Torso printed with new detailed spacesuit

Black gloves

Mac The captain of the Solar Explorer may look relaxed and laid-back, but make no mistake—Mac runs a tight ship! His minifigure only appears in the Solar Explorer (7315).

Large helmet and breathing apparatus cover torso detail

Front **Back**

Breathing apparatus

Studs

Simple face detail with messy orange hair

BB's Helmet BB's headgear has two studs on the back, which allow him to attach to space vehicles, so he can "hover™" above the ground.

BB Mac's copilot in the Solar Explorer is very young and very eager. He wears the same helmet as his hero Mac over his unique, tousle-haired head.

LEGO JACK STONE

Jack Stone focused on hero Jack saving the day in various guises. The figures were "mid-figs," midsized figures that could not be taken apart.

Helmet worn when piloting rescue boat

Torso printed with rescue overalls

Res-Q Worker This figure shows Jack Stone in his role as an intrepid rescuer at the Aqua Super Station (4610).

MARTIAN COLONY

All named after stars, the Martians used an air pump and tube transport system to get around. They had more vehicles than the astronauts, so it's lucky they were friendly!

MY JUMPSUIT IS OUT OF THIS WORLD!

Air tube mask printed on martian head

Torso design indicates leader status

Cassiopeia Rigel's daughter Cassiopeia is the only female Martian in the theme.

Lime freckle pattern

Angled legs are only used for Martians

Pollux Like all the Martian figures, Pollux is taller than a standard LEGO minifigure.

Rigel This green Martian has years of experience at leading his people. He's also the General of the Aero Tube Hangar (7317), a Biodium mining outpost on Mars.

LEGO STUDIOS

Fans had gone wild for the LEGO Studios Steven Spielberg MovieMaker set in 2000. To follow up on its success, 14 more sets were released this year, all designed to be part of LEGO fans' homemade films. Two of the sets were based on the making of the *Jurassic Park III* movie, with LEGO® Adventurers Johnny Thunder and Pippin Reed taking the place of the real stars.

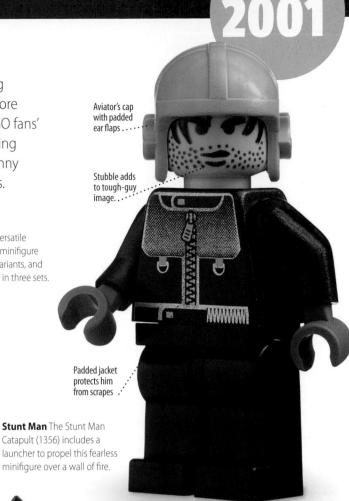

Aviator's cap with padded ear flaps .....

Stubble adds to tough-guy image....

.... Casual outfit can be swapped for a costume

Screwdriver close to hand

Grip This versatile technician minifigure has three variants, and he appears in three sets.

.... Headset for communicating with crew

ID badge ....

Padded jacket protects him from scrapes ....

Actress This red-haired minifigure appears in her own Studios themed polybag set (4062).

White-capped Cameraman This minifigure has a unique jacket with a zipper and a large LEGO logo printed on his back.

Grip This versatile technician minifigure has three variants, and he appears in three sets.

Stunt Man The Stunt Man Catapult (1356) includes a launcher to propel this fearless minifigure over a wall of fire.

LEGO® TOWN

It turned out to be an unusually quiet year for the usually bustling LEGO Town. Only three sets were released: two promotional sets for real-world airlines (1100 and 2718) and a reissue of 1992's Gas N' Wash (6472).

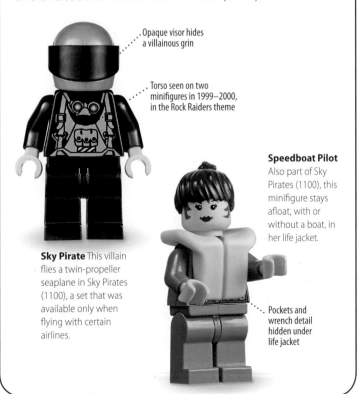

Opaque visor hides a villainous grin ....

Torso seen on two minifigures in 1999–2000, in the Rock Raiders theme ....

Speedboat Pilot Also part of Sky Pirates (1100), this minifigure stays afloat, with or without a boat, in her life jacket.

Sky Pirate This villain flies a twin-propeller seaplane in Sky Pirates (1100), a set that was available only when flying with certain airlines.

Pockets and wrench detail hidden under life jacket ....

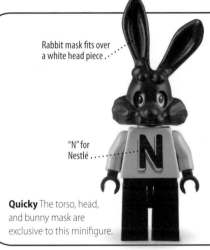

Rabbit mask fits over a white head piece ....

QUICKY

Quicky the bunny is the cute mascot of Nesquik®, Nestlé's popular flavored milk drink. His minifigure, which appeared in three promotional sets under the LEGO Studios banner, was designed to show an actor portraying Quicky for a movie.

"N" for Nestlé ....

Quicky The torso, head, and bunny mask are exclusive to this minifigure.

LEGO® TIME TEACHING CLOCK

Young fans could now learn to tell the time with a buildable clock. It came with a minifigure whose collection of hats included a chef's hat for meal times, a baseball cap for play times, and a ghost mask for bedtimes!

Wizard's hat shows that it's time for learning ....

Pocket to hold tools for mending the clock ....

Clock Man This minifigure always has time for LEGO fans. Designed to fit on top of a working clock, he appears this year only. He has a standard LEGO head and blue legs.

LEGO ALPHA TEAM

Super-spies took on a malevolent mind manipulator in the first LEGO secret agent theme—Alpha Team. Evil Ogel sought to transform the population into Skeleton Drones using mind control orbs. The seven agents of Alpha Team battled him on land, sea, and in the air in six new sets featuring nine new minifigures. Alpha Team and Ogel would be back for rematches in 2002 and 2004.

Unique new head piece

Alpha Team logo on necklace

Utility belt holds mechanic's tools

Cam Attaway Alpha Team's mechanic wears her purple glasses for the first and only time in the Alpha Team ATV (6774).

HEY, THAT'S SUPPOSED TO BE A SECRET!

Headset for communicating with the team

Dash Justice At the first sign of trouble, team leader Dash will be there in a flash! Brave Dash pilots the Alpha Team Helicopter (6773).

Utility belt worn over buttoned jacket

Black levers act as antennae

TV display screen

Tee Vee This first variant of Alpha Team's communications robot is fully programmed and switched on—as you'd expect of a TV set on minifigure legs!

Purple hair is unique to 2001 and 2002 variants.

Mouth clenched in concentration

Explosives attached to clothes

Crunch Working for Alpha Team is a real blast for Crunch. He's the team's dedicated explosives expert.

Three pockets on utility belt

Radia Quick-thinking and super-clever, Radia has a mind as bright as the lasers that she works with.

DID YOU KNOW?
"Ogel" is LEGO spelled backward—he represents the opposite of LEGO fun and play.

Moveable chrome gold visor

Aviator-style protective helmet

Pockets on legs for tools

Flex No problem is too knotted for Flex, Alpha Team's ropes expert. He's just happy to be on the team—delighted, in fact!

DIDN'T SEE THAT EVIL ORB COMING!

Skeleton head

Epaulettes appear only on first variant

Minion Commander A mindless drone with a head of bone, this minifigure is the first variant of Ogel's minions.

Menacing red eye

Elaborate shoulder armor

Protective armor clips over torso

Ogel The Alpha Team's foe appears in his first variant with plain black legs and torso. His armored shoulder protection is so bulky, it almost covers his scowl.

Ogel Control Center (6776) This set saw Ogel's first minifigure appearance. He was protected by two Minion Commanders.

LEGO *STAR WARS*

It was another year of firsts for LEGO *Star Wars*, with the debuts of two classic characters from Episodes IV, V, and VI: the crimson-clad Royal Guard and the iconic Stormtrooper. But they were not the only *Star Wars* rookies. Watto, from *Star Wars: Episode I The Phantom Menace*, made his first appearance in his very own set—Watto's Junkyard (7186).

Ventilated helmet

Imperial emblem on helmet

Special black armor with life-support system

Simple black uniform with belt

TIE Pilot The original variant of the Imperial Pilot flies the much feared TIE Fighter (7146).

Imperial Pilot This minifigure pilots Emperor Palpatine's Shuttle (7166). Later variants are much less cheerful!

Royal Guard
This red-robed warrior minifigure, with his black spear, is one of Emperor Palpatine's personal guards.

Hood mold specially designed for the Royal Guards

Hood conceals black LEGO head piece with no face details

Utility belt with blaster power cell reserves

Stormtrooper This year saw the debut of the original Stormtrooper minifigure. There would be many future variants.

Imperial Shuttle (7166) Palpatine's infamous spaceship was introduced in 2001 along with four minifigures, including two Royal Guards.

Plain head, wings and torso fit over standard LEGO torso

Watto Appearing only in Watto's Junkyard (7186), this minifigure variant of the winged Toydarian junkyard dealer is both unique and rare.

LEGO® SOCCER

The Women's Team, a brand-new set in the LEGO Soccer theme, was released in conjunction with the Women's European Championships, this year held in Germany. No new pieces were used, but it scored a memorable first nevertheless: a women's team had never before appeared in a LEGO Soccer set.

Country flag sticker can be stuck here

LET'S GET IT IN THE LEGO NET!

Blonde Player This woman has one aim—putting the ball in the back of the net. She's playing with her teammates for the first time in the Women's Team (3416), and they're going for goal.

Plain blue Women's Team shirt

Dark cap and keeper's gloves

Ponytail detail on hair piece

Brunette Player
It takes more than 90 minutes to win a match. This minifigure trains for hours every day in her yellow team bib.

Bib pieces fits over neck

Black-haired Player
This defender is ready to tackle anything—or anyone—the opposition might throw at her.

Goalie The Goalie, with smiling LEGO face, looks more carefree than her pals. She's a safe pair of hands, and she knows it!

Helmet exclusive to Phase I, Episode II Clone Troopers

Stripes indicate Clone Army rank

Body armor shown by gray markings

Utility belt carries survival gear

DC-15 blaster

MY UNIT IS ME, MYSELF, AND I.

Clone Trooper
This Phase I Clone minifigure is the first variant of the Clone Trooper.

LEGO® STAR WARS™

The 25th anniversary of *Star Wars* had arrived. The occasion was celebrated with the release of *Star Wars:* Episode II *Attack of the Clones* and with seven LEGO sets tied to the movie. Their memorable minifigures included a grown-up Anakin Skywalker and villains Jango Fett and Count Dooku, who troubled the Jedi for the first time.

Vernon Dursley from the Harry Potter™ theme also wears this hair piece this year

Padawan hair braid printed on torso

Padawan Anakin Skywalker
This minifigure is the first adult version of Anakin. He has lost the freckles of his 1999 younger self.

Original Yoda head has molded but no printed eyes

Shorter, nonposable leg piece debuts this year

Yoda Unique printing on the aged Grand Master's torso includes a blissl—an instrument like a tiny panpipe—worn around his neck.

NEVER TRUST ANYONE NAMED DARTH.

Female hair piece recreates the long hair of the movie character

Headset lets him talk to other Jedi while chasing Jango Fett

Torso printed with loose-fitting tan Jedi tunic

Obi-Wan Kenobi Two variants of this Obi-Wan minifigure exist: the other has no headset but is otherwise identical.

2002

A GLITTERING CAST of famous movie characters entered the minifigure world in 2002. Licensed lines were the hot LEGO® news, with new sets based on *Star Wars™*: Episode II *Attack of the Clones, Harry Potter and the Chamber of Secrets™,* and Spider-Man all flying off the shelves. The big Hollywood stars didn't entirely steal the scene, however. The LEGO® Alpha Team was back for Mission Deep Sea, and Pepper Roni from the successful LEGO® *Island* video game made his debut as a minifigure in the Island Xtreme Stunts line.

Unique head with gray beard and wrinkled skin

Cape clasp and belt on torso unique to Count Dooku

Jedi Starfighter (7143) This set contains a Jedi Starfighter spacecraft and Obi-Wan Kenobi to pilot it. Obi-Wan's droid R4-P17 is also included in the set.

Count Dooku Dooku has fallen to the dark side, and his clothes are a little on the dark side, too—they are all black or brown. His minifigure came with Jedi Duel (7103).

IF ONLY THERE WERE MORE OF ME ....

J-12 jet pack and helmet are one piece

Boba's face is a childish version of Jango's

Custom-made blasters are actually LEGO revolvers

Short LEGO legs are unposable

Young Boba Fett Yoda and this child variant of Jango's clone son are among the first minifigures to feature the short LEGO legs.

Jango Fett A minifigure mercenary and bounty hunter, Jango appears in set 7153. His head is plain black on one side with a stubbly face and balaclava outline on the other side.

BATTLE DROIDS

Although the Separatist Battle Droids had appeared as LEGO figures before, this was the first year for Super Battle Droids and Droidekas. The Clone Wars were about to get a lot tougher!

Head is molded as part of torso

Head clips on to shoulder section of torso

Battle Droid arm holds binoculars

Droideka This heavy Destroyer Droid is made up of 26 pieces, including its weapons.

Super Battle Droid Towering over ordinary Battle Droids, this imposing figure boasts all-new parts in a unique metal blue color.

Security Battle Droid A red torso identifies this Battle Droid as one of a few advanced enough to act as prison guards.

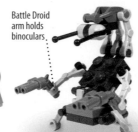

Veil worn by Zam when she is posing as a human

Zam Wesell Like Jango, Zam is a bounty hunter. Unlike him, she is also a Clawdite shape-shifter, so her minifigure head has both a human face and a reptilian Clawdite one.

Unique torso and hips with specialized equipment and armor

Mask and goggles offer protection from sun and sand

Humidifier to make dry air easier to breathe

Tusken Raider This mysterious minifigure moves through deserts in his sand-colored shroud and crossed utility belt.

LEGO® SPIDER-MAN™

The web-head swung into the LEGO line-up for the first time, as a subtheme of LEGO® Studios. The Spider-Man Action Studio (1376) featured the first Spider-Man and Peter Parker minifigures, and Green Goblin (1374) included the Green Goblin and Mary Jane. Fans could now drop Spidey into a variety of sticky situations in their own stop-motion movies.

Features not printed on mask

Green Goblin Mask

LEGO® SPACE

This promotional pair hold a special place in LEGO history. After their appearance at the World Space Congress, images of them were launched into space on the NASA Mars Exploration Rovers *Spirit* and *Opportunity* in 2003.

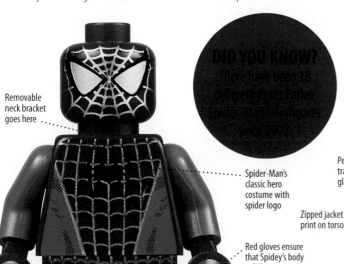

Removable neck bracket goes here

DID YOU KNOW?
There have been 18 different Peter Parker/Spider-Man minifigures since 2002.

Spider-Man's classic hero costume with spider logo

Red gloves ensure that Spidey's body is fully protected

Spider-Man
The first-ever version of Spider-Man features an exclusive neck bracket, which allows him to be clipped onto a long bar piece and moved around to "climb" walls.

Green Goblin
Spidey's archenemy, Norman Osborn, hides his identity under a grotesque mask. Sadly, his minifigure face isn't much prettier. Armor is printed on his legs and torso.

Peter's trademark glasses

Chinese design on torso

Zipped jacket print on torso

Peter Parker Spider-Man's alter ego has a two-sided head—one side with glasses, one without.

Two-sided head piece: happy and scared

Mary Jane Watson Peter's red-haired love interest is dressed for a trip to the carnival in the Green Goblin set (1374).

Classic LEGO® helmet with chrome visor

Biff Starling It's not obvious, but this minifigure is nervous—he's hoping he doesn't meet any Blacktron astronauts on his mission.

Gold ribbing

Torso pattern exclusive to these two minifigures

Sandy Moondust This space robot or "astrobot" shares a torso with only one other minifigure—her space colleague, Biff Starling.

LEGO® HARRY POTTER™

The boy wizard returned for a second magical year in 2002. This time, the sets focused not just on Hogwarts, but on other places in Harry's world, too, such as the house of Harry's Muggle relatives, the Dursleys. Ten sets were released based on the second movie, *Harry Potter and the Chamber of Secrets*™, with three more based on the first movie, *Harry Potter and the Sorcerer's Stone*™.

SORCERER'S STONE

The new *Harry Potter and the Sorcerer's Stone*™ sets introduced two new species: goblins and trolls. Goblins would return in 2011.

Goblin
This short-legged minifigure is an employee in Gringotts Bank (4714).

- Specially molded head
- Bank teller's uniform

Troll
The body, legs, and arms of this creature are one huge piece. It is topped by a standard minifigure head.

- Scary expression
- Movable right arm has loop to hold club
- Loincloth on elastic waistband
- Unposable legs

Ron Weasley™ This is the last minifigure of Ron to feature a yellow head and the only variant released in 2002.

- Casual zipped checkered jacket

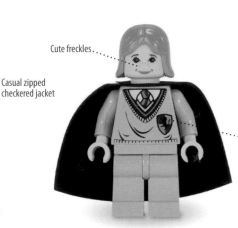

Ginny Weasley™ As a first-year student at Hogwarts, Ginny gets her first minifigure. It is her only variant to feature a yellow head.

- Cute freckles
- Gryffindor crest

CHAMBER OF SECRETS

The 2002 LEGO Harry Potter sets had several new minifigures, including Dobby the house-elf, Professor McGonagall, Professor Lockhart, Tom Riddle, Lucius Malfoy, and Madam Hooch, plus three new variants of Harry.

DID YOU KNOW?
Professor McGonagall is the only LEGO Harry Potter minifigure to wear a green wizard's hat.

Gilderoy Lockhart™
The ornately printed torso and light-pink hips and legs are unique to this minifigure.

- Groomed blond hair
- Carefully chosen pink outfit

Green Lockhart
This stylish variant of the professor is seen in two LEGO Harry Potter sets in this year (4733 and HPG01—a promotional release in Hong Kong).

- Elaborate gold design on vest

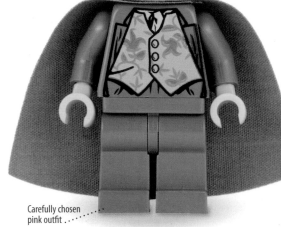

Madam Hooch™ The gray striped robe is unique to this variant of the Hogwarts flying instructor.

- Pilot's goggles

Professor McGonagall™ This strict professor's printed sloped piece was seen in two sets released this year (4729 and HPG04—a promotional set).

- Green wizard's hat
- Spell book
- Face has wrinkle printing

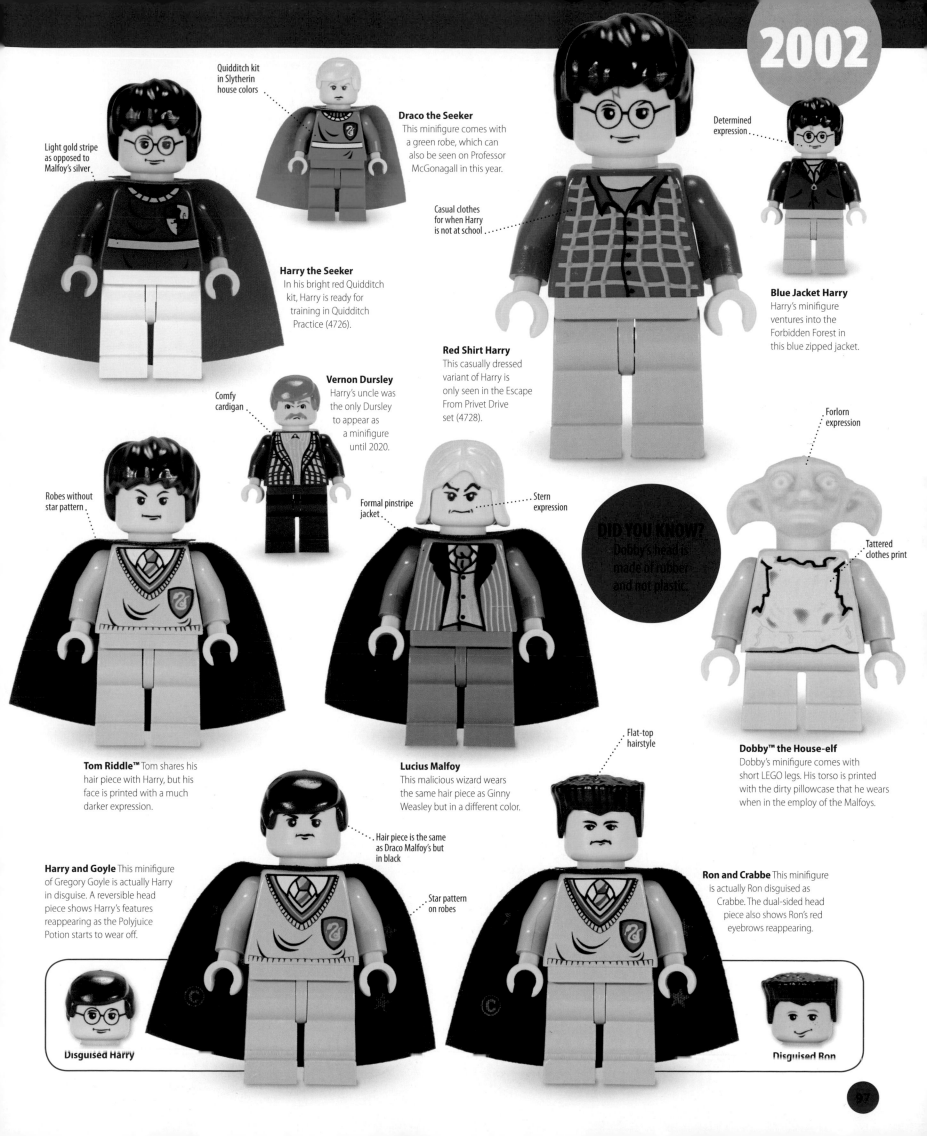

Quidditch kit in Slytherin house colors

Draco the Seeker
This minifigure comes with a green robe, which can also be seen on Professor McGonagall in this year.

Light gold stripe as opposed to Malfoy's silver

Casual clothes for when Harry is not at school

Determined expression

Harry the Seeker
In his bright red Quidditch kit, Harry is ready for training in Quidditch Practice (4726).

Red Shirt Harry
This casually dressed variant of Harry is only seen in the Escape From Privet Drive set (4728).

Blue Jacket Harry
Harry's minifigure ventures into the Forbidden Forest in this blue zipped jacket.

Comfy cardigan

Vernon Dursley
Harry's uncle was the only Dursley to appear as a minifigure until 2020.

Forlorn expression

Robes without star pattern

Formal pinstripe jacket

Stern expression

DID YOU KNOW?
Dobby's head is made of rubber and not plastic.

Tattered clothes print

Tom Riddle™ Tom shares his hair piece with Harry, but his face is printed with a much darker expression.

Lucius Malfoy
This malicious wizard wears the same hair piece as Ginny Weasley but in a different color.

Flat-top hairstyle

Dobby™ the House-elf
Dobby's minifigure comes with short LEGO legs. His torso is printed with the dirty pillowcase that he wears when in the employ of the Malfoys.

Harry and Goyle This minifigure of Gregory Goyle is actually Harry in disguise. A reversible head piece shows Harry's features reappearing as the Polyjuice Potion starts to wear off.

Hair piece is the same as Draco Malfoy's but in black

Star pattern on robes

Ron and Crabbe This minifigure is actually Ron disguised as Crabbe. The dual-sided head piece also shows Ron's red eyebrows reappearing.

Disguised Harry

Disguised Ron

2002

LEGO ALPHA TEAM

Ogel took his evil beneath the waves in the second year of Alpha Team, called Mission Deep Sea. His plan: to use his orbs to mutate sea creatures into monstrous slaves. It took all of Alpha Team's skill—and some awesome underwater vehicles—to put a stop to him and his modified Skeleton Drones.

Stubble

Communication unit for talking to the team

Pockets for storing equipment

Crunch Explosives expert Crunch has been underwater for so long, he just hasn't found the time to shave.

Radia The 2002 version of Radia has purple hair and the 2004 version has black hair—she gets bored easily!

Helmet with diving mask

Air tube

Detachable flippers

Dash Justice With a determined, steely look in his eyes, this minifigure is looking forward to taking on the evil Ogel.

Movable diving mask

Cam Attaway This minifigure of Alpha Team's Cam is dressed in full diving gear, ready to accompany her boss, Dash, on a sea mission.

Scuba tank This scuba attachment fits between the torso and head piece.

Flex retains the right orange arm from the 2001 variant

Huge smile

Bubble-shaped transparent neon green helmet

Flex Scuba-diving Flex is happiest working the Sub-Surface Scooter (set 4791), as can be seen from his huge grin.

Vital diving equipment

LEGO Alpha Team logo

Commander The medal print on the torso of this minifigure indicates that he is the appointed commander of the Skeleton Drones.

Red-and-black uniform is the same as 2001 version, apart from medal

Charge This version of the electricity expert, in diving gear, pilots a diving mech in Alpha Team Robot Diver (4790).

LEGO® SOCCER

Soccer was king for the third year, with sets tied to the 2002 FIFA World Cup™ and a new version of the LEGO Championship Challenge (3420). The Grand Championship Cup (3425) was the largest Soccer set ever released, with 22 minifigures, and would be the last LEGO Soccer stadium set for four years.

V-neck soccer strip

Black Stripe Defender From the Defender 1 set (4443), this player is one of several 2002 FIFA World Cup minifigures to wear Coca-Cola branding.

Cockerel logo on shirt

French Soccer Player This player sports the French team colors of blue, red, and white. His legs display the Adidas logo.

French Football Federation logo

LEGO® CASTLE

This was a relatively quiet year for LEGO Castle—only two sets were released. Black Falcon's Fortress (10039) was a rerelease of a 1986 set, and Blacksmith Shop (3739) was a fan-designed model available only through the LEGO Shop At Home website. These would be the last Castle sets until 2004.

Shiny scale mail

Blacksmith There are two things that this minifigure takes great pride in: the armor he makes and his mustache.

LEGO® ISLAND XTREME STUNTS

Based on the successful LEGO *Island* and LEGO *Island 2* video games, the new theme Xtreme Stunts introduced pizza delivery guy and ace skateboarder Pepper Roni and his enemy, the Brickster, in minifigure form. The sets combined skateboard, boat, and all-terrain vehicle (ATV) stunts with Pepper's efforts to keep LEGO Island safe. After 2002, the theme featured only three promotional sets.

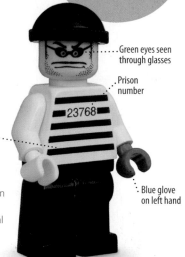

WANT YOUR PIZZA WITH A SIDE OF KICKFLIPS?

Pizza pattern on torso

Knee pads protect from falls

Pepper Roni A skateboard expert, Pepper Roni keeps the Island safe from criminals. He is also a pizza delivery boy.

Green eyes seen through glasses

Prison number

Jail stripes pattern common on all three con men

23768

Brickster LEGO *Island Xtreme Stunts'* main villain is always scheming to escape from jail and steal bricks from other buildings on the Island.

Blue glove on left hand

STUNT MANIACS

Pepper was joined by all his friends from the PC game, including Sky Lane. This theme used a bracket and bar system (see Sky Lane, right) to allow the minifigures to perform their stunts, similar to the LEGO® Gravity Games™ stunt sticks introduced in 2003.

White mustache

Stylish red vest and bow tie

Infomaniac
The creator of LEGO Island has an angled "i" logo on his torso to stand for his name. He appears only in one set this year—Xtreme Tower (6740).

Infomaniac's 1999 variant has black pants

Xtreme Tower (6740) The largest set released this year from this theme, Xtreme Tower includes six minifigures, the Xtreme Tower, a helicopter, and a skateboard.

Bar attaches to stud on neck bracket

Tube top with string ties

Neck bracket A bar fits into the stud on the back of the neck bracket so that Sky can do her daring skateboard stunts.

Sky Lane Pepper Roni's daring friend often helps him fight criminals. She wears a neck bracket while performing stunts.

LEGO® STUDIOS

The monsters came out to howl in 2002, as LEGO Studios unleashed four horror movie sets. The Mummy, the Vampire, the Monster, and the Werewolf were all there—along with directors, cameramen, and actors and actresses to be the "victims." It was all good film fun, and also the first time there had ever been a Vampire minifigure.

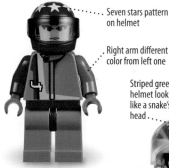

White, lifeless hands

Vampire This scary Vampire is thirsty for minifigure blood! Turn his head around to see his mouth open, ready for a bite.

Seven stars pattern on helmet

Right arm different color from left one

Striped green helmet looks like a snake's head

Scorcher Although his torso says "4," this minifigure always comes first in the Hot Scorcher set (4584).

Storming Cobra
From the Storming Cobra set (4596), this racer minifigure drives a green race car over a ramp—just for fun.

LEGO® RACERS

LEGO Racers spun off from Town Race in 2001. This year brought Drome Racers, a subtheme that featured an extensive story and multiple minifigure characters. Centering on a vast indoor racing arena called the Drome, it featured six teams racing for glory. Each instruction booklet included a Drome Racers comic.

Jacket pattern with straps

I'M GOING TO BLOW THIS CASE WIDE OPEN!

Gray beard

New torso complete with striped tie and gold badge

Police Chief Late nights working a case in the Police HQ (7035) has added wrinkles to the Police Chief's minifigure head.

2003

THE LEGO® MINIFIGURE celebrated its 25th birthday in grand style. After decades of almost exclusively yellow-skinned minifigures, some of these iconic toys got a major redesign as natural skin tones were introduced. A minifigure of Lando Calrissian from the LEGO® *Star Wars™* theme was among the first to receive this more realistic treatment. 2003 also saw big changes in LEGO® Town, LEGO® Sports expanded to include a wider range of sports (including LEGO® soccer and basketball), and the most ambitious LEGO® Adventurers line ever was released.

LEGO® WORLD CITY

LEGO Town became LEGO World City in 2003, and the emphasis was on action. Police sets dominated, with Trains and Coast Guard still featuring, while Construction and Airport took a back seat for a short while. World City would last for two years before being replaced by LEGO® CITY.

POLICE

The World City Police featured in six sets in 2003, including a new Police HQ (7035) and a Surveillance Truck (7034). Only two of the sets contained minifigure crooks.

Knitted cap

Wicked smile revealing a gold tooth

Torso with inmate number is new and unique to this minifigure

Wireless radio

I SPEND ALL DAY STUCK IN TRAFFIC.

Highway Patrol Officer
This minifigure works with the Highway Patrol and Undercover team—nothing gets past his minifigure eyes.

Rank symbols on collar

Police Officer
A smiling Policeman is always reassuring. This one is from the Police HQ (7035).

Jail Prisoner Unfortunately for this jailbird, he was arrested and has been locked up in the Police HQ (7035).

Silver sunglasses for flying in sunny skies

He has the same smiling head as the Police Officer

Patrolman torso is new this year

Radio to call for backup

Police Pilot
The Police Pilot fights crime from the skies, and he looks cool doing it, with new silver shades and a leather jacket.

The belt has pouches for storing vital equipment

Scowling head piece is new this year

Motorcycle Patrolman
It looks like the Motorcycle Patrolman has spotted some minifigures speeding!

Capped Patrolman
This Patrolman is smiling for a reason—not only does he appear in World City set Squad Car (7030), he also gets to help Spider-Man chase a thief in Spider-Man's First Chase (4850).

CITY FOLK

It wasn't all big adventures in World City. Minifigures were still traveling by train, going through Grand Central Station on their way to their destinations.

Necklace has golden pendant

Tapered jacket print

Heavy luggage to heave onto the train

Passenger Boarding the High Speed Train (4511) is quite an occasion for this minifigure—she's wearing a brand-new jacket and red lipstick.

Square glasses

Open-collared shirt

Orange train ticket

Commuter
The commuter minifigure is wearing a new blazer; he'd love to shout about it, but he can't—he's a minifigure.

Flat, gelled hair gives a professional look

Dark glasses keep identity hidden

BE COOL. DON'T BLOW MY COVER.

Tailored suit

Slick suitcase full of secret documents

Undercover Cop
Dark hair, dark glasses, and a dark suit ensure that this minifigure cop blends into the background when he's on the lookout for crooks and thieves.

DID YOU KNOW?
Approximately 15 minifigures are produced every second.

Coast Watch HQ (7047) This set comes with a platform, radar dish, speedboat, helicopter, and four minifigures.

COAST GUARD

The only Coast Guard sets released in a span of 10 years, Coast Watch HQ (7047) and Hovercraft Hideout (7045) featured plenty of World City action as the heroes confronted smugglers for the first time.

Hair piece also seen on Charge from the LEGO® Alpha Team subtheme in 2001

Serious head piece is new this year

MY HOBBIES INCLUDE WATCHING PAINT DRY.

Coast Guard Coast guarding is a serious business—as you can tell from this minifigure's pursed lips.

LUCKILY FOR ME, MINIFIGURES FLOAT!

Silver sunglasses shield eyes from sun's reflection on the water

Zipped pockets keep out water

Coast Watch Crew
Part of the Coast Guard crew, this minifigure constantly monitors the coast for criminal activity.

Safety straps for a snug fit

Gray gloves for extra grip on the boat steering wheel

New Boat Driver The Boat Driver is very happy indeed—he's the only minifigure to wear this new stickered flotation jacket, exclusive to set 7047.

LEGO SPORTS

LEGO Sports was a new theme for 2003, incorporating LEGO Soccer with extreme sports and basketball. But this meant more than just designing new sets—it required the redesign of the minifigure for basketball. The addition of the stunt stick to the Gravity Games sets meant that minifigures could be played with in a whole new way!

Helmet with checked pattern is new this year

Race number is a sticker

Light gray gloves

The course features jumps and drops

Snowboard features red minifigure outline

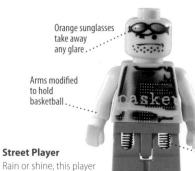

Snowboard Boarder Cross Race (3538) In this set, two minifigures race to the finish line at the bottom of the snowy and tricky competition course.

GRAVITY GAMES

The LEGO® Gravity Games™ sets featured special stunt sticks that could be attached to the minifigures to allow them to do midair stunts. Vertical ramps also made for even more excitement.

Plain black helmet worn by more than 250 minifigures

Gray Snowboarder Being up against the Tough Snowboarder doesn't scare this minifigure—he has years of experience on the slopes.

Even super-cool snowboarders need gloves to keep warm!

Helmet first seen in the 2002 Racers theme

Big Air Snowboarder
This minifigure has the same head piece as Madam Hooch from the LEGO Harry Potter theme, but she prefers snowboards to broomsticks.

Tough Snowboarder
This snowboarder looks tough, but he still likes to protect his minifigure skin from the sun's glare with colored sunscreen.

Gravity Games silver-and-black logo is printed on her torso

Monobrow and goatee printed on head piece

Cool graphics on T-shirt

Stunt Skateboarder
Helmet and goggles keep this minifigure safe as she performs stunts at the Skateboard Vert Park Challenge (3537).

Park Skateboarder
The Skateboarder's bearded head piece appears on six other sporty minifigures.

NBA AND STREET BASKETBALL

Minifigures underwent a radical redesign for the NBA Basketball subtheme and their street basketballer counterparts. Springs were built into their legs, and arms and hands were specially constructed to hold, throw, and slam dunk the ball.

Blue strip of NBA All-Star Game East team

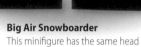

Orange sunglasses take away any glare

Arms modified to hold basketball

Street Player
Rain or shine, this player is always ready to play some b-ball.

Springs to "jump" and shoot

East NBA Player
Springing off to shoot some hoops is sure to make this minifigure player's team happy.

Sunglasses printed on forehead

Jacket seen on the Stuntman in the LEGO® Studios theme in 2001

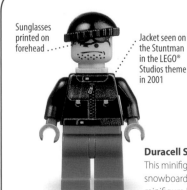

Duracell Snowboarder
This minifigure has a snowboard featuring a LEGO minifigure head design.

LEGO GRAVITY GAMES PROMOTIONAL SETS

Half of the LEGO Gravity Games sets were promotions for companies including Duracell, something that continued into 2004. Each set featured a minifigure and stunt stick.

LEGO ADVENTURERS

ARE YOU READY FOR AN ADVENTURE?

LEGO® Orient Expedition was the last Adventurers subtheme, released with 15 standard sets and three promotional minifigure sets. The brave adventurers set off on a daring quest to recover the Golden Dragon of Marco Polo. In addition to having the most detailed storyline of any Adventurers line, the sets also came with pieces of a board game that could be assembled and played.

Johnny Thunder
A new version of the adventurer minifigure returns with a new head with sideburns and a chin dimple.

- Desert outfit for his Orient adventure
- Gun tucked under belt

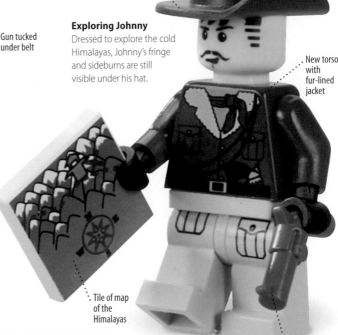

Exploring Johnny
Dressed to explore the cold Himalayas, Johnny's fringe and sideburns are still visible under his hat.

- Wide-brim hat
- New torso with fur-lined jacket
- Tile of map of the Himalayas
- Revolver for protection

Head gear also seen on Professor Karkaroff and Victor Krum from the Harry Potter™ theme in 2005, but in black

- New head with red lips
- Red wool scarf
- New and exclusive torso with fur-lined jacket
- Black gloves

Pippin Reed Brave Pippin scares off a yeti in Yeti's Hideout (7412) and manages to get her minifigure hands on a jewel!

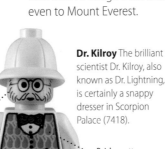

- Pith helmet
- New green torso with red scarf
- White, wispy beard

Reporter Pippin
This version of Pippin appears in Elephant Caravan (7414), where the race is on against Lord Sinister—who will get to the treasure first?

ADVENTURERS

Many favorite characters were back for 2003, including Johnny Thunder and Pippin Reed. Their thrilling journey would take them through India and China and even to Mount Everest.

Dr. Kilroy The brilliant scientist Dr. Kilroy, also known as Dr. Lightning, is certainly a snappy dresser in Scorpion Palace (7418).

- Paisley pattern on vest

- Monocle over eye
- Revolver fits into hand
- Holster pattern on torso

Lord Sam Sinister
A hook for his left hand and a battle-scarred face give this minifigure a new look.

UP TO NO GOOD

Four villains confronted the Adventurers: fiendish Emperor Chang Wu, ruthless Maharaja Lallu, crooked yeti hunter Ngan Pa—and the baddest of all, perennial nemesis Lord Sinister.

DID YOU KNOW?
The LEGO Orient Expedition subtheme introduced the scimitar, elephant, and sherpa hat elements.

- Red turban
- New torso with blue vest and yellow embroidery pattern

Babloo Seen only in Elephant Caravan (7414), Babloo fights off the bad guys with his scimitar.

- Ponytail hair piece

FRIENDS AND ALLIES

Three new faces joined the team: Babloo, from India; Sherpa guide Sangye Dorje; and Jing Lee, the only newcomer who became a permanent part of the group.

- New torso with Chinese shirt print

Jing Lee Martial arts are this minifigure's expertise—those baddies had better watch out!

Sherpa Sangye Dorje
The young mountain guide knows that snow shoes are essential wear when traveling to the Temple of Mount Everest (7417).

- Identical head gear to Pippin Reed
- Ax to cut through slippery ice
- Backpack filled with supplies
- Red sash tied around waist
- Snow shoes attach to legs

LEGO *STAR WARS*

It was a year almost as huge as Jabba the Hutt himself, as the first Jabba's Palace (4480) was released. New minifigures included Bib Fortuna, Lando Calrissian, and Greedo—plus a green figure of Jabba, of course.

Skull and lekku (head-tails) are all one head piece

Scarlet eyes

Long navy cape

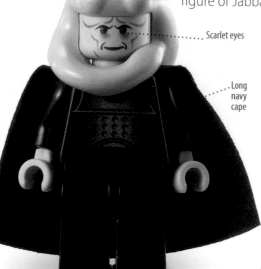

Bib Fortuna Jabba's chief of staff was the first minifigure of the Twi'lek species to be made.

DID YOU KNOW?
Boba Fett from Cloud City (10123) is one of the rarest and most collectible minifigures.

I'M SO RARE, THERE'S A BOUNTY ON MY HEAD!

Boba Fett This unique variant of the bounty hunter—in set 10123—is the first minifigure to have printed arms.

Green Mandalorian armor

Armored knee pads

Blaster

Jabba the Hutt Jabba's head and torso are made from a single mold, but the tail comes in two separate parts.

Plain, unmarked eyes

Fingers molded on hands

Tail pieces fit into torso socket

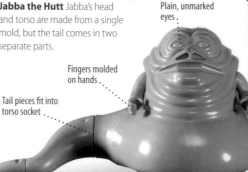

Molded antennae

Elongated snout

Arms with painted tan stripes

Brown hips and sand blue legs are unique to Greedo

Greedo A bumpy head mold was designed specially for Greedo. His large eyes are fitted with light reflectors.

YOU ARE NOT THE DROID I AM LOOKING FOR.

Breathing filters

Oxygen-filled rebreather pack

Commanders wear orange pauldrons

Black glove

Printed belt holds blaster ammo

Sandtrooper To aid breathing in the extreme desert climate, this minifigure wears a rebreather pack.

Cloud City (10123) In part of this set, which features seven minifigures, the villainous Darth Vader has trapped Han Solo in carbonite. The Lando minifigure tries to rescue the Han Solo minifigure.

Release lever fits into Lando's hand slot

Tile with carbonite Han Solo print

Darth Vader

Boba Fett

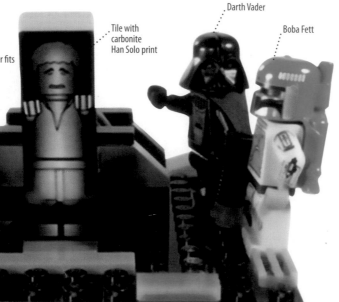

Shirt with dark blue collar

Lando Calrissian Lando's brown head piece is the first human flesh-colored minifigure head for the *Star Wars* theme.

Dual-colored cape is blue outside and yellow inside

Blaster made from megaphone piece

LEGO SPIDER-MAN

The second year of the LEGO Spider-Man theme moved away from LEGO Studios, with three sets based on the first Spider-Man movie. Major new minifigures introduced were the Green Goblin's alter ego, Norman Osborn, as well as Peter Parker in his wrestling costume.

New balaclava print covers mouth and nose

> I'M YOUR FRIENDLY NEIGHBORHOOD SPIDER-MAN.

> I'M JUST NOT SURE GREEN IS MY COLOR.

Determined expression

Spider-Man's wondrous web

New faded spider and web print on torso

White gloves

Double-faced The other side of Osborn's dual face shows a scared expression.

Norman Osborn This shirtless, yellow-torsoed minifigure represents Norman Osborn before his transformation into the Green Goblin in The Origins (4851).

Wrestling Peter For his fight against Bone Saw McGraw, Parker fashions this costume, which is only found in Spider-Man's First Chase (4850).

LEGO® EXPLORE® LITTLE ROBOTS™

The Little Robots from the BBC children's series of the same name was a LEGO Explore theme for two years, starting in 2003. Five sets were released featuring Tiny, Sporty, and the team.

Red shoulder pads

Sporty This beefy robot helps out in the Junk Yard. He has a green, red, and gold body.

Torso has switch pattern

Tiny Specially molded hands help this little robot hold the Day and Night lever in the Junk Yard.

Belt molded around waist

Prominent black nose for sniffing

Messy Tiny's green-and-golden robot-dog pet from the Tiny and Friends set (7441) is always running away.

LEGO® RACERS

This year saw the release of the second Williams F1 Racer set, a 1:27 scale race car with a driver. The set was based on the well-known British racing team and preceded Ferrari and Lamborghini as Racers licenses. This was the last Williams F1 set and minifigure produced.

New torso with polo shirt and jacket

Eyes printed with green eyeshadow

New white-and-pink torso

Peter Parker A studious-looking Parker is off on a school trip to the science lab in The Origins (4851). Watch out for spiders, Peter ….

Mary Jane Appearing only in The Final Showdown (4852), Peter Parker's minifigure love interest features an exclusive torso piece.

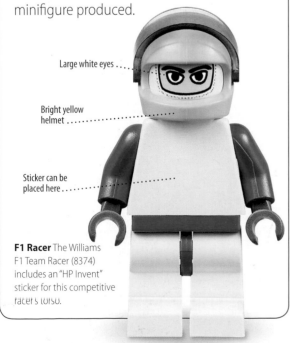

Large white eyes

Bright yellow helmet

Sticker can be placed here

F1 Racer The Williams F1 Team Racer (8374) includes an "HP Invent" sticker for this competitive racer's torso.

LEGO® DISCOVERY

LEGO Discovery was a one-year theme focusing on real-life space flight. Only one of the six sets featured minifigures: The Lunar Lander (10029). The other sets were replicas of NASA spacecraft

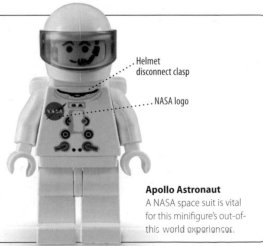

Helmet disconnect clasp

NASA logo

Apollo Astronaut A NASA space suit is vital for this minifigure's out-of-this world experiences.

Ogel has one red eye and one black

I CAN'T FAIL THIS TIME ... CAN I?

Black, mechanical shoulder pads

Blue hook replaces red one on 2002 version

Ogel The minifigure's only design change since 2002 is the color of his hook. Now, Ogel feels ready for his final battle against Alpha Team.

Transparent blue bubble helmet

New silver outline around scarab logo

Black and red torso and legs

Super Ice Drone The black skull head piece with white printing and red eyes is unique.

Ogel's ice orbs can freeze anything

OGEL AND HIS MINIONS

Ogel's plan is to freeze the world with the help of his Skeleton Drones and ice orbs. Thanks to his powerful mind control orbs, the skeletons follow the evil minifigure's orders without hesitation.

Ogel Minion This skeleton minifigure has a new helmet to stop him from freezing himself!

2004

2004 SAW THE COMEBACK of some old favorites, as LEGO® Alpha Team and LEGO® DUPLO® returned. LEGO® Harry Potter™ and BIONICLE® also remained strong. LEGO® Spider-Man™ swung back into action as *Spider-Man 2* arrived in movie theaters. Ferrari sets were released for the first time, and LEGO® *Star Wars*™ continued to flourish with the launch of iconic classic sets and sets from the Expanded Universe.

LEGO ALPHA TEAM

GOOD THING I WORE MY THERMAL UNDERWEAR!

After a year's absence, Alpha Team returned to stop evil Ogel in Mission: Deep Freeze. With a new logo, redesigned minifigures, and two new minifigure heroes—Diamond Tooth and Arrow—it was a new team for a new era.

New head piece features black sunglasses and a grimacing expression

New, triangular Alpha Team logo

Dash Alpha Team leader Dash has a completely new look in 2004.

New uniform with blue sleeve and silver zipper details

ALPHA TEAM

This year, agents Cam and Crunch were replaced by Arrow and Diamond Tooth. All six of the year's sets featured Alpha Team vehicles in icy colors, including Flex's Chill Speeder (4742) and Charge's Ice Blade (4743).

Magnifying glass

Red robot eyes

Tee Vee Alpha Team's communications expert has appeared in three very different guises—a TV with legs; an underwater vehicle; and now, finally, an android minifigure.

Special magnifying lens

Bandanna printed on head piece

Arrow Alpha Team's new mechanic has the same torso as Diamond, apart from his right arm.

Diamond Tooth New for 2004, Diamond Tooth is the mining expert for Alpha Team, and he pilots the Tundra Tracker (4744).

Hoth Princess Leia
This variant features Leia's iconic bun hairstyle. In 2011, the rebel leader has braids instead.

NEXT TIME, I'M DRIVING!

Print details on torso include the rebel leader's insignia

Flesh-colored hands—the 2011 variant has white-gloved hands

LEGO *STAR WARS*

The year 2004 saw the release of a number of classic *Star Wars* sets, including a new version of the *Millennium Falcon* (4504). This version of the ship featured both Han Solo and Princess Leia in their Hoth outfits from *Star Wars: Episode V The Empire Strikes Back.*

Printed fur-trimmed hood—Han's 2011 variant comes with detachable hood

Furry hood protects Han in a chilly blizzard

Large sensor dish

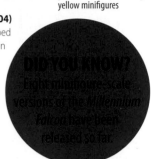

Chewbacca and Han sit in the cockpit of the promotional set, featuring yellow minifigures

Hoth Han Solo The rebel pilot is dressed warmly for the icy conditions on Hoth.

Han's handy electrobinoculars hang from a strap

Hoth Han Solo Variant This rare yellow variant featured in a promotional version of set 4504 with all-yellow minifigures.

***Millennium Falcon* (4504)**
The ship's triangular-shaped panels can be pulled open on their hinges to reveal all the action inside.

DID YOU KNOW?
Eight minifigure-scale versions of the *Millennium Falcon* have been released so far.

LEGO® RACERS

Ferrari was introduced to LEGO Racers in 2004, with minifigures of pit crew members and real-life Formula 1 drivers Michael Schumacher and Rubens Barrichello. Four System sets were released this year, as well as Ferrari-based LEGO® Technic sets. The LEGO Racers relationship with Ferrari would prove to be a long-lasting one.

Removable helmet

F1 Ferrari Pit Crew Member
Underneath his helmet, the minifigure wears a red balaclava. The head piece was also used in 2003 for Spider-Man.

Mechanic In 2004, this figure appeared in a second LEGO DUPLO Ferrari set complete with pit stop and fuel truck.

Racer The racer figure appeared in his race car in both DUPLO Ferrari sets released in 2004.

Simpler race car design for younger fans

I'M RUBENS ... HE'S MICHAEL!

Unique pattern printed on the top of the helmet

Unique head piece resembles real-life driver

Sponsors' logos

Brazilian flag represents driver's nationality

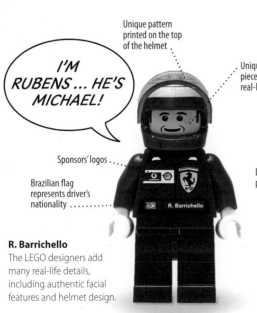

R. Barrichello
The LEGO designers add many real-life details, including authentic facial features and helmet design.

Driver's name is printed on torso

Famous Ferrari stallion logo

German flag represents driver's nationality

M. Schumacher
This minifigure's unique head piece is designed to closely resemble race car driver Michael Schumacher.

DID YOU KNOW?
The first LEGO sets to feature Ferrari cars were promotional items released in 1997.

LEGO® DUPLO®
Little builders had the chance to race to the finish line with this LEGO DUPLO Ville (formerly known as DUPLO Town) Ferrari F1. It came with a driver figure, podium, and silver trophy.

RUBEUS HAGRID

This was the second version of Hagrid to be produced. As before, he stands a head taller than a standard minifigure. The 2004 version features a flesh-colored face and hands.

··· Crossbow

Hagrid This figure comes with a barrel of tools, a key, and a crossbow to help in his job as gamekeeper of Hogwarts.

Ron has his trademark red hair piece ···

Neville has the same torso and legs as the 2004 variants of Harry and Ron ···

Flesh-colored version of 2001 head ···

Casual Ron Weasley Ron's torso with striped sweater and open shirt is unique to two Hogwarts Express sets released in 2004.

Neville Longbottom™ Harry's friend Neville is a minifigure for the first time. His unique head piece has a nervous face in Professor Lupin's Classroom (4752).

Time-Turner Hermione Granger Hermione has a unique detail on her Gryffindor uniform—a magical Time-Turner. A robed variant was also released.

Harry Potter has a flesh-colored head for the first time ···

Harry's tie and sweater are printed with the Gryffindor house colors ···

Third-Year Harry Potter
Three minifigures of Harry in his Gryffindor uniform were released this year. Each has the same head, torso, and legs, but two have robes.

STUDENTS

This year brought new versions of Harry Potter, Hermione Granger, Draco Malfoy, Ron Weasley, and Neville Longbottom. Harry actually appeared in six different incarnations, although many of the variations were very minor.

LEGO HARRY POTTER

Harry Potter and the Prisoner of Azkaban™ got the LEGO treatment in 2004. Sets included new versions of Hogwarts Castle (4757), Hagrid's Hut (4754), and the Hogwarts Express (4758), along with several models depicting key scenes from the film. There were nine new sets in total, plus the first mini-set—the Knight Bus (4755). In this year, all the minifigures were remade with the new flesh tones, apart from Snape, who retained his glow-in-the-dark head.

DID YOU KNOW?
2004 saw the release of the first and only motorized version of the Hogwarts Express train (10132).

The head is printed with a gaping mouth but no eyes ···

The 2011 version has a gray head and arms instead of green ···

Shimmering blue gown with purple accessories ···

Tattered gray robe and hood ···

Dementor™ The first version of the spooky Azkaban guard was released in four sets. It comes with a LEGO dish piece that can be attached to the base to keep it upright.

Unique light-purple witch's hat ···

Unposable sloped piece ···

Professor Trelawney Harry's Divination teacher stands out from the other minifigure professors, wearing a unique outfit.

Snarling mouth

Werewolf mask This removable piece can be put over Lupin's human head in place of his hair piece.

TEACHERS

New teacher minifigures graced the LEGO Harry Potter line this year. Professor Sybill Trelawney appeared for the first time in minifigure form, as did Remus Lupin (in both human and werewolf forms). A new version of Albus Dumbledore and two of Professor Snape were also released, including a Boggart.

Gray robes ···

Professor Lupin The scratches on his face and his tattered suit hint at this minifigure's secret. A full moon would reveal it ····

Glow-in-the-dark head ···

Unique torso is printed with Neville's grandmother's cardigan and scarf ···

Boggart
This minifigure is Neville Longbottom's worst fear—a shape-shifting version of Professor Snape.

LEGO® CASTLE

The second LEGO Castle subtheme to be called Knights' Kingdom appeared this year, both as a subtheme and as buildable action figures. The evil Vladek and his army of Shadow Knights battled the forces of King Mathias and his four brave knights, Rascus, Danju, Jayko, and Santis. Seven sets were released in this first year of the line.

Gold crown first seen on Royal Knights in 1995

Underneath his helmet, Jayko is smiling

Jayko The youngest of the four knights, Jayko is often known as "the Rookie." His main color, medium blue, is new.

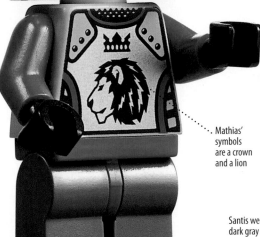

Crown covers the sides of the head and the nose

Danju's hair is dark tan underneath his helmet

Danju The oldest of King Mathias' four knights, Danju is also the wisest. His dark purple color is also new this year.

Underneath his helmet, Rascus has a goatee beard

Printed torso

Removable armor

Rascus The four knights have detachable, printed armor, with plain torsos underneath.

Rascus Without Armor Rascus is a great warrior, and he is famous for his agility and flexibility.

Angry expression

Medieval helmet protects face

Red breastplate with scorpion symbol

Mathias' symbols are a crown and a lion

King Mathias Appearing in two sets this year, King Mathias rules his kingdom, Morcia, with wisdom and nobility.

Santis wears dark gray gloves

Santis This knight is famous for his great strength. Santis was also released as a larger action figure, along with six other Knights' Kingdom characters.

Brown torso and legs with gray details

The Guardian does not have a hat or hair piece—just printed hair

Detachable gray beard

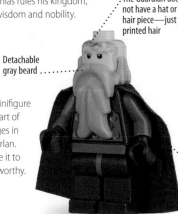

The Guardian This wise old minifigure protects the Heart of the Shield of Ages in the Citadel of Orlan. He will only give it to those who are worthy.

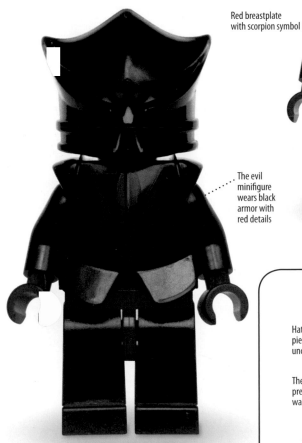

The evil minifigure wears black armor with red details

Vladek Leader of the Shadow Knights, the wicked Vladek kidnaps King Mathias and tries to take his place as ruler.

Shadow Knight Vladek's loyal Shadow Knight minifigures help him carry out his evil schemes.

Hat and head pieces are unchanged

The tie on the previous version was black

Pilot The LEGO pilot has a slightly updated torso with a new red tie and revised gold plane logo.

LEGO® WORLD CITY

Ten years after its first release, the classic Century Skyway airport set (6597) was rereleased in 2004. The 12 minifigures that came with the new set had minimal changes from their original 1994 versions.

The passenger is casually dressed

Passenger The 2004 version has a new head, featuring eyebrows and a wide smile.

Spider-Man's Street Chase (4853)
Spider-Man tries to stop two jewel thieves in this set—can he catch them?

Escaping jewel thief

Web line

City rat

HEY, COME BACK HERE WITH THAT!

DIAMONDS

VARICK ST.

DID YOU KNOW?
The year 2004 included the first appearances of J. Jonah Jameson and Harry Osborn as minifigures.

Mary Jane Watson
Like Peter Parker, M. J. gets a new outfit. Her facial features are also updated.

Pretty patterned sweater.

LEGO SPIDER-MAN

LEGO Spider-Man returned in 2004 as *Spider-Man 2* hit movie theaters. This time, Aunt May, Mary Jane, and the other minifigures had faces and hands matching their skin tones. The line included five new sets and 17 minifigures, including four different versions of Dr. Octopus. This was the final year of the Spider-Man play theme until 2012, when it returned as part of the LEGO® Marvel Super Heroes theme.

Aunt May is the only minifigure with this light gray ponytail

Head piece is unchanged since 2003

Aunt May
Peter Parker's Aunt May's minifigure is unique to Doc Ock's Bank Robbery (4854).

Unimpressed expression

J. Jonah Jameson It might be Peter Parker's boss's first appearance, but his black flat-top hair piece can be found on more than 20 other minifigures.

Scruffy collar and tie

Spider-Man The wall-crawler keeps the same head seen on his 2002 and 2003 versions but has an updated web design on his torso and legs.

New web design in 2004

Flat-top hair piece

Casual vest over zipped jacket

Spider-Man's costume is also a darker blue in 2004

This blue suit can also be seen on Bruce Wayne in 2006

Hand piece

Casual blue pants

SPIDER-MAN AND FRIENDS

This was the third time Spider-Man had appeared in minifigure form. Along with the webbed wonder, the 2004 sets showcased all the major characters, including Aunt May, Peter Parker, Harry Osborn, J. Jonah Jameson, and Mary Jane Watson. The new Peter Parker figure was more casually dressed than previous versions, and he was not wearing glasses.

Peter Parker Not only does Spider-Man's alter ego have a slight image makeover in 2004, he also has a head that matches his skin tone for the first time.

Harry Osborn Peter Parker's best friend has two minifigures in 2004: one wearing a blue suit (above) and the other wearing a gray pinstripe suit.

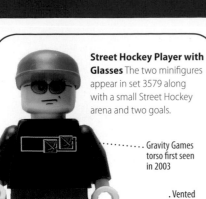

Street Hockey Player with Glasses The two minifigures appear in set 3579 along with a small Street Hockey arena and two goals.

.... **Gravity Games torso first seen in 2003**

Vented helmet

Gravity Games torso with white and silver logos

Red Street Hockey Player These minifigures are designed for a one-on-one game, involving two players.

STREET HOCKEY

This Street Hockey set (3579) featured two minifigures on movable bases controlled by levers. One seemed to be much more confident about winning than the other!

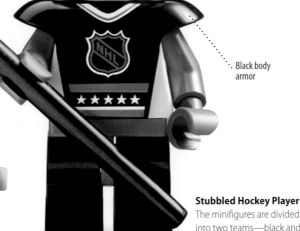

This minifigure's head piece has stubble and "angry" eyebrows

Black body armor

WHAT DO YOU MEAN I HAVE TO BUILD MY OWN PENALTY BOX?

Stubbled Hockey Player The minifigures are divided into two teams—black and white. Their body armor shows their team colors.

LEGO® SPORTS

The Hockey subtheme of Sports first appeared in 2003, but there were no minifigures—just brick-built players. In 2004, one set featured minifigures: NHL Championship Challenge (3578). There were eight ice hockey players, each with a different face. They were attached to movable bases, controlled by levers, and designed for a two-player game.

Safety helmet

White body armor

Determined Hockey Player Ice Hockey can be dangerous, so the minifigures protect themselves with body armor and helmets.

Doc Ock uses his tentacle arms to crush his foes

Dr. Octopus Thanks to his grabber arms, Dr. Octopus is slightly more complex than the other 4+ figures.

Doc Ock: Frowning Due to his unique design, Doc Ock is made up of 26 different LEGO pieces.

Bendable tentacles

I GIVE GREAT HUGS!

A special neck clip attaches Doc Ock's robotic arms to his minifigure

DR. OCTOPUS

The villainous Doc Ock came in four versions in 2004: frowning, smiling, angry, and in his Fusion Lab outfit.

Green suit

Spider-Man's Train Rescue (4855) In this set, Spider-Man battles Doc Ock on top of a subway train. The set also features minifigures of J. Jonah Jameson and a subway train conductor.

Peter Parker Unlike traditional minifigures, the 4+ versions have molded noses.

Spider-Man The 4+ figure has similar costume detailing to the regular minifigure.

SPIDER-MAN™ 4+

LEGO Spider-Man was the only licensed theme in the 4+ line, which was first introduced in 2003. At 2 in (10 cm) tall, the figures were larger than minifigures, with little or no building required—perfect for little hands.

Classic grin · 1978
· Male Person · LEGOLAND Town

Beard, mustache, and eyepatch ·
1989 · Captain Redbeard
· LEGO Pirates

Full lips · 1989 · Female Pirate
· LEGO Pirates

Mustache and stubble
· 1989 · Blue Pirate · LEGO Pirates

Headset and eyebrows
· 1992 · Space Police Chief
· LEGO Space

Droid head with large eye shield
· 1997 · Blue Droid · LEGO Space

Huge grin · 2001 · Flex
· LEGO Alpha Team

Purple eyeshadow and glasses
· 2001 · Cam Attaway
· LEGO Alpha Team

Princess curls · 2002
· Maiden · LEGO Castle

Evil black skull head
· 2004 · Super Ice Drone
· LEGO Alpha Team

HEADS UP, EVERYONE!

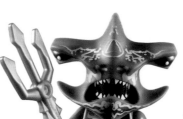

Hammerhead shark head · 2011
· Hammerhead Warrior
· LEGO Atlantis

Ancient Egyptian jackal head
· 2011 · Anubis Guard
· LEGO Minifigures

THE BASIC DESIGN of the standard minifigure head—a rounded piece with a stud on top—has not changed since the early years. The first heads always smiled, but in 1989, LEGO® Pirates introduced new face prints that included beards, eyepatches, and a range of different facial expressions. The launch of licensed themes in 1999 saw a massive innovation—specially molded heads created for less humanlike characters, and soon many other themes introduced these, too. The reversible head was introduced in 2001, which allowed a minifigure to change his or her expression when they felt like it.

Modified snake head with fangs
· 2012 · Lizaru · LEGO NINJAGO

Two-headed modified snake head · 2012 · Fangdam
· LEGO NINJAGO

Windswept face · 2013
· Skydiver · LEGO Minifigures

Cookie-shaped head · 2013
· Gingerbread Man
· LEGO Minifigures

Freckles · 1992 · Vendor
· LEGO Paradisa

Cool shades · 1992 · Pool Guy
· LEGO Paradisa

Printed droid head · 1994 · Spyrius
Droid · LEGO Space

**Cross-eyed, glasses, and facial
hair** · 1996 · Dr. Cyber
· LEGO Time Cruisers

Glow-in-the-dark shroud · 1997
· Ghost · LEGO Castle

Scared face · 2007 ·
· Crown Knight · LEGO Castle

**Open-mouthed modified alien
head** · 2009 · Kranxx · LEGO Space

**Bug-eyed modified head with
tongue** · 2009 · Squidman
· LEGO Space

Cold cheeks · 2009
· Carol Singer · LEGO Creator Expert

Large-jawed alien head · 2011
· Alien Trooper · LEGO Space

Big-eyed alien head · 2012
· Classic Alien · LEGO Minifigures

**Block-shaped head with large
blue eyes** · 2012 · Clockwork Robot
· LEGO Minifigures

Green face with spiked tiara
· 2012 · Lady Liberty
· LEGO Minifigures

**Modified minotaur head with
horns** · 2012 · Minotaur
· LEGO Minifigures

Gray zombie face · 2012
· Zombie Bride · LEGO Monster
Fighters

**Lion head mask with crown
pattern** · 2013 · Laval
· LEGO Legends of Chima

Eagle mask with gold tiara · 2013
· Eris · LEGO Legends of Chima

One-eyed monster head · 2013
· Cyclops · LEGO Minifigures

Robot head · 2013
· Robot Sidekick · LEGO Space

Insectoid head · 2013
· Winged Mosquitoid · LEGO Space

Queasy face · 2014
· Queasy Man · LEGO Creator Expert

Alien head with tentacles
· 2013 · Alien Trooper
· LEGO Minifigures

Hairy monster head · 2015
· Square Foot · LEGO Minifigures

Fairground face paints · 2019
· Girl · LEGO CITY

Possessed face · 2019
· Mr. Branson · LEGO Hidden Side

113

Breathing apparatus

Air tanks

Protective visor

Fire extinguisher

> *THIS YEAR WAS SMOKING HOT!*

Heroic Firefighter
This firefighter looks every bit the rugged hero, with a dimpled chin and determined expression.

2005

IT WAS A YEAR full of new play themes and new innovations for the LEGO Group. A new LEGO® CITY theme (an evolution of LEGO® Town and World City), plus LEGO® Dino Attack, LEGO® Power Racers, and LEGO® Tiny Turbos all made their first appearances. The LEGO® Factory initiative allowed fans to design sets for other fans to order. Sets based on *Star Wars*™: Episode III *Revenge of the Sith* and *Harry Potter and the Goblet of Fire*™ helped fans bring the movies to life. Minifigure star power was also on display in new LEGO® *Star Wars*™ video games and mini-movies.

LEGO CITY

A new LEGO CITY theme took over from World City this year and immediately expanded its scope by adding construction to the traditional police and fire sets. LEGO CITY gave builders the chance to play in the "real world," with minifigures representing both everyday heroes and the ordinary folks who keep a city running.

Cool Firefighter
Appearing on Day 1 of the 2005 CITY Advent Calendar has given this minifigure a confidence boost!

White helmet

Reflective stripes

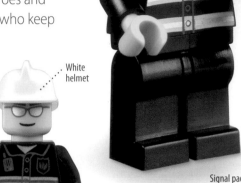

First time this helmet appeared in a color other than black or white

FIRE

The LEGO CITY Fire minifigures were on the job in 2005, with a new Fire Station (7240), Fire Truck (7239), Fire Helicopter (7238), and Fire Car (7241). To the rescue!

Flame on badge

Radio

Happy Firefighter
With a cheerful smile, this minifigure is always happy to help his fellow citizens.

Signal paddle

Working flashlight

Flashlight Cop
This police officer has a light-up flashlight to shed some light at crime scenes.

Traffic Cop
His angry scowl suggests that this cop is not to be messed with!

POLICE

The LEGO CITY Police Force made its first appearance in two years with four new sets, including a Police Station (7237). After this, the theme would virtually disappear until 2008.

> *SOUND THE ALARM! SOMEONE DRANK MY COFFEE!*

Gray beard and mustache

Stern Policeman
This Policeman shares the same head as the chess piece version of Jayko from Knights' Kingdom in 2005.

DID YOU KNOW?
Police dogs made their debut in LEGO CITY sets this year.

Knitted cap

Inmate number

Gold tooth

New head with dark blue shades

Leather jacket

Prison Inmate With an arched eyebrow and a menacing grin, this new minifigure looks like trouble!

Police Biker
This minifigure comes with a new torso, designed to look like a leather jacket.

Cool shades

Aviator cap first seen in the LEGO® Adventurers theme in 1998

Flippers

Torso featuring the Octan logo

Gas Station Worker
Wearing blue overalls printed with the famous Octan logo makes this Gas Station Worker proud.

Only two minifigures have this torso

LEGO CITY workers love red caps

Radio for communicating with colleagues

Pearl necklace

Red lipstick

Diver Girl
All ready to dive beneath the LEGO ocean waves, this minifigure wears a floral swimsuit and black flippers and carries air tanks on her back.

Sleeveless Man This dude's head was first seen in the LEGO Adventurers theme in 2003.

Office Worker
This stylish minifigure loves accessorizing—her pearl necklace is her favorite.

CITY LIFE
Along with Police, Fire, and Construction, 2005 saw a new Community Workers minifigure set, a LEGO CITY Advent Calendar, and one Airport set—the Desert Biplane, complete with pilot.

Stubble

Head appears on one other minifigure— another chef!

Chef's hat

Torso with overalls print is new for this year

Desert Biplane Pilot This Pilot minifigure pilot looks a bit disgruntled. Could it be the fact that his torso isn't unique? It is also seen on Lucius Malfoy from the LEGO® Harry Potter™ theme in 2003.

Crane Operator
Bright orange overalls mean that this construction worker is easy to see on the construction site.

Pizza Chef This cheerful pizza chef has a large, curly mustache and a huge grin.

Six-point Star of Life symbol

Doctor This doctor wears a new, buttoned shirt featuring the blue EMT Star of Life emblem.

HOSPITAL
The first hospital-themed model in 17 years appeared in 2005, with a promotional Paramedic set offered in the Czech Republic and at LEGOLAND® Windsor, UK. A new torso design with the Star of Life symbol also made an appearance this year.

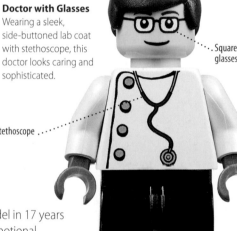

Doctor with Glasses
Wearing a sleek, side-buttoned lab coat with stethoscope, this doctor looks caring and sophisticated.

Square glasses

Stethoscope

Construction helmet

Head only seen on Construction and Train minifigures

Formal shirt and tie

Foreman As the head of the team, the foreman must look the part—he wears a shirt and tie under his jacket.

Tired eyes

Worker with Broom
Construction workers work hard all day, so it's no wonder this minifigure looks tired!

CONSTRUCTION
LEGO CITY was on the move, and the minifigure Construction workers helped it grow. The foreman minifigure kept an eye on the workers as they operated heavy machinery and started another new building.

Classic smiling face

De Bouwsteen minifigure
The back of the minifigure features the LEGO logo.

Light blue torso

DUTCH TREAT
This minifigure was produced with special permission from the LEGO Group, and only 1,000 were ever released. The extremely rare minifigures were accompanied by a certificate and given out to members of De Bouwsteen, a group of Dutch Adult Fans of LEGO (AFOLs), at LEGO World Netherlands in 2005.

Construction Site (7243)
This set includes a large crane, a dump truck, a rock crusher with a conveyor belt, and three minifigures to operate all the machinery.

LEGO *STAR WARS*

Star Wars: Episode III Revenge of the Sith dominated the LEGO assortment in 2005, with 13 sets devoted to the new movie. As well as several new minifigures, light-up lightsabers were added to some sets. Anakin Skywalker's transformation into Darth Vader provided the climax to the three prequels and a compelling LEGO set.

Head button turns lightsaber on and off

Lightsaber and minifigure are one complete assembly

Gray tunic

Brown Jedi robe

THEY PUT THE "LIGHT" IN LIGHTSABER!

Light-up Lightsaber Mace Windu
This Mace Windu minifigure is pretty special—he is the only minifigure to wield a purple light-up lightsaber.

Molded hood

Obi-Wan Kenobi
This new variant of Obi-Wan features a light-up lightsaber. He appears in Ultimate Lightsaber Duel (7257), where he must fight his former apprentice, Anakin Skywalker.

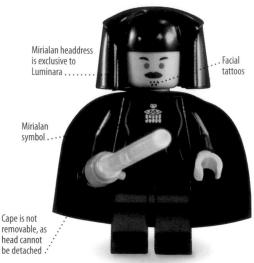

Mirialan headdress is exclusive to Luminara

Facial tattoos

Mirialan symbol

Cape is not removable, as head cannot be detached

Luminara Unduli This skilled Jedi Master has a unique head piece with facial tattoos that represent her physical accomplishments.

JEDI AND MORE

The year 2005 saw the first appearance of Jedi Mace Windu and Luminara Unduli in minifigure form, plus Owen Lars and a Wookiee warrior. There was also a new version of Obi-Wan Kenobi.

THE DARK SIDE

The *Star Wars* villains have their share of minifigures, too, with two versions of battle-scarred Anakin, a new Darth Vader, and an exclusive and highly valued Scout Trooper.

Orange eyes glow with mischief

Jawa This shady character hides under a large hood element. It's perfect for snooping around and carrying out shifty droid deals.

Ion blaster

Hilt of the light-up lightsaber is joined to arm piece

Battle scars

Cyborg hand

Specially fitted cloak for short-legged minifigures

Anakin Skywalker This powerful Jedi is the only minifigure to have this hair piece in this color.

Gray, scarred head under helmet

Single-piece helmet used for all Vader minifigures until 2015

Control panel

Darth Vader This Vader minifigure appears more machine than man in his black life-support suit.

Plain black head visible through visor

Ammo pouches

Scout Trooper Camouflaged armor keeps this minifigure well hidden during operations in the jungles and swamps.

FIRST APPEARANCES

Fierce cyborg General Grievous made his debut in LEGO form in 2005, as did the Buzz Droid, the FX-6 Surgical Droid, and the Dwarf Spider Droid.

Unique skull-like head piece

Grievous has two blue lightsabers and two green ones

General Grievous This fearsome cyborg figure can hold four lightsabers at once.

Republic symbol

Air supply hose

Life-support pack

Clone Pilot With a life-support pack on his torso, this minifigure is ready for takeoff!

CLONE TROOPERS

Two new styles of Clone Trooper, an Aerial Trooper and a new Clone Pilot, were released in 2005. All featured a new clone helmet based on Episode III.

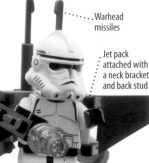

Warhead missiles

Jet pack attached with a neck bracket and back stud

Blaster

Aerial Trooper This minifigure has a jet pack and specializes in air attacks.

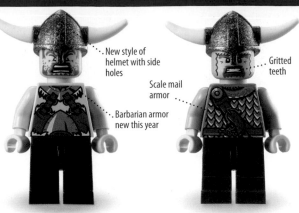

Barbarian Armor Viking
Barbarian-style armor really helps this Viking channel his inner rage.

- New style of helmet with side holes
- Scale mail armor
- Barbarian armor new this year

- Gritted teeth

Scale Mail Viking
Despite a new torso with scale mail resembling the scales of a fish or a reptile, this Viking still seems angry!

LEGO® VIKINGS

Courageous Scandinavian warriors battled mythological monsters in five exciting LEGO Vikings sets in this theme. Minifigures featured many new torsos and heads, as well as a new small, white barb piece used as the horns for the helmets. Vikings would be replaced by the new Castle line in 2007.

- Dragon figurehead
- Fearsome Viking Warrior
- Cage prison

Viking Ship Challenges the Midgard Serpent (7018) This set features the first galley made by the LEGO Group and is the first set to include a sea serpent (not shown). It features the Viking King minifigure and six Viking warriors.

- Dimple

Handsome Viking This Viking has a rugged charm and is one of the few Viking minifigures to have a happy expression.

- White barb used as horn
- Armor breastplate

Stern Viking Featuring the new speckled armor breastplate, this Viking is ready to defend his village from fearsome monsters.

- Studded collar
- Leather belt
- Patterned round shield

Serious Viking This minifigure is included in only one set—Viking Fortress (7019), in which the Vikings fight the Fafnir Dragon.

Golden helmet reflects his status

White beard and sideburns

Black cape

Viking King As leader of the Vikings, it's only right that the caped Viking King is regally dressed in red.

DID YOU KNOW?
Most of the monsters in the Vikings sets came from Norse myths.

LEGO DINO ATTACK

Dangerous dinosaurs go on a rampage, and only the Dino team can stop them in this new theme. Each set included a Dino team vehicle and a mutant dinosaur. Minifigures featured new heads and new torsos with equipment or weapons printed on them for each character.

DID YOU KNOW?
LEGO Dino Attack was released in Europe as Dino 2010 with some changes to the sets and story.

- Battle scar
- Ammunition belt

Viper Viper's vest holds many weapons to fight the war against the dinosaurs.

Digger This Digger minifigure features the new torso with red harness and binoculars pattern.

- Utility belt

A steady hand even in the face of danger

- Balaclava

Specs The balaclava-clad head on this minifigure is also featured on a LEGO® Mars Mission astronaut from 2007.

Specs with Tools Specs' new torso has tools with lime green handles and a red book.

- Clothes hold various tools and a book
- Rope

Shadow This minifigure's new head is specially camouflaged for creeping up on the dinosaurs undetected.

Danju wields his sword with skill

Blue sword

Each of the knights' visors is slightly different in design

Vladek is an expert sword fighter

Dark Lord The new Vladek minifigure now features a red breastplate with an image of a scorpion.

Wolf emblem

Hawk emblem

Beneath the helmet is a scowling face

Monkey emblem

The bear's ferocious teeth are visible

Sir Rascus In combat Rascus is agile and flexible, just like the monkey emblem on his shield and armor.

Sir Santis A new shield and breastplate features a bear, reflecting Santis's strength and fortitude.

Sir Danju The wise Danju's emblem is a wolf, printed on his new armor breastplate and his shield.

Sir Jayko Although he is the youngest of the knights, Jayko is powerful and fast. The new hawk emblem design reflects this.

Head is also used on the Jing Lee the Wanderer minifigure from the LEGO Adventurers theme in 2003.

LEGO® CASTLE

LEGO® Knights' Kingdom returned for its second year in 2005, with seven sets. Both the story—King Mathias and four brave knights versus Vladek and his Shadow Knights—and the majority of the minifigures remained largely the same as in 2004. Many of the new minifigures released for this theme were part of a chess set.

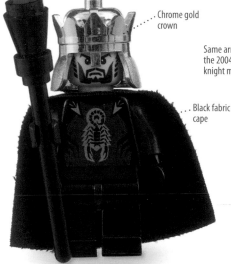

Black ponytail hair piece

Royal staff.

Chrome gold crown

Evil skull face

Same armor as the 2004 Jayko knight minifigure

Black fabric cape

Sloped piece

Black Chess Queen This sinister, skeleton-faced minifigure is a chess piece.

Black Chess King Chess minifigures were only released as part of the chess set (851499).

White Chess Queen This minifigure is one of the queens from the Knights' Kingdom chess set.

LEGO® CLIKITS™

LEGO CLIKITS was an arts and crafts line aimed at girls that allowed them to create room decorations, gifts, and accessories. Only three CLIKITS figures were released, and each one came in a separate set.

Hip hairstyle.

Flower in hair.

Star With the name Star, it's no surprise that this figure came in a set (7535) with lots of star pieces.

Daisy This figure was included in set 7534 with pieces designed to make jewelry.

Aqua skirt

BIONICLE®

The year 2005 brought more ways to play in the BIONICLE universe. Characters previously depicted only as buildable models became smaller single-piece figures, battling new Visorak spider pieces. Despite having no articulation, each one was posed for action.

Toa Hordika Nokama All in blue, this figure is the Toa of Water. She can create anything from water—from a stream to a tidal wave.

Base fits on to standard LEGO studs

Distinctive design based on larger buildable version

Toa Hordika Matau All four of this year's playsets included the same six Toa Hordika figures, including the brave Matau.

White and black mandibles

Visorak Keelerak Agile and strong, this figure has large mandibles and razor-sharp legs.

LEGO® HARRY POTTER™

The LEGO Harry Potter play theme focused on *Harry Potter and the Goblet of Fire* in 2005, with four new sets. Three of the four sets dealt with the three deadly tasks from the Triwizard Tournament. Three new versions of Harry appeared this year, and new minifigures included Viktor Krum, Professor Karkaroff, and Mad-Eye Moody.

Bowl-cut hair

Ron Weasley This minifigure's head is reversible—turn it around to see Ron sleeping!

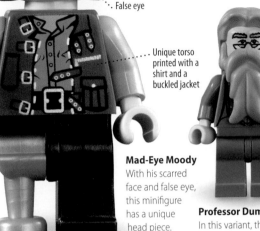

False eye

Unique torso printed with a shirt and a buckled jacket

Mad-Eye Moody
With his scarred face and false eye, this minifigure has a unique head piece.

Until 2018, all versions of Dumbledore have the same beard

Professor Dumbledore
In this variant, the headmaster wears blue dress robes.

Hermione Granger
This minifigure has a reversible head. The other side shows her in an enchanted sleep.

Same uniform as the 2004 minifigure

Torn uniform

"POTTER" is printed in large letters on the back of torso piece

Harry Potter™ This is one of three Harry Potter minifigures released for *Harry Potter and the Goblet of Fire*. Each one wears a different outfit suitable for the trials Harry must face.

Whiskery facial markings

Ratlike teeth

Gloved, replacement hand

Wormtail This minifigure's unique head shows signs of his Animagus form—a rat.

DID YOU KNOW?
In set 4767, LEGO designers created a dragon's egg with a magnetic piece on one side. Harry has a magnetic handle so he can hold it.

Head glows in the dark

Face now has smaller nostrils and eyes changed from red to clear

Lord Voldemort This is the first actual minifigure of Lord Voldemort. Prior to this, he featured only as a face on one side of Professor Quirrell's head.

Large, furry hat

Fur-lined Jacket with toggle fastenings

Viktor Krum This torso piece is identical to Igor Karkaroff's, but Victor's younger-looking face makes it easy to distinguish between the two.

Igor Karkaroff
The scowling face with goatee is unique to this minifigure.

Shark head piece fits over minifigure head

Durmstrang crest

Shark Head Viktor
This minifigure shows Viktor Krum when he is half-shark, half-human.

Graveyard Duel (4766) This set, which shows a graveyard scene, also came with ideas for other builds using the bricks, such as this one.

Lord Voldemort

Wormtail

Black skeleton is unique to this set

Death Eater

Death Eater
This Death Eater resembles Lucius Malfoy and has a reversible head.

Black Death Eater mask

Robe used on the minifigures of Voldemort and the Dementors

Merperson This Merperson's unique head, torso, and tail prints are not found on any other minifigure.

Hair piece also used for Poison Ivy from LEGO® Batman™

The first LEGO merperson tail

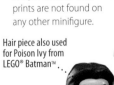

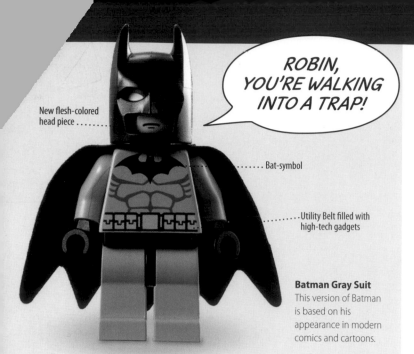

New flesh-colored head piece

Bat-symbol

Utility Belt filled with high-tech gadgets

Batman Gray Suit
This version of Batman is based on his appearance in modern comics and cartoons.

> ROBIN, YOU'RE WALKING INTO A TRAP!

2006

A CAPED CRUSADER, a powerful Airbender, a yellow sponge from beneath the sea, brave young warriors in mighty battle mechs—these were just some of the new LEGO® minifigure "faces" to appear in 2006. Building on its success with *Star Wars*™, LEGO play themes embraced pop culture by welcoming some of the hottest licenses around. Lines such as LEGO® EXO-FORCE™ and LEGO® Aqua Raiders would also provide the adventure and role-play LEGO fans craved, while new soccer sets revived LEGO® Sports.

LEGO® BATMAN™

LEGO fans and comic fans both had reason to cheer when the new LEGO Batman theme premiered in 2006. The Dark Knight appeared with some of his best friends and his worst enemies in six sets (a seventh, the Ultimate Batmobile set, featured no minifigures). Many of the minifigures also appeared in three magnet collections.

Wavy hair piece

New torso this year with "R" symbol and yellow Utility Belt

Robin The minifigure of Batman's ally is based on the third Robin from the comics, Tim Drake. He was the first to wear long pants instead of shorts.

DID YOU KNOW?
Batman's "blank" eyes are created by printing a white band across the minifigure's forehead.

New head piece with mustache and laugh lines

Alfred
Bruce Wayne's loyal butler, Alfred, wears a new torso this year, with suit jacket, gray vest, and blue bow tie.

Alfred is always impeccably dressed

New masked head

Nightwing symbol

Silver goggles visible underneath mask

Unique feline mask

Dual-sided head

Nightwing After retiring as Robin, Dick Grayson became Nightwing. His hair piece is also seen on Hitomi, from the LEGO EXO-FORCE theme.

Catwoman This jet-black catsuit, new this year, allows Catwoman to remain undetected during her nocturnal criminal activities.

THE BATMAN FAMILY

Two versions of the Batman minifigure, plus Robin, Alfred the butler, Nightwing, and Batman's alter ego Bruce Wayne are featured in the 2006 sets.

> I'D WIPE THAT SMILE OFF YOUR FACE, RIDDLER, IF YOU WEREN'T PLASTIC!

Batman Black Suit
This all-black variant resembles Batman's suits from the comics of the late 1990s. It features gold torso details.

Well-groomed hair

Handsome features

Suit is pressed to perfection

Bruce Wayne The Caped Crusader's civilian torso was first seen in 2004 on Harry Osborn from the LEGO® Spider-Man™ theme.

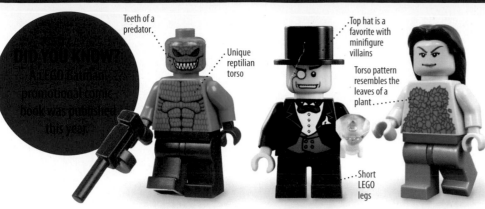

Teeth of a predator.

Unique reptilian torso

Top hat is a favorite with minifigure villains

Torso pattern resembles the leaves of a plant

Short LEGO legs

Killer Croc The scaly-skinned menace has the appearance and the strength of a crocodile.

The Penguin This dapper crook wears a tuxedo, with a vest and bow tie, and a monocle over one eye.

Poison Ivy This female villain has a brand-new, unique head with green lips and red eyebrows.

DID YOU KNOW? A LEGO Batman promotional comic book was published this year.

First time a hair piece is printed

Acid damage

Two-Face's black-and-white suit reflects his split personality

Two-Face This criminal has all-new elements that are unique to him. His head is regular on one side but purple and scarred on the other, with a large exposed eye.

THE VILLAINS

Most of Batman's minifigure archenemies surfaced in 2006, either individually in sets or together in Arkham Asylum (7785). The Joker, Penguin, Two-Face, and Killer Croc all had their own vehicles in the assortment.

Question mark emblem

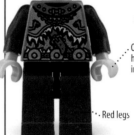

The Riddler Nothing makes The Riddler happier than leaving complex clues to his crimes for Batman to solve. This year, the Riddler has a new head with purple mask detail.

Green jumpsuit

Permanent grin

The Joker Calling Card

The Joker This Joker minifigure featured in a limited-edition box set, given away at the 2008 San Diego Comic-Con, as well as in set 7782.

Mr. Freeze This cool character's clear bubble helmet was first seen on minifigures from the LEGO® Insectoids theme in 1998.

Freezer blaster

Cryogenic suit

Pointed black hat made originally for LEGO® Castle witches and wizards

Scythe

The Scarecrow This sinister red-eyed minifigure has a transparent head that glows in the dark. His torso has printed stitching and a rope belt.

LEGO® VIKINGS

White facial hair makes him appear old and wise

In 2006, the LEGO Vikings Chess Set was released, as well as two Vikings sets. These included the Army of Vikings with Heavy Artillery Wagon (7020), which came with seven minifigures— the most included in any Vikings set.

Red Chess King The Viking chess pieces have the same torso pattern as the Fantasy Era dwarf minifigures from the Castle theme in 2008.

Horns are glued to helmet

Red Chess Bishop So that the chess minifigures did not get mixed up, some of the pieces were stuck together with glue.

Gray hair piece

On the chessboard, he holds a sword in each hand

Red legs

Blue Chess Queen The blue and red queens in the Viking chess set are the only ones that have happy expressions. They must be enjoying the game!

Gray sloping piece for skirt

LEGO® TECHNIC

This minifigure is unusual, as it was included in an educational LEGO Technic set—Science and Technology Base Set (9632). The set came with 25 booklets with building directions for 12 different models.

Black ponytail hair piece

Pretty orange flower pattern

Floral Shirt Girl Minifigures aren't usually featured in LEGO Technic sets, but this girl seems very happy about it!

NO, I DON'T KNOW WHAT I'M SMILING ABOUT EITHER.

LEGO® AVATAR™ THE LAST AIRBENDER™

Based on the popular animated Nickelodeon series, *Avatar: The Last Airbender* was a one-year theme in 2006. Two sets were released, featuring six new minifigures. Aang is the only minifigure to appear in both sets and, like the others in the theme, he features manga-style eyes.

Master Airbender Tattoo

Aang As the last Airbender, Aang must try to save the world, but as his smile suggests, he would rather have fun than fight the Fire Nation!

Bright yellow torso

Orange poncho

New brown legs with yellow printing on the thighs

Strap holds a boomerang on his back

Smirk

Blue robes

Sokka Katara's warrior brother, Sokka is brave and loyal. His unique torso has a printed strap detail.

Classic Castle helmet but in a new color

Armor breastplate

New head has ponytail on the back

Fire Nation Soldier Serving fiery Prince Zuko is no joke—this soldier is the only minifigure with this new, serious head.

Firebender This scary-looking minifigure has the power to control fire. He has a new head piece with a skull-like mask.

Prince Zuko
The exiled heir to the Fire Nation throne has quarreled with his father. The scar on his face was caused by his father's fire during a duel.

Fireproof armor pattern is unique to the Zuko minifigure

Loop of hair

Dark blue robe with white trim

Katara This minifigure has a brand-new, unique head that features loops of hair that drape over her face.

Flying Doctor
This air ambulance doctor has a new torso with a jacket print that includes a radio, zippers, and the EMT Star of Life logo.

Radio

Zipper

Star of Life logo

LEGO® CITY

When there was an emergency, the LEGO CITY Emergency Medical team was on the job in 2006. Doctors and air ambulance pilots made up just some of the minifigures released with four Emergency sets. Also in 2006, LEGO Train (now a subtheme of CITY) converted to remote control, with two sets featuring seven minifigures.

Doctor with Stethoscope
With a new torso featuring pens and a stethoscope, this Doctor is ready to help the ailing citizens of LEGO CITY.

Open collar

Stethoscope

Silver shades

Tools in pocket

Construction Worker
New overalls with a handy pocket for storing essential tools have made this construction worker's day.

Glasses

The conductor wears his uniform with pride

Train logo

Conductor Charlie
This friendly conductor really enjoys helping passengers.

LEGO® CASTLE

LEGO Knights' Kingdom continued the story of the heroic knights of Morcia and their battle against the evil Vladek. The struggle shifted to the mighty Mistlands Tower, and King Jayko was promoted to the throne from his previous rank of knight. Apart from Lord Vladek and King Jayko, all the other characters were new for 2006, including noble hero Sir Adric.

Gray beard fades to white at edges

Black cape

Hawk symbol

King Jayko This royal minifigure has a new pearl gold armor breastplate. It features a silver and black hawk pattern.

Bushy eyebrows meet in the middle

Evil sneer on face

Dracus The warlord of the evil Rogue Knights, this menacing minifigure stands out in his yellow pants and sleeves.

Fierce facial expression for battle

Bronze studs

Karzon Vladek's wicked weapons master is very proud of his bronze armor and likes to show it off with plenty of bad-tempered shouting.

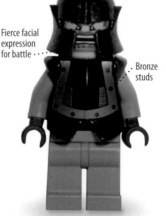

Little of Vladek's face is visible under visor

Scorpion emblem

Bright red cape

Lord Vladek The evil knight now wears a black armor breastplate, embellished with a large silver scorpion.

Helmet has also been worn in red by the knight Santis in 2004

Striking red armor

Sir Adric Raring to defend King Jayko in battle, Sir Adric just needs to make sure he can see out of his chunky helmet first!

SpongeBob SquarePants
This minifigure has a unique head piece printed with SpongeBob's face, which fits over a plain yellow torso.

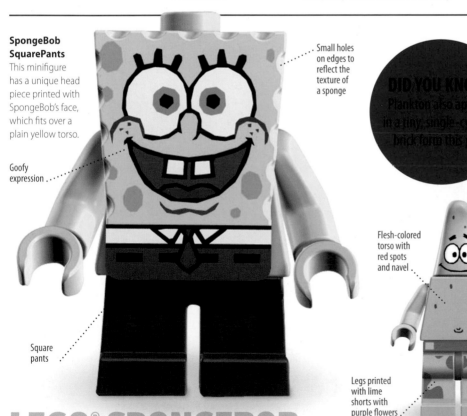

Goofy expression

Square pants

Small holes on edges to reflect the texture of a sponge

DID YOU KNOW?
Plankton also appears in a tiny, single-cylinder brick form this year.

Flesh-colored torso with red spots and navel

Legs printed with lime shorts with purple flowers

Patrick Star SpongeBob's dopey best friend Patrick has a unique, cone-shaped head piece.

High-waisted blue pants

Short LEGO legs

Mr. Krabs The owner of the Krusty Krab restaurant has a unique molded head piece and eyes on stalks.

Unique features

Shirt collar pattern

Squidward Tentacles SpongeBob's grumpy neighbor has a regular head piece that is printed with a big nose and large yellow-and-red eyes.

Small lever

Sticker with Plankton's features

PLANKTON!
This large version of Plankton is made from three round bricks covered by a sticker. This was the only figure in Build-A-Bob (3826). The set references the TV episode in which Plankton takes over SpongeBob's mind.

LEGO® SPONGEBOB SQUAREPANTS™

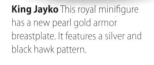

Who lives in a LEGO set under the sea? SpongeBob SquarePants! Three sets appeared this year, featuring minifigures of all the major characters. The SpongeBob theme earned a reputation for having many interesting elements and variations of minifigures over the years.

LEGO® STAR WARS™

The year 2006 saw the return of some well-loved minifigures and the arrival of some new ones. The Bespin Security Guard, Dengar, and Ten Numb all made their debuts this year. Luke Skywalker, Princess Leia, Han Solo, and Lando Calrissian returned in the all-new Jabba's Sail Barge (6210).

Green lightsaber

Skin-colored hand. On the 2010 variant, it's black

Jedi robe pattern

Face printed with lines to reflect his Sullustan features

Lando Calrissian Disguised as a skiff guard on Jabba's Sail Barge, Lando intends to help his friends.

Helmet with face guard is unique

Vibro-ax

Jedi Knight Luke Variants of this minifigure all have the same legs and torso with black Jedi robes.

Ten Numb Ten is a Sullustan minifigure. He is exclusive to the B-wing fighter (6208).

Torso has gold trim and the guards' emblem

Relby-K23 blaster pistol

Brown tunic and gold armor

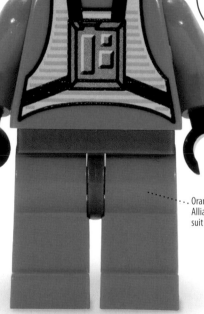

X-wing pilot helmet

The torso on the 2010 variant has creases on the shirt

Arms printed with red marking to show rank of sergeant

LUKE ISN'T THE ONLY SUPERSTAR PILOT AROUND HERE!

Han Solo This version of Han Solo is the only one that doesn't have a gun holster printed on his legs.

Bespin Security Guard This is the only minifigure to have the standard head piece in reddish brown.

Orange Rebel Alliance flight suit

Sail

Lando Calrissian

Boba Fett

Gamorrean Guard

Jabba's Sail Barge (6210) This set comes with eight minifigures. The sides of the barge open to reveal Jabba's throne room, prison, and kitchen.

Luke Skywalker

Han Solo

R2-D2

Jabba the Hutt holding Princess Leia's chain

Wedge Antilles Also new to the minifigure party this year was pilot Wedge Antilles., appearing in X-wing Fighter (6212).

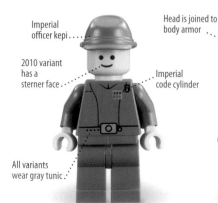

Imperial officer kepi

2010 variant has a sterner face

Head is joined to body armor

Imperial code cylinder

Deadly vibro-ax

Dengar always wears a turban

Torso pattern unique to this minifigure

All variants wear gray tunic

Imperial Officer This minifigure is a high-ranking soldier in the Emperor's huge army.

Gamorrean Guard This boarlike creature has a new modified head with snout and tusks.

Dengar This bounty hunter is hired by Darth Vader to capture the *Millennium Falcon*.

DRINK ANYONE?

R2-D2 is forced to be a servant on Jabba the Hutt's Sail Barge, so this variant comes complete with two drinks and a serving tray attachment.

R2-D2 This little droid comprises a head piece, a body piece, and two leg pieces that are joined to its body with LEGO Technic pins.

Camera eye

Goblet

Tray

LEGO EXO-FORCE

LEGO minifigures met Japanese manga in this exciting new line. Daring young fighters in massive mechs challenged the might of an army of evil robots with their equally massive mechs in 16 sets. The human minifigures featured new torsos and new, cartoon-style hair pieces, as well as anime-inspired facial designs.

New angular hair piece

New torso with EXO-FORCE uniform

Orange visor

Ha-Ya-To As the joker of the team, Ha-Ya-To is always smiling—even in the face of danger.

Hikaru The serious Hikaru has a new hair piece and dual-sided head with an orange visor printing.

DID YOU KNOW?
Every 2006 LEGO EXO-FORCE set features a light-up brick called a "power core."

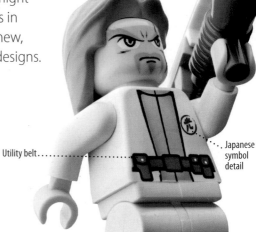

Utility belt

Japanese symbol detail

Keiken The leader of the EXO-FORCE team is the eldest and most experienced. Turn his head around to reveal his fighting face.

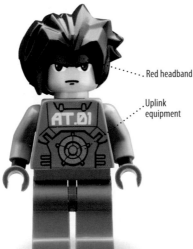

Scar

Intense expression

Red headband

Uplink equipment

Takeshi This minifigure has a new torso design with a dark gray armor breastplate over a red suit.

Ryo The technical expert of the team, there's nothing Ryo can't fix or invent!

Claw

Large feet for stability

Blaster

Meca One This cunning golden figure is the leader of the robots.

Blue Devastator These cold and calculating robots have terrifying mechanical claws.

Iron Drone The drone figures are the strongest robots but are less intelligent than the Devastators.

THE ROBOTS

The enemy robots have a clear hierarchy, beginning with the Iron Drone figures, moving up to three different colors of Devastator (red, blue, and green), and finally to the golden leader, Meca One.

LEGO® RACERS

Four more Ferrari sets sped toward the finish line for LEGO Racers this year. Along with a new version of driver Felipe Massa and a number of pit crew members, this year's line-up included announcers, cameramen, and a race official. A Fuel Filler minifigure was also introduced, wearing modern protective gear.

Checkered pattern

TV Press

DID YOU KNOW?
Five new minifigure characters make their first appearances in the 2006 LEGO Racers sets.

Head piece also used for the 2004 Rubens Barrichello minifigure

Felipe Massa This new minifigure represents the real-life race car driver Felipe Massa. A torso sticker shows his name and the Brazilian flag.

Cameraman Capturing all the race action with his camera, this minifigure wears a stickered bib to show that he's a member of the press.

Torso printed with name

Scuba tank

Weight belt

Spear guns doubled as legs for the 2006 LEGO® EXO-FORCE™ Mini Venom Walker

Aqua Raider Diver The divers are armed with spear guns to fend off savage sea creatures.

2007

THE EXCITEMENT was building in 2007, as the LEGO Group helped celebrate the 30th anniversary of *Star Wars™* with a host of new sets and a special 14-carat gold C-3PO minifigure. Harry Potter™ returned in one set, his last until 2010. Meanwhile, new LEGO play themes took center stage, including the undersea LEGO® Aqua Raiders, the out-of-this-world LEGO® Mars Mission, and the fantasy-themed LEGO® Castle. LEGO® Modular Buildings made their first appearance, giving experienced builders the chance to assemble realistic buildings in scale to their minifigure residents.

Mechanical robot arm

Lobster Strike (7772) A fearsome giant lobster, an underwater exploration rover to defeat it, and two minifigures are included in this set.

Dinosaur tail end piece is also used on the Jabba the Hutt minifigure, first released in 2003

Huge claws

Antennae also used as Barraki spines in BIONICLE® sets

Spinning drill for collecting underwater crystals

LEGO AQUA RAIDERS

Aqua Raiders plunged beneath the ocean waves in 2007 in seven sets. Unlike previous underwater teams, the Aqua Raiders don't fight other minifigures, but search for treasure along the sea floor. They need to watch out, though—dangerous sea creatures stand between them and their prizes!

Knitted hat has kept more than 140 minifigures warm, including robbers and farmers

Aqua Raiders trident logo

Hatted Diver After a long day seeking treasure deep in the ocean, this minifigure dons a knitted hat to keep warm.

LEGO® SPACE

The year 2007 saw the first new LEGO Space theme in six years: LEGO Mars Mission. Considered a sequel of sorts to 2001's LEGO® Life on Mars, it differed by making the alien figures a menacing rather than peaceful force. Eight sets were released in 2007, featuring astronauts with new torsos and glow-in-the-dark aliens.

Air pressure regulator

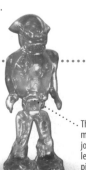

Alien The mysterious alien figures are made of two unique transparent green, glow-in-the-dark parts—legs and torso.

The figures can move only at the joint where their legs and torso pieces meet

Angry Spaceman Space travel is no picnic, but this grumpy minifigure is proud to wear the Classic Space logo on his suit.

- Zipped black mask and red eyes
- Unique torso with yellow Utility Belt

Dark Blue Knight
Batman receives a makeover with a dark blue mask, cape, hips, and hands.

Bane This mighty minifigure only ever appears in one set, The Bat-Tank: The Riddler and Bane's Hideout (7787). He gets a redesign in 2012 and switches to a black suit.

- Bulging muscles and scars

LEGO® BATMAN™

Two sets appeared in 2007, featuring a new dark blue costume for the Caped Crusader. Only one new character was released—the muscle-bound Bane.

- Specially molded head piece

Kalmah This fearsome figure may be small, but he strikes fear into the hearts of his Toa Mahri foes.

- Movable legs

BIONICLE®

The final year of the miniature BIONICLE theme featured three sets and 11 new figures of the warring Toa Mahri and the Barraki. The sets included both vehicles and Rahi beasts for transporting the figures.

LEGO MODULAR BUILDINGS

Modular Buildings sets were launched this year, giving minifigures the most realistic and detailed street scenes yet to hang out in. The first was Café Corner (10182), part of the Advanced Models theme, which features more challenging models. This was followed by Market Street (10190), a LEGO® Factory exclusive created by talented fan Eric Brok. Both sets came with three very busy minifigures.

Male Worker
This worker's torso is mostly featured on LEGO CITY minifigures.

- Green overalls

Spiky hair, seen on EXO-FORCE minifigures and LEGO DC's Nightwing minifigure

NOW, WHERE DID I PUT MY GLOVES?

Super Goalie The Super Goalie's hair piece is usually enough to distract the opposition.

LEGO® SPORTS

This exclusive Goalie minifigure was part of a promotional set given out free with the purchase of some types of Adidas trainers. It also included a golden soccer ball and a stand for the figure. The minifigure came with flat gloves with Adidas goalie glove pattern stickers, which attached to his regular minifigure hands.

- Neat ponytail

City Worker This man's hair piece was also used for the LEGO Harry Potter Mad-Eye Moody minifigure.

- Blue jacket

Office Worker
This businesslike minifigure is dressed for a day at the office.

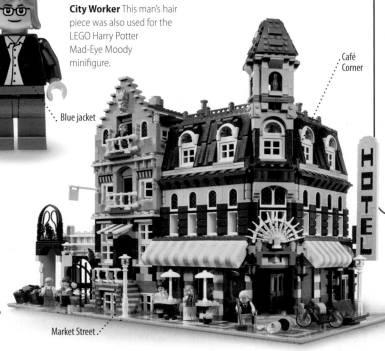

- Café Corner

Market Street (10190)
This modular set contains a marketplace and a four-story townhouse, plus three minifigures.

- Market Street

Café Corner (10182)
This modular construction set can be combined with other LEGO sets, as it is here, to create a whole neighborhood.

LEGO® HARRY POTTER™

The year 2007 saw the release of one set in the LEGO Harry Potter theme, the third version of Hogwarts Castle (5378), from *Harry Potter and the Order of the Phoenix*™. Nine minifigures came with the set, including Harry Potter in a new school uniform and new versions of Hermione Granger, Draco Malfoy, Professor Snape, and a Death Eater.

Death Eater
This version of the Death Eater is exclusive to set 5378.

Ornate silver mask

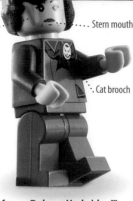

Pink blush to match pink suit
Stern mouth
Molded hair
Cat brooch

Smart school tie

Harry Potter™ Harry's tie is printed with the colors of his house—scarlet and gold for Gryffindor.

Professor Dolores Umbridge™
The unpleasant Umbridge makes her minifigure debut in Hogwarts Castle (5378). Her hair is also seen on a worker minifigure in the Modular Green Grocer (10185) from 2008.

Double-sided sleeping/smiling head

Gryffindor uniform

Frowning expression

Hermione Granger This version of Hermione is unique to set 5378, but the individual parts have been used in other sets.

Professor Snape Like the Hermione minifigure, this version of Professor Snape is also unique to set 5378.

DID YOU KNOW?
The mandrake plants from Hogwarts Castle (5378) included their very own unique minifigure heads.

Hogwarts Castle (5378)
This version of the famous castle was the only LEGO model released for *Harry Potter and the Order of the Phoenix*.

The castle's interior has hidden items for Harry and his friends to find

Owl perched in alcove

LEGO® EXO-FORCE™

LEGO EXO-FORCE returned for a second year in 2007 with 11 new sets. Inspired by Japanese manga and animation, the theme featured a team of human pilots battling against the cunning robot army for control of their mountain home. Most LEGO EXO-FORCE sets were battle machines that both sides created to try to win the war.

Hair piece is also used for LEGO Sports Goalie minifigure

New reversible head. Turn it around to see her angry expression

New gold amulet-patterned armor torso

Hitomi The granddaughter of Sensei Keiken, this is courageous Hitomi's first and only appearance in minifigure form in Fight for the Golden Tower (8107).

Bright red angular hair

New gold-and-violet flight suit torso

Ha-Ya-To Ha-Ya-To's specialty is flying, which explains his windswept hair.

DID YOU KNOW?
Hitomi serves as leader of EXO-FORCE when the Sensei disappears.

LEGO® RACERS

The Ferrari 248 F1 Team roared into action in 2007 in a new set for LEGO Racers. It included eight minifigures: a new variant of Felipe Massa, the minifigure debut of Kimi Raikkonen, two crew members, three engineers, and a record keeper. A second edition of this set contained different race cars and a Michael Schumacher minifigure in place of Raikkonen.

F. Massa With a new torso and new standard helmet, Massa is ready to burn some rubber.

Ferrari red legs and torso

Crown Princess
Daughter of the Crown King, this fair maiden's smiling face suggests she is safe from the evil Skeleton Warriors. For now ….

..... Gold crown-trimmed corset

.... New dark blue sloped skirt

CROWN KNIGHTS

Led by the brave Crown King, the Crown Knights are made up of foot soldiers and horsemen. They have new torsos with armor breastplate printing and appeared in every 2007 Castle set.

.....Broad-brim helmet

Chest strap .....

Crown emblem .....

Crown King with Cape
Ruler of the Crown Knights, the caped Crown King has new pearl gold armor to protect him in battle.

Chrome gold crown

..... Golden broadsword

I MAY BE A PLASTIC KING, BUT DON'T CALL ME A RULER!

Dark blue cloth cape

Scared Crown Knight
Maybe this scared Crown Knight has just spotted an evil skeleton?

LEGO CASTLE

The new LEGO Castle series featured human Crown Knights battling against a scary Skeleton Army led by an evil wizard. This popular theme, referred to as "Fantasy Era" by LEGO fans to distinguish it from Classic Castle sets, lasted for three years. Seven sets were released this year, along with a Castle Chess Set (852001) and Tic Tac Toe (Noughts and Crosses) game (852132).

Crown Knight with Visor The Crown Knight's standard helmet and pointed visor is metallic silver for the first time this year.

Hood .

Crown Bishop
From the Fantasy Era Chess Set, the Crown Bishop is hoping his angry expression will scare the Skeleton Army.

Studded breastplate.

Staff with lightning bolts

.... New torso with scale mail and belt detail

Double-headed ax

Skeleton Warrior shield

Shield with printed crown emblem .....

Skull head is new this year

Red robed torso underneath breastplate

Evil Wizard His hat and legs are exclusive, but the Wizard's head is similar to Ogel's in the Alpha Team theme.

Evil red eye

Wizard hat with printed skull and lightning bolts.

Skeleton Warrior
This warrior's speckled armor was first seen on the Vikings minifigures in 2005.

... Evil scowl

THE SKELETON ARMY

The Evil Wizard's army consists of Skeleton Warriors who ride skeleton horses. Other sinister minifigures, such as the Evil Queen and Evil Bishop, appear only in the Fantasy Era Chess Set.

Evil Queen The red-headed Evil Queen wears a new armor breastplate, with a silver-studded ribcage pattern and skeleton head detail.

Charms for sorcery .

Black Skeleton The standard Fantasy Era skeleton is black instead of white. Its body and limbs have also been redesigned to hold poses.

LEGO® STAR WARS™

The year 2007 brought the 30th anniversary of *Star Wars* and new excitement to the LEGO *Star Wars* play theme. There were new sets from across the original and prequel trilogies, new and exclusive minifigures, a special commemorative 30th anniversary C-3PO minifigure, and the release of one of the largest LEGO *Star Wars* sets to date!

GUESS WHAT I'M GOING TO BE WHEN I GROW UP?

Tousled hair

Freckled face

Anakin Skywalker The third representation of Anakin as a young child, this version features a new head and torso.

Short LEGO legs

Light blue lightsaber

Obi-Wan Kenobi This young version of the Jedi Padawan is exclusive to the Republic Cruiser set (7665).

Hood with cape

Green lightsaber

Qui-Gon Jinn The wise Jedi Master has a new head with mustache, beard, and chin dimple.

Jedi robe first seen in 2005

EPISODE I

One of the highlights of the new Episode I LEGO sets was the new version of Anakin Skywalker, the first to feature short LEGO legs. Short LEGO legs had been introduced to minifigures in 2002, three years after the last young Anakin minifigure.

Red markings

Clone troopers are always ready for battle

Unique torso with Jedi robes and silver belt detail.

Back of specially designed head has more sensory tentacles

New torso, with black shadow armor design, is exclusive to this minifigure

White C-3PO head

K-3PO Exclusive to the Hoth Rebel Base set (7666), this minifigure is highly collectible.

New helmet with red Imperial symbols.

Tentacles

EPISODE III

Four new sets for *Star Wars: Episode III Revenge of the Sith* were released this year, featuring a new Specialist Clone Trooper minifigure, as well as Battle Droid and Super Battle Droid figures.

Shock Trooper Every Clone trooper is created from the DNA of bounty hunter Jango Fett, but this minifigure has a unique helmet and torso.

Kit Fisto Jedi General Kit Fisto is the first LEGO *Star Wars* minifigure to have a head made from soft rubber rather than ABS plastic. Plo Koon and Yoda would soon follow suit.

Shadow Trooper This shady Shadow Trooper is ideal for undercover work, with its advanced dark armor.

Torso with breathing equipment detail is new this year.

AT-AT Driver This clone driver pilots an All-Terrain Armored Transport (AT-AT).

Pilot helmet

General Veers The stern Imperial Officer Veers makes his debut this year.

Officer torso first introduced in 2005

General Grievous
The cyborg general is without his cape in this version, but he is still just as dangerous!

Two pairs of mechanical arms

Droid legs

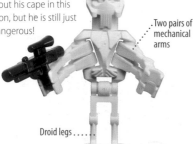

Super Battle Droid
The Super Battle Droid figure comes in two colors—metal blue and dark gray.

Strong, bulky body

Mechanical arm

Snow gear for fighting on the ice planet Hoth

Hoth Rebel This is the second version of this character and features a new flesh head.

Backpack for equipment

EPISODE IV, V, AND VI

A handful of brand-new LEGO *Star Wars* minifigures appeared this year, including the Shadow Stormtrooper, K-3PO, and General Veers. The character of K-3PO did not appear again for nine years until 2016 in Assault on Hoth (75098).

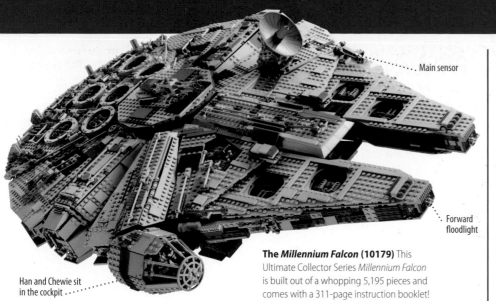

Main sensor

Forward floodlight

The *Millennium Falcon* (10179) This Ultimate Collector Series *Millennium Falcon* is built out of a whopping 5,195 pieces and comes with a 311-page instruction booklet!

Han and Chewie sit in the cockpit

EPIC SET

One of the most sought-after LEGO *Star Wars* sets was also the biggest ever made at the time—the Ultimate *Millennium Falcon* (10179). It featured five minifigures of classic characters— Luke, Han, Leia, Obi-Wan, and Chewbacca.

Lines under eyes

Obi-Wan Kenobi Obi Wan's minifigure has a furrowed brow and gray hair.

Smirking expression

Han Solo There have been 40 different Han Solo minifigures released since the first one in 2000.

Side buns

Tatooine Luke Skywalker An update of a 1999 variant, Luke now has longer hair, a flesh-toned head and hands, and new torso and leg printing.

Leia is wearing red lipstick

Princess Leia A flesh-toned Princess Leia is dressed in her all-white senator's uniform.

Belt pouch.

Tan pants

Only 10,000 limited-edition C-3POs were made.

R2 SAYS HE INTENDS TO STAY 29 FOREVER.

DID YOU KNOW? As well as the chrome gold C-3POs, five solid gold versions were given away in a competition.

C-3PO To celebrate 30 years of *Star Wars*, the LEGO Group created this limited-edition chrome gold painted C-3PO. No LEGO *Star Wars* collection is complete without it!

2007

Service Station Worker This minifigure stays warm in his scarlet jacket—but looks cool in his silver shades and visor helmet!

Classic Space logo

Service with a smile

Chef whites

Chef This cheerful chef is a promotional minifigure and wears classic chef whites and a chef's hat.

LEGO® CITY

Adventure had no limit in the 2007 LEGO CITY sets. From Fire Station (7945) and Harbor (7994) to the busy Train Station (7997), LEGO CITY was a bustling place to be. The vast majority of minifigures introduced this year used new combinations of existing elements to make nonetheless compelling new characters.

This megaphone has featured in many sets, from Batman to *Star Wars*.

Construction Worker With his bright orange jacket and megaphone, this worker is both seen and heard on the building site.

Silver hard hat matches shades

Silver shades to protect eyes from the glare of fires

Firefighter The brave LEGO CITY firefighters battle fires and rescue any people or animals that need their help.

Helmet with visor

Police badge

Anchor logo

Policeman The citizens of LEGO CITY are safe thanks to this Policeman.

Gray beard

Neat tie.

Boat Captain This minifigure's torso is new, with an anchor logo and blue tie and pocket detail.

I'M WORKING ON A SPELL TO MAKE LEGO SETS BUILD THEMSELVES ...

Beard piece fits between the wizard's head and torso pieces

New hat print with gold buckle and stars

Good Wizard Four LEGO Castle minifigures and a Viking have previously used this head, with its stern but kind face.

Potion, pouch, and amulet hang from belt

2008

THIS YEAR WAS a memorable one in the history of LEGO® play. As well as being the 50th anniversary of the patent of the LEGO brick and the 30th anniversary of the LEGO minifigure, it brought fans an amazing array of new themes. LEGO® *Star Wars*™: *The Clone Wars*™ made its debut, along with the action-packed LEGO® *Indiana Jones*™. LEGO® Agents went on their first secret mission and the Vintage Minifigure Collection brought back favorites from the past. All in all, a year to remember!

Magic lightning bolt for zapping unsuspecting minifigures

Green eyeshadow and black lipstick

Spider necklace

Evil Witch The potion bottles on this minifigure's belt may contain poison or possibly her makeup!

LEGO® CASTLE

The Crown Knights of LEGO Castle got a new enemy this year—the mighty Troll Warriors. Fortunately, they also acquired a new ally in the equally fierce Dwarf Miners. Six major LEGO Castle sets were released this year, plus three smaller sets. An exciting new Castle Advent Calendar also made its appearance as the holiday season approached.

New head with extra-wide smile

Fantasy Era torso with crown buckle

Jester This all-new Jester lurks behind the day 24 window of the Castle Advent Calendar (7979). He is clearly having a happy holiday.

DWARVES

The brave dwarves appeared in four sets, including the impressive Dwarves' Mine (7036). The minifigures were armed with war hammers and battle axes—all elements from past Viking sets.

Broom popular with minifigure witches

Intricately braided beard

Winged helmet exclusive to Dwarves

Apron keeps dust off her skirt

Maid Don't get mud all over the Maid's freshly swept floor. This medieval minifigure will not be happy.

Tasty drumstick

Dwarf Pawn In LEGO Castle Giant Chess (852293), Dwarf minifigures like this one serve as pawns.

Advent Calendar Dwarf This minifigure from the Advent Calendar is making the most of the festive fare.

TROLLS

Two kinds of Troll were made: regular minifigures and Giant Troll figures. Natural enemies of the Dwarves, Trolls battled the Crown Knights, too, using siege engines and a warship.

Copper troll helmet with cheek guards

Belts, chains, and buckles on chest

Copper Troll Pawn This Troll pawn is one of 33 minifigures in the LEGO Castle Giant Chess Set.

Silver-black variant of troll helmet.

Troll symbol on buckle

Silver Troll Pawn Another Troll pawn variant wears a breastplate with integral shoulder guards.

Spikes run from his head down his back

Giant Troll At 3 in (7.5 cm) tall, this muscle-bound, club-wielding Giant Troll is twice the size of a standard minifigure.

Hands attach via LEGO Technic pins

LEGO AGENTS

Agents replaced Alpha Team as the LEGO super-spies theme and leapt into action by sending secret operatives up against the evil Dr. Inferno. The eight sets were numbered ("Mission 1, Mission 2," and so on), and each included a comic strip on the box. Unlike Alpha Team, most of the henchmen minifigures in Agents had unique names and powers.

Agent Chase As team leader, Chase appears in six of this year's eight sets—more than any other Agents minifigure.

Reversible head

Same head as standard Chase (this is the reverse face)

... piece in reddish brown

Agents logo on left of torso

Powerful glasses for detailed work

ID card attached to belt

Gun is hose nozzle piece

Agent Trace Trace is the sole female Agent, and will remain so until next year.

Radio keeps him in touch with the team.

Diver Chase Chase may be ready to go under, but he'll still come out on top in the Deep Sea Quest (8636).

Agent Charge Unlike most Agents, Charge has only one face. No wonder he looks so angry about it!

Helmet with visor—he is an air, land, and sea pilot

Rocket Charge In Mission 2 (8632), Charge swaps his hair for a helmet to ride a high-tech rocket cycle.

AGENTS

The Agent minifigures came equipped with jet packs, speedboats, and an awesome Mobile Command Center (8635). They needed them all to fight not only Dr. Inferno and his minions, but also a glow-in-the-dark octopus!

Agent Fuse This Agent minifigure gets his name because he is an expert in electronics, not because he has a short temper!

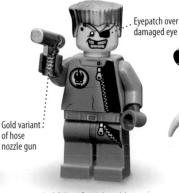

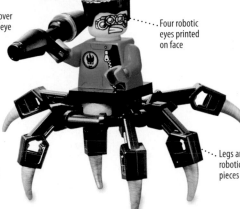

Gun made from camera and cones

Robber's knitted cap

Metal plate attaching arm to torso

Eyepatch over damaged eye

Gold variant of hose nozzle gun

Four robotic eyes printed on face

Legs are robotic arm pieces

Unique face with thick monobrow

Inferno Henchman There are no fancy robotic parts for this Henchman. He's just plain bad!

Fire Arm This minifigure has a huge double gun instead of a right hand. He has a robotic eye, too.

Gold Tooth With gold teeth, hair, and gun, this must be one of the shiniest minifigure minions ever.

Spy Clops This multilegged figure is a creation of Dr. Inferno. He is made up of 19 parts, including 6 helmet horns used as feet.

Break Jaw The helmet of this thuggish minifigure makes him look like he has a fierce underbite!

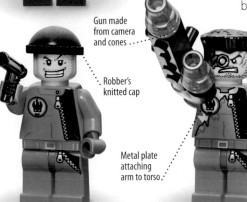

She gets her name from her claw hand

Black is dominant color in outfit

Same head as Evil Witch from LEGO Castle

Mechanical arm and claw

Claw-Dette This wicked-looking minifigure is Dr. Inferno's right-hand woman. Or should that be his right-claw woman?

THEY'RE JUST JEALOUS OF MY HAIR!

Unique hair piece is one of the most unusual ever

Flat-top hair piece in black

Clear, bubble-style helmet

Chainsaw piece in use since 1993

Slime Face This henchman minifigure's head is colored trans-neon green to make it look like slimy green jelly.

Badge design based on his own hairstyle

INFERNO AND CREW

Dr. Inferno planned to conquer the world, aided by his team of minions with their futuristic weapons and gigantic laser cannon. They were a strange and scary group, with names like Break Jaw, Slime Face, and Spy Clops. None of these minifigures would reappear after 2008.

Dr. Inferno There are two variants of this minifigure, but only their claw color varies. This one has pearl light gray; the other has silver.

Slime drips printed on torso

Saw Fist This cyborg henchman is aptly named! He is the only minifigure to use the LEGO chainsaw piece as a limb.

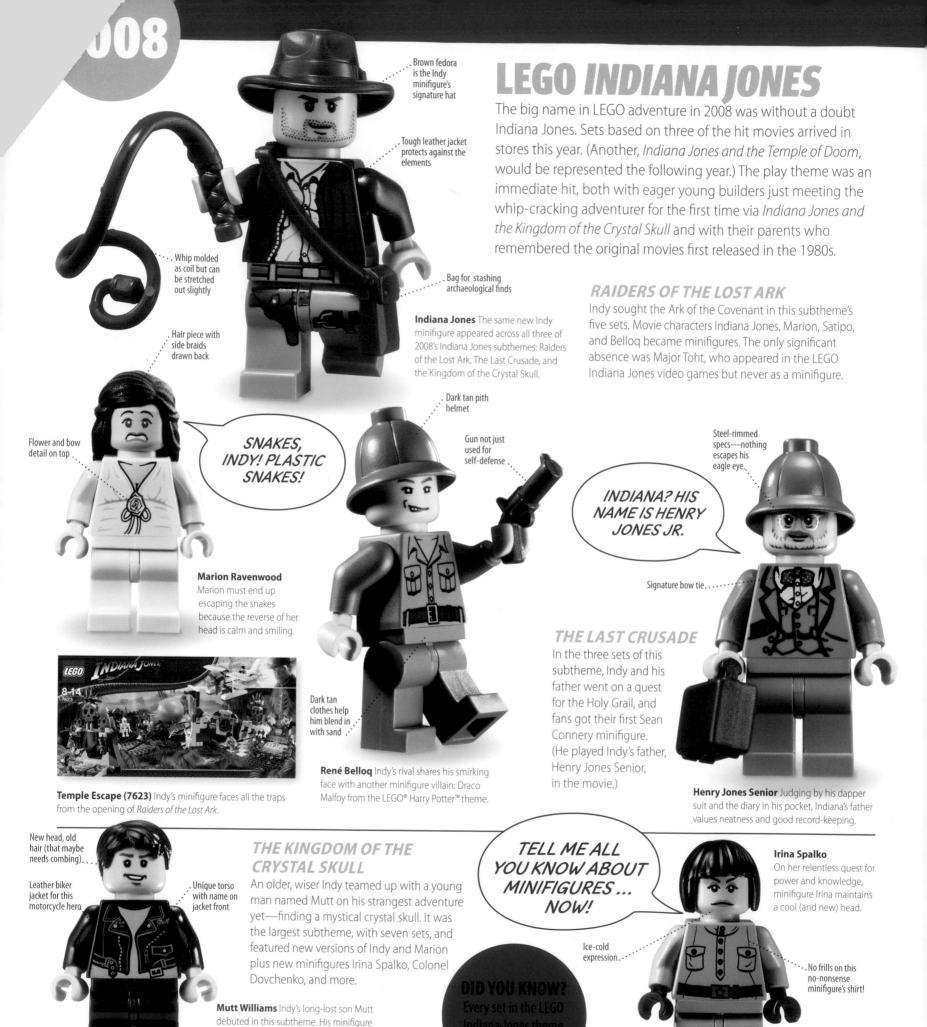

LEGO INDIANA JONES

The big name in LEGO adventure in 2008 was without a doubt Indiana Jones. Sets based on three of the hit movies arrived in stores this year. (Another, *Indiana Jones and the Temple of Doom*, would be represented the following year.) The play theme was an immediate hit, both with eager young builders just meeting the whip-cracking adventurer for the first time via *Indiana Jones and the Kingdom of the Crystal Skull* and with their parents who remembered the original movies first released in the 1980s.

Brown fedora is the Indy minifigure's signature hat

Tough leather jacket protects against the elements

Whip molded as coil but can be stretched out slightly

Bag for stashing archaeological finds

Indiana Jones The same new Indy minifigure appeared across all three of 2008's Indiana Jones subthemes: Raiders of the Lost Ark, The Last Crusade, and the Kingdom of the Crystal Skull.

RAIDERS OF THE LOST ARK

Indy sought the Ark of the Covenant in this subtheme's five sets. Movie characters Indiana Jones, Marion, Satipo, and Belloq became minifigures. The only significant absence was Major Toht, who appeared in the LEGO Indiana Jones video games but never as a minifigure.

Hair piece with side braids drawn back

Flower and bow detail on top

SNAKES, INDY! PLASTIC SNAKES!

Marion Ravenwood
Marion must end up escaping the snakes because the reverse of her head is calm and smiling.

Dark tan pith helmet

Gun not just used for self-defense

INDIANA? HIS NAME IS HENRY JONES JR.

Steel-rimmed specs—nothing escapes his eagle eye

Signature bow tie

THE LAST CRUSADE

In the three sets of this subtheme, Indy and his father went on a quest for the Holy Grail, and fans got their first Sean Connery minifigure. (He played Indy's father, Henry Jones Senior, in the movie.)

Dark tan clothes help him blend in with sand

René Belloq Indy's rival shares his smirking face with another minifigure villain: Draco Malfoy from the LEGO® Harry Potter™ theme.

Temple Escape (7623) Indy's minifigure faces all the traps from the opening of *Raiders of the Lost Ark*.

Henry Jones Senior Judging by his dapper suit and the diary in his pocket, Indiana's father values neatness and good record-keeping.

New head, old hair (that maybe needs combing)

Leather biker jacket for this motorcycle hero

Unique torso with name on jacket front

THE KINGDOM OF THE CRYSTAL SKULL

An older, wiser Indy teamed up with a young man named Mutt on his strangest adventure yet—finding a mystical crystal skull. It was the largest subtheme, with seven sets, and featured new versions of Indy and Marion plus new minifigures Irina Spalko, Colonel Dovchenko, and more.

Mutt Williams Indy's long-lost son Mutt debuted in this subtheme. His minifigure was included in three sets: Jungle Duel (7624), Temple of the Crystal Skull (7627), and Peril in Peru (7628).

TELL ME ALL YOU KNOW ABOUT MINIFIGURES ... NOW!

DID YOU KNOW?
Every set in the LEGO Indiana Jones theme features a minifigure of Indy himself.

Irina Spalko
On her relentless quest for power and knowledge, minifigure Irina maintains a cool (and new) head.

Ice-cold expression

No frills on this no-nonsense minifigure's shirt!

LEGO® CITY

LEGO CITY continued to be a busy place in 2008, and a safer one for its minifigure citizens, too. Not only was there a brand-new Police Station in town, but the Coast Guard was back after many years away. The new Coast Guard minifigures kept watch on the shoreline of LEGO CITY, rescuing surfers and boaters from sharks, spills, and stormy weather.

Alert, ever-watchful expression

Patroller This is one of two Patroller minifigures in the Coast Guard Patrol Boat and Tower (7739).

Fully waterproof jacket

Crash helmet often used for sports minifigures

THE OCEAN IS MY BEAT.

Determined look—nobody gets lost at sea on his watch!

Life jacket is old piece in use since 1990

Helicopter Pilot The pilot flies his chopper over treacherous seas to rescue minifigures from such hazards as snapping sharks!

Radio used to report back to base

POST OFFICE

The Cargo subtheme entered its second year, with two of its four sets centered on delivering mail. Both the Postal Plane (7732) and Mail Van (7731) sets included a postman minifigure.

COAST GUARD

After a five-year absence, Coast Guard returned under the LEGO CITY banner, with the minifigures sporting new blue-and-yellow uniforms. Eight sets included Coast Guard Platform (4210), Quad Bike (7736), Helicopter and Life Raft (7738), and Patrol Boat and Tower (7739).

Speedboat Pilot Under his life jacket, this minifigure wears the standard 2008 Coast Guard top with zippers, logo, and radio printed on it.

Mail taken from mailbox for delivery

Glasses help him read badly addressed mail

Front of mailbox opens

New envelope logo for 2008 Post Office workers

Mail Van Worker There's no chance of this Mail Van Worker deserting his mail! He's never far from his trusty yellow van.

LEGO® VINTAGE MINIFIGURE COLLECTION

Old minifigures were suddenly new again with the launch of the LEGO Vintage Minifigure Collection. Each set in this series would feature five reissued minifigures, usually with little to no change from the original. The first set featured a Red Spaceman, Firefighter, Octan Driver, Mad Scientist, and prisoner named Jailbreak Joe.

Astronaut wears the updated helmet, first seen in 1987

Classic planet logo on torso

Red Spaceman This minifigure from the classic Space theme was launched into the LEGO® Universe in 1978.

BREEZY TODAY, HUH?

"V" logo comes as a sticker to be applied to the torso

Vestas Worker The worker minifigure drives the Vestas maintenance van.

WIND POWER

Sometimes, LEGO sets are made in conjunction with real companies. A limited-edition set appeared in 2008 promoting Vestas, a Danish wind power company. Vestas Wind Turbine (4999) featured a maintenance van and a motorized wind turbine on a small house.

Red cap with peak shades his eyes

Octan Driver Fourteen sets (other than this one) have included this fuel truck driver minifigure.

Logo of Octan—the LEGO fuel brand

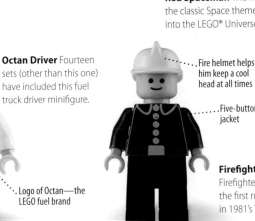

Fire helmet helps him keep a cool head at all times

Five-button jacket

Firefighter This cheerful Firefighter got his foot on the first rung of the ladder in 1981's Town theme.

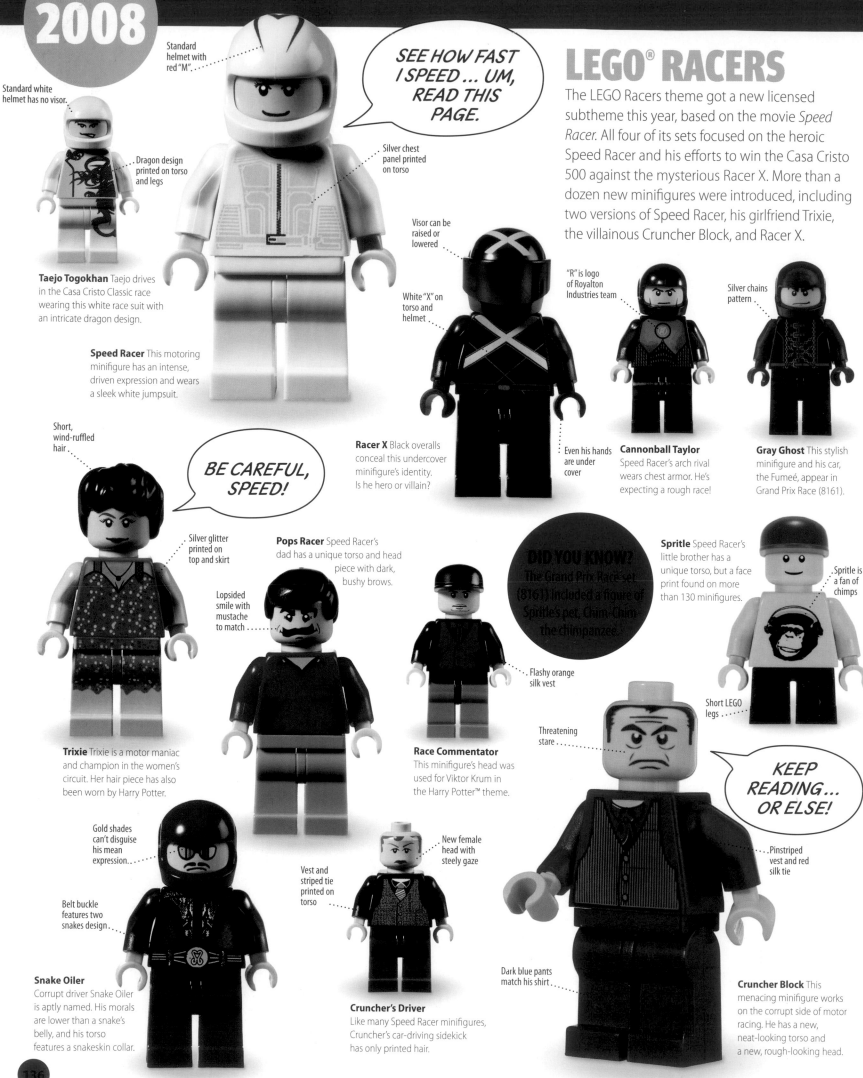

Standard white helmet has no visor.

Standard helmet with red "M".

SEE HOW FAST I SPEED ... UM, READ THIS PAGE.

Dragon design printed on torso and legs

Silver chest panel printed on torso

LEGO® RACERS

The LEGO Racers theme got a new licensed subtheme this year, based on the movie *Speed Racer*. All four of its sets focused on the heroic Speed Racer and his efforts to win the Casa Cristo 500 against the mysterious Racer X. More than a dozen new minifigures were introduced, including two versions of Speed Racer, his girlfriend Trixie, the villainous Cruncher Block, and Racer X.

Taejo Togokhan Taejo drives in the Casa Cristo Classic race wearing this white race suit with an intricate dragon design.

Speed Racer This motoring minifigure has an intense, driven expression and wears a sleek white jumpsuit.

Visor can be raised or lowered

White "X" on torso and helmet

"R" is logo of Royalton Industries team

Silver chains pattern

Short, wind-ruffled hair

BE CAREFUL, SPEED!

Racer X Black overalls conceal this undercover minifigure's identity. Is he hero or villain?

Even his hands are under cover

Cannonball Taylor Speed Racer's arch rival wears chest armor. He's expecting a rough race!

Gray Ghost This stylish minifigure and his car, the Fumée, appear in Grand Prix Race (8161).

Silver glitter printed on top and skirt

Pops Racer Speed Racer's dad has a unique torso and head piece with dark, bushy brows.

Lopsided smile with mustache to match

DID YOU KNOW?
The Grand Prix Race set (8161) included a figure of Spritle's pet, Chim-Chim the chimpanzee.

Spritle Speed Racer's little brother has a unique torso, but a face print found on more than 130 minifigures.

Spritle is a fan of chimps

Flashy orange silk vest

Threatening stare

Short LEGO legs

Trixie Trixie is a motor maniac and champion in the women's circuit. Her hair piece has also been worn by Harry Potter.

Race Commentator This minifigure's head was used for Viktor Krum in the Harry Potter™ theme.

KEEP READING... OR ELSE!

Gold shades can't disguise his mean expression.

New female head with steely gaze

Pinstriped vest and red silk tie

Belt buckle features two snakes design

Vest and striped tie printed on torso

Snake Oiler Corrupt driver Snake Oiler is aptly named. His morals are lower than a snake's belly, and his torso features a snakeskin collar.

Cruncher's Driver Like many Speed Racer minifigures, Cruncher's car-driving sidekick has only printed hair.

Dark blue pants match his shirt

Cruncher Block This menacing minifigure works on the corrupt side of motor racing. He has a new, neat-looking torso and a new, rough-looking head.

FIRST LEGO® LEAGUE

The 2008 *FIRST* LEGO League Challenge was Climate Connections, its theme being the effects of climate and climate change on the Earth. Teams had to identify a climate problem in their area and use LEGO® MINDSTORMS® technology to design and build a working robot to solve it. Twelve accessory minifigures were included in the set.

Male Skier
This minifigure's ski goggles have served as aviator, engineer, and miner's goggles in other themes.

White gloves keep hands toasty warm

Female Skier Four of the Climate Connections minifigures wear these skis. They are exclusive to the subtheme.

Black crash helmet

Skis connect to feet

SPECIAL EVENTS

The big event for the LEGO Group this year was the 50th anniversary of the stud-and-tube brick, followed by the LEGOWorld 2008 celebration in the Netherlands. As ever, special events meant special minifigures that would become highly sought-after by fans.

Anniversary Minifigure This minifigure bears the original and classic yellow head.

The "50" stands for 50 glorious years of LEGO bricks

Wispy red hair printed on head

White backpack

De Bouwsteen A Dutch group of adult fans of LEGO (AFOL) called De Bouwsteen gave out 750 of these minifigures to members at LEGOWorld 2008.

Classic head

Plain clothing; as a mascot, he represents all minifigures.

Universe Promo As a promotion for 2008's LEGO Universe online game, the website mascot was finally made into a real minifigure.

LEGO® FACTORY

The LEGO Factory theme started in 2005 and gave us three sets in this year. Two of these were space-themed and the third a Custom Car Garage (10200). Factory was tied to LEGO® Digital Designer, a software program that allowed for virtual LEGO building. The theme was replaced in 2009 by LEGO® DesignbyME.

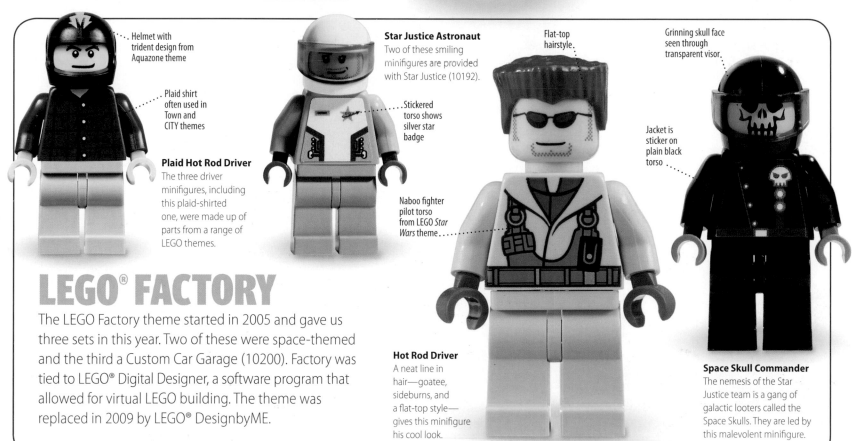

Helmet with trident design from Aquazone theme

Plaid shirt often used in Town and CITY themes

Plaid Hot Rod Driver The three driver minifigures, including this plaid-shirted one, were made up of parts from a range of LEGO themes.

Star Justice Astronaut Two of these smiling minifigures are provided with Star Justice (10192).

Stickered torso shows silver star badge

Naboo fighter pilot torso from LEGO *Star Wars* theme

Flat-top hairstyle

Hot Rod Driver A neat line in hair—goatee, sideburns, and a flat-top style—gives this minifigure his cool look.

Grinning skull face seen through transparent visor

Jacket is sticker on plain black torso

Space Skull Commander The nemesis of the Star Justice team is a gang of galactic looters called the Space Skulls. They are led by this malevolent minifigure.

LEGO® STAR WARS™

LEGO *Star Wars* went from strength to strength in 2008. An exciting development was the launch of the first ever sets based on *The Clone Wars* TV series. Classic *Star Wars* was well represented, too, with sets from Episode IV, Episode V, and the Expanded Universe. With so much to smile about, LEGO *Star Wars* fans may have found their only problem was keeping up with the new releases.

Rebel Trooper The first ever Rebel Trooper minifigure wears a new helmet exclusive to these troopers. Its clip-on visor, however, has been seen before.

- Helmet chin strap printed on head
- Short blaster gun is easy to handle when on the move
- New torso with blue shirt and black vest

Emperor Palpatine
This Emperor Palpatine minifigure from the Death Star (10188) shows him in the black robes of a Sith Lord.

- Like all Sith lightsabers, Palpatine's has a red blade
- New bluish-gray head with heavily wrinkled face
- Head made in one-off black color
- Standard protocol droid design on torso

Imperial Protocol Droid
Unlike most protocol droids, this minifigure has no name or model number. He will forever remain anonymous.

- Black gloves for handling dark deeds
- Long black cloth cape

- This hair piece is most often worn by female minifigures
- Belt holds blaster power cell reserves

Luke Skywalker
Old parts are used for this minifigure but in a new combination. Luke's 2007 head and hair top a standard stormtrooper torso and legs.

LEGO *STAR WARS* EPISODES IV, V, AND VI

The highlight of the year in classic LEGO *Star Wars* was the release of a fantastically detailed, multidecked Death Star (10188). It came with 24 characters, six of which were exclusive to the set. These included Luke Skywalker and Han Solo in borrowed stormtrooper armor, an Assassin Droid, and an Interrogation Droid.

- New head and side parting hair piece
- Clone trooper-style armor

WHEN DO I GET TO SING "SEND IN THE CLONES"?

Obi-Wan Kenobi
Like other *Clone Wars* minifigures, Obi-Wan has the big, cartoonlike eyes of his animated TV character.

- Blue lightsaber shows he fights for the light side

- Scared eyes—well, he has been kidnapped by Asajj Ventress!
- Arms attach to bulbous body

Rotta the Huttlet
This tiny baby Hutt figure can attach to other elements by a single stud.

- A tense tussle has left his hair tousled
- Green lightsaber used by Ahsoka in the Clone Wars
- New torso with black tunic over brown shirt

- Mask is not detachable, as Plo Koon rarely removes it
- Head made from rubber rather than plastic

- Undershirt seen at neck of Jedi robe
- Detachable head piece has montrals (points)

Plo Koon This minifigure Jedi Master has a unique head. He wears a special mask that protects him from breathing a harmful excess of oxygen.

THE CLONE WARS

LEGO *Star Wars* went storming into the Clone Wars era in 2008 with 10 new sets. New minifigure versions of Anakin Skywalker, Yoda, and Obi-Wan Kenobi were joined by a host of debuting characters, including Ahsoka Tano, Plo Koon, and General Grievous's MagnaGuards.

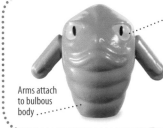

Anakin Skywalker
This heroic minifigure's new head is scarred and battle-worn. His hair and torso are new for 2008, too.

- Brown crop top matches belt and gloves

Ahsoka Tano A bright orange torso and head mark out Anakin's Padawan as a minifigure member of the Togruta species.

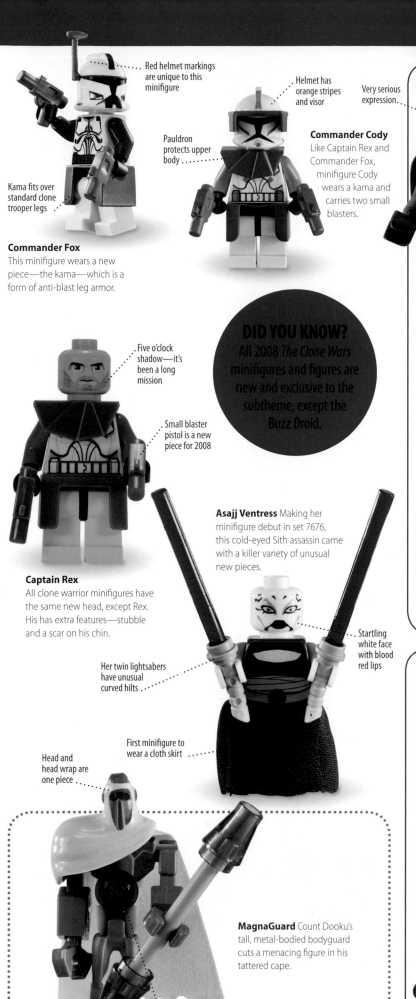

Red helmet markings are unique to this minifigure

Kama fits over standard clone trooper legs

Commander Fox
This minifigure wears a new piece—the kama—which is a form of anti-blast leg armor.

Helmet has orange stripes and visor

Pauldron protects upper body

Commander Cody
Like Captain Rex and Commander Fox, minifigure Cody wears a kama and carries two small blasters.

DID YOU KNOW?
All 2008 *The Clone Wars* minifigures and figures are new and exclusive to the subtheme, except the Buzz Droid.

Five o'clock shadow—it's been a long mission

Small blaster pistol is a new piece for 2008

Captain Rex
All clone warrior minifigures have the same new head, except Rex. His has extra features—stubble and a scar on his chin.

Asajj Ventress Making her minifigure debut in set 7676, this cold-eyed Sith assassin came with a killer variety of unusual new pieces.

Her twin lightsabers have unusual curved hilts

Startling white face with blood red lips

First minifigure to wear a cloth skirt

Head and head wrap are one piece

MagnaGuard Count Dooku's tall, metal-bodied bodyguard cuts a menacing figure in his tattered cape.

Photoreceptor attaches to tube in figure's torso

I'LL BE BACK, HARLEY—AND THAT'S NO JOKE!

Very serious expression

Body armor printed on new torso

Batman This updated Batman minifigure wears an outfit like that of the character in the newly released *The Dark Knight* movie.

New design for Utility Belt

Domino mask

Harley Quinn Harley wears a new dual-colored jester cap in The Batcycle: Harley Quinn's Hammer Truck (7886). She and Batman were the only minifigures in the set.

Giant hammer for committing large-scale crimes

Diamond shapes printed on legs

LEGO® BATMAN™

The Caped Crusader was back this year for what were to be his last four sets until 2012. The big news was the release of an all-new minifigure. Harley Quinn—mischievous villain, Joker's sometime girlfriend, and Poison Ivy's best buddy—arrived on the scene to give Batman some ha-ha-hard times.

LEGO® EXO-FORCE™

The anime-inspired EXO-FORCE theme came to an end in 2008, delivering seven sets that included a massive Hybrid Rescue Tank (8118). Minifigures making a final stand against their robotic foes included new versions of the EXO-FORCE battle machine pilots. Sensei Keiken also appeared for a second time.

Other side of head has angry expression

Blue tubes run between the armor and belt

Camo patterns feature on all 2008 pilot torsos

Ryo The 2008 version of repair expert Ryo is back in his orange suit, this time with a new, armored torso.

Reversible head with closed-mouth expression

Ha-Ya-To The third and last Ha-Ya-To minifigure has the same head, hair, and legs as earlier versions, but his torso is new. He now wears body armor printed over a camouflage pattern suit.

HOW LONG DO I HAVE TO HOLD THIS? TAKE THE PICTURE ALREADY!

Pickax

Helmet with breathing gear and headlamps, first introduced in 1999 in the LEGO Rock Raiders theme

Star logo

Doc The team's leader and also the medic, Doc has been on many adventures. His head is also double-sided—determined and grinning.

2009

IT WAS AN EVENTFUL year in the world of LEGO® minifigures. A new theme, LEGO® Power Miners, was launched, with the help of an animated mini-movie. LEGO® *Star Wars*™ celebrated its 10th anniversary in *Clone Wars* style. Old favorites LEGO® Pirates were reintroduced after more than a decade's absence, and the LEGO® Space Police patrolled the galaxy again. The games figure also made its first appearance this year as LEGO® Games hit the shelves, giving board games an exciting LEGO makeover.

Duke

Rotating drill

Doc

Energy Crystals

LEGO POWER MINERS

Considered by many to be the follow-up to 1999 to 2000's LEGO® Rock Raiders, LEGO Power Miners would become one of the most popular LEGO play themes, until the arrival of LEGO® NINJAGO® in 2011. It was the ninth play theme in which all the minifigure characters were given names.

Metal plate in forehead

Safety goggles

Hair piece seen on more than 240 minifigures

Bomb logo

Flashlight

Stubbly Rex Rex's other variant has a head with two stubbly faces. One looks determined, while the other looks scared.

Duke This veteran miner thinks he has seen it all—until he meets the Rock Monsters!

Rex This minifigure's job is to handle explosives, so he has a bomb logo on his uniform.

POWER MINERS

Doc, Rex, Duke, and Brains made up the team of minifigure miners in 2009. The brave Power Miners dug beneath the Earth, discovering amazing powerful crystals and fearsome Rock Monsters.

Glasses with power lens

Stored Energy Crystals

Articulated arms can launch rocks . . . or smaller rock monsters!

Boom! LEGO dynamite

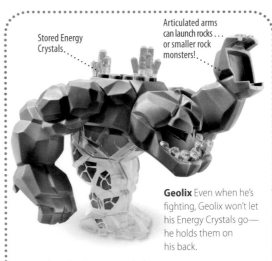

Geolix Even when he's fighting, Geolix won't let his Energy Crystals go—he holds them on his back.

ROCK MONSTERS

The Rock Monster figures used all-new molds and came in five colors. Small versions were included with most sets, and two larger versions were included with the Fall 2009 releases.

Brains The Power Miners' scientist, Brains, can also be found in 2010's LEGO® Atlantis theme.

Hinged mouth can open and close to gobble up crystals

Thunder Driller (8960)
With this powerful, double-geared drill, the Power Miners Doc and Duke can easily tunnel through solid rock.

Firox If this Rock Monster is allowed to eat an Energy Crystal, it becomes super fast.

LEGO PIRATES

LEGO Pirates minifigures sailed the seas for the first time in 12 years. Eight new sets appeared in 2009, featuring Captain Brickbeard along with a new female pirate and new versions of the Imperial Guard. However, after the release of the exclusive Imperial Flagship (10210) in 2010, the pirates mostly went back into hiding until 2015.

Cutlass

Bicorne hat with skull and crossbones

Customary pirate's eyepatch

WE WILL HAVE TO SEARCH THE SEVEN SEAS FOR THOSE PIRATES!

Bicorne hat

Red epaulettes

Gray mustache and stern expression

Grand blue uniform

Hopeful wave

Tattered vest

Patched and ragged pants

Castaway In the 12 years since the last LEGO Pirates release, the castaway has had no hope of rescue. His pants have become ragged and his beard shaggy.

Gold detail on outfit

Gold epaulettes

Gold hook piece is new for 2009

Peg leg

Governor This important minifigure is in charge of the Soldiers' Fort (6242). He resembles the Admiral from 2010's Imperial Flagship advanced building set (10210), but with red rather than gold epaulettes.

Eyepatch

Long, brown hair

Green bandanna worn at a jaunty angle

Treasure map

Telescope Pirate This treasure-hungry pirate debuts new head and torso pieces for this year. Her map tile has appeared in 15 sets since 2008.

Captain Brickbeard
The pirates' new leader replaces Captain Redbeard. This greedy pirate is only interested in one kind of treasure—gold.

IMPERIAL GUARD

The new Imperial Guard had wore updated red jackets with blue epaulettes. The Governor wore a blue jacket with red epaulettes. In 2009, for the first time, the good guys sailed a bigger ship than the pirates.

Matching green pants

Green Bandanna Pirate
This pirate doesn't see why he can't look good while being bad. His bandanna and his pants match perfectly!

PIRATES

Captain Brickbeard led a crew of minifigure pirates in search of treasure. The pirates had a variety of heads, hats, and leg colors. New elements included a gold hook on Brickbeard, a grizzled head with an eyepatch on another pirate officer, and a new castaway minifigure.

Tricorne hat

Nervous Officer
This minifigure has good reason to worry—he's a lowly pawn in a LEGO Pirates chess set.

Impressive plume of red feathers

Blue epaulettes

This soldier has a knapsack printed on his back

CLASSIC PIRATES

Two classic LEGO Pirate theme minifigures were reissued in 2009 as part of the Vintage Minifigure Collection. The soldier was originally produced in 1989 and the pirate in 1996.

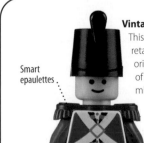

Vintage Soldier This minifigure retains all the original pieces of the 1989 minifigure.

Smart epaulettes

The pirate's original vest was darker

Vintage Pirate The LEGO designers kept all the details from the 1996 version, apart from the pirate's vest color.

Imperial Officer Attention! This soldier could win the prize for best dressed minifigure, thanks to his plumed hat and fine epaulettes.

There have been two variants—the original had solid black pupils

Celebration Luke Skywalker
Originally available only as part of DK's LEGO *Star Wars Visual Dictionary*, this exclusive minifigure celebrates the rebels' victory over the Empire at the end of Episode IV *A New Hope*.

The 2009 Wicket has detailed printing on his face

Exclusive torso with gold medal

> HEY DAD, WANT TO SEE THE MEDAL I GOT FOR DEFEATING YOU?

Gun belt detail on brown pants

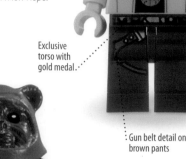

Wicket W. Warrick
Wicket was one of the first Ewoks to appear in minifigure form in 2002. This year, he's given a makeover and is seen in his distinctive orange hood.

Combined head-and-torso piece fits over standard torso

LEGO *STAR WARS*

The 10th anniversary of LEGO *Star Wars* meant special minifigures. Among the treasures from this year were Luke Skywalker with a celebration medal, a chrome Darth Vader, a silver Stormtrooper magnet, and the first minifigure appearance of Admiral Ackbar. Of these celebration minifigures, only Ackbar appeared in a standard LEGO set. The brave Ewoks also received a more realistic look.

This Mon Calamari head piece can be seen on two other minifigures from the LEGO *Star Wars* theme

Unique torso with Mon Calamari officer's uniform

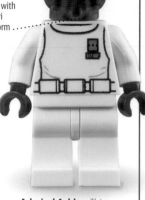

Admiral Ackbar This version of the rebel leader appeared in just three sets, so it is especially prized by collectors.

Underneath his helmet, the stormtrooper's head is blank

This minifigure has the same helmet and torso pattern as a regular white stormtrooper

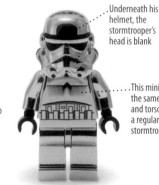

Silver Trooper This shiny minifigure appears in a magnet set in 2009 and in an exclusive polybag for Toys 'R' Us in 2010.

Underneath his shiny helmet lies Vader's scarred human face

> KIDS, HUH? WHAT CAN YOU DO?

Chrome Vader This 10th anniversary Darth Vader is shinier and more evil than ever, thanks to his chrome-black finish. Only 10,000 were produced.

This version has a cape but no lightsaber

LEGO® *INDIANA JONES*™

The minifigure archaeologist with the famous hat was back in 2009 with two new sets based on *Indiana Jones and the Temple of Doom*—the only movie not featured in the theme's 2008 debut. The highlight of the 2009 theme was the Temple of Doom set (7199), featuring not only six new minifigures but also a thrilling temple/mine rollercoaster track build that was over 3 feet (nearly 1 meter) long.

These detachable horns also appear on the Minotaur in LEGO Minifigures Series 6 from 2012

Red crown piece

Willie Scott Ready for a performance at Club Obi Wan in Shanghai, singer Willie Scott wears a glamorous outfit.

Unique red outfit with gold details

Elusive diamond

Mola Ram The Thuggee High Priest has many unique details, including his headdress (excluding the horns), his torso, and the red paint on his forehead.

Indy is dressed up to visit Club Obi Wan in Shanghai

Indiana Jones This version shows Indy dressed in a smart tuxedo, with his 2008 head piece.

Rock bin trap

Thuggee guards pursue Willie and Short Round

Glow-in-the-dark spikes

Temple of Doom

Temple of Doom (7199) This set boasts many exciting features including a trap door, several booby traps, and glow-in-the-dark spikes.

LEGO SPACE

The intergalactic law enforcers were back after 11 years with a new play theme, chasing down the galaxy's worst thieves in 10 sets. Nicknamed Space Police III by fans, the theme featured numerous new alien heads, and every set included at least one alien minifigure, from the four-armed Frenzy to the eight-eyed outlaw Snake!

- Alien head piece also used on Rench in the Space Police III subtheme in 2010
- A large skull is also printed on the back of Kranxx's vest

Kranxx The leader of the Black Hole Gang, Kranxx is also a skilled pilot with a taste for high speeds.

- Spiked helmet on top of green alien head.

Slizer This spiky alien criminal is the chief mechanic of the Black Hole Gang.

- Spiked armor printed on torso and legs

- Unique torso with cracked marble details

Classic Space Statue This statue of the first LEGO Space Astronaut features only in the Space Police III Galactic Enforcer set (5974). It's stolen by Kranxx and Slizer and the Space Police must get it back.

- Unique head piece
- Red cape—to match his eyes

Squidman This alien criminal is always thinking up schemes to make himself rich, but they usually fail.

- Scales and muscles printed on torso

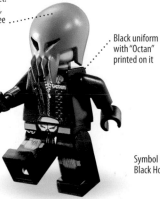

- Extra-large eyes
- Extra arms
- Torso extension piece

Frenzy This four-armed bad guy has a unique head piece featuring a huge, gaping mouth.

- Dual-sided head underneath the helmet. One side has two eyes, the other side has three

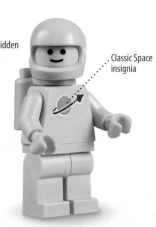

- Black uniform with "Octan" printed on it

Skull Twin Just one of these criminals would be bad, but unfortunately there are two evil Skull Twins. Double trouble!

- Visor can be used to hide his identity
- Eighth eye

Snake Variant In Space Speeder (8400), slimy Snake appears without his visor.

- Protective helmet
- Symbol of the Black Hole Gang
- Knee pads printed on legs

Snake This prolific criminal appears in five sets—more than any other alien villain in this theme.

CLASSIC SPACE

Four brave astronaut minifigures returned to outer space in 2009 as part of the Vintage Minifigure Collection. These minifigures were originally produced in the first nine years of the Classic Space line. The reissued versions looked identical, apart from their helmets, which were given a more modern shape.

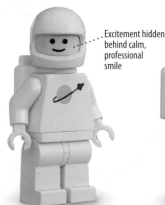

- Excitement hidden behind calm, professional smile
- Classic Space insignia

White Spaceman This intergalactic explorer has been on ice since 1987. He can't wait to journey into the 21st century.

Yellow Spaceman It's been a long time since he last piloted a rocket, but it's a bit like riding a bike . . . .

- Flick-fire missile launcher
- Space Police badge

Rookie Officer This officer is on his first mission. He seems confident enough, but his alternative face looks scared.

Special Ops Officer Orange glasses ensure that this minifigure looks good, even in space.

- Large visor

Female Officer In 2009, the Space Police got their first female recruit. She wears the same uniform as her male minifigure colleagues.

Lava Dragon—Knight
In this two-to-four-player game, the winner is the first knight to reach the top of a fiery mountain.

Minotaurus—Red Spartan
Playing as red, blue, white, or yellow Spartans, the object is to travel to the center of a maze, avoiding the Minotaur.

Ramses Pyramid—Blue Explorer
Blue, red, yellow, and orange explorers try to get to the top of Ramses Pyramid.

Lunar Command—Green
Players must build space stations to launch a Lunar Rocket.

LEGO GAMES
Standing two bricks tall with a stud on the head, the games figure burst onto the scene in 2009 in LEGO Games such as Lava Dragon, Minotaurus, Lunar Command, and the award-winning Ramses Pyramid.

Farm Hand
The hardworking farm hand has some familiar parts: her shirt was worn by Cloud City Luke Skywalker in 2003.

- Cheerful red pants

- Crouching cat from set 7637

LEGO® CITY

Farm made its first appearance in a LEGO System theme in 2009 as part of LEGO CITY. Five sets and eight new minifigures and various animals populated this line, which lasted for two years. Three of the minifigures were farmers, each with a different head and torso. Prior to this release, Farm was primarily a LEGO® DUPLO® theme for younger fans.

GREAT CROP OF BRICKS THIS YEAR!

- Tan sun hat

Printing continues on the back of the torso

- Head piece popular in LEGO CITY theme and also used for several policemen and construction workers

Farmer The Farmer has a new torso with a red plaid shirt and green overalls.

Green overalls for doing dirty farm work

Spotless pants are free from mud—so far!

- Casual blue plaid shirt

Four-wheel Driver
This minifigure is taking his four-wheel drive with horse trailer for a spin in the country. He's no farmer!

This hat piece is more commonly seen as a construction helmet.

DID YOU KNOW?
LEGO CITY Farm (7637) includes a grain silo, barn, cow pen, tractor, and three minifigures.

- The horse cannot be disassembled

Horse Rider
This well-dressed rider and her horse are found in 4WD with Horse Trailer (7635).

Hat piece often used for LEGO Police.

Red jacket with horn logo printed on torso.

YOU GOT MAIL!
This LEGOLAND Town post office worker was a reissue of a classic minifigure from 1982. He has appeared in six sets and was one of two post office minifigures released this year.

Smart black pants

Postman
This vintage minifigure hasn't delivered any LEGO mail since 1991, so he's probably got a sack full of letters waiting for him!

- Retro orange sunglasses

- Camera

New Hawaiian shirt is also seen on later CITY minifigures

Alternative face with cheesy grin

THE TOURIST
Although essentially a CITY minifigure, this Tourist actually appeared in the LEGO® Agents set Robo Attack (8970). The unsuspecting out-of-towner finds himself in the path of a rampaging robot!

Scared Tourist
This minifigure has a unique, dual-sided head that can be smiling or scared.

Troll King
This green minifigure is the leader of the wicked Troll Warriors. He plans to capture the Crown King and imprison him in his Mountain Fortress.

Tattered cloak is new this year

LEGO® CASTLE

The year 2009 was the last one for the fantasy-based LEGO Castle theme before LEGO Kingdoms took up the quest in 2010. In 2009, a mighty minifigure king and his knights battled the evil forces of the Troll King in three sets.

Golden sword

Detachable breastplate armor

Crown King
The 2009 version of the King has new printing on his torso and legs and a blue plume in his crown. Unlike the 2007 version, this minifigure does not have a cape.

First hair piece to feature a hole for accessories

Medieval-style blue dress

Crown Queen
The Queen has a dual-sided head: now she is happy and smiling, but she can easily turn to her annoyed expression if something makes her royally angry.

VINTAGE CASTLE

Three vintage minifigures were reissued this year: a Forestman and Knight from the classic Castle sets and a ninja warrior from the Ninja sets.

Ninja head wrap later used in NINJAGO play theme in 2011

Red Ninja The Red Ninja minifigure first adventured in 1999 in sets such as Ninja's Fire Fortress (3052).

Red feather

Simple hat

Forestman This vintage Forestman was last seen in 1990 in the Crusader's Cart (1877) and Hay Cart with Smugglers (1680) sets.

Pilot torso

DECK THE HALLS WITH LEGO BRICKS! FA LA LA ....

Male Carol Singer The two exclusive carol singers from Winter Village Toy Shop (10199) have a new head piece with an open, singing mouth and rosy cheeks.

Chimney

Santa with Fireplace
Perhaps not surprisingly, Santa can be found behind window 24 on the LEGO CITY Advent Calendar.

Sack for presents

Traditional Santa outfit and beard

Roaring fire

Stocking

LEGO® SEASONAL

LEGO minifigures have always been a great holiday gift for LEGO fans. This group from the Winter Village Toy Shop and LEGO CITY Advent Calendar were the first of many designed to double as holiday decorations. They did not appear in any other sets. One set in this festive line would come out each year from 2009 onward.

Unique caroler's head piece

Song book

Female Carol Singer
This carol singer's double cloak should keep her warm during those chilly winter nights.

Festive red cap keeps the snow off

Messenger pouch was first seen in various LEGO *Indiana Jones* sets from 2008

Holiday Postman
This minifigure appears behind the tenth window of the LEGO CITY Advent Calendar.

Classic Castle helmet

Knight This noble minifigure debuted in 1978 as part of the Castle Mini Figures set (0016). He reappears, unchanged, as a vintage Knight for 2009.

Shield printed on torso

ULTIMATE FAN

This exclusive minifigure was a giveaway at the 2009 LEGO Fan Weekend in Skærbæk, Denmark. Since then, he has become a very rare and much sought-after collectible!

LEGO logo and event details make this torso unique

LEGO Fan Weekend 2009 The head, hair, and legs parts are common LEGO pieces, but the torso is unique with details of the 2009 event printed on it.

2010s

Minifigures went massive in the 2010s! First, they received their own dedicated theme, introducing hundreds of new characters across the decade. Then LEGO® NINJAGO®: *Masters of Spinjitzu* took the small screen by storm, before THE LEGO® MOVIE™ and its follow-ups turned minifigures into genuine film stars. Meanwhile, pop culture icons from Fred Flintstone and The Beatles to Mickey Mouse and Minecraft "mobs" all got the minifigure treatment— along with dozens of Super Heroes and super-villains from Marvel and DC Comics!

I LIKE LEGO CLUB. WHACK!

Underneath his removable hair and beard, the Caveman has a unibrow and a wide smile

The spiked club is new for this Minifigure

Hairy chest and animal-hide clothes

Caveman This Minifigure loves inventing things. If only he would invent a razor, then everyone could see his unique face!

2010

FROM THE SANDS of Persia to the depths of the ocean, LEGO® minifigures were everywhere in 2010. LEGO® *Star Wars*™ celebrated the 30th anniversary of Episode V *The Empire Strikes Back*, while new licensed themes *Prince of Persia*™ and *Toy Story*™ combined Disney action and adventure with LEGO building know-how. Meanwhile, daredevil divers went in search of Atlantis, LEGO® Kingdoms brought the classic Castle theme back, and high-octane World Racers hit the track. And, not to be forgotten, the colorful, charming, and completely unique LEGO® Minifigures became the stars of their very own collectible theme.

LEGO MINIFIGURES

The collectible LEGO Minifigures theme was a major hit in 2010, with the first two series each providing 16 exclusive Minifigures to excited fans. Each character was packed individually in a series-colored polybag so collectors wouldn't be able to tell which Minifigure they were getting until they opened it.

Clown face is unique to this Minifigure

A black version of this hair piece can be seen on the Disco Dude in Series 2

Torso and legs are also exclusive to this Minifigure

Ninja katana, used for slicing sandwiches!

Horn

Ninja hood

Ninja He might look like a cool, scary Ninja, but this Minifigure is really a clumsy scaredy-cat.

Red cape has been seen on more than 20 other minifigures, including a 2002 Quidditch Harry Potter™

Circus Clown This Minifigure can't talk, but fortunately he can honk his horn.

Rare blue head piece with unique red mask printing

Super Wrestler Life's just one big wrestling match for this Minifigure, and he's determined to win!

Wrench

Head, torso, and legs are exclusive to this Minifigure

Demolition Dummy This unique Minifigure has a one-track mind: he just wants to dismantle everything.

PA7 70

License plate from a dismantled car

Zombie The LEGO Group's first-ever Zombie Minifigure would be followed by four more in 2012's LEGO® Monster Fighters theme.

Turkey leg

Shovel

This hair piece is making its debut in blonde

Hands fit inside pom-poms

SERIES 1

The Series 1 line-up featured nine new LEGO parts. The new theme was more popular than anticipated, and supply issues made this first series of collectible Minifigures the rarest in the entire theme.

Cheerleader "2, 4, 6, 8, LEGO bricks are what we rate!" This enthusiastic pom-pom-shaking Minifigure is the first to feature rare side printing on her legs.

SERIES 2

LEGO Minifigures Series 2 introduced more new Minifigures and also redesigned some old ones, including the Vampire. The series included 13 new elements and innovations, such as giving the Mime three interchangeable heads.

Stud so that decoration can be attached to the headdress

This head piece was also used on a rocker in a store-exclusive Minifigure three-pack in 2012

Pharaoh This Minifigure was a king back in Ancient Egypt, but now he's all alone in the modern world, without a pyramid to call home. He wants his mummy!

GET UP AND GROOVE TO THE PLASTIC BEAT!

Retro record

1970s outfit including medallion and white suit

Gold cobra-head staff, specially created for this Minifigure

New spear has a soft plastic tip

Helmet, head, torso, and legs are unique to this Minifigure

Spartan Warrior He'd love to meet another Spartan Minifigure to fight with, but the Spartan Warrior is just too unique.

New microphone piece

Shield has a handle on the back and a stud on the front

Sandals printed on feet

Disco Dude Remember when pop music was played on funky vinyl things called records? No? The Disco Dude can!

Exclusive pink outfit with silver details

New, textured version of the witch/wizard's hat

The witch was the first to have a bright green head

This is the first appearance of the sloped base in the Minifigures theme.

Pop Star She might be one of the LEGO world's most popular singers, but the Pop Star is just an ordinary Minifigure at heart.

Witch This Minifigure spells trouble. Watch out for her in 2012; she reappears in a Halloween accessory set.

Beret is also seen on the Artist in Series 4

SHHH! THE FANS WANT TO HEAR MY MARACAS!

New sombrero hat piece is unique to this Minifigure

This hair piece was first seen on the Cheerleader in Series 1

Rescue float can be gripped by two Minifigures

Two alternative heads: frowning and frightened

Mime The Mime can convey extreme emotions and make other Minifigures fall over laughing without even making a sound.

Unique poncho made of two new patterned cape pieces

Maraca Man When this colorful but mysterious character shakes his maracas, the other Minifigures get into a party mood.

Maracas were specially created for this Minifigure

Lifeguard This Minifigure scans the seas looking for swimmers in trouble. The initials of LEGO sculptor Gitte Thorsen can be seen printed on her swimsuit.

LEGO® CASTLE

In 2010, the new LEGO Kingdoms series took over from the 2007–2009 LEGO Castle theme, focusing on a battle between the rival Lion and Dragon kingdoms. Eight new sets were released this year, featuring wizards, knights, royalty, and other new minifigures. A Kingdoms Advent Calendar was the jewel in the crown of this year's assortment.

WHY DID THE DRAGON CROSS THE ROAD?

Dual-sided head: smiling and sad

1x1 round plates for juggling

Quiver of arrows

Broad-brimmed helmet in shiny dark gray

Dragon Bowman Who knows what this Bowman is up to with his cheeky smirk? Perhaps he has a plan up his sleeve to ambush the Lion Kingdom knights?

If the Queen kisses him, this LEGO frog may turn into a prince!

Jester This medieval clown is only the second Jester minifigure ever created. The first wore a similar outfit in blue and red and was in the 2008 Fantasy Era sets.

The Prince wields a sword

Smiling head piece with chin dimple

Lion Prince The heir to the throne has the same torso and legs as the King, without the armor. The Prince only appears in the 2010 Kingdoms Advent Calendar.

The Queen's dress has lace-up details printed on the back

Queen She has a new outfit in 2010 with gold details and a sloped skirt piece, but her head and crown were used on the Fantasy Era Queen in 2009.

Gold crown with detachable plume of feathers

Hair piece also seen on Hermione in the LEGO® Harry Potter™ theme

Dragon Knight One of five knights in the Green Dragon Knights Battle Pack (852922), the Dragon Knight features the new dragon torso printing.

Green is the color of the Dragon Kingdom

Dragon insignia

The Dragon Knight wears a cape instead of armor

Standard LEGO cape found in more than 200 sets

Lion Princess The Princess's regal torso and matching sloped skirt piece are new for 2010.

Hat with dragon print is unique to this minifigure.

New torso can be found underneath this armor

This wizard is the first minifigure to have this beard piece in black

DRAGON KINGDOM

The Dragon Kingdom had no king, so the Dragon Wizard minifigure usually acted as the leader. The Dragon Knights used the same helmet as the Lion Knights but wore dark and pale green armor with a golden dragon on the breastplate.

LION KINGDOM

The heroic Knights of the Lion Kingdom featured a new helmet with a cross shape on the front and a new breastplate with a golden lion print. They were led by the Lion King, who had a new crowned head, a new torso, and new legs.

Dragon Wizard This powerful minifigure would love to defeat the Lion Kingdom. He really doesn't like the Lion King!

New printed legs with gold detail

Lion King As befits the noble leader of the Lion Kingdom, the King has many new elements, including a torso with Lion head medallion and fur trim pattern.

LEGO® ATLANTIS

Minifigure divers went in search of the mysterious city of Atlantis in this underwater play theme, but aquatic guardians were determined to stop them. Many exciting new elements and molds were introduced to create the amazing undersea creatures of LEGO Atlantis. The theme was a huge success, leading to more sets and minifigures in 2011. The new Atlantis elements also provided LEGO fans with colorful and unique pieces to use in their own creations.

FIRST THING I DO IN ATLANTIS? VISIT THE SWIMMING POOL!

Eyepatch is unique to Ace minifigures

Propeller blade attached to air tank

Ace Speedman
The leader of the Salvage Crew, Ace Speedman pilots the Neptune Carrier. He wears a distinctive eyepatch—his eye is fine, he just thinks an eyepatch looks cool!

Standard-issue green diving flippers

Shark Warrior
Comprising three unique pieces, the Shark Warrior has the head of a shark but the torso and legs of a human.

There is no standard minifigure head underneath, unlike Viktor Krum's 2005 LEGO Harry Potter minifigure

Gold-and-black speckled helmet

Trident

Gold-and-black speckled breastplate

Portal key

ATLANTIS DEEP SEA SALVAGE CREW

The lime-green-and-silver Atlantis minifigures featured a new breathing apparatus mold, new torsos (printed front and back), and new heads. All but two of the Atlantis sets came with specially molded portal keys, which were the object of the divers' quest in the 2010 storyline.

UNDERSEA GUARDIANS
Atlantis featured some of the most innovative minifigure designs to date, particularly its fierce underwater warriors. The Portal Emperor included a new helmet with a never-before-seen gold-and-black speckled paint pattern.

Portal Emperor
This minifigure is made of five parts, four of which are unique. Only his breastplate appears on another minifigure—the Atlantis Temple Statue in 2011.

DID YOU KNOW?
Atlantis was the first LEGO play theme to feature 3D content on its website.

Dual-sided head: smiling and annoyed

Detachable headgear

Manta Warrior
Featuring unique head, headgear, and torso pieces, this Manta Warrior is a fearsome foe for the Salvage Crew. His trident can fire blasts of electricity!

Headgear reflects the shape of a manta ray fish

Detachable headgear

Squid Warrior
Instead of legs, the Squid Warrior has a new tentacle piece. The piece was used in a different color on the 2011 Alien Commander in the LEGO® Alien Conquest theme.

Detachable headgear

Harpoon gun

Professor Samantha Rhodes
Although not technically a member of the Salvage Crew, scientist Sam Rhodes accompanies them because she is determined to prove that Atlantis exists.

Unique torso

Like the other underwater warriors, the Squid Warrior wields a gold trident—new for 2010

New tentacle piece instead of regular legs

Portal key

2010

Luna Lovegood™ She's a unique character in many ways, and Luna Lovegood was also the only Ravenclaw minifigure for many years.

Spectrespecs

Exclusive pink jacket

Unique skirt-over-pants design

LEGO® HARRY POTTER™

LEGO Harry Potter reappeared after a two-year absence in 2010 with six fun sets. Rebranded for the new movie *Harry Potter and the Half-Blood Prince™*, the characters had mostly been released before. One set, The Burrow (4840), was brand new and taken from that film.

White wand piece

Voldemort™ Look out, Harry Potter! He Who Must Not Be Named looks more evil than ever in 2010. He can be found in Hogwarts Castle (4842).

Unique torso

Hair piece is dark brown version of ones used on Draco Malfoy

Fenrir Greyback™ This snarling werewolf has bared teeth for biting other minifigures, even when there isn't a full moon.

Unique torso and head

STUDENTS

All of Harry's friends got minifigure redesigns this year. The only new character was Luna Lovegood, complete with reversible head with Spectrespecs on one side and a smile on the other.

Wavy hair piece

Ron Weasley™ Harry's best friend has a new haircut in 2010, and a dual-sided head featuring smiling and scared faces.

Dementor The gray-and-green 2004 Dementor figures were scary enough, but the spooky 2010 ones are terrifying. Their gaping mouths look ready to suck out a minifigure's soul.

Dementors have a skeleton body underneath their tattered robes

Long, curly hair piece is unique

Bellatrix Lestrange™ The evil personality and unique style of one of Voldemort's most loyal supporters is brought to life as a minifigure for the first time in 2010.

Torso and skirt piece are decorated with silver and blue details

DARK LORD AND FOLLOWERS

The vicious (and redesigned) Lord Voldemort had new minifigure allies this year. Those joining his wicked crew included the dangerous witch Bellatrix Lestrange and the vicious fiend Fenrir Greyback.

Same torso and legs as Hermione, Ron, and Ginny

Harry Potter™ In set 4842, this version of Harry Potter comes with his Invisibility Cloak.

Dual-sided head: frowning and smiling

Ginny Weasley™ Ron's sister's minifigure looks much more grown up than its 2002 version.

2010 Quidditch minifigures have a helmet that can be placed on head when hair piece is removed

Marcus Flint The Slytherin captain wants to win the Quidditch Cup. His unique head piece shows his large sneer.

QUIDDITCH™

Game on! The year 2010 saw new minifigures of Harry Potter and Draco Malfoy in redesigned Quidditch robes and a new character, Marcus Flint.

Blond hair piece is unique to both 2010 versions of Draco

Gloved hands

Draco Malfoy For 2010, Malfoy's Quidditch minifigure has a new dark green outfit with white pants. His dual-sided head can look worried or smug.

Green is color of Slytherin house

Only nine other minifigures wear this colored robe

Lion badge denotes Gryffindor house

Gloved hands

Harry Potter Unique to Quidditch Match (4737), this version of Gryffindor's scarlet Quidditch gear appears twice—on Harry and on Captain Oliver Wood, also released in 2010.

TEACHERS AND OTHERS

Four new minifigures joined the supporting cast this year: Professor Flitwick, Argus Filch, and Ron's parents Arthur and Molly Weasley. The Molly minifigure went through numerous prototypes before the final look was achieved.

Hair piece also seen on Dumbledore

Unique head and torso

Hair piece also used on Mary Jane Watson in the 2004 LEGO® Spider-Man™ theme

Molly Weasley Ron Weasley's caring and hardworking mother is portrayed in a unique minifigure with a lined face and homey apron.

Crumpled outfit is unique to this minifigure

Argus Filch™ Making his first appearance in 2010, the Hogwarts caretaker has a hefty collection of keys hanging from his belt.

Arthur Weasley It was easy for the LEGO designers to make Mr. Weasley look like his sons—they just used the same red hair piece as Fred and George's minifigures.

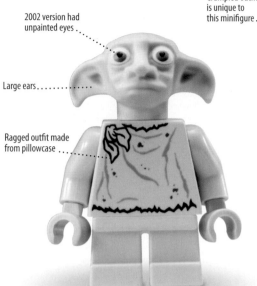

2002 version had unpainted eyes

Large ears

Ragged outfit made from pillowcase

Dobby™ The heroic house-elf's minifigure had an impressive makeover in 2010. His unique head mold and authentic outfit bring his character to life.

Small silver glasses

Bushy brown mustache

Professor Flitwick™ The Charms Professor's tiny stature is reflected in his short LEGO legs.

Rumpled vest and bow tie

Plain head piece underneath helmet

Gryffindor Knight Statue This statue of a Knight appears in the Gryffindor common room in Hogwarts Castle (4842).

Movable hands

Hagrid™ A head taller than most other minifigures, this version of Hagrid the Hogwarts gamekeeper appears in one set in 2010 and two more in 2011.

LEGO SPECIAL EDITIONS

Standard sets are not the only place minifigures can be found. Minifigures have been used as promotional items, bonuses with books and video games, and even appeared in LEGO® Education sets. Unique minifigures such as the LEGO® Club Max are rare and highly collectible. Nothing says LEGO building like a minifigure, and fans around the world know it!

LEGO Club Max This promotional minifigure was available for a limited time to LEGO Club members, LEGO VIP members, and at LEGO events in the UK and US.

The head and hair pieces are new in 2010.

Exclusive torso with details of event.

Exclusive birthday cake design

Birthday Party Boy Only available in two birthday party sets released this year, the torso is exclusive to this minifigure.

LEGO Fan Weekend This promotional figure was given to exhibitors at the LEGO Fan Weekend in Skærbæk, Denmark.

One-off torso and leg design

New and unique torso with LEGO® Universe Nexus insignia

Pocket printing on side of leg

Nexus Astronaut This limited-edition space traveler came in a polybag for fans who preordered the LEGO Universe Massively Multiplayer Online Game.

Smart scarlet zip-up jacket

Post Office envelope logo

Postal Worker This minifigure featured in 2010's CITY Buildings (9311), a LEGO Education set specially developed for use in kindergartens and schools. She was the first female worker at the LEGO Post Office.

LEGO® WORLD RACERS

World Racers was a new theme in 2010, the first racing-related theme since *Speed Racer* to have minifigures and a story behind it! World Racers pitted two teams—the Backyard Blasters and the Xtreme Daredevils—in a bruising series of races all over the globe.

Team logo on helmet

Removable goggles

Dirtbike Helmet REX-treme
Rex has four variants. Three are distinguished by their helmet, but the fourth, from a promotional set, has plain white legs.

Another variant has the same helmet but with a red visor

Torso exclusive to Bart Blaster variants

Detachable goggles

Aviator Helmet Bubba Blaster
This monobrowed minifigure has three variants.

Racing Helmet Bart Blaster
There are four variants of this minifigure released in 2010, each with different helmets.

Unique torso with Backyard Blasters logo

Suit pattern continues on legs

Aviator-style helmet

Helmet with red visor

Dual-sided head: evil grin and determined expression

Red Visor Billy Bob Blaster
Underneath his helmet, Billy Bob has red eyes and an unusual glasses pattern.

All the Backyard Blasters have the same legs

TEAM X-TREME DAREDEVILS

MAX-treme, DEX-treme, and REX-treme made up the heroes of World Racers, driving sleek vehicles armed with an array of missiles. All three featured new, dual-sided heads and torsos printed front and back.

Aviator Helmet Bart Blaster
This determined driver has a dual-sided head—one face is scowling and the other is half-covered by a balaclava.

Torso is unique to all variants of this minifigure

BACKYARD BLASTERS

The Backyard Blasters were the "bad guys" of this theme. Bart, Billy Bob, and Bubba would try anything to beat their opponents. The team drove large, chunky vehicles with an array of explosive and destructive weapons, such as giant cannons and saws.

Lime green helmet is exclusive to variants of Dex and Max

Green Helmet DEX-treme
The three Dex variants all feature the same torso with radar detail on the front and belt detail on the back.

Radar detail

CREW AND OFFICIALS

Other minifigures came along for the World Racers ride—three Team X-Treme crew members and three race officials. The latter minifigures had little to do, since no one was paying attention to the rules anyway ....

Each crew member variant has the same torso

Orange legs also used on rebel pilots from the LEGO Star Wars theme in 1999

Race Official The three versions of the race officials had the same torso but different heads and head gear.

Crew Member Three crew members were released with different heads.

Visor can be worn up or down

Black gloves to protect hands

Standard Helmet MAX-treme One side of his head is grinning and the other is determined, but thanks to his shades, it can be hard to tell what Max is really thinking.

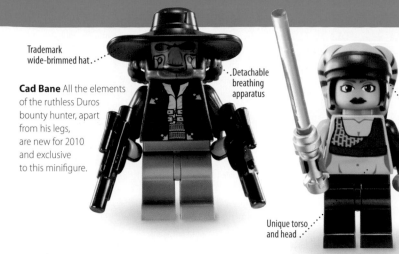

Trademark
wide-brimmed hat.

Cad Bane All the elements
of the ruthless Duros
bounty hunter, apart
from his legs,
are new for 2010
and exclusive
to this minifigure.

Detachable
breathing
apparatus

Aayla Secura Twi'lek Jedi
Knight Aayla Secura makes her
first minifigure appearance
in 2010 in the *Clone Wars* set
Clone Turbo Tank (8098).

Exclusive
Twi'lek
head-tails

Unique torso
and head

Head piece is the
same as the 2008
Clone Trooper,
although Senate
Commandos are
not clones

Lightsaber

Printing also
continues on
the back
of the torso

Exclusive white
markings
denote rank
of captain

Luke Skywalker The fifth variant
of Luke as an X-wing pilot features
more details on his g-suit and helmet.
The g-suit is also worn by fellow rebel
Zev Senesca, also released this year.

LEGO *STAR WARS*

The year 2010 proved to be a great one for LEGO *Star
Wars* collectors, as new characters and new versions
of fan favorites entered a galaxy not-so-far-away.
Ruthless bounty hunter Boba Fett was back with a
more movie-accurate look, and Aayla Secura, Cad
Bane, and Bossk became minifigures for the first time.

Detachable
range finder.

Senate Commando Captain
Tasked with guarding Chancellor Palpatine
and the Senate, this minifigure's elite status
is reflected in his unique helmet and torso.

Unique
sand-green
head

Flight suit
has breathing
apparatus
printed on
the back

Bossk The Trandoshan bounty
hunter's reptilian head piece
and flight suit torso were
specially created for this
minifigure. This version of
Bossk is exclusive to two sets.

Blaster rifle

Battle-damaged
helmet with new,
battle-scarred
head underneath.

Blaster with LEGO
Technic piece
on barrel.

*YOU'RE
WORTH A LOT
OF CREDITS
TO ME.*

Removable jet
pack on back

Boba Fett This new variant
of the famous bounty hunter
is available only in *Slave I*
(8097). The minifigure has a
new torso and cape.

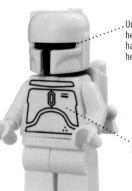

Underneath his
helmet, Boba Fett
has a plain black
head piece

Minimalist black
line printing

Limited-edition Boba Fett Designed to
look like the original all-white concept art
for Boba, this promotional minifigure was
given away as part of the 30th Anniversary
of *Star Wars: The Empire Strikes Back*.

LEGO® ADVANCED MODELS

Since 2000, LEGO builders wanting a bigger challenge have looked to the
Advanced Models theme. These LEGO sets were larger in size and piece
count and generally used more advanced building techniques. Popular
Advanced Model subthemes in 2010 included Modular Building and Space.

**Mannequin Bride and
Groom** The huge
clothing store Grand
Emporium (10211)
featured wedding
mannequins, a cashier,
a window cleaner,
a child, and two
shopper minifigures.

Wedding dress used
again in a LEGO
Education set in 2011.

Head piece is turned to
show blank side—the other
side features face printing

Detachable
gold visor

Astronaut This
minifigure appears
in Space Shuttle
Adventure (10213),
which was the
second ever LEGO
Space Shuttle set.

LEGO® SEASONAL

The holidays meant more fun minifigures
this year. This unusually undressed Santa
minifigure is from the LEGO CITY Advent
Calendar. He's fresh from the bathtub!

Santa keeps his hat on,
even in the bath!

Nude yellow
torso and legs.
Black hips
represent briefs

Bathtub Santa
He makes an unusual appearance on
day 18 of the 2010 LEGO CITY Advent
Calendar, but by day 24, Santa is
dressed again.

DON'T TELL ANYONE, BUT SPINJITZU MAKES ME DIZZY!

Detachable beard covers goatee printed on head

Traditional Japanese hat

Spinner

First release minifigure wears black obi sash

Master Wu Ninja practice the art of Spinjitzu—spinning at high speed—to fire up their energy. Spinners such as this one allow Master Wu and his students to practice Spinjitzu.

Katana is a traditional ninja sword

Gold fireball pattern

A mask hides Nya's identity.

Nya One of the few NINJAGO minifigures with a reversible head, Nya is Kai's sister. Her alternative face has a mask covering her mouth.

Bushy eyebrows

Cole As the Ninja of Earth, the Cole minifigure wears black to represent the energy stored below the ground.

Earth symbol attached to cords

LEGO NINJAGO

LEGO NINJAGO was one of the most ambitious play themes ever launched, and its success proved to be beyond anyone's expectations. Combining colorful and exciting ninja sets with a social game (NINJAGO Spinners), it boasted a successful TV series and a best-selling graphic novel line. Originally planned to be a three-year line, the popularity of NINJAGO later led to it being extended far beyond that.

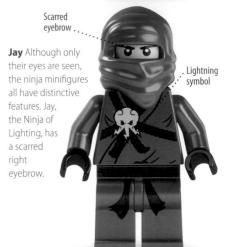

Scarred eyebrow

Jay Although only their eyes are seen, the ninja minifigures all have distinctive features. Jay, the Ninja of Lighting, has a scarred right eyebrow.

Lightning symbol

2011

THIS WAS A BIG YEAR for the LEGO Group. LEGO® NINJAGO®, one of its most successful play themes, was introduced; aliens invaded Earth in the new Alien Conquest line; LEGO® CITY launched a successful space program; bold adventurers went on a Pharaoh's Quest; and LEGO® Master Builder Academy taught fans new and better ways to build. And with new sets appearing in the LEGO® Atlantis, LEGO® SpongeBob SquarePants™, and LEGO® *Stars Wars*™ themes, action continued from the depths of the ocean to the farthest reaches of outer space and everywhere in between!

Red robes indicate that Kai is the Ninja of Fire

Kai DX This variant of the Kai minifigure bears a golden dragon design. It shows that he has tamed a dragon and attained Dragon Extreme (DX) status.

Dragon breathing fire design

Tail of dragon printed on legs

DID YOU KNOW?
Although the Kai minifigure has scars around his left eye, these were not present in the TV series.

Zane The Ninja of Ice, Zane, wears all-white robes. He is the fourth of the four original ninja minifigures in the LEGO NINJAGO theme.

Ice symbol on robe

Gray sash keeps robes in place

NINJA

The four ninja minifigures each wear different-colored robes tied to their element: red for Fire, blue for Lightning, white for Ice, and black for Earth. The colored robes were featured in play theme sets and spinner packs.

Removable bone trophy.

Gnashing teeth.

Silver samurai helmet.

> DOESN'T EVERYONE HAVE A DOG BONE ON THEIR HAT?

VILLAINS

Lord Garmadon's plot to escape the underworld leads to a conflict that spans all NINJAGO. Aided by General Samukai and the Skeleton Army, Garmadon quests for the Four Golden Weapons of Spinjitzu.

Lord Garmadon Nemesis of the ninja, Garmadon cuts a suitably sinister minifigure in black. The bone on his helmet marks him out as the commander of the Skeleton Army.

Removable armor

Metal plate replaces lost eye

New booted leg piece

Kruncha The General Kruncha figure wears a military cap that cannot be removed.

Frakjaw This Frakjaw figure hides his metal-plated head firmly under his hat.

Nuckal The skeleton figures have vertical grip arms—their hands are rotated 90 degrees to their arms.

Dual-colored jester hat

Bonezai Like the ninja, each skeleton has his own theme. Bonezai is the Skeleton of Ice.

Krazi Skeleton Krazi's hat was last seen on a jolly court jester in 2009's LEGO® Castle theme.

Chopov The first Chopov figures were hatless, but he later gained this simple black helmet.

SKELETONS

Soldiers of Lord Garmadon, skeleton figures each have a unique weapon. They appear in both play theme sets and spinner packs. Despite their fearsome look, they play a comic role in the story.

Bamboo hat

Protective chestplate of a skeleton general

Wyplash His torso may be standard skeleton issue, but the General Wyplash figure's worm-eaten head and bone armor are all his own

Sideswept hair with front curl

Superman
The promotional Superman minifigure would later reappear in 2012's Superman vs. Power Armor Lex (6862).

Famous S-shield

Muscles printed on torso

Red cape

LEGO® DC UNIVERSE SUPER HEROES

Super Hero excitement started to build in July with the announcement at San Diego Comic-Con that the DC Universe would be coming to LEGO sets in 2012. Batman and Green Lantern minifigures were given away at that show as a free promotion, with a Superman minifigure offered at New York Comic-Con that fall.

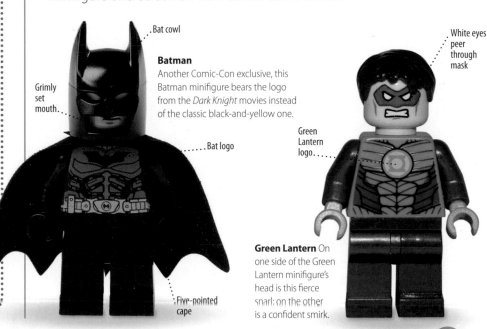

Bat cowl

Batman
Another Comic-Con exclusive, this Batman minifigure bears the logo from the *Dark Knight* movies instead of the classic black-and-yellow one.

Grimly set mouth

Bat logo

Five-pointed cape

White eyes peer through mask

Green Lantern logo

Green Lantern On one side of the Green Lantern minifigure's head is this fierce snarl; on the other is a confident smirk.

LEGO® PHARAOH'S QUEST

A brave team of minifigure adventurers battled an ancient Egyptian Pharaoh in this play theme that lasted for one year. Pharaoh's Quest featured six sets and 12 new minifigures. The sets also included six mystical treasures, such as swords and scarabs, all but one of which were colored gold.

Extravagant sideburns

Rifle

Jake Raines
With a wry grin, bold stare, and facial scar, this dashing minifigure conveys Jake Raines's fearless nature.

Pistol—for self-defense

Earnest expression

Cross-body bag to store finds

Map

Large pickax

Helena Tova Skvalling
Two versions of Helena's minifigure exist—one with yellow hands and one wearing brown gloves.

Professor Archibald Hale
The pith helmet may be old hat, but the bespectacled head is brand new for the Professor Hale minifigure.

READY FOR ADVENTURE

Professor Hale is aided by a team of brave minifigure heroes. Their names all refer to types of weather—an homage to the names of the original LEGO® Adventurers, including Johnny Thunder and Charles Lightning.

Battle spear

Striped headdress worn by pharaohs

Amset-Ra Turn his head, and Amset-Ra's serene death mask becomes a grim mummy face.

Mummy wrappings

Flying Mummy The falcon headdress of this minifigure represents the god Horus.

Wings attach to minifigure's neck

PHARAOH FOE

The heroes' enemy is evil pharaoh Amset-Ra. His forces include jackal-headed Anubis Guards, Flying Mummies with beak-shaped headdresses, and dim but dedicated Mummy Warriors.

Jackal-head mask

Scarab-shaped shield

Anubis Guard
No standard minifigure head lurks under the jackal mask of the Anubis Guard.

LEGO MASTER BUILDER ACADEMY

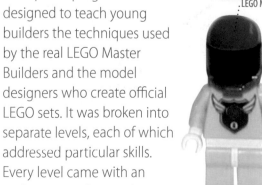

LEGO MBA Level 1 logo on shirt

Aviator's cap and goggles

Level 1 Minifigure
A minifigure in lime green represented Skill Level 1—the easiest.

LEGO MBA Level 2

Level 2 Minifigure
This minifigure's helmet was part of his gear from the Level 2 Auto Designer kit.

This special program was designed to teach young builders the techniques used by the real LEGO Master Builders and the model designers who create official LEGO sets. It was broken into separate levels, each of which addressed particular skills. Every level came with an exclusive minifigure whose color represented its level.

MINIFIGURE MANIA

Some LEGO minifigures do not fit into a theme, but they are no less popular. They have played a part in all sorts of celebrations, from topping cakes at weddings to being a giveaway at LEGO Fan Weekends in Denmark. The fellow in the red and blue even came with his own speech bubbles—he always had something to say.

Simple, smiling face

Speech Bubbles Minifigure
Minifigures got to talk—in a way—with the LEGO Speech Bubbles Minifigure (81087). It came with a minifigure, attachable speech bubbles, and stickers with quotes.

Top hat

Tiara and veil

Bride and Groom
Fans could now tie the knot in LEGO style with these Bride and Groom cake toppers.

Sloping piece forms skirt

LEGO® MINIFIGURES

The second year of the collectible LEGO Minifigures series featured three assortments, totaling 48 new Minifigures. The bar code—which in the past allowed some people to work out which Minifigure was in a package—was removed, so the selection was truly random. Forty-eight new parts featured this year.

It's *very* warm inside the gorilla suit!

Standard minifigure head visible through mask

Gorilla Suit Guy This Minifigure is not a real gorilla—just a guy dressed up in a suit!

Giant banana

Pointy elfin ears

Stag head emblem on shield

Scale mail armor

Elf The Elf warrior is the first minifigure to have ears attached to his hair piece.

SERIES 3

Fans were particularly excited to get their hands on the first LEGO Elf Minifigure in Series 3. New parts for this series included the Elf's bow and arrow, the Tennis Player's racket, and the Hula Dancer's maracas.

Tennis racket

Tennis outfit printed on torso and legs

Tennis Player This sporty Minifigure wears traditional tennis whites.

Upturned alien eyes

Space Alien Lime green is the LEGO Group's go-to color for aliens. This one has a contrasting red tongue.

Breathing tubes

Rapier with cup-shaped hilt

Plumed hat with turned-up brim

Musketeer The *fleur-de-lis* on the Musketeer's torso is a classic symbol of French royalty.

Bright orange hazard suit and helmet

Traditional Japanese makeup

Dark red fan

New hair piece with quiff

Sailor hat unique to this minifigure

SERIES 4

Among the new parts created for Series 4 were Kimono Girl's fan and the Sailor's hat. The Ice Skater and a Hockey Player shared the ice—and the limelight—as they both debuted new minifigure ice skates.

Radioactivity warning symbol

Hazmat Guy Judging by his terrified expression, the Hazmat Guy Minifigure is in the wrong job.

Kimono Girl A delicate floral pattern adorns the kimono of this graceful Minifigure.

Removable fabric skirt fits over legs

Ice Skater Silver skates attach to the Ice Skater Minifigure's feet.

Telescope for spotting land

Sailor This skilled seafarer is the first collectible Minifigure to have a winking facial expression.

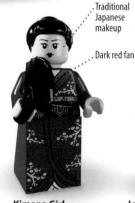

Winged metal helmet

Winged scarab printed on hair

SERIES 5

Series 5 Minifigures showcased 20 new parts, including the Boxer's gloves, the Evil Dwarf's round shield, and the Egyptian Queen's sharp bob.

Two blades attach to ax individually

Minifigure hands replaced with a new glove element

Venomous green snake

Boxer The Boxer packs a real punch in his flashy all-red gear. Instead of ordinary minifigure hands, he has two boxing gloves.

Egyptian Queen The ancient Queen's snake has appeared in various colors in around 100 sets.

Evil Dwarf This beard piece debuted in 2008 in the LEGO Castle theme. It is only used for dwarf minifigures.

Cave Woman One of the locks on the Cave Woman's hair piece acts as a clip to attach her bone ornament.

Rock club

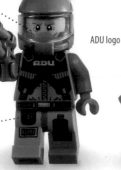

Mature features

ADU-issue azure blue suit

ADU logo

Helmet protects his powerful brain

Detachable jet pack

ADU Sergeant
Gray facial hair and wrinkles mark this minifigure out as the senior ADU member.

Computer Specialist
Orange glasses protect this minifigure tech expert's eyes from screen glare.

ADU Rookie The slightly overconfident Rookie isn't laughing on the other side of his face!

ALIEN DEFENSE UNIT

The brave minifigures of the ADU have new torsos, printed legs, a belt pattern on the hips, and reversible heads. The team includes a prominent female minifigure who appears only in Earth Defense HQ (7066).

Breathing apparatus

> THOSE ALIENS HAVE MADE THEIR LAST CROP CIRCLE!

High-grip gloves

Double-barreled blaster gun

ADU Soldier This soldier scans the horizon for UFOs, ready to launch into action.

Specs for spotting toxic spills

Radio to transmit warnings

Scientist Cleaning up alien toxin is this green-spattered scientist's job.

LEGO® SPACE

Aliens invaded Earth for the first time in a LEGO line in this one-year Alien Conquest theme. The strange aliens and their UFOs were opposed by the Alien Defense Unit, who drove the invaders off Earth at the end of 2011. The Alien Conquest story crossed over into numerous other play themes, including LEGO City Space.

Shocked expression

Farmer Except for his standard hair piece, this agricultural abductee is made of all new parts.

Sharp, sleek hairdo

Microphone

Clipboard

Lotta Brix
A new head and torso grace this pushy news reporter minifigure who is about to get the full scary story!

CIVILIANS

The Aliens need brainpower to make their ships go, and they have realized that Earth people are a good supply. These civilian minifigures all have reversible heads so they can look scared when the Aliens appear.

Staring, single eye

Alien Clinger The Alien Clinger can fit onto any civilian minifigure's head. Once in place, it sucks out their brainpower to fuel the Alien ships.

> I RULE AN EMPIRE, BUT I CAN'T FIND PANTS THAT FIT!

Gold epaulettes show rank

Alien ray gun

Six tentacles swirl around him

Alien Commander
Separate brain and face elements make up the head of the self-styled "Supreme Overlord" alien.

ALIENS

Four new Alien minifigures were introduced in this line, with new head pieces and new torsos. Their ray guns had previously only appeared in the collectible Minifigures theme. The Alien Commander has tentacles instead of standard LEGO legs.

Alien Android The easily fazed android sports the standard Alien Conquest Alien colors—black, magenta, silver, and lime green.

Semitransparent brain

Mechanical eye

Mechanical arm with barb

Metal peg leg

Very small brain

Pronounced underbite

Alien Trooper This ferocious minifigure is the land soldier of the alien invaders.

LEGO® HARRY POTTER™

The LEGO Harry Potter theme featured two sets related to *Harry Potter and the Deathly Hallows*™ in 2011, as well as the largest LEGO Harry Potter set at the time, Diagon Alley (10217). This year saw the release of 28 minifigures, with some—including Narcissa Malfoy, Mr. Ollivander, and the Weasley twins—appearing in minifigure form for the first time.

Ron Weasley™ The 11th Ron minifigure has had his old bowl haircut restyled into a shaggy side part.

Red and brown color scheme

Two-colored hair piece

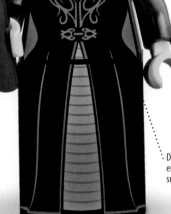

Narcissa Malfoy™ Narcissa's sleek minifigure has fancy blue-gray embroidery on both sides of her torso.

Dress print emphasizes small waist

DID YOU KNOW?
The strip of paint on some minifigures' torso pegs (underneath the head piece) helps the printing machine recognize which side of the torso is the front or back.

Lightning bolt scar

Familiar Harry Potter hairstyle

White bow tie and dress shirt

Witch's hat with buckle

Professor Sprout A sprig of leaves adorns the torso of Hogwarts' Herbology teacher.

Conductor's cap is a purple version of a police hat

Stan Shunpike
This Knight Bus conductor minifigure doesn't have printed sideburns, unlike his 2004 predecessor.

Magic wand

Hollow, lined cheeks

Teeth gritted in concentration

Zipped cardigan

Side braids drawn back

Hermione Granger
The new 2011 Hermione minifigure has swapped her school uniform for casual clothes.

Knitted cardigan with hood

Casual pants

Yule Ball Harry Potter DK's book LEGO® *Harry Potter™ Building the Magical World* came with this minifigure, looking suave in his Yule Ball dress robes.

Neville Longbottom™
Unlike the 2004 version, Neville's new minifigure has a reversible head.

LEGO ATLANTIS

The adventure beneath the sea continued in 2011, as the minifigure heroes of LEGO Atlantis found the lost city itself, complete with a Poseidon statue that turned out to be its Golden King. The King would be the only Atlantis minifigure to appear as a microfigure in the LEGO® Game Atlantis Treasure. Ten minifigures and five sets rose from the depths this year.

Grecian-style building

Gold fish ornament

City of Atlantis (7985)
A ruined city, a deep sea sub, five minifigures, and a giant crab come with the City of Atlantis set.

Barracuda Guardian

Spartan warrior's helmet

Poseidon Statue A yellow human face is printed on the reverse of this golden minifigure's head.

Lobster Guardian
This fierce fellow guards the temple with a golden trident gripped in one of its big claws.

Long, spiky spines

Strong pincers

I USED TO STYLE WOOKIEE HAIR IN MY OLD JOB.

Curved top to helmet

Breathing apparatus

Lightweight armor

Black gloves

T-shaped visor

Unique ponytail plugs into stud on head

Twin blaster guns

Head piece and hair piece have both been seen before

Mandalorian A detailed new head, with glaring blue eyes, is concealed by the minifigure soldier's helmet.

Eight-horned head top piece

Orange jumpsuit

Aurra Sing Aurra's torso and legs are printed with an ammo vest and holsters.

Savage Opress A yellow pattern on Opress's head represents clan tattoos.

Bowcaster

Embo The printed radar dish helmet is unique to the Embo minifigure.

Padmé Naberrie This is the first update of the Padmé minifigure since the *Star Wars* theme's debut in 1999.

Rare double-ended lightsaber

Yellow eyes of dark side devotee

LEGO *STAR WARS*

The LEGO *Star Wars* theme went from strength to strength this year, with both fan-requested minifigures and minifigures based upon The Clone Wars appearing. Some characters, such as the crimson R-3PO, had never before been seen in LEGO form. Others became exclusive minifigures unlikely to reappear in future sets. All of this helped make 2011 a great year for LEGO *Star Wars* collectors.

DID YOU KNOW? The R-3PO minifigure uses the same mold and printing as C-3PO. Only its color is different.

New torso details for fourth Darth Maul minifigure

Darth Maul The spiked piece on top of Maul's head is the same as that of Opress, his minifigure brother, but with different printing.

Shadow ARF Trooper A new, black Advanced Recon Force Trooper came free with some online purchases as part of a *Star Wars* Day promotion.

Removable turban

Patched-together armor

Dengar Bounty hunting has left its mark on Dengar's battle-scarred minifigure.

Photoreceptor eyes

Pattern also on back of torso

R-3PO This protocol droid minifigure is only available with the Hoth Echo Base set (7879).

New, tousled hair piece

Breathing mask on reverse face joins air tube

Bacta Tank Luke The latest Luke Skywalker minifigure shows the hero ready for immersion in a healing bacta tank.

HALLS TO BE DECKING I HAVE!

Straight ears

Backpack attaches at neck

Short LEGO legs

Santa Yoda A festive Yoda minifigure appeared in the 2011 LEGO *Star Wars* Advent Calendar (7958).

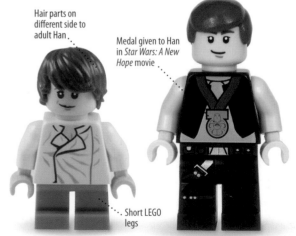

Hair parts on different side to adult Han

Medal given to Han in *Star Wars: A New Hope* movie

Short LEGO legs

Young Han Solo This Han minifigure came only with the *Star Wars™: The Padawan Menace* Blu-ray.

Han Solo with Medal Another exclusive Han minifigure came with the first edition of DK's LEGO® *Star Wars™ Character Encyclopedia*.

THREE OF A KIND!

All three of these were limited-edition exclusives, appearing as promotional minifigures with LEGO *Star Wars* books and DVDs, or as part of the 2011 LEGO *Star Wars* Advent Calendar. Hard to find they are!

LEGO® TRAIN

The Mærsk Container Train (10219) left the station in 2011, with a diesel engine and two container cars. It came with three train worker minifigures, all with the same body but with different heads. This was a follow-up to the rerelease of the Mærsk Container Ship (10155), which also came out this year.

High-visibility bib

Mærsk Train Workman
This gray-bearded minifigure wears a Mærsk-blue construction helmet, first seen in 1980.

LEGO® SEASONAL

This year's addition to the Winter Village line was the Post Office set (10222), featuring seven minifigures. Hooray—they finally had somewhere to go to buy their holiday cards!

Reversible head with smile or frown

White envelope logo worn by PO staff

Post Office Worker
The Winter Village Post Office set featured a female Post Office worker—the second ever to appear in a LEGO set.

LEGO® CASTLE

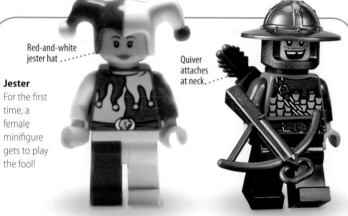

Red-and-white jester hat

Jester
For the first time, a female minifigure gets to play the fool!

Quiver attaches at neck

Dragon Knight Of the six Dragon Knight variants released this year, only this one is missing a tooth.

LEGO® Kingdoms was a subtheme of the LEGO Castle line and featured the Lion Kingdom battling the evil Dragon Kingdom. Five sets were introduced in 2011, with a dozen minifigures, many of whom appeared in more than one set. The Milkmaid was exclusive to her set, Mill Village Raid (7189).

Corset bodice in rough fabric

Reverse face has cross expression

Milkmaid The last thing this minifigure maid wants is an arrow hole in her milk bucket accessory!

LEGO® ADVANCED MODELS

The Pet Shop (10218) was the first Modular Building set to include two structures—a three-story pet shop and a townhouse. This was the sixth set released for this line. LEGO fans blasted off into outer space again with Shuttle Expedition (10231), which was a slightly revised version of the Space Shuttle Adventure set (10213) from 2010.

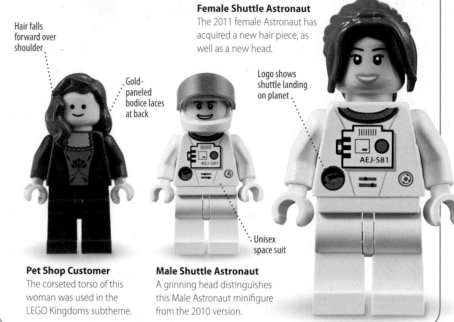

Hair falls forward over shoulder

Gold-paneled bodice laces at back

Female Shuttle Astronaut
The 2011 female Astronaut has acquired a new hair piece, as well as a new head.

Logo shows shuttle landing on planet

Unisex space suit

Pet Shop Customer
The corseted torso of this woman was used in the LEGO Kingdoms subtheme.

Male Shuttle Astronaut
A grinning head distinguishes this Male Astronaut minifigure from the 2010 version.

LEGO® BRAND STORE

The year 2011 saw the tradition of exclusive LEGO sets offered at LEGO Brand Store openings continue. These sets featured one or more minifigures, some specially made for the sets, others reissues of classic minifigures. Several new shops opened this year in North America, Canada, Denmark, and the UK.

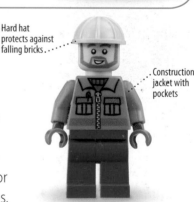

Hard hat protects against falling bricks

Construction jacket with pockets

Mission Viejo Worker
This construction worker from Mission Viejo, California, shares a head with the Mærsk Train Workman, above.

I'M ON A KNIGHT SHIFT.

Helmet with nose guard

Sunrise Lion Knight
The Sunrise, Florida, Knight has a new torso, but his other parts are all reused.

Long side fringe

Pretty yellow flowers

San Diego Lady
This minifigure from San Diego, California, wears a vest worn by four other Brand Store minifigures so far.

Standard wizard's hat ·····

Gandalf the Gray As you might expect, all parts of Gandalf's minifigure but the face and hands are gray.

New torso with rope and belt pattern ·····

Gray beard encircles smiling face

2012

EXCITEMENT GREW in 2012, with adventure stepping up to the next level. New licensed themes LEGO® *The Lord of the Rings*™, LEGO® DC Universe Super Heroes, and LEGO® Marvel Super Heroes spawned some of the most sought-after building sets yet. Brand-new play themes such as Monster Fighters delighted fans, while continuing favorites LEGO® NINJAGO®, LEGO® Minifigures, LEGO® *Star Wars*™, and LEGO® CITY found new ways to spark their imaginations. Of the huge number of new and refreshed minifigures released this year, many represented some of the greatest characters in fiction. Little surprise, then, that 2012 became a banner year for collectors of every age.

Dark brown hobbit hair

Gray cloak ·····

Frodo's other face has an expression of wide-eyed terror!

Ornate helmet with cheek protectors ·····

Braided dwarfish beard ·····

Gimli The huge new beard worn by this minifigure is the largest in the theme.

Short sword is a new weapon for 2012

Frodo Baggins Frodo is the main character in the theme, and his minifigure appears in four of the seven sets.

The One Ring fits over the minifigure's hand

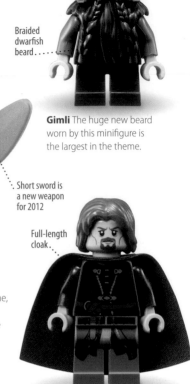

Full-length cloak ·····

Boromir A grimacing face appears on the reverse of this brave warrior's head.

LEGO *THE LORD OF THE RINGS*

It was one of the most hotly anticipated LEGO play themes launched in 2012, with seven sets based on the three hit *The Lord of the Rings* movies. All the major characters appeared as minifigures, with new heads, torsos, and printed legs. The many new elements included swords, shields, and helmets, and an entirely new element was created to represent the One Ring.

Gold crest on helmet

Breastplate covers entire torso ·····

King Théoden The heroic Rohan king minifigure has new ornate legs, helmet, torso, and breastplate.

Scale mail pattern on legs

Elvish ears attached to hair piece

Slightly bigger bow and arrow version introduced in 2011

Legolas This minifigure's new hair piece is worn by all 2012 elves in this theme and for *The Hobbit* in 2013.

Elven tailcoat

EXCLUSIVE ELF
This exclusive version of Second Age Elrond was available only with preorders of LEGO® *The Lord of the Rings*™: The Video Game.

Same hair piece as fellow elves Legolas, Haldir, and Tauriel, but in brown

Open-mouthed angry expression

Pearl gold spear

Elrond Young Elrond carries a long spear and has a reversible face: open-and closed-mouthed.

GOLLUM

This small LEGO figure requires a minimum 2x2 brick to stand on because of his hunched shape. He appears in two variants and in two sets, one from 2013's *The Hobbit* theme and one from *The Lord of the Rings*.

Head and body are one piece

Arms must be attached

Gollum The other (equally precious) variant of Gollum has sinister narrowed eyes.

I WONDER IF THE DINO FOLKS ARE HIRING?

Boa crest on hood

Gray scale markings

Ready to grip Constrictai Fang Blade

Snike Short, unposable legs set the tunneling Constrictai apart from the other Serpentine tribes.

LEGO NINJAGO

Now in its second year, NINJAGO upped the action as the ninja challenged the tribes of the Serpentine. The snakes featured new serpent heads, new scaly torsos, and new printed legs. Kai's sister, Nya, returned this year clad in samurai gear in Samurai Mech (9448).

All-black outfit includes tattered cloak and hood

Ringwraith The shadowy Ringwraiths, also known as Nazgûl, have only appeared in one set to date (9472).

Terrifying warpaint printed on face beneath helmet

White hand of Saruman

In set 9476, an Uruk-hai can be found with a handprint on his helmet.

Standard gray breastplate piece

Uruk-hai Four variants of these fierce warrior creatures have been released, with and without helmets and armor.

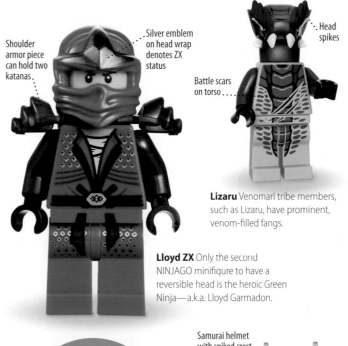

Shoulder armor piece can hold two katanas

Silver emblem on head wrap denotes ZX status

Head spikes

Battle scars on torso

Lizaru Venomari tribe members, such as Lizaru, have prominent, venom-filled fangs.

Lloyd ZX Only the second NINJAGO minifigure to have a reversible head is the heroic Green Ninja—a.k.a. Lloyd Garmadon.

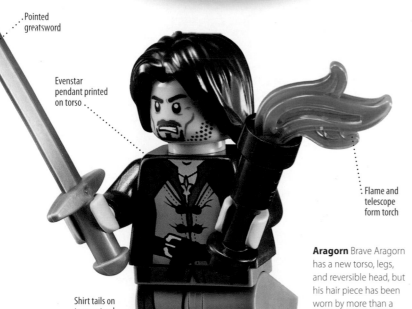

Pointed greatsword

Evenstar pendant printed on torso

Flame and telescope form torch

Aragorn Brave Aragorn has a new torso, legs, and reversible head, but his hair piece has been worn by more than a dozen other minifigures in this color since 2010.

Shirt tails on torso extend to legs

DID YOU KNOW?
All Serpentine tribes carry small, hand-held vipers that they use as toxic weapons.

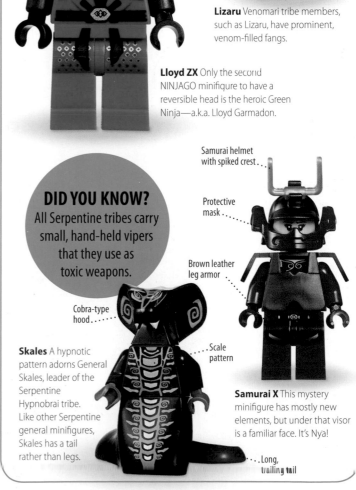

Samurai helmet with spiked crest

Protective mask

Brown leather leg armor

Cobra-type hood

Scale pattern

Skales A hypnotic pattern adorns General Skales, leader of the Serpentine Hypnobrai tribe. Like other Serpentine general minifigures, Skales has a tail rather than legs.

Samurai X This mystery minifigure has mostly new elements, but under that visor is a familiar face. It's Nya!

Long, trailing tail

Bizarro This rare minifigure of Superman's troubled clone was a prize in a raffle at the 2012 San Diego Comic-Con.

Unique head has sad expression on other side

One-off torso

Purple cape

Tiara is part of hair piece

Halter top with gold trim

Star-spangled shorts

Wonder Woman The minifigure Amazon warrior comes complete with a golden lasso accessory.

Angry expression

Stylish black suit

Lex Luthor Lex is one of three minifigures in the Superman vs. Power Armor Lex (6862).

SUPERMAN
The giveaway Man of Steel from 2011's San Diego Comic-Con made a welcome return in 2012. This time he was packaged with Wonder Woman and Lex Luthor who, unlike Superman, were new and exclusive to the set.

Cowl piece in use since 2006

Headband visible through cowl eyeholes

Utility Belt is larger than on other Batman minifigures

Electro pattern on cowl

I TAKE CRIME APART, BRICK BY BRICK.

Bat-symbol in blue

Five-pointed cloth cape

Electrical wires and plates printed on legs and torso

Electrosuit Batman This minifigure was exclusive to LEGO® *Batman*™ *The Visual Dictionary*, published by DK.

Batman Two variants of this minifigure exist: this one and another with a new-style cowl.

LEGO DC UNIVERSE SUPER HEROES

After releasing a few exclusive minifigures at Comic-Cons in 2011, the DC Universe burst into life with an explosion of LEGO minifigures in 2012. It was the first year that non-Batman DC sets joined the assortment, a trend that would continue in 2013. New characters, including Wonder Woman and Lex Luthor, made their debuts and old favorites got an exciting new look.

DID YOU KNOW?
The Cowgirl Minifigure from series 8 wielded a brown version of Wonder Woman's lasso.

Lined cheeks give serious expression

Expensive gray business suit

BATMAN II
The Dark Knight returned in five sets this year, with a new minifigure head and torso. Many other minifigures were similarly refreshed for 2012, including Poison Ivy, The Joker, The Riddler, Two-Face, and Catwoman.

Bruce Wayne Batman's alter ego shares his new head with a less heroic minifigure from the LEGO Marvel Super Heroes theme: Loki.

Robin The first new Boy Wonder minifigure since 2008 wears all red instead of the classic red and green.

WHICH ROBIN AM I? I GET CONFUSED.

Cord printed on torso represents cape attachment

Lightning bolt symbol

Shazam! Another San Diego Comic-Con raffle prize, this was the only Shazam! minifigure until 2019.

Bat wing tail fins

Reverse of head has expression of open-mouthed alarm

"R" logo appears on all Robin minifigures

Black cape is the same as Batman's

Batman in cockpit

Black on yellow bat-symbol

Batmobile and the Two-Face Chase (6864) This set comes with two vehicles, five minifigures, and a bank with a safe.

Hubcaps same color as bat-symbol

Whip to whisk stolen goods into her grasp

Classic jester hat

Wrestler mask printed on head

Zipped catsuit printed on torso

Diamond pattern on legs

Catwoman The feline minifigure has a new torso, mask, and head—complete with purple lipstick.

Harley Quinn Aside from her classic hat, the Joker's mischievous minifigure sidekick has all new parts.

Bane Tubes that carry a strength drug to Bane's brain are printed on the back of his torso and head.

NEW HEAD, NEW TORSO... SAME SENSE OF HUMOR! HA HA HA!

Old hair piece appears in green for first time

Torso printed with lime vest, bow tie, and squirting flower

White hands match face

Same hair piece as 2006 Two-Face

New head has a pupil missing on the scarred side

Split colors continue on back of legs and torso

Two-Face Bold new colors give this updated good guy/bad guy minifigure an eye-catching look.

Leaves printed on hair piece

Bowler hat in light gray

Crowbar resembles a question mark

The Joker It's smiles all around for the Joker. His new head has a different kind of grin on the reverse.

DID YOU KNOW?
The Riddler's hat is a gray version of the one debuted by the 2011 collectible LEGO Minifigures Small Clown.

Leaves emit potent pheromones

Riddler's question mark motif

Poison Ivy A printed vine trails its leaves all over this minifigure's torso and legs.

The Riddler Three question marks on this minifigure's new torso and hat leave no doubt as to the trickster's identity!

Vest laced up with string

Fedora shields eyes from sun

T-REX ... MMMM, TASTES LIKE CHICKEN!

Belt holds gun and compass

Rex Tyrone If you want a rampant Raptor roped, Rex is your man. His fedora hat—in a variety of colors—has also been worn by bandits; gangsters; cowboys; and, of course, Indiana Jones.

LEGO® DINO

Deep in the jungle, LEGO adventurers discovered dinosaurs that had somehow survived into the modern era. Armed with tranquilizer guns, the minifigure heroes tried to capture the dinos alive in the seven-set theme. Each set came with a dinosaur, at least one hero minifigure, and a vehicle.

Utility vest holds screwdriver and radio

Nervous expression

Tousled hair

Binoculars for spying dinosaurs

GPS device to help locate T-rex

"Tracer" Tops A chin dimple and cool shades give Triceratops hunter Tracer his rugged look.

Belt holds pocket for pen and paper

Chuck "Stego" Jenkins A new head is introduced for this wildlife photographer. He clearly has bigger things to worry about than shaving.

ID tag necklace

Sue Montana Ponytailed Sue is ready to face the action dressed in hardy safari gear.

Loosely tied scarf

Josh Thunder This minifigure hero is a descendant of Johnny Thunder from the LEGO® Adventurers theme.

Belt pocket

167

LEGO MARVEL SUPER HEROES

Spider-Man had first spun his webs in a LEGO set in 2002. Ten years later, he was back—this time as Ultimate Spider-Man—along with a whole wave of Marvel characters making their minifigure debuts. They included the X-Men, the Avengers, and some of their most formidable foes!

Scabbard on back holds two katanas.

Muscled torso

Extra utility belt on leg

Deadpool A black-and-red mask is printed directly onto the minifigure mercenary's head.

Sideburns printed on head.

Wolverine
The X-Men's wild mutant minifigure has a hair piece previously seen only on vampires.

Claws attach to minifigure hands

Flaming red hair.

Symbol of phoenix rising from flames

Phoenix
This minifigure shows fiery X-Men telepath Jean Grey in her classic costume as Super Hero Phoenix. Her reversible head has two faces—one friendly and one fierce.

Gray eyebrows show his age

First minifigure to wear cape in medium lilac color

Gray platform

Magneto The platform supplied with this X-Men foe minifigure represents the metal disk on which he flies.

X-MEN

Wolverine was the first X-Men mutant to achieve minifigure status, in Wolverine's Chopper Showdown (6866). Phoenix would show up next, as a promotional giveaway at San Diego Comic-Con in July of this year.

Wolverine's Chopper Showdown (6866)
In set 6866, Wolverine needs his chopper motorcycle to escape the Magneto and Deadpool minifigures and their helicopter.

HEY DOC OCK, CAN YOU SCRATCH MY BACK?

Small spider logo

Mask has rounded eye shapes and black webs

Large white eyes

Black suit is really a living alien being!

Black Suit Spider-Man
Raffle winners at the 2012 San Diego Comic-Con got this special minifigure as a prize.

Mask printing covers half of minifigure's head

Dragon symbol

On reverse face, red eyeglass shades are lowered

Arms attach to neck bracket

Life-preserving technology on chest panel

Iron Fist The symbol on this minifigure's torso shows that he fought the magic dragon Shao Lao.

Doc Ock The Doc Ock minifigure has four arms that are all detachable and posable.

Spider-Man
The new Spidey minifigure is modeled on the cartoon version from the *Ultimate Spider-Man* animated TV series.

The usual red Spidey gloves

SPIDER-MAN

Spidey and martial arts master Iron Fist teamed up to take on Dr. Octopus in Spider-Man's Doc Ock Ambush (6873). It was one of three 2012 sets to include minifigures based on characters from the *Ultimate Spider-Man* TV series.

DID YOU KNOW?
The 2012 Doc Ock minifigure is made up of an amazing 26 parts.

Thor The Norse god minifigure wears an angry snarl on the other side of his head.

- Only Thor has this hair piece in light yellow
- Unique torso with circular armor plates

AVENGERS

Smash hit movie *The Avengers* became an exciting LEGO subtheme in 2012, with four action-packed sets. Black Widow, who appeared only in Quinjet Aerial Battle (6869), was the most sought-after minifigure.

- Striped panel is straighter than on Toy Fair variant

Captain America There have been more than a dozen Captain America variants since this one.

- "A" for America (but it could also be for Avengers)

- Printed mask has white eye covers

Toy Fair Cap A special promotional Captain America minifigure came packaged as a set with Iron Man at the International Toy Fair in New York.

- V-shaped red-and-white panel

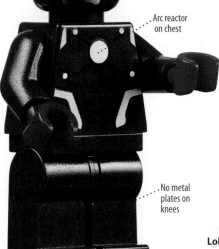

Toy Fair Iron Man Just 125 minifigures like this one were given away at the International Toy Fair in New York.

- Mask printed on head
- Arc reactor on chest
- No metal plates on knees

Iron Man Transparent bricks attach to Iron Man's hands to represent repulsor beams.

- Gold mask fits over helmet
- Repulsor beam

- Unique horned helmet
- Armor based on *The Avengers* movie costume

Loki All subsequent variants of the god of mischief have worn the same helmet.

- Strap for archer's quiver

Hawkeye A black bow was designed specially for this minifigure.

- Gloved hand for holding bow

- Black, tousled hair
- Well-muscled torso

Incredible Hulk This Hulk minifigure was an exclusive gift-with-purchase at LEGO Stores and the online LEGO Shop.

Black Widow Unlike the movie character, this sleek minifigure wears one of her belts diagonally.

- Eyebrows and lipstick colors match hair
- Weapon holsters strapped to both legs

- Head, torso, and legs are one piece
- Detachable hands turn at wrist

HULK GROW!

The Hulk figure in Hulk's Helicarrier Breakout (6868) is far from mini. He's been scaled up to match Hulk's relative size in the movie. Call him a minifigure and he'll get angry, and you wouldn't like him when he's angry ….

HULK SMASH BIGGER HULK!

- Pants molded on figure, as well as printed

Large Hulk Huge, specially molded hands enable the large Hulk to grip standard minifigures by their legs.

LEGO CITY

LEGO CITY left town for a while in 2012, with the introduction of the CITY Forest Police subtheme. New Forest Police minifigures and their adversaries appeared in seven sets, including a new Forest Police Station (4440). Forest firefighters also got four sets. Ranger, pilot, and crook minifigures featured new heads and torsos, and firefighter minifigures had new torsos.

- New torso with life jacket worn over it
- Forest Police campaign hat
- Aviator-style sunglasses
- Torso common to Forest Police

Boat Policeman On his new head, the Boat Policeman wears a new hat made just for 2012's Forest Police.

- Standard crash helmet
- Police badge

Vehicle Policeman The Police driver has the same new head as his colleague, left. He appears only in Police Pursuit (4437).

- Respirator attaches to neck

Fireman This hose-wielding hero is one of four in the LEGO CITY Firemen Minifigure Pack (853378).

- Water cannon with water jet
- Fireproof suit

LEGO MINIFIGURES

The LEGO collectible Minifigures line returned for its third year in 2012, with 48 new Minifigures spread over three series. As in previous years, many new elements were featured in each of the series.

Clockwork Robot A bracket that fits over the Clockwork Robot's neck holds a turnable key.

Block-shaped head with stud on top

Panel of gauges, knobs, and screen

Bright colors as seen on vintage toys

Throwing spear

Metal rivets on feet

Makeup matches pink hair streak

Skater Girl Series 1 and 4 also included skater Minifigures, but this one is the first female.

"Pretty" skeleton head logo

Winged heart design

Pants with pockets and studded belt

Removable surgical cap

Surgical mask printed on head

Surgeon This smooth operator comes with syringe and X-ray minifigure accessories.

Patient's X-ray shows a broken rib!

Helmet has cheek pieces and neck guard.

Roman Soldier From helmet to sandals, this Soldier Minifigure's costume is fully authentic.

Lightning wings and arrows pattern

Sandals printed on sides as well as front of feet

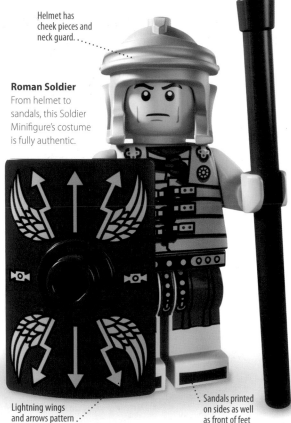

SERIES 6

Series 6 introduced 18 new pieces and contained the largest number of new head molds in any assortment at that point—three. The Roman Soldier, Clockwork Robot, and Surgeon were among the most sought after Minifigures from this set.

DID YOU KNOW?
Series 6, 7, and 8 featured an exciting range of fearless female Minifigures, such as the Intergalactic Girl, Viking Woman, and Downhill Skier.

Seven-pointed crown

Torch made from plume and telescope pieces

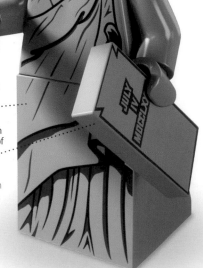

All parts except flame are sand green

Tile printed with America's date of independence

Lady Liberty The green color of Lady Liberty mimics the copper patina on the Statue of Liberty monument.

LEGO® FRIENDS

The new LEGO line for girls, LEGO Friends, proved to be an incredible success. Larger than standard minifigures and more stylized, the characters in these sets are known as mini dolls.

Shoe straps printed on legs.

Andrea A top with a musical note design is a perfect fit for songbird Andrea.

Ice-cream sundae

Dark red tie

Emma Mini doll Emma enjoys a refreshing ice cream by the pool in Emma's Splash Pool (3931).

Peter In the theme's launch year, its only male mini doll was Peter, Olivia's father.

Head cover has rabbit ears

Gold shell crown

Ocean King The stormy sea king's gold trident is right out of the LEGO® Atlantis theme.

Fish tail with silver scales

So far, only this little Minifigure has worn this hood in red

Rubbery basket used in LEGO Friends theme

Grandma Visitor This is the first female in the LEGO Minifigures theme to have short legs.

Aztec Warrior This Aztec knight wears a gold eagle helmet and feathered breastplate.

Green warpaint

Gold spear

Eagle feathers design

Bunny Suit Guy
A veggie diet has put a spring (or a hop) in this Minifigure's step.

Giant carrot accessory

Swim cap so tight it has wrinkles

Winner's medal

SERIES 7
When Series 7 hit the stores, it brought 16 new parts and more printing than any LEGO Minifigures collection to date. Its rarest Minifigures were the Aztec Warrior, Bunny Suit Guy, and Ocean King.

Swimming Champion
The swimmer's medal would resurface in the Team GB series.

Brawny Boxer
Team GB's lion head logo appears on the Brawny Boxer's headguard.

Blue mouth guard protects smile

Large boxing gloves

Horse Rider
The Rider's helmet will later be worn by two minifigures in the LEGO Friends theme.

Helmet and hair molded as one piece

Team GB sash

TEAM GB
Nine Minifigure athletes were produced to commemorate the 2012 London Olympic Games. Each came with a white stand and gold medal. All of these Minifigures were available only in the United Kingdom and Ireland.

New Santa hat

Short, detachable beard

Glaring red eyes

Sack bulging with gifts

Santa Santa's sack accessory can be gripped by minifigure hands or attached to a brick.

Helmet has antennae

RESISTANCE IS ... JUST GOING TO BE FRUSTRATING FOR YOU.

Magenta skis coordinate with jacket

Conquistador
This seeker of gold wears a metallic gold breastplate over his dark red torso.

Detachable plume

Helmet is metallic gold

Goggles shield eyes from glare

Standard Skull

Ruffle is separate

Actor Alas, poor Actor! He wears a scratchy ruffle that feels a bit uncomfortable during long plays.

Claw arm

Laser weapon made from ray gun and red bar

Evil Robot
Robot armor covers this Minifigure's torso and legs. Under his helmet, his face is silver metal with rivets.

Ski poles

Downhill Skier Colors taken from the LEGO Friends theme adorn this Minifigure's gear.

SERIES 8
Series 8 had a more even distribution of Minifigures than past releases, making it easier for fans to collect a complete set. The Downhill Skier was possibly slightly more difficult to find.

LEGO® MONSTER FIGHTERS

The LEGO Monster Fighters theme focused on Lord Vampyre's evil plan to use the powerful Moonstones to help monsters to rule the world. Only the valiant Monster Fighters could stop him! Heroes and Monsters clashed in nine sets in this one-year line. Although some of the Monsters had appeared in previous LEGO sets, they all got new heads and torsos for this play theme.

Blunt-ended foil keeps vampires at bay

I KNOW THE MONSTERS ARE DOWN THERE ... THAT'S WHY I'M UP HERE!

New color for bowler hat this year

Harpoon clips to topknot

Crossbow

Garlic and stakes attached to belt

Ann Lee Ann's two faces—one smirking and one scowling—both bear a scar left by a witch's nail.

Blunderbuss weapon topped by pearl gold cone

Telescopic eye

Unique steam-powered artificial leg

Dr. Rodney Rathbone
The dapper minifigure team leader appears in three Monster Fighters sets.

Silver bullets to take down werewolves

Major Quinton Steele This old-school minifigure hunter has werewolf teeth as a trophy on his printed belt.

Hammer held by steam-powered artificial arm

Slicked-back hair

Bushy beard and eyebrows

Twin pistols

Pink moonstone coveted by zombies

Jack McHammer Jack's hammer was first wielded this year by the Thor minifigure in the LEGO Marvel Super Heroes theme.

Frank Rock Biker Frank rarely takes his shades off, but his alternative face shows him with uncovered eyes.

FIGHTERS

All five Monster Fighter minifigures in the theme feature new heads, new torsos, new printed legs (except Rathbone), and all appear in at least two sets.

Head bandages coming undone

Mummy This is the first mummy minifigure with glow-in-the-dark details.

Tightly wrapped torso and legs

Hair piece has huge bat ears attached

New arm pieces have bat wings attached

Shaggy fur pattern printed on torso

MONSTERS

One of the Monsters—the Swamp Creature—had never appeared in any LEGO set prior to this. Like the Werewolf, Swamp Creature, Mummy, and the Zombie Bride and Groom, he appeared in just one set in the theme.

Unique head with bared teeth

Glow-in-the-dark claws attach to minifigure hands

Detachable head cover with fins

Manbat Two toothy Manbat minifigures defend Lord Vampyre's abode in the Vampyre Castle (9468).

Hair piece has widow's peak

Special bat moonstone accessory

Werewolf Both the torso and legs of the minifigure Werewolf are printed with ripped clothing.

Seaweed and scales pattern on legs

Swamp Creature Big, froglike eyes peer through eyeholes in this minifigure's head cover.

Cloth cape with huge, pointed collar

Lord Vampyre A red moonstone gives Lord Vampyre power over all other Monster minifigures.

Double-ended saberstaff

Zabrak tattoos on face

Darth Maul This same Maul also came in an equally rare Mini Sith Infiltrator set, available only at the 2012 San Diego Comic-Con.

Yellow eyes on chrome silver head

Pattern on both sides of torso

TC-14 The only existing female protocol droid minifigure was the second promotional giveaway on May the Fourth.

Exposed wires on torso

"REVENGE OF THE FIFTH"

The unofficial *Star Wars* Day on May the Fourth was followed by a cleverly titled "Revenge of the Fifth" day. To celebrate, the LEGO Group offered two exclusive minifigures free with LEGO.com and LEGO store purchases.

New hair piece with integral gold headdress

Gold patterns on royal robe

IF YOU ONLY KNEW HOW LONG IT TAKES TO PUT ON THIS GET-UP ....

Queen Amidala This is the first Padmé minifigure to show her dressed as the Queen of Naboo.

Unique new piece for skirt

Helmet with breathing mask and vision enhancer

LEGO *STAR WARS*

The big news for LEGO *Star Wars* in 2012 was the arrival of Queen Amidala. Padmé Amidala (or Padmé Naberrie) minifigures had been around since 1999, but this was her first appearance as queen. It featured in only one set, Gungan Sub (9499). Other highlights of the year were a more detailed Gamorrean Guard and the debut of bounty hunter Boushh.

Thermal detonator

Boushh Removing this minifigure's helmet reveals its true identity. It isn't Boushh the bounty hunter at all—it's actually Princess Leia in disguise!

Helmet dented by past battles

Short blaster gun

Gun is pistol set in a lightsaber hilt

Boba Fett A new Boba minifigure has orange kneepads and silver boots

Stormtrooper The 2012 Stormtrooper has a new head with a black balaclava hidden under his old standard helmet.

Dotted mouth

Spatters on classic helmet

Orange pauldron shoulder pad

Tatooine Stormtrooper Dirt stains cover 2012's second new Stormtrooper.

Armor printed on new torso

DID YOU KNOW?
Padmé has appeared in five minifigure versions, three of them under her family name of Naberrie.

LEGO® CUUSOO

LEGO CUUSOO was the original name for the LEGO Ideas theme, which allows fans to design sets and submit them online to the LEGO Group. The best designs may be made into real LEGO sets. The Hayabusa Unmanned Asteroid Explorer (21101) was the second CUUSOO set produced, and the first available worldwide. It featured this minifigure of a Hayabusa project manager.

Junichiro Kawaguchi The only minifigure in the Hayabusa set (21101) is the space project's manager.

JABBA THE HUTT

This second version of Jabba is more detailed than the one that appeared in 2003, and features a head that can swivel 360 degrees. His hands are capable of holding minifigure accessories.

Jabba the Hutt The head and torso of this Hutt figure are made as one piece.

Tattoo on right arm

Faint stripes indicate skin wrinkles

Seagull The Sea Captain's faithful friend perches on his hand when it wants a rest.

Hockey stick Over the years, sporting minifigures have made use of tennis racquets, baseball bats, and pool cues, too!

Frying pan Watch out! The Governor's Daughter is wielding a big silver frying pan and she looks pretty cross!

Maracas It's party time! Clip on the Maraca Man's colorful maracas and watch him shake them to the beat.

Shovel Minifigure shovels have been around since 1978, but 2019 saw the first green one—for scooping up after dogs!

Briefcase and ticket This Passenger minifigure looks businesslike with his briefcase accessory. Clip his ticket to his hand and off he goes to board the train.

MINI GEAR

MINIFIGURES WERE given C-shaped hands so they could carry things—and they have certainly carried a lot of things! LEGO® minifigure gear can be practical, such as a sword for defending the king's treasure or a tool used on the job, or just for fun, such as a piece of sports equipment or a magic wand. The kind of gear they carry helps to distinguish one minifigure from another and is great for role-play. For example, the crook might have the stolen money in his hand but the police officer is ready for him with the handcuffs! Watch for new gear every year.

Money There's a sinister squid on the loose! The Squidman minifigure flees the scene of the crime, carrying his stolen loot in his hand.

Pom-poms
The Cheerleader's hands fit securely inside her blue and white pom-poms.

Handcart The Railway Employee minifigure transports the passengers' luggage. He doesn't look very thrilled about it!

Sword Cole from LEGO NINJAGO clutches tightly to the engraved hilt of his long katana sword.

Tarot cards The Fortune Teller is never seen without her trusty tarot cards. Printed on 1x2 tiles, one shows the sun and the other a tower.

Magic wand Abracadabra! Clip the Magician's wand into his hand and he's ready to conjure up a spell.

Parrot Pieces of eight! Every good pirate needs a parrot pal.

Tools The Harbor Worker is a busy man, but luckily tools like his handy wrench and mallet make life a little easier.

Trophy The Karate Master carries a golden miniature minifigure statuette. The perfect prize!

Paintbrush and palette
The Artist's paint-splattered palette and brush accessories were brand-new for 2011.

Steak and cleaver
The Butcher's brand-new T-bone steak has a bone to make it easier to hold.

Ax Minifigure firefighters have always carried axes, but 2019's CITY sets introduced the most realistic choppers on the block!

Police badge and handcuffs
The Policeman's badge is printed on a 1x2 tile. His handcuffs have a cylinder-shaped piece for a firm grip.

Pearl gold CHI harness gives Longtooth awesome power.

Battle scar on unique head mask

LET ME AT THOSE CROCS!

Longtooth This older foot soldier has spent many years on the Lion Tribe's front line, where all the action is—and his minifigure has the battle scars to prove it!

LEGO LEGENDS OF CHIMA

Tribes of sentient animals clash over a mysterious source of power called CHI in this exciting new theme. Its story centers on the battle for control of CHI between the powerful Lion and Crocodile Tribes, which then draws other tribes of Chima into battle. In 2013, LEGO Legends of Chima featured more than 30 new minifigures, all with completely new designs and accessories.

Eagles have the same wings as Ravens, but in white

Unique head mask features flowers and happy grin!

G'lonna This lovable little girl Gorilla likes to adorn her fur with braided vines and pretty pink flowers.

Eris The gleaming gold tiara on Eris' head shows that she is the daughter of one of the Eagle Tribe's Ruling Council Members.

G'lonna stores her CHI in a decorative harness

Legs feature feathers, talons, and Eagle Tribe armor

2013

LEGO® FANS WERE INTRODUCED

to a whole new world of play in 2013 with the launch of LEGO® Legends of Chima™, a fantasy theme set in a world where animals rule and the power of CHI is the key to peace… or empire. But there were plenty of other high-stakes conflicts going on this year, as the ninja of Ninjago battled a Stone Army, LEGO® Galaxy Squad fought off a bug invasion, and two new licensed themes— LEGO® Teenage Mutant Ninja Turtles™ and LEGO® *The Lone Ranger*™—took the battle between good and evil to new heights.

Only Laval is important enough to wear this unique head mask!

HEROIC TRIBES

The brave Lions, quirky Eagles, and laid-back Gorillas are allied in an effort to preserve peace and harmony in Chima. They want to ensure fair distribution of CHI for all tribes—even their hostile enemies!

Powerful CHI staff is a symbol of his high status in the tribe.

Lagravis Laval's father commands great respect as king of the Lion Tribe. The aging leader is the only Lion minifigure with a gray mane.

CHI-orb-encrusted crown

Royal armor features Lion Tribe symbols

Laval Dressed in a gleaming gold crown, a regal cape, and dark blue battle armor, Laval looks every inch the royal prince of the Lion Tribe!

Only Lagravis wears this elaborate CHI armor in pearl gold

LEGO® DC Universe Super Heroes Riddler has same purple hands in 2012.

Head mask with beak and feather texture fits over regular minifigure head piece

Peg leg is also worn by Alien Android in 2011 in LEGO® Alien Conquest theme

Rizzo This ragtag Raven has a silver peg leg and eyepatch made from scavenged metal.

Jagged scales poke through his gold head mask

King Crominus The gruff, tough king of the Croc Tribe has gold teeth to match his royal head mask.

I'M THE KING—DO WHAT I SAY AND MAKE IT SNAPPY!

Razcal This minifigure is in charge of valuing the Ravens' stolen treasures. The gold markings on his head mask suggest that he keeps some for himself!

Only Croc royalty wear capes

Battle scars over both eyes from numerous dogfights

TIME TO CHI UP!

Worriz is first minifigure to wear this jagged cape

Wakz wears scary-looking fangs on his leg straps

Wakz Bushy eyebrows and white whiskers mark this minifigure out as the oldest warrior of the Wolf Tribe.

Red robe features animal bones

Sharp claws

Crawley This formidable foot soldier's tough scales provide natural body armor, so all he wears in battle is a red bandanna and a loin cloth.

VILLAIN TRIBES
Motivated by greed, the Crocodiles want to seize control of all the CHI in Chima. They persuade the ferocious Wolves and sharp-tongued Ravens to side with them and do battle against the Lions and their allied tribes for power.

Vine necklace has a place for storing CHI

Worriz His minifigure's gray cape shows that Worriz is the lead negotiator of the Wolf Tribe, but that doesn't mean he is the boss—all members of the pack are equal.

Freckled face

Pepper Potts Iron Man's loyal assistant is exclusive to Iron Man: Malibu Mansion Attack (76007). Turn her head around to see her scared expression.

Iron Man This minifigure has an updated torso, with arc reactor and gold Heartbreaker armor.

Arc reactor

Transparent blue jets

LEGO® MARVEL SUPER HEROES

The armored Avenger Iron Man flew into battle in sets based on the movie *Iron Man 3*. From his Malibu mansion to a high-speed chase over water, Tony Stark challenged the forces of the Mandarin with the help of War Machine. Other minifigures this year included Dr. Doom, Nova, and Venom.

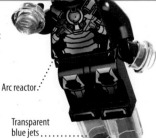

Dual-sided head: confident and scared

Tony Stark The first ever minifigure of Tony Stark appears in Iron Man: Malibu Mansion Attack (76007).

War Machine Wearing the same helmet as Iron Man, but in gray, this minifigure comes with a shoulder gun and transparent red repulsors and jets.

Shoulder gun

Dual-sided head: neutral and angry

"Danger" printed on torso

LEGO® MINIFIGURES

The collectible LEGO Minifigures theme reached its landmark tenth series in 2013, celebrating with the rare and remarkable Mr. Gold. But the year's shiny star would have been the first to admit: none of it could have been possible without the hardworking Minifigures of series 9, and the characters in series 11 were some of the very best yet!

I'D LIKE TO THANK MY DESIGNER.

Award for her role in "The 7-Stud Brick"

Diamond pendant

Hollywood Starlet This icon of the plastic screen wears a stylish dress with precisely 372 stars printed on it.

Tattered top hat

Mr. Good and Evil This character has a split personality after an experiment went wrong. Even his clothes and face are divided—one side torn and messy, the other side neat and tidy.

Potions bottle containing suspicious purple liquid

WHY DID I CROSS THE ROAD?

Large wings

Chicken Suit Guy This is the first minifigure to have a torso with arms that are the same from the front and back.

Claws for pretending to scratch the soil

SERIES 9

The year's first series could hardly have been more varied, boasting monsters, movie stars, and more! A new roller skate piece also made its debut—in the first of almost 100 set appearances to date.

Traditional British court dress

Brand-new gavel

Judge The ceremonial wig worn by this formidable character is new this year.

Helmet with unique star printing

Roller Derby Girl Don't try to stop this roller-skater— her super-fast wheels mean she's not going to slow down for anything!

New roller skate design can attach to LEGO studs

EXCLUSIVE MINIFIGURE

This 19th-century Toy Soldier minifigure is exclusive to DK's LEGO® *Minifigures Character Encyclopedia*. Although he carries a rifle, this is just for dress purposes and his real mission is to find a fun adventure and make new friends.

A black version of this helmet first appeared in the LEGO® Pirates sets in 1989.

Toy Soldier This smiling, bright-eyed and rosy-cheeked minifigure wears the uniform of a Napoleonic era British soldier.

SERIES 10

Not everyone could own a Mr. Gold, but there were no disappointments to be found in the series 10 mystery bags! The Roman Commander had legions of fans, and there was a real buzz around Bumblebee Girl . . . .

Helmet first appeared on the Roman Soldier.

Reading glasses

"Shhh!" is written on the mug—a message for those who make noise!

Librarian The *Oranges and Peaches* title on the Librarian's book comes from a joke about a mishearing of *On the Origin of Species* by Charles Darwin.

A comb-over to hide balding

Grandpa Although he dislikes anything new, Grandpa's bald cap is a brand-new hair piece.

Bumblebee Girl This is the first female costumed LEGO Minifigures character.

Wolf symbol represents Rome

Classy gold monocle

Roman Commander Fans requested this character to command the Roman Soldier from Series 6.

Stylish gold tie

Mr. Gold Just 5,000 editions of this dazzling character were created to celebrate the 10th series of LEGO Minifigures. Mr. Gold is also the only character that can't be found in every box of Minifigure bags.

Hiked-up pants

Old news is good news

Fancy gold suit

First time this pot has featured printing

Same wings as the Series 8 Fairy, but clear rather than transparent-blue

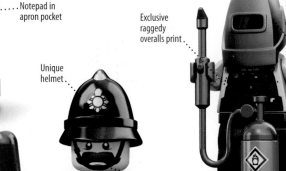

I LOVE WORKING ON SUNDAES!

Hair like whipped cream

Ice cream piece has come in 11 colors since 1995

Diner waitress LEGO designer Tara Wike inspired the look of this retro roller-skater, hence her "Tara" name badge.

Notepad in apron pocket

Hair is braided into pigtails at back

Pretzel piece found in more than 20 sets

Printed fabric skirt piece

Pretzel Girl This traditionally dressed Bavarian minifigure shares her passion for pretzels with the Lederhosen Guy from series 8.

SERIES 11

Minifigures conquered the world in series 11! Diner Waitress, Constable, and Pretzel Girl were icons of American, British, and Bavarian culture respectively, while the Yeti hailed from the dizzy heights of the Himalayas!

Crow can be detached from hat

Buttons for eyes and stitched-on smile

Pitchforks first seen in LEGO Castle theme

Scarecrow His bird friend might not think he's scary, but this straw man is always outstanding in his field!

Ear of corn in top pocket

Unique helmet

Exclusive raggedy overalls print

Welding mask hides oil-spattered face

Gloved hands protect against the heat

Truncheon later used by dentist in Assembly Square (10255)

Chinstrap printed on head piece

Constable There have been lots of LEGO police officers over the years, but none as smartly dressed as this classic British bobby!

Welder This masked Minifigure wields a new welding torch piece. It has since been used as a fancy light fitting!

Same head mold used for 2015's Square Foot Minifigure

Yellowed fangs

Ice lolly piece introduced in 1998

Yeti Some call him abominable, but the only scary thing about this snowman is the state of his teeth!

Frosty fur printed on legs

LEGO® TEENAGE MUTANT NINJA TURTLES™

Turtle power was back with this new theme based on the Nickelodeon TV series. Leonardo, Raphael, Donatello, and Michelangelo minifigures teamed up to fight the evil Shredder and the Kraang, aliens from Dimension X who resemble brains and inhabit robot minifigure bodies. Sets included the Turtle Lair Attack (79103) and the Stealth Shell in Pursuit (79102).

Sculpted red bandanna

The four Turtles have different torso designs

Raphael Hot-headed Raph has a chip knocked out of the shell on his torso.

Raph carries a sai—a traditional martial arts weapon—in each hand.

Angry grimace

Leo always wears blue

Katana sword

Leonardo Like his brothers, Leo has a specially molded head with a unique facial expression and colored bandanna.

Knee pads are essential when crawling through sewers

Long rat ears

Furry chest peeks through

Fierce, gap-toothed grin

Bō staff with extra blade

Sloped piece with kimono flower pattern

Splinter The Turtles' sensei debuts a new sculpted rat head piece.

Burn scars to face and eye.

Claws are also worn by Setam, a warrior minifigure in the 2010 LEGO® *Prince of Persia*™ theme.

Shredder The Turtles' archenemy looks fearsome in spiky armor and wielding trademark shredder claws.

Donatello This brainy minifigure prefers talking to fighting, but he can use his deadly Bō staff when he needs to.

New turtle shell piece. The shell is also printed on the back of the Turtles' torsos.

Shell attaches to back with neck bracket

Michaelangelo Mikey's tongue is stuck out in concentration. Another 2013 variant has an excited smile.

Unique orange elf hair piece

Armed with two daggers

Elvish ears attached to hair piece

Camouflaged warrior clothing printed on torso and legs

Tauriel The Elvish Guard of Mirkwood wields gold-and-silver daggers that originated with the 2010 *Prince of Persia*™ theme.

Same hair piece as 2012 Legolas, with braid running down back

Legolas Greenleaf This version of the elf appears in just one set, dressed in forest attire for Escape from Mirkwood Spiders (79001).

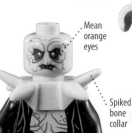

Golden chain mail

Mean orange eyes

Spiked bone collar

Yazneg Scars and wrinkles mark the torso and bare head of the Orc commander minifigure.

High-rise pants printed on torso and legs

Arms uniquely printed in pearl gold

Bald patch printed on hair piece

Unique beard piece includes extra padding to bulk out stomach

Tasty sausage

Bombur The many dwarves in the LEGO *The Hobbit* theme all have beard and hair pieces unique to their individual figure.

Goblet raised for a toast

Balin Like his fellow dwarf minifigures, Balin stands on short LEGO legs. His alternative face bears a frown.

Unique new one-piece hair and beard

New hair piece worn by all hobbits.

Mouth opened wide in worried expression

Torso printed with traditional hobbit clothing

Bilbo Baggins The first of two Bilbo minifigures wears a full hobbit suit. The other wears just pants, a shirt, and braces.

The One Ring

Chain mail seen through shirt opening

Thorin Oakenshield Dwarf leader Thorin shares his new hair piece mold with minifigures Kili and Fili, also from *The Hobbit* theme.

LEGO® *THE HOBBIT*™

Based on the prequel films to *The Lord of the Rings* trilogy, the launch of LEGO *The Hobbit: An Unexpected Journey* featured eight sets depicting movie scenes. All of the major characters were represented, with Gandalf, Gollum, and Legolas also appearing in *The Lord of the Rings* sets. It was a fantastic year for hobbits and dwarves, who also turned up as microfigures in a new LEGO game.

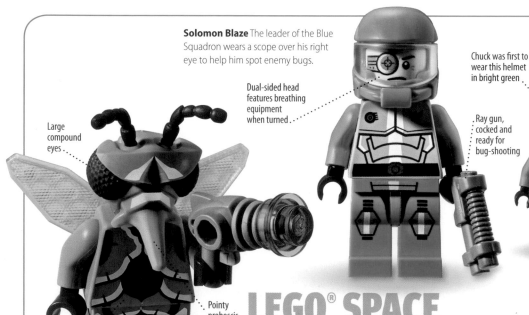

Solomon Blaze The leader of the Blue Squadron wears a scope over his right eye to help him spot enemy bugs.

Dual-sided head features breathing equipment when turned

Large compound eyes

Exoskeleton

Pointy proboscis

Winged Alien Mosquitoid This minifigure has a winged element, introduced in 2013, which attaches with a neck bracket.

Chuck was first to wear this helmet in bright green

Ray gun, cocked and ready for bug-shooting

Exclusive head features thick eyelashes and blue lips

Chuck Stonebreaker This minifigure is cross. Very cross. He hates the color green.

Ashlee Starstrider This Orange Squadron team member wears the latest fashion in space—blue lipstick!

Sharp fangs

Alien Mantizoid If his face isn't enough to scare the Galaxy Squad, then this Alien's two sharp blade weapons certainly will!

Only Billy wears this helmet in red

Billy Starbeam As leader of the Red Squadron, Billy tells his team what to do—which is always to get the bugs. Zap!

LEGO® SPACE

Got a flyswatter handy? The year 2013 saw the launch of a new Space subtheme: LEGO Galaxy Squad. Summoned to Earth by Lord Vampyre from the LEGO Monster Fighters theme, the alien bugs swarm through space—and only Galaxy Squad can stop them! The subtheme features Red, Blue, Green, and Orange teams versus a powerful (if not too smart!) menace.

Frodo Baggins The adventuring hobbit comes with a new, double-sided head in 2013, and no longer wears a cape.

Worried expression

Brown jacket, with red vest, as in 2012

Frodo's other face displays an angry scowl.

Gríma Wormtongue The evil adviser to King Théoden looks sinister in his dark, subdued robes.

Sunken eyes

Patterned neckline

Ornate chain necklace

New hair piece similar to Elrond's, but without the braided detailing

Double-sided head can be either smiling or frowning

Elven dress printed on torso and sloped piece

Arwen This elf became the first female minifigure of the theme, appearing alongside her father Elrond in set 79006.

LEGO® THE LORD OF THE RINGS™

The most famous fantasy series of all continued its epic journey in 2013. Five more sets depicted some of the best-known scenes from all three movies. New versions of minifigures were revealed, and even more joined the action, with many featuring new headgear and hair pieces. The adventure continued with new releases later in the year.

Aragorn This version of the heir of Gondor has a new torso and legs, ready for battle in set 79007.

Red elvish cloak

Bears same expression as in 2012 sets

White tree of Gondor printed on armor

Braided hair with silver detailing

Orange fabric cloak

Long red coat continues on to legs

Elrond The Third Age version of Elrond shows him to be older, with silver lining his hair, and dressed for life in Rivendell rather than battle.

Wrinkled face partly concealed by bushy beard

Black-and-white wizard's staff

Saruman
Saruman the White battles Gandalf the Gray in The Wizard Battle (79005).

Standard cloth cape, in white

Unique helmet

Snarling teeth

Silver chains printed on torso

Ghostly skeleton features printed on face and torso

Crown in an eerie green color

Simple belt detailing on torso

White wizard's staff

Mouth of Sauron This evil messenger makes one exclusive appearance. The face beneath his helmet has a mouth but no eyes.

King of the Dead The leader of the Soldiers of the Dead marshals his minifigure troops to battle in Pirate Ship Ambush (79008).

Gandalf the White His cloak and clothes might be all-new, but Gandalf's distinctive bushy eyebrows and kindly eyes are clearly visible beneath his new white hair and beard piece.

LEGO® FRIENDS
Following on from its massive success in 2012, LEGO Friends returned in 2013. Twenty-three new sets continued to expand the world of Heartlake City and the adventures of the original five girls.

Glasses printed on unique face

Surfer-style ruffled hair piece

Ms. Stevens The teacher at Heartlake High is one of several brand-new mini dolls for 2013.

Matthew The third male mini doll to feature in the theme, artistic Matthew attends Heartlake High.

Legs also used on Peter's mini doll figure in 2012

Aquaman
Usually seen wielding his powerful trident, Aquaman wears a belt with the symbol of Atlantis on it.

Muscular torso with scales

LEGO® DC UNIVERSE SUPER HEROES

Batman returned to the world of LEGO building this year, accompanied by Superman. The Caped Crusader battled his foes in a new version of Arkham Asylum (10937) and teamed up with Aquaman against Mr. Freeze. Superman was kept busy challenging General Zod in sets based on the *Man of Steel* movie.

Arctic Batman
Wearing an Arctic camouflage Batsuit in preparation for taking on Mr. Freeze, this variant is exclusive to Arctic Batman vs. Mr. Freeze: Aquaman on Ice (76000).

Dual-sided head: frowning or determined

White headband worn underneath cowl

Cape is shorter than previous variants

Staff

Movie Batman Exclusive to set The Bat vs. Bane: Tumbler Chase (76001), this minifigure features a copper-colored belt and black Batman logo.

Robin The addition of a hood rather than a hair piece makes this variant of Robin look unusually scary!

New suit with silver-and-gold detail

Superman Something has made Superman angry—one side of his dual-sided head features red eyes.

Hair piece is the same as the Black Widow from the LEGO® Marvel Super Heroes theme, seen in 2012

Lois Lane Making her debut in minifigure form this year, Lois appears in Superman: Black Zero Escape (76009).

Gray buttoned vest and shirt

DID YOU KNOW?
This is the first minifigure appearance of Dr. Harleen Quinzel, although she was seen as Harley Quinn in 2012.

TIME FOR ANOTHER "FOWL" CRIME!

Freeze gun

Eye can now be seen through monocle

2013 head piece features more wrinkles than the 2006 variant

Silver fish accessory

The Penguin Back to rain on Batman's parade, this version of the Penguin features a new torso, legs, and head piece.

Harley Quinn costume poking through

ID badge

2006 variant is wearing a black wizard hat

The other side of head features red eyes

Mr. Freeze
Minus his trademark goggles, Mr. Freeze's icy blue eyes are revealed. His helmet was first seen in 2011 in the Atlantis theme.

Sunken red eyes

General Zod's emblem: a sideways omega symbol

Dr. Harleen Quinzel
Psychiatrist Dr. Quinzel's hair piece can be interchanged with a red-and-black jester's hat.

Scarecrow
The nightmarish Scarecrow has a new, more detailed head and a dark brown wizard hat.

General Zod There are two variants of General Zod; in the other, he is wearing his combat armor.

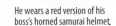

Each of the ninja received a new elemental sword this year

Silver, three-point crown shows he has reached ZX status

Kozu is armed with two scimitar swords

He wears a red version of his boss's horned samurai helmet

> WOW, WHO'S YOUR TAILOR, KOZU?

> THIS GUY IN THE UNDERWORLD.

This jagged sword element is only carried by the NINJAGO warriors

Protective shoulder pauldrons

Blue-and-silver color scheme for the Ninja of Lightning

Jay Kimono This new variant of ninja Jay wields a powerful new Lightning blade!

Elaborate red-and-white armor covers his torso extension piece

General Kozu
Look out, ninja! Lord Garmadon's scariest soldier is taller than a regular minifigure thanks to his unique torso extension piece.

Lower body is a standard minifigure torso

Lloyd Golden Ninja When Lloyd Garmadon turns into the Ultimate Spinjitzu Master, he becomes gold from minifigure head to foot!

Green-and-gold elemental robes

Sword hilt is a telescope piece

LEGO® NINJAGO®

Entering its third year, NINJAGO ramped up the action as the ninja faced off against Lord Garmadon and an army of ancient stone warriors. The ninja now wore elemental robes and carried powerful new weapons, but it took the appearance of a gold ninja and an awesome new dragon to finally end the latest threat.

Ice-white ninja head wrap

Gold warrior symbol

Arms are in Kai's elemental color

New helmet with crest and mask

Horned staff matches his intimidating helmet

Evil-looking red eyes

This torso extender piece was first introduced on his 2012 variant

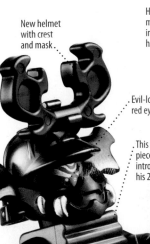

Lord Garmadon
Master Wu's four-armed, evil brother has a special torso extender piece to fit his extra limbs!

Zane Kimono Ninja of Ice Zane wears a black, white, and gold kimono for the first time in Garmatron (70504).

Kai Kimono Kai and his fellow ninja minifigures wear their elemental robes when they battle Lord Garmadon and his Stone Army.

Ninja leg wraps

Cole Kimono This variant of Cole has ZX (Zen Extreme) ninja status, but he wears a formal kimono instead of his regular ZX robes.

Purple belt extends from lower torso to leg piece

LEGO® BRAND STORES

These three minifigures were offered to 300 lucky customers in a promotion at the grand opening of the LEGO Store in Watford, United Kingdom. Packaging for the range featured Watford Junction railway station.

Signaling paddle

LEGO Friends Mia also rode this skateboard in 2012

Passenger
Dressed warmly for a long wait, the Passenger looks happy that his train isn't delayed.

Station Master
This busy worker lets the train driver minifigures know when the train is ready to depart.

Skateboarder
The Skateboarder isn't allowed to ride his board at the station.

LEGO® STAR WARS™

A big drum roll in the LEGO *Star Wars* universe this year was for the debuts of a whole host of new characters in minifigure form and new versions of familiar minifigures, including Yoda and Darth Maul. Also, 2013 heralded the release of *The Yoda Chronicles*, an animated mini-series created by the LEGO Group featuring the wise green Jedi Master and other favorite characters.

Poggle the Lesser With his specially sculpted head, the Archduke of Geonosis makes his debut in Duel on Geonosis (75017).

Beardlike tendrils

Gold armor printing

Trans-clear wings

Jango Fett The redesigned variant of the renowned bounty hunter features silver armor and knee pad printing on the legs.

Pistol accessory

The Gran species has three eyes

Prominent head crest

Same head piece as Professor Snape from the Harry Potter™ theme

Same hair piece as Draco Malfoy from the Harry Potter™ theme, but in white

General Rieekan This brave rebel general appears for the first time in 2013, sporting a new thermal jacket to keep him warm on icy Hoth.

Count Dooku With distinctive eyebrows and slicked-back hair, the third incarnation of Dooku bears a close resemblance to actor Christopher Lee, who played him in the movies.

Two-sided head has a snarling expression on the other side

Coleman Trebor Making his minifigure debut in AT-TE (75019), the Vurk Jedi Master has a specially molded gray head piece.

Ree-Yees With a three-eyed head created just for him, this lawless creature works on Jabba's Sail Barge (75020).

THE MOVIE SAGA

Among the many sets released this year were the all-new Rancor Pit (75005) and a new version of Jabba's Sail Barge (75020). The Rancor Pit set was designed as an add-on to Jabba's Palace (9516), released in 2012.

Bulbous eyes

Long, droopy ears of the Ortolan species

Wrench for fixing starfighter equipment

Alternative face print has no visor

Rebel insignia

Snowspeeder Luke Wearing a pressurized g-suit, Luke is ready for action against the Imperial forces in the Battle of Hoth (75014).

Max Rebo Jabba the Hutt's musician is entirely blue; 75020 is the character's sole set appearance in more than 20 years of LEGO *Star Wars*.

A-wing Rebel Pilot This redesigned pilot, who first appeared in 2000, has a completely new helmet and a new dark green flight suit.

Loose white straps

Life-support chest pack printing is more detailed than on Luke's 2010 flight suit

Printed braid is longer than on 2002 variant

Padmé was the first minifigure to wear this hair piece

Printed eyes seen on classic Yoda for the first time

Small curved ears

Two-sided head piece also shows determined face

Pockets and straps printed on legs

Episode II Anakin Skywalker This variant of Anakin features him wearing Hawkeye's hair piece from the LEGO Marvel Super Heroes theme.

Padmé Amidala Padmé may look happy, but her back features scratch marks made by the Nexu beast in the Geonosian Arena.

Yoda It's all about Yoda in 2013! He has a new molded head piece featuring a focused expression.

THE CLONE WARS

The Clone Wars raged throughout LEGO *Star Wars* in 2013, with new sets including Z-95 Headhunter (75004) and the Mandalorian Speeder (75022), which featured a new Maul minifigure.

Huge bounty hunter blaster rifle

Rako's trademark facial tattoo

Rako Hardeen This minifigure is really Obi-Wan Kenobi in disguise. Luckily for him, the face tattoo isn't permanent!

Double-sided head shows eyes crackling with power

Jek-14 The Force-enhanced clone is the first minifigure to have a transparent arm.

Modified clone trooper helmet

THE YODA CHRONICLES

The Jek 14's Starfighter set (75018) was based on three-part animated mini-series *The Yoda Chronicles*. It featured the first *Star Wars* character to be created jointly by The LEGO Group and Lucasfilm—the mighty Jek-14.

Togruta have striped head-tails

HEADS OR TAILS ... OR BOTH?

Turn Ahsoka's face and her expression changes to a huge grin

Ahsoka wields two lightsabers to defeat the Umbarans

Ahsoka Tano The 2013 minifigure features the same hair piece as her younger 2010 self, but she has a more grown-up look with new head, torso, and leg printing.

Four arms means Krell can wield two double-bladed lightsabers and still have a free pair of hands!

Krell has an extended torso with an additional pair of arms

Pong Krell The head, torso extension, and arms are all one piece, designed to show this all-new minifigure's distinctive jowled features.

Rare darksaber

Cyborg Maul Maul now walks on powerful cybernetic legs. Nothing can stop this fierce Sith warrior!

New torso for 2013

Clawlike robotic legs

Different head mold to classic Yoda in a brighter green, with longer ears and cartoonlike eyes.

White tufts of hair can be seen on the back of his head

Yoda This variant of Yoda features new torso printing with a hood on the reverse.

Two-sided head piece also shows Obi-Wan with a stern expression

Obi-Wan Kenobi This calm Jedi minifigure prefers to use his lightsaber to defend rather than to attack.

Jedi robes extend to legs

LEGO® CITY

Police and Fire took center stage this year, with a new Elite Police Force providing a lot of the action. Chase McCain and the Elite Police team tackle the toughest crimes and criminals, both in LEGO CITY sets and in a 2013 video game. Meanwhile, the Fire team got a new Fire Station (60004).

Conspicuous red crowbar

City Burglar Could you pick this minifigure out in a police line-up? His unique head with stubble and a scowl might help!

Police radio

Chase McCain This Chase first appeared in 2013, but an exclusive variant was also given away with preorders of the LEGO *CITY Undercover* video game in 2012.

Fireproof helmets have been worn by minifigures since 1978

New torso features a utility belt and air pressure gauge for breathing equipment

Firefighter This minifigure is wearing the regulation LEGO CITY firefighter uniform from 2013.

New striped torso features a rope for scaling buildings

Colorful hair printed on hood piece

Graffiti tag torso print

Drops of paint on foot

Wyldstyle Streetwise Lucy (to use her real name) appears in seven 2014 sets but wears her hood up in just one.

2014

MINIFIGURES WERE BIGGER than ever when they hit cinema screens in 2014! THE LEGO® MOVIE™ was a worldwide box office smash and, of course, there were plenty of themed LEGO sets to go with it. The year also saw minifigures and other LEGO creatures starting to populate the LEGO® Minecraft™ world, plus the debut of the LEGO® Ultra Agents and their fiendish foes. Things got a bit chilly in LEGO® CITY as brave explorers set off for the Arctic, and over in Chima a whole new range of tribes made their mark, from Bats to Mammoths!

THE LEGO MOVIE

The first ever big-screen LEGO adventure introduced the world to happy-go-lucky minifigure Emmet and his many friends in Bricksburg and its surrounding brick-built worlds. More than 20 sets depicted epic scenes from the movie, from Bad Cop Pursuit (set 70802) to Lord Business's Evil Lair (set 70809). Meanwhile, 16 collectible Minifigures included some of the movie's best cameo characters.

Unique metallic beard piece

Treasure chest stomach

LEGO Technic peg leg

MetalBeard The captain of the Sea Cow ship has a minifigure head and hat, but no other minifigure parts!

Only Emmet wears this hair piece

Emmet "The Special" wears the mysterious bright red Piece of Resistance on his back in eight THE LEGO MOVIE sets.

Neck bracket holds Piece of Resistance in place

DID YOU KNOW?
In THE LEGO MOVIE, the Piece of Resistance is really just the top from a tube of glue!

THE GOODIES

As "the Special," Emmet meets a host of heroes, from brave Wyldstyle and mystical Vitruvius to swashbuckling MetalBeard and star-trekking Benny. But it is the ordinary citizens of Bricksburg who finally save the day.

Deliberate broken look to helmet

Classic Space logo shows decades of wear

*SPACESHIP SPACESHIP **SPACESHIP!***

Flexible rubber horn piece

Unikitty Seven versions of the Cloud Cuckoo Land princess appeared in 2014, including Angry Kitty and Astro Kitty.

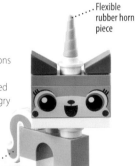

Brand-new tail element

Braces on teeth

Fabu-Fan This smiling inhabitant of Bricksburg wears her love for the 1980s' LEGO FABULAND theme (see p.21) with pride!

Logo used on sets from 1979 to 1989

Mike Monkey appeared in several FABULAND sets

Benny Based on LEGO Space minifigures from the 1970s and '80s, Benny is designed to look very well played with!

New hat mold with printed sheriff's star

Pistol piece found in more than 100 sets

Mustache cleverly disguises robot features

This smile is found in just one set.

Bad Cop A turn of the head transforms this tough guy into his alter ego, the far less intimidating Good Cop!

IS THERE SOMETHING STUCK IN MY TEETH?

Super Secret Police emblem

Same uniform worn by Officer Toque in THE LEGO® NINJAGO® MOVIE™

Helmet and cape shaped like a giant necktie

Unique shoulder armor

Boot tops are part of special leg piece

Each giant heel built from 28 pieces

THE BADDIES
No minifigure in THE LEGO MOVIE is really, really bad, but some of them give it a decent try! President Business is the big bad guy on the block, aided by his Super Secret Police force.

Sheriff Not-a-robot The shiny sheriff of the Super Secret Police in the Old Wild West is (whisper it) a robot!

Posable horse figure introduced in 2010

Lord Business President Business is ready to give Bricksburg the boot (or both very big boots) in his towering super-villain guise!

LOOKING FOR A SQUARE MEAL?

Poncho print matches hat and legs

Tacos are 1x1 tile pieces

Top hat and beard are all one piece

COLLECTIBLE MINIFIGURES
Variants of Emmet, Wyldstyle, President Business, and Bad Cop all feature in the first THE LEGO MOVIE collectible Minifigure range. Mostly, however, the selection is a chance for their lesser-known co-stars to shine!

Taco Tuesday Man Bricksburg's most famous marketing mascot is made from all-exclusive parts—with the exception of his tacos!

Exclusive Hawaiian shirt print

Opening lines of Gettysburg Address on printed tile

Abraham Lincoln The first minifigure of a US President is revealed to be a Master Builder in THE LEGO MOVIE!

They're literally right here!

Exclusive concerned face print

Mrs. Scratchen-Post This animal lover comes with one of her many feline friends and a unique cat-hair-covered costume!

Pouch for carrying cat treats

Unique hat slots into hair piece

"Where Are My Pants?" Guy The first minifigure to come with two sets of legs carries his spare pair as pants!

White hip piece serves as underpants

Ginger cat piece found in eight sets

Antique musket appears in almost 90 sets

Calamity Drone This Wild West dancer is secretly a robot agent for the villainous President Business. Can you tell?

Detailed dress print on sloped brick

LEGO® MINECRAFT™

The first LEGO set based on building-and-battling video game Minecraft was part of the LEGO® Ideas theme in 2012. A dedicated LEGO Minecraft theme launched the following year, and in 2014, this spawned the first Minecraft minifigures. Cube-shaped head pieces set these characters apart from traditional minifigures, while other new pieces were introduced to build the world's other blocky inhabitants.

Standard minifigure torso and legs

Pixelated pickax

Steve The theme's hero appears in all of 2014's minifigure-scale sets, armed with different tools, weapons, and armor. In some sets, Steve is brick-built.

DID YOU KNOW?
The heads of LEGO Minecraft minifigures are 1.5 studs wide.

New cube-shaped head

ZOMBIES? WE'RE JUST A MINER THREAT!

Blocky open collar print

Zombie These mean, green monsters menace Steve in two 2014 sets: The Cave (set 21113) and The Mine (set 21118).

New blocky bow-and-arrow piece

Skeleton Minecraft's bony bad guys have new square skulls on top of standard skeleton pieces found in other themes.

Torso first seen in LEGO® Castle sets

Enderman Three of these towering terrors go about their block-carrying business in The Ender Dragon (set 21117). Don't disturb them!

Squarely scary features!

Arms are sideways tile pieces

Torso, legs, and feet are all one piece

All four feet are one piece

Creeper This multilegged monster is made from just four pieces, including a new block-footed piece for creepy creeping!

Red minifigure head visible through eye slits

Breez This galactic hero was one of 15 robot figures released in 2014. She is made up of nine pieces.

LEGO® HERO FACTORY

A theme based around large figure builds (much like LEGO® BIONICLE®), LEGO Hero Factory ran from 2010 to 2015. It was not until 2014, however, that the sets started to include minifigure-scale characters.

LEGO® ULTRA AGENTS

Minifigure play met app-based missions with the launch of LEGO Ultra Agents. Each 2014 set related to a free-to-download story for smartphones and tablets, and playing through six interactive adventures unlocked exclusive building instructions. The action took place in Astor City and saw Solomon Blaze and his trainee Ultra Agents taking on a rogues' gallery of catastrophe-causing villains!

Scar beside right eyebrow

Cybernetic right leg

Solomon Blaze Last seen in 2008's LEGO® Space Galaxy Squad sets, the chief Ultra Agent is now an older and wiser minifigure!

Max Burns Just like his fellow Ultra Agents, this firebrand stunt driver has a name with flaming connotations!

ID badge with Ultra Agents symbol

Targeting visor is hidden when head piece is turned

Stud shooter new for 2014

Caila Phoenix This heroic martial artist and demolitions expert flies a jet pack in Ultra Agents Mission HQ (set 70165).

Unprinted areas of helmet reveal green details

Space Invader shirt print

Terabyte This techno-terror wears a unique transparent bright green hacking helmet, printed to mostly look like metal.

Cyber hacking blaster weapon

Transparent bright green head

Slime bombs strapped across chest

Retox A bowler hat can't disguise this radioactive wrongdoer! He is the slimy sidekick of chemical crime queen Toxikita.

Keychain hangs from belt

Helmet, shoulder armor, and chest plate are all one piece

Tremor Giant fighting fists and exclusive silver metallic armor make this bad guy look quite unlike any other minifigure!

Fists first seen in LEGO® Legends of Chima™ theme

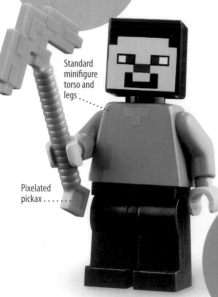
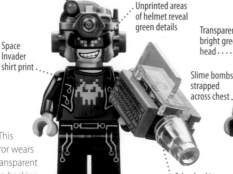

LEGO® MINIFIGURES

In its fifth year, this collectibles theme went digital with the LEGO® Minifigures Online game. Each Minifigure in Series 12 came with a code to access its counterpart in the massively multiplayer online world, with characters from older series unlocked via in-game achievements. The game was discontinued in fall 2016, but the physical Minifigures from 2014 are still going strong! This year also saw the release of The Simpsons as collectible Minifigures, with 16 familiar faces from Springfield.

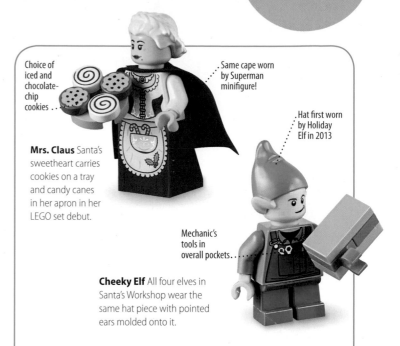

Spider kept in her pocket

Striped tights print under fabric skirt

Spooky Girl The first Minifigure to be entirely black, white, and gray carries the second all-monochrome bear!

Plume plugs into helmet

Pickax piece introduced in 1978.

Battle Goddess With an exclusive shield print, a new helmet piece, and a unique skirt, this warrior wins every time!

Long spear also wielded by Series 10 Warrior Woman in darker brown

Braces curve over plump belly

Headgear also used in a 2019 Chinese New Year set

Mythical winged horse design

Prospector This gold-digger's brand-new beard piece is also worn by Wiley Fusebot in THE LEGO MOVIE, albeit in reddish brown.

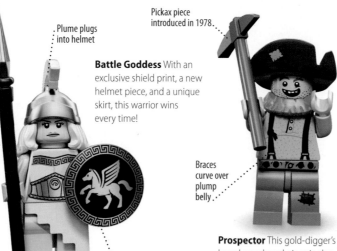

Choice of iced and chocolate-chip cookies

Same cape worn by Superman minifigure!

Hat first worn by Holiday Elf in 2013

Mrs. Claus Santa's sweetheart carries cookies on a tray and candy canes in her apron in her LEGO set debut.

Mechanic's tools in overall pockets

Cheeky Elf All four elves in Santa's Workshop wear the same hat piece with pointed ears molded onto it.

LEGO® CREATOR EXPERT

Advanced builders met many new minifigures in 2014. Parisian Restaurant (set 10243) and Fairground Mixer (set 10244) were populated by colorful townspeople, while Santa's Workshop (set 10245) featured four friendly elves, a minifigure Mrs. Claus, and the jolly red-suited fellow himself. This new addition to the Winter Village subtheme boasted 883 parts, including bricks to build four adult reindeer and a smaller calf without full antlers.

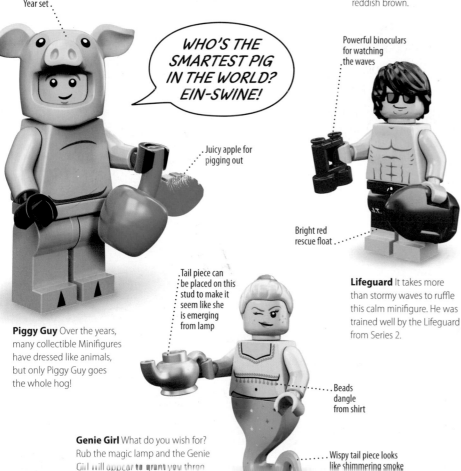

WHO'S THE SMARTEST PIG IN THE WORLD? EIN-SWINE!

Juicy apple for pigging out

Piggy Guy Over the years, many collectible Minifigures have dressed like animals, but only Piggy Guy goes the whole hog!

Powerful binoculars for watching the waves

Bright red rescue float

Lifeguard It takes more than stormy waves to ruffle this calm minifigure. He was trained well by the Lifeguard from Series 2.

Tail piece can be placed on this stud to make it seem like she is emerging from lamp

Beads dangle from shirt

Genie Girl What do you wish for? Rub the magic lamp and the Genie Girl will appear to grant you three wishes. Be sure to choose wisely!

Wispy tail piece looks like shimmering smoke

Clock tower

North Pole sign

Santa is ready to set off

String of Christmas lights across roof

Elf strokes a reindeer

Santa's Workshop (10245) Time to load up the sleigh! The set features four wrapped presents and four toys, including a yellow car and a blue spaceship.

Scutter The largest member of the Scorpion Tribe has six creepy-crawly legs and a spiky posable stinger!

Stinger tail made from click-hinge pieces

Unique firebird head mask

Exclusive head mask

Wings can move back and forth

Braptor The leader of the Bat Tribe boasts brand-new wing pieces that clip on to his armor.

Six eyes on head mask

Each leg is a LEGO Hero Factory talon

Two eyes visible through mask

Fire CHI in exclusive harness

Sparacon Two fangs, eight limbs, and eight beady eyes make this Spider Tribe soldier a scary sight!

Flame pattern on ceremonial robe

Fluminox This fiery Phoenix leads the only Legends of Chima tribe to be based on a mythical creature.

Ragged, battle-worn cape

Sir Fangar Like other members of the Ice Tribes, the leader of the Saber-Tooth Tigers has transparent icy body parts.

Transparent limbs new for 2014

Research Scientist This lab-coated chemist works alongside an astronomer and a paleontologist in the 165-piece Research Institute set.

Focused expression

Access-all-areas pass

More robust helmet than those of other classic astronauts

Space logo unchanged since 1978.

Yve Classic LEGO Space minifigures had never been seen in green before Yve and her fellow astronaut Pete.

LEGO® LEGENDS OF CHIMA™

At the start of its second year, Legends of Chima ventured into the Outlands, where tribes of Spiders, Scorpions, and Bats plotted to steal all the CHI in Chima for themselves! Then, in summer 2014, a wave of "Fire vs. Ice" sets introduced the ancient Phoenix Tribe and their Ice Clan enemies—made up of Saber-Tooth Tigers, Mammoths, and Vultures!

One of two facial expressions

The Flash Who knows why it took the Fastest Man Alive so long to make his debut as a minifigure!

Lightning bolt logo

Red hair and cowl are one piece

Batgirl For her first LEGO look, Barbara Gordon wears the costume seen in 2011's "New 52" comic books.

Exclusive lavender cape

Bat ears are part of hair piece.

Man-Bat This big-eared bad guy uses parts designed for the similarly named Manbat from the LEGO® Monster Fighters theme.

Wings move as part of special arms

LEGO® IDEAS

In 2014, LEGO® CUUSOO changed its name to LEGO Ideas but stayed focused on releasing sets suggested by fan designers. This year's sets included Exo Suit (set 21109)—featuring minifigures based on fan builder Peter Reid and his girlfriend Yve—and Research Institute (set 21110), based around three female scientist minifigures, intended to inspire girls with an interest in science.

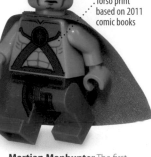

Piercing alien eyes

Torso print based on 2011 comic books

LEGO® DC COMICS SUPER HEROES

This year's DC Comics sets drew on the publisher's 80-year history to bring fans the first-ever minifigures of various heroes and villains. Nine sets were released in total, including two San Diego Comic-Con exclusives and two promotional minifigures. Batman's Tumbler (set 76023) became the largest set of the theme to date, boasting 1,869 pieces, including two special minifigures.

Martian Manhunter The first minifigure of this Justice League member was exclusive to LEGO Stores and LEGO.com.

Cowl hides second, more intense face

Batman of Zur-En-Arrh This colorful San Diego Comic-Con exclusive is the Batman-inspired protector of an alien world.

Costume first seen in a 1940 comic book

LEGO® CITY

CITY minifigures had to wrap up warm this year as they headed to the Arctic for the first time. A bright orange color scheme made the adventurers and vehicles stand out against the snow, and new polar bear and husky dog figures added animal magic to their missions. Ten Arctic sets were released in all, including ships, planes, plows, and snowmobiles.

Tinted glasses protect against Arctic glare

Clip-on ID badge

Arctic Research Assistant A hat, a gilet, a sweater, and gloves all contribute to the warmth of this minifigure's smile!

Arctic Captain This smiling sailor delivers vital supplies to the exploration team in his intrepid icebreaker ship.

Open version of Arctic Explorer's jacket

Chunky fisherman's sweater

Goggles are part of face print

NOBODY WARNED ME IT WOULD BE SO COLD!

Arctic Explorer Four sets feature this polar pioneer, who tries to keep nice and cozy inside her new hood piece.

Pole Star emblem on jacket

Climbing gear hangs from belt

Head turns to reveal super-angry face

Tiara, hair, and elven ears are all one piece

Witch-King If you dare take this minifigure into a darkened room, you'll see Sauron's second-in-command glow in the dark!

Unique crown piece

Glow-in-the-dark head

Galadriel The mightiest and fairest of all the elves is made from all-exclusive parts, including a sparkling cape.

LEGO® *THE HOBBIT*™

The final year for the Middle-earth theme focused on the third film in the Hobbit trilogy, *The Battle of the Five Armies*. Four sets depicted scenes from the film, with the largest—The Lonely Mountain (set 79018)—featuring an enormous figure of Smaug the fire-breathing dragon! Others included the fearsome Witch-King and Orc leader Azog, plus the first Galadriel minifigure.

Exclusive hook hand

Azog A special head-and-shoulders piece allows this mighty Orc to tower over most other minifigures.

Spider legs can clutch a minifigure

Spider Bytez This moody mutant comes with his human alter ego Victor in TV-inspired Mutation Chamber Unleashed (set 79119).

Totally unique body piece

Exclusive body mold

Building studs on both arms

Leatherhead The Turtles' alligator ally is a massive presence in the TV series set Turtle Sub Undersea Chase (set 79121).

Bandanna covers top of head

Neck bracket holds half-shell in place

Sunglasses hang from bead necklace

Dark green body parts

Michelangelo Muted green body parts and printed nostrils set Mike's movie minifigures apart from earlier versions.

Raphael Like the other movie Turtles, Raph wears his new half-shell piece higher on his back than his 2013 minifigure did.

LEGO® TEENAGE MUTANT NINJA TURTLES™

The Turtles really came out of their shells in 2014, with starring roles in a brand-new movie, as well as in their ongoing Nickelodeon TV series. Both were the subject of new LEGO releases, with five TV-themed sets appearing in April and three movie tie-ins showcasing new-look Ninja Turtle minifigures in July.

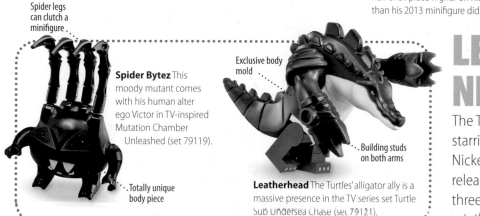

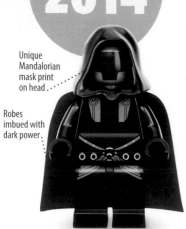

Darth Revan This Sith Lord from the Old Republic era was released to mark *Star Wars* Day on May 4th.

Unique Mandalorian mask print on head

Robes imbued with dark power

Festive Astromech Half droid, half Christmas tree, this unique figure lit up Day 22 in the 2014 Advent Calendar.

Printed baubles

Leg parts are exclusive in this color

Detailed new head piece

Tunic print continues on back

Bith Musician Three identical minifigures depict lead singer Figrin D'an and the Modal Nodes band in 2014's Cantina set.

C-3PO The famous droid gets his first printed legs with this Sandcrawler variant, which also shows a restraining bolt on his torso.

Jawa restraining bolt

Leg repaired with silver spare parts

THE ORIGINAL TRILOGY

Episode IV inspired several sets in 2014, from an updated Mos Eisley Cantina (set 75052) to the Ultimate Collector Series Sandcrawler (set 75059). The latter boasted 3,296 pieces, including seven new or redesigned droids.

STAR WARS LEGENDS

This year's characters from outside established *Star Wars* lore included names from the *Knights of the Old Republic* video game and *The Yoda Chronicles* TV series. A new LEGO *Star Wars* Advent Calendar (set 75056) also brought festive fun.

Ithorian Jedi Master The first Ithorian minifigure goes by the nickname Rusty in *The Yoda Chronicles* TV show.

New "hammerhead" piece

Bare legs and feet under short robes

DID YOU KNOW?
C-3PO's head piece can be found on fellow protocol droids R-3PO and K-3PO, and RA-7, the Death Star droid.

Santa Vader This seasonal Sith could feel your presents when he escaped from Advent Calendars on Christmas Eve!

Gifts attached to belt

Fur-lined pockets printed on legs

Treadwell Droid This brick-built droid from the 2014 Sandcrawler set has four skeleton arms on a rotating body!

Binoculars piece for eyes

Base made from LEGO® Technic parts

LEGO® STAR WARS™

Animated TV series *STAR WARS® REBELS™* took the galaxy by storm in 2014, charting the rise of resistance at the height of the Empire's power. The accompanying LEGO subtheme featured five key rebels in its first year, as well as their two connecting vessels. Not too far, far away, sets based on the movies and more also continued to thrive.

The Ghost (set 75053) Jedi Kanan Jarrus joins Hera and Zeb at the controls of the rebels' stealth ship.

The Phantom (set 75048) can dock between these two engines

Flying goggles printed on helmet

Dual-sided head print

Hera Syndulla The Twi'lek captain of the *Ghost* has a unique helmet piece that includes her long head-tails (lekku).

Lasat head piece found in just one set

Shark-tail design on shoulder

Zeb Orrelios To date, this Lasat rebel is the only member of his species to be made into a minifigure.

STAR WARS REBELS

Of the six main rebels—Hera Syndulla, Ezra Bridger, Kanan Jarrus, Zeb Orrelios, Sabine Wren, and Chopper the droid—five appeared in 2014 sets. Sabine did not make her debut until the following year.

Gleaming robot eyes

P.I.X.A.L. Circuit-style markings and silver metallic hair make it clear that Cyrus Borg's sidekick is a highly advanced android.

LEGO® NINJAGO®

In its fourth year, Ninjago City was rebooted as a techno wonderland, where there was nothing at all to worry about. Well … only the fact that Master Wu and genius inventor Cyrus Borg had fallen under the control of the Digital Overlord! Luckily, Borg's android assistant P.I.X.A.L. was on hand to help the ninja put things right once again.

Possessed red eyes

Techno Wu Even Wu's hat gets a metallic makeover when he allows himself to be captured by the Digital Overlord!

Only time Wu wears a black beard

Metallic print under unique tech-head

Cyrus Borg When technology gets the better of him, this friendly inventor becomes the terrifying OverBorg!

Smiling face can be swapped for sterner look

Wings attached at neck

Falcon The huge wings worn by this hero are one wide piece made from jewel-like transparent red plastic.

AVENGERS

Two sets in 2014 were based on the animated TV series *Avengers Assemble*. As well as featuring fresh looks for Captain America, Thor, and the Hulk, they also introduced the first minifigures of some unusual characters.

Mind-beam weapon on forehead

MODOK This big-brained villain has the hugest head of any minifigure! Amazingly, it slots on to a standard torso.

Golden chest plate is part of head piece

LEGO® DISNEY PRINCESS™

The second theme to feature mini dolls (after LEGO® Friends) introduced new figure parts, such as a tail for Ariel from *The Little Mermaid* and floor-length dress pieces for the likes of Rapunzel and Cinderella.

First mini doll to wear this hairstyle

Ariel The Little Mermaid is joined by her best friend, Flounder the fish, in Ariel's Amazing Treasures (set 41050).

No other character has this piece in green

New hair piece with band

Cinderella Cinders shall go to the ball, thanks to the horse-drawn coach in Cinderella's Dream Carriage (set 41053).

Magical sparkle print on dress

LEGO® MARVEL SUPER HEROES

This year's big Marvel moment was the Earth premiere of the *Guardians of the Galaxy* movie. Three LEGO playsets captured most of its heroes in minifigure form. Away from the movie theater, the comic-book exploits of the X-Men and the animated TV adventures of the Avengers also found new form in LEGO sets.

Skin tone printed on blue head piece

Cyclops This hero's figure-hugging costume is recreated using printing alone, with no need for a helmet or other extras.

Belt buckle is an "X" symbol

X-MEN Until 2014, Wolverine and Phoenix were the only X-Men with their own minifigures. That changed with X-Men vs. the Sentinel (set 76022), which added Storm and Cyclops to the mix, along with a new-look Wolverine.

Shoulder straps are part of head piece

GUARDIANS OF THE GALAXY

Intergalactic outlaws Rocket Raccoon, Groot, Star-Lord, Drax, and Gamora all feature in 2014's *Guardians of the Galaxy* sets, with antagonists the Sakaaran, Nebula, and the Collector (a San Diego Comic-Con exclusive minifigure) also putting in appearances.

Tail piece fits between torso and leg

Rocket Raccoon The smallest Guardian might just be the fiercest! He wears this orange outfit in just one set.

Long hair hides alternative face print

Storm A unique cape loops around this minifigure's wrists, making it ideal for striking dramatic Super Hero poses!

Classic 1970s comic-book costume

Kai Both the Fire Ninja and Cole the Earth Ninja feature in the first wave of LEGO DIMENSIONS sets.

Tournament of Elements robe

"Toy Tag" stand interacts with brick-built portal

TRAVEL TO A NEW DIMENSION? THAT MUST BE MAGIC!

Classic "Gandalf the Gray" look

Minifigures can be detached from Toy Tags

Gandalf This wizard from *The Lord of the Rings* is one of three minifigures included with the DIMENSIONS Starter Pack.

LEGO® DIMENSIONS

The Lord of the Rings, LEGO® NINJAGO®, *The Simpsons*, *Doctor Who*, *The Wizard of Oz*, and more all came together in the LEGO DIMENSIONS video game! To begin, players built a portal from LEGO bricks and connected it to their games console. They then placed minifigures with special stands on the portal to bring them to life within the game!

2015

WORLDS COLLIDED with the launch of LEGO® DIMENSIONS in 2015. A blend of LEGO® building and console gaming, the theme mixed minifigures from different pop culture realities to create a unique and expandable play experience. The year also marked the minifigure debuts for Rey, Finn, and friends in the first LEGO® *Star Wars*™: *The Force Awakens* sets. Elsewhere, sea shanties were sung for the return of LEGO® Pirates, and engines revved in anticipation of the new LEGO® Speed Champions theme.

LEGO DIMENSIONS Starter Pack (set 71200) Four versions of the Starter Pack made the game available to owners of PS3, PS4, Xbox One, and Xbox 360 owners.

Wyldstyle from THE LEGO® MOVIE™

Brick-built portal

Alternative calm face print on reverse of head

Fire CHI weapon can be used in the game

Ornate leg armor printing

Eris Chima's eagle princess has exclusive leg and torso printing for her LEGO DIMENSIONS debut.

Same hat mold as Gandalf

New bright-green head piece

Wicked Witch of the West This *Wizard of Oz* minifigure can really fly once she gets inside the game's reality!

Longbow really works in gameplay

Swirling Middle-earth design on Toy Tag

Same Batsuit seen in six DC Comics Super Heroes sets.

Taller cowl than other 2015 Batman minifigures

Batman The Caped Crusader comes with a 3-in-1 Batmobile, Batblaster, and Batray build in the DIMENSIONS Starter Pack.

Legolas Like all DIMENSIONS minifigures, this *The Lord of the Rings* Elf has his own Toy Tag stand with unique, elven-inspired printing.

- Gold shades printed on transparent head piece
- T-shirt printed with money

Invizable This show-off likes to be seen, so he dresses to impress to make up for being completely see-through!

LEGO® ULTRA AGENTS

The second year of Ultra Agents sets introduced AppBricks to the LEGO world as the heroes took on eight Antimatter Missions. Each set included at least one carbon-infused AppBrick, which activated interactive comic strips when placed alongside an app-enabled tablet or smartphone screen. New minifigure agents included Trey Swift and Steve Zeal, who faced a fresh array of fantastical foes.

- Scary cyborg face
- Mechanical spider legs

Spyclops This cyber spider is always on the web! His bug-spray weapon gets used on any agent that bugs him.

- Rare printed brain piece
- Lower body made from 13 pieces

Professor Brainstein This scientist comes in two sets—once as a good guy, and once as a mega-brained monster!

- New bandanna and flowing hair piece
- You can't swashbuckle without buckles!

Pirate Queen Ask this royal rogue about her noble heritage, and she'll show you all the priceless antiques she's stolen!

PIRATES

As ever, the LEGO Pirates crew is led by a classic captain with an eyepatch, peg leg, and hook hand. But there is also a sea change with the first ever Pirate Cook, Pirate Boy, and Pirate Queen!

- Only one bottom tooth
- Bare chest under apron
- Rope holds oversized pants up
- New-look bandanna piece

Pirate Cook This scruffy chef keeps a wide selection of exotic cooking sauces. Unfortunately, he keeps them on his apron ....

Pirate Boy The *Brick Bounty*'s freshest face may have based his look on Bo'sun Will from 1989's LEGO Pirates sets.

- Adventurous grin

Governor's Daughter This young civilian is just as handy with a sword as her father's most accomplished soldiers.

- Elegant 18th-century outfit

- Plume is a status symbol

- Gaudy gold epaulettes

Governor The graybeard boss of the Bluecoats cuts quite a dashing figure in his unique bicorne hat with decorative cockade printing.

LEGO® PIRATES

Six years after the LEGO Pirates were presumed lost at sea, they sailed into view once more with new recruits, new-look enemies, and even their very own chess set! This time around, the marauders made their daring raids on board the 745-piece ship *Brick Bounty* (set 70413) and hid their loot behind a giant skull on Treasure Island (set 70411).

- Wig first worn by Revolutionary Soldier in 2013

Admiral This seasoned sailor wears the same uniform as the Governor but pairs it with a stylish powdered wig piece.

BLUECOATS

These stuffy soldiers have tried to sink the pirates' spirits since the earliest days of the theme. For 2015, they return with their most stylish uniforms to protect the Governor's Daughter from harm.

PIRATES CHESS SET

With 857 pieces, including 20 minifigures, this is 2015's biggest LEGO Pirates set. Bluecoats and pirate minifigures play the kings, queens, and pawns, while brick-built pieces are used for the rooks, knights, and bishops.

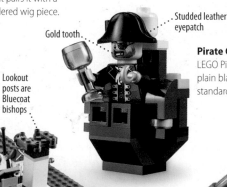

- Variant Pirate Queen
- Pirates have parrots for rooks
- Lookout posts are Bluecoat bishops
- Gold tooth
- Studded leather eyepatch

Pirate Chess King No other LEGO Pirate captain combines a plain black bicorne hat with two standard legs.

Pirates Chess Set (set 40158) This serious strategy game is full of fun details, like the pawn with a banana instead of a sword.

- Bodice first worn by a LEGO Castle princess

Bluecoat Chess Queen This VIM (Very Important Minifigure) in Bluecoat society has her own throne on the LEGO Pirates chessboard.

LEGO® JURASSIC WORLD

In 2001, the LEGO® Studios theme included two sets based around the filming of *Jurassic Park III*. But it was not until 2015's *Jurassic World* that the modern-day dino film franchise got its own LEGO theme. Six sets followed the story of the spectacular new movie, all boasting brand-new minifigures and at least one large dinosaur figure each.

Choice of stern and worried face prints

Printed cell phone tile introduced in 2014

I SAID SEND ME A TEXT NOT A T-REX!

Smile can be swapped for angry look

Knife sheath on belt

Owen Grady Owen shares his head printing with Marvel character Star-Lord, both of whom are played by actor Chris Pratt.

Wings move up and down on hinges

Dilophosaurus A whole new species in the LEGO ecosystem, this colorful creature has a brand-new frill-necked head piece.

Tooth-lined jaw can be snapped shut.

Pteranodon This mold was first seen in 2001's LEGO® Dino theme, but got a new color scheme for 2014.

Claire Dearing It's just another day at work for Jurassic World's manager when she faces two Velociraptors in Raptor Rampage (set 75917)!

Overworked expression

Shoulder holster

Vic Hoskins Security chief Vic tackles a T-rex that is four times his height in his only 2015 set appearance.

LEGO® ELVES

The third mini doll theme followed the adventures of Emily Jones in the magical world of Elvendale. It introduced many new parts, including mini doll hair pieces with sculpted Elf ears.

Elemental symbol on forehead

Unique die-cut cape

Skyra This Wind Elf guards the portal between Elvendale and the human world. She is found in just one set.

LEGO® SPEED CHAMPIONS

Speeding into stores in 2015, this new theme got the green light from car fans everywhere. All seven of the first year's sets featured realistic recreations of famous race cars in minifigure scale, and came with minifigure drivers decked out in authentic team colors. The largest set also included a pit stop, a finish line, and a huge Ferrari team truck.

Helmet piece introduced in 1987

Exclusive "Porsche Motorsport" branding

Porsche Driver Eye-catching bright green arms and legs make this minifigure hard to miss—even at 93 mph (150 kph)!

Silver metallic helmet

McLaren speedmark logo

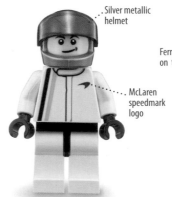

McLaren Driver This smiling sportsman knows he'll soon be back behind the wheel of his McLaren P1™ hybrid supercar.

Ferrari badge on torso

Confident face print found in more than 90 sets

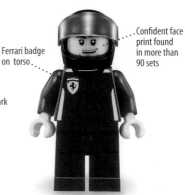

Ferrari Driver Clad in Italian racing red, this driver is every bit as stylish as his LaFerrari hypercar (set 75899).

SERIES 13

Kings, goblins, aliens, and wizards rubbed shoulders in the 13th series of collectible Minifigures. But some of the most lovable characters turned out to be the everyday folk doing the thing that they loved.

ANYONE WANT A SNACK?

Beauty spot

Ripped green crop top

Bone clasp pins skirt together

Lady Cyclops She may wield a heavy club, but Lady Cyclops mostly uses it for playing baseball and scratching her back.

Groovy print on torso and arms

Disco Diva From the top of her perm to the wheels on her roller skates, this singing sensation is pure 1970s!

Roller skate piece introduced in 2013

Hot dog piece goes over standard head and torso

Squirt of mustard

Hot Dog Man With his buns of plastic, this meaty mascot just wants to feed the world—with frankfurters!

Snaking tendrils extend from arms

Plant Monster The face in the mouth of this walking plant belongs to its most recent meal!

Vines cover legs and torso

SERIES 14

Released in time for Halloween 2015, the Monsters series of Minifigures included witches, werewolves, gargoyles, and ghosts. For the easily frightened, it also featured one or two characters who were simply playing at being paranormal!

DID YOU KNOW?
Series 13 was the very first to feature a Minifigure dressed as food.

Peep through the grille to find a grinning face

Foil is also used by the Series 12 Swashbuckler Minifigure, but in gold

Fencer On guard! The eager Fencer wears a pristine white outfit. His torso, legs, and protective masked helmet are all unique.

Mask-string loops around the whole head

Skeleton Guy This harmless trick-or-treater isn't just dressed like a skeleton—he's dressed like a classic LEGO skeleton!

Pumpkin basket for Halloween treats

LEGO skeleton limb designs printed on sides

Unusual pigtails piece

Pom-poms have hand grips inside

Zombie Cheerleader Zombies are well represented in the Monsters series, with Zombie Pirate and Zombie Businessman also on the team.

LEGO® MINIFIGURES

With its 16 unrelated characters, 2015's first wave of Minifigures followed a familiar and much-loved formula for Series 13. The second wave followed on from the previous year's *The Simpsons* series, while the third was more of a departure. For the first time in the main Minifigures series, each character in Series 14 was linked by a theme—each one was a monster of some sort!

I AM NAILING THIS PROJECT!

Unique saw piece

Low-slung tool belt packed with essentials

Carpenter This blue-collar craftsman carries a standard 1x4 LEGO tile printed to look just like a plank of wood.

Patched hat and scraggly hair are all one piece

Broomstick has appeared in nearly 80 sets in different colors

Striped leggings underneath cloth skirt

Wacky Witch Hubble, bubble .... how does it go again? This poor witch just can't remember— she's been too busy trying to improve her flying skills!

Black cat is not impressed

197

Daphne Like the rest of the gang, danger-prone Daphne has a scared face print, as well as a happy one.

Magnifying glass really works!

Unique hair piece

Shaggy Found in all five sets, Scooby Doo's best friend is more interested in sandwiches than mystery-solving!

Shaggy always needs a shave!

Turtleneck collar

Scooby snack found in Haunted Lighthouse (set 75903)

Velma The smartest member of the gang can never lose her glasses—they are printed on her face!

LEGO® SCOOBY-DOO™

"Jeepers, Scoob, we've got our own theme!" Shaggy and his cartoon buds starred in five fright-filled sets in 2015. Each one was packed with monsters and g-g-g-ghosts, but on closer inspection, they all turned out to be crooks in elaborate costumes! The theme also included a brick-built version of the adventure-loving gang's iconic camper van, The Mystery Machine (set 75902).

Pumpkin piece also appears in Halloween sets

Stalk can be held by minifigure hands

Mask mold first used in LEGO® Monster Fighters theme

Golden trident from LEGO® Atlantis theme

Swamp Monster Turning the head piece under this monster mask reveals the face of villainous Mr. Brown!

Fred's alternative scared face is not quite so confident!

Ascot tie over white sweater

Fred This dashing detective drives the Mystery Machine through a spooky forest in his only set appearance.

Single LEGO stud on back

Head is a separate, posable piece

SCOOBY-DOOBY-S-S-S-SWAMP MONSTER!

Scooby-Doo The greatest of Great Danes appears in all five sets—as happy, scared, standing, and sitting variants.

Headless Horseman The face of cunning Elwood Crane is exposed when this new pumpkin-head piece is removed.

LEGO® DC COMICS SUPER HEROES

The Justice League and their enemies boosted their numbers in this year's DC Comics sets. Goodies Supergirl, Cyborg, and Hawkman all made their minifigure debuts, while the forces of darkness were joined by Black Manta, Captain Cold, Gorilla Grodd, and Darkseid. The last two were the first big figures to be seen in the theme, and towered over their adversaries!

Pipes made from flexible plastic

Top of helmet slots on over neck section

Black Manta This fishy foe wears a diving helmet with built-in tubes connected to a breathing tank on his back.

Calm expression can be substituted for gritted teeth

Symbol of the House of El

Scuba suit printing continues on back

Bulky body

Hands and arms are posable

Darkseid It takes four members of the Justice League to fight this big blue brute in Darkseid Invasion (set 76028).

Unfastened pouch on upside-down Utility Belt

Vampirelike teeth

Upside-down bat-symbol

Batzarro This corrupted clone of Batman came as part of a limited-edition LEGO DC Comics Super Heroes DVD set.

DID YOU KNOW?
Raffle winners at 2015's San Diego Comic-Con took home an exclusive minifigure of DC Comics hero Arsenal.

Supergirl Teenage Kara Zor-El fights beside her Kryptonian cousin Superman in Brainiac Attack (set 76040).

LEGO® IDEAS

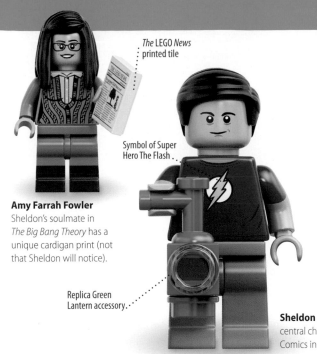

Amy Farrah Fowler
Sheldon's soulmate in *The Big Bang Theory* has a unique cardigan print (not that Sheldon will notice).

The LEGO News printed tile

Symbol of Super Hero The Flash

Replica Green Lantern accessory.

Sheldon Cooper The Big Bang Theory's central character shows off his love for DC Comics in his minifigure form.

Two out of four fan-designed sets came with minifigures in 2015. First up was *The Big Bang Theory* (set 21302), which recreated the set of the TV sitcom complete with lead characters Sheldon, Leonard, Howard, Raj, Amy, Bernadette, and Penny. Then it was the turn of the world's longest-running science-fiction show in *Doctor Who* (set 21304), with a bigger-on-the-inside TARDIS build!

Swiveling eyestalk

Tough Dalekanium shell

Dalek Two of these minifigure-scale monsters menaced the Doctor and his best friend Clara in the *Doctor Who* set.

SWAMP POLICE

Helicopters and hovercraft keep the Swamp Police one step ahead of the crooks and crocodiles in the City's murkiest waters! Thirteen new minifigures in the subtheme include eight new-look cops and five fugitives from justice.

Protective vest

Large, practical pockets

Female Swamp Police Officer Wearing one of two standard Swamp Police uniforms, this ranger rides out in two different sets.

Same hat style as 2012's Forest Police

Radio clips on to shirt placket

Bearded Crook A distinctive look sees this bad guy catch the eyes of the cops in three separate sets!

Dark-orange beard

Missing tooth

Ragged braces

Male Swamp Police Officer The second standard outfit in the Swamp is more lightweight than the version with vest protection.

LEGO® CITY

It was another big year in LEGO CITY, with a new fleet of demolition vehicles needed to keep up with the ever-changing face of LEGO urban life! The long arm of the law reached into the City swamps—and even the sea proved no boundary for City explorers. CITY minifigures even went out of this world via the cutting-edge Space Port!

Reflective visor protects against solar glare.

Stylish half-rim glasses

Space Scientist Away from work, this smiling minifigure enjoys reminding all of her friends that what they do isn't rocket science.

Red pen in lab coat pocket

Astronaut Two seemingly identical spacewalkers in Utility Shuttle (set 60078) have different faces (male and female) under their golden visors.

CONSTRUCTION

This year's Construction sets were just as much about knocking things down as building them up! Demolition sites and vehicles featured in four sets, assisted by a Service Truck (set 60073) carrying an all-important portable toilet!

Brown shirt under high-vis vest

Pneumatic hammer drill

Construction Worker A brand-new hard hat-and-headphones piece protects this worker's invisible ears from the blare of his drill.

Depth and pressure gauges

Scuba Diver Standard City divers' gear gets an update when paired with this explorer's detailed wetsuit print.

DEEP SEA EXPLORERS

Six sets left LEGO CITY for the seabed in 2015, discovering shipwrecks, sawfish, treasure chests, and whalebones! Each set included at least one exploratory vehicle, closely based on the latest real-world submersibles.

Crowbar for prying open treasure chest

Deep Sea Diver This explorer's heavy-duty helmet with built-in air tanks was first seen in 2010's LEGO® Atlantis theme.

Metal toecaps

SPACE PORT

Realistic shuttles and satellites set this returning CITY subtheme apart from the science fiction of LEGO® Space. Scientists, technicians, and trainee astronauts worked together on the ground, while space-suited minifigures ventured out into orbit.

LEGO *STAR WARS*

Ten years after the last live-action *Star Wars* movie, the Skywalker saga returned to movie theaters in December 2015 with *The Force Awakens*. Three months earlier, on "Force Friday," LEGO *Star Wars* sets based around the new film made their debut in stores. They introduced the world to minifigure versions of a new generation of Resistance heroes and their First Order enemies.

Finn This friendly ex-stormtrooper and reluctant hero appears in just one 2015 set, the new *Millennium Falcon* (75105).

New hair piece

Jacket "borrowed" from Poe Dameron

THE RESISTANCE

Led by General Leia (who would become a minifigure in 2016), this brave band of freedom fighters combines newcomers including Rey, Finn, and BB-8 with seasoned rebels such as Han Solo and Chewbacca.

Untidy short collar

Older Han Solo The 24th Han minifigure is the first to have gray hair (though he retains a boyish grin).

Photoreceptor "eye"

BB-8 It's true that this droid is made from just two pieces, but both are new and boast exclusive printing!

Base connects to a single stud

Hair piece worn instead of mask

Rey The future Jedi comes with a scavenger's bag and a protective desert mask piece in Rey's Speeder (set 75099).

Staff for self-defense

Helmet hides snarling face

Flametrooper First Order stormtroopers come in several guises, but few are as fearsome as these fire-throwing thugs.

Brick-built fuel pack

Exclusive cruciform lightsaber

Kylo Ren Ren's helmet comes in just one 2015 set. Four years passed before it appeared again (with a different printing).

THE FIRST ORDER

Inspired by the old, defeated Empire, the First Order wants to see the galaxy ruled by fear once again! Its figurehead is the dark side master Kylo Ren, who answers to the mysterious Snoke.

Battle-ravaged cape

Unique silver metallic armor

Black fabric cape with red trim

Captain Phasma The commander of the stormtroopers has a plain head piece under her helmet to keep her identity a mystery.

THE SHIELD HELICARRIER

By far the biggest ever LEGO Marvel Super Heroes set, The SHIELD Helicarrier (set 76042) is built from 2,996 pieces at microfigure scale. Twelve microfigures are included, along with five hero minifigures.

SHIELD Agent Eight identical microfigures patrol the deck of the Helicarrier, emblazoned with SHIELD emblems.

Microfigure stands 0.6 in tall (15 mm), including base

Printing even includes pockets!

Nick Fury The director of SHIELD's eyepatch and goatee beard are both less than a millimeter tall on this microfigure.

Transparent red visor built into helmet

LEGO® MARVEL SUPER HEROES

Big-screen adventure *Avengers: Age of Ultron* dominated both at the box office and in the LEGO Marvel Super Heroes theme of 2015. Six sets included all the familiar heroes, including newcomer Scarlet Witch. A single *Ant-Man* set represented the year's other entry to the Marvel Cinematic Universe, while two sets explored the web-slinging world of animated TV series *Ultimate Spider-Man*.

Ant-Man Shrinking Super Hero Scott Lang rides a giant brick-built bug in Ant-Man Final Battle (set 76039).

Powered-up red eyes on reverse

Scarlet Witch This villain eventually teams up with the Avengers, and two face prints show her good and bad sides!

Energy bolts in both hands

Skin-tight mask printed on head piece

Darker suit than Peter Parker wears as Spidey

Miles Morales Spider-Man One of many spider-heroes in the Multiverse, Miles makes his minifigure debut in an *Ultimate Spider-Man* set.

Tendrils built on the back of neck bracket

Scary alien smile

Carnage This red menace from *Ultimate Spider-Man* turns his tendrils on Miles Morales in Carnage's SHIELD Sky Attack (set 76036).

LEGO® NINJAGO®

The ninja had gone their separate ways at the start of 2015, but were brought back together at the Tournament of Elements. Here, they met villainous Master Chen and his daughter Skylor, a.k.a. the yellow ninja. Later in the year, they battled ghosts in the City of Stiix, and Lloyd the Green Ninja was possessed by Morro the Master of Wind!

Kanji symbol for number six

Only ninja to wear this color

Skylor The Elemental Master of Amber is the sixth ninja to appear in NINJAGO and wears a symbol denoting this.

Evil red eyes

Serpent-tooth necklace

Master Chen This sneaky snake-worshipper wears a unique serpent skull helmet with trailing spiky tails!

Sickly skin tone under cowl

Mask and armor are two separate pieces

Evil Green Ninja Lloyd gets a ghostly new look for 2015. He's soon back to his healthy green self, though.

Face print on transparent green head piece

Scythe Master Ghoultar One of 18 Ghost Warrior minifigures, Ghoultar has a brand-new multicolor part in place of legs.

Ghostly lower body connects to LEGO studs like standard legs

Ponytail print on torso

Alex The minifigure version of Minecraft's default female avatar has appeared in more than 20 sets since 2015.

LEGO® MINECRAFT™

Armored Skeletons, Zombie Pigmen, and new brick-built nasties roamed the LEGO Minecraft world in 2015. But most importantly, protagonist Steve no longer had to face these dangers alone, as he was joined by fellow adventurer Alex! She appeared in The Desert Outpost (set 21121) and The Nether Fortress (set 21122), once with a helmet and once without.

Wings clip on to back of armor

Tribe-specific printing on armor piece

Bladvic A member of the Bear Tribe, Bladvic wears distinctive new flame wings and Fire CHI armor.

Rinona The Rhino Tribe debuted in 2014, but Rinona and her brother Rogon returned for the Fire vs. Ice showdown!

Printed Fire CHI harness

Hardy rhino-hide leg print

LEGO® LEGENDS OF CHIMA™

Bears and Beavers joined the tribes of Chima for the final year of this theme, and there were reinforcements for the Rhinos, Tigers, and more. Nine sets concluded the "Fire vs. Ice" storyline introduced in 2014, tying in with the third season of the animated *Legends of Chima* TV show, which ended with peace returning to the land of CHI.

Same head mold as LEGO Minifigures Yeti from 2013

Breezor This beaver is the only Chima minifigure not to have a standard head piece beneath an animal mask.

Only second use of short legs in Chima theme.

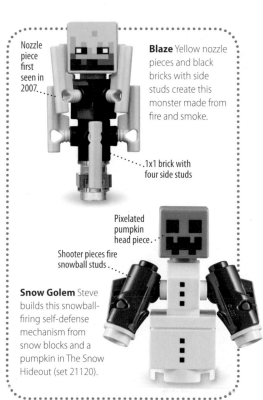

Nozzle piece first seen in 2007.

Blaze Yellow nozzle pieces and black bricks with side studs create this monster made from fire and smoke.

1x1 brick with four side studs

Pixelated pumpkin head piece

Shooter pieces fire snowball studs

Snow Golem Steve builds this snowball-firing self-defense mechanism from snow blocks and a pumpkin in The Snow Hideout (set 21120).

Ultimate Macy Knighton's royal princess is more interested in being a knight than a noblewoman—especially in her Ultimate armor!

- Six-stud shooter built on to armor
- Power mace weapon
- Scannable shield makes maces rain down in the NEXO KNIGHTS app

LEGO® NEXO KNIGHTS™

Peace reigns in the Kingdom of Knighton—until Jestro the jester messes with the Book of Monsters! As fiery fiends burst forth from its pages, it falls to five brave NEXO KNIGHTS to save the day …. More than 50 new minifigures plus other new figures featured in the first year of this fantasy theme, including knights, robots, and lava monsters!

THE KNIGHTS

All five NEXO KNIGHTS came in standard and Ultimate versions in 2016. Each Ultimate minifigure came with three scannable shields, which unlocked NEXO Powers inside the LEGO NEXO KNIGHTS: MERLOK 2.0 app.

Lance The most laid-back (some would say laziest) knight likes fame, fashion, and fighting monsters!

- Only Lance wears this pointed visor
- Cutout in armor reveals fox print on torso

Aaron This thrill-seeking knight wears a slightly more serious expression on the reverse of his head piece.

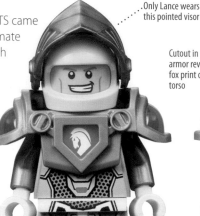

2016

THERE WERE KNIGHTS to remember in 2016, as LEGO® NEXO KNIGHTS™ powered into toy stores, a TV show, and a dedicated app. Mixing medieval adventure with ultramodern tech, the sets came with special minifigure shields that could be scanned by a smartphone to unlock powers in the app. And as if that wasn't enough excitement, the year also saw some all-time icons becoming minifigures, in the shape of rock band The Beatles, E.T. The Extra-Terrestrial, and a host of Disney favorites.

- New helmet mold shared with Aaron and Axl

Ultimate Clay In his Ultimate outfit, the leader of the NEXO KNIGHTS wears exclusive transparent blue armor and visor parts.

- Arms move like a standard minifigure's

Axl By far the biggest of the NEXO KNIGHTS, Axl has an all-new extended torso part and unique armor-clad arms.

THE VILLAINS

Long ago, the evil wizard Monstrox was transformed into a book and locked away in a dusty library. But when Jestro gets his hands on the book, Monstrox's power compels him to free its monstrous contents!

Jestro He was never a good jester, but Jestro's run-in with Monstrox turns him into a really bad one.

- Skulls were bells before Jestro turned bad
- Cape torn in battle with Merlok

Book of Monsters Two hinged parts make up Monstrox's book-bound form, which can be held by a minifigure.

- Printed face found in two sets

- Detachable horn pieces
- One of four different Scurrier faces

Scurrier All the monsters in NEXO KNIGHTS' first year are based around fire and lava, including this pear-shaped pest.

THE OTHERS

One of Knighton's most important citizens is the wise wizard Merlok, who becomes a computer program after an explosive encounter with Jestro. The Kingdom is also kept running smoothly by teams of tiny robots!

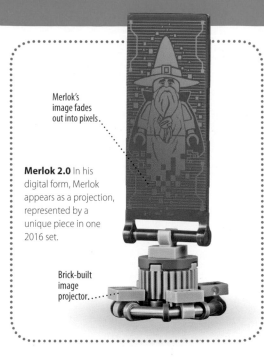

Merlok's image fades out into pixels.

Merlok 2.0 In his digital form, Merlok appears as a projection, represented by a unique piece in one 2016 set.

Brick-built image projector.

Beard hides memory stick pendant print

Merlok The only minifigure version of Merlok came with the DK book, LEGO® NEXO KNIGHTS™: *The Book of Knights.*

All-exclusive printing

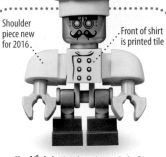

Shoulder piece new for 2016

Front of shirt is printed tile

Chef Éclair Knighton's royal chef is built to the same design as five Squire Bots that assist the knights.

LEGO® CITY

New-look firefighters blazed a trail through the City in 2016, while an aerial display team lit up the sky. Beyond the urban sprawl, police officers dealt with daring escapees on isolated Prison Island, and scientists discovered secrets waiting to be found in active volcanoes! Meanwhile, ordinary citizens from every age group enjoyed a relaxing day out in the park.

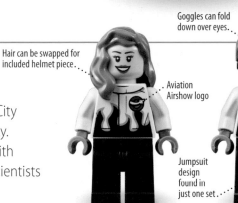

Hair can be swapped for included helmet piece

Goggles can fold down over eyes.

Aviation Airshow logo

Jumpsuit design found in just one set.

Zip-up top under life jacket

Police Officer Island life clearly agrees with this perky patrolman, who appears in two of the year's Prison Island sets.

Female Stunt Pilot This daredevil performs wing-walking stunts in one of five airport-themed sets from 2016.

Male Stunt Pilot The wing-walker's identically dressed partner flies their vintage biplane in Airport Air Show (set 60103).

New kindly face print

Both knitwear designs new for 2016

Grandparents These two older city-dwellers enjoy the outdoors in People Pack—Fun in the Park (set 60134).

Dog Owner This minifigure is the first to use a wheelchair piece. He loves to take his faithful pooch to the park.

New rear wheel piece

Same front wheels as LEGO skateboards.

New uniform print with flashlight

High-vis stripes printed on legs

Firefighter This first responder keeps her cool when she attends an oil barrel blaze in Fire Ladder Truck (set 60107).

Young Family A new baby figure was born in 2016, proudly parented by two minifigures from the Fun in the Park set.

Body is all one piece

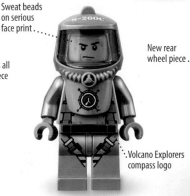

Sweat beads on serious face print

Volcano Explorers compass logo

Vulcanologist This scientist wears a silver heat suit to explore a lava flow in volcano Heavy-Lift Helicopter (set 60125).

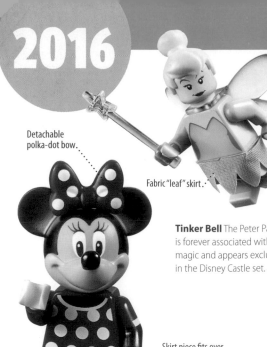

Detachable polka-dot bow.

Wings first worn by LEGO Minifigures Fairy in 2008

Fabric "leaf" skirt.

Tinker Bell The Peter Pan pixie is forever associated with Disney magic and appears exclusively in the Disney Castle set.

I THINK YOU'LL FIND I'M A MICKEY-FIGURE!

Same head piece as Minnie with different printing

Firework launcher

Disney Castle (set 71040) This 4,080-piece set recreates the famous Cinderella Castle at Walt Disney World Resort in Orlando, Florida.

Daisy Duck

Skirt piece fits over standard legs

Minnie Mouse Both Minnie and Mickey wear exclusive outfits in the Disney castle set. Minnie's includes a new skirt piece.

Legs have printed dress-suit piping on sides

Mickey Mouse A fabric coattails piece completes Mickey's formalwear look, which fits between his torso and legs.

Unique horned headdress

Magical staff.

Two-tone fabric collar

Bottle labeled "Drink Me".

Maleficent This Minifigure depicts the animated antagonist of *Sleeping Beauty* (1959) rather than the live-action version of more recent movies.

Alice The title character of *Alice in Wonderland* comes with a potion that might just restore her to human size!

Same skirt mold as Minnie Mouse.

LEGO® DISNEY™

This year saw the LEGO Group and Disney celebrate their long-standing relationship with one of the biggest sets ever. Standing 29 in (74 cm) tall and 19 in (48 cm) wide, Disney Castle (set 71040) played host to seven minifigures, including Mickey Mouse and Donald Duck. The year also saw a host of classic Disney characters making magical appearances in the LEGO® Minifigures line.

Same head mold as original

Alien A native of the Pizza Planet restaurant, this little green guy first appeared in the LEGO® *Toy Story* theme in 2010.

Brand-new lower body piece

All printing updated from LEGO *Toy Story* variant.

Clamshell bikini print

Ariel The star of *The Little Mermaid* comes with a unique hairstyle and an opening oyster shell accessory.

DISNEY MINIFIGURES SERIES 1

Favorites from across the Magic Kingdom came together in the first Disney Series of collectible LEGO Minifigures. Eighteen lucky-dip characters included Aladdin and the Genie, Mr. Incredible and Syndrome, and Alice and the Cheshire Cat.

Iconic round glasses

Paul McCartney Paul's shirt is almost invisible beneath the waves of his enormous kipper tie, worn with a fab frock coat.

Printed LOVE tile

John Lennon Purple flowers sail on a sea of green on John's psychedelic shirt—the perfect match for his two-tone pants!

LEGO® IDEAS

Fifty years after Beatlemania made them the world's most famous faces, the Fab Four reformed—as minifigures! The Beatles Yellow Submarine (set 21306) was based on the band's 1968 animated film of the same name and began life as a design by fan builder Kevin Szeto. It also included an exclusive figure of The Beatles' furry cartoon friend, Jeremy Hillary Boob.

Sideburns printed on head piece.

Ringo Starr When the band begins to play, it's Ringo's drums, not his style, that sets the pace!

Submarine motor accessory.

George Harrison Though his friends are all aboard, George just isn't up for wearing such groovy-colored clothing!

- Detachable tiara

SERIES 15

There were lots of unusual parts to play with in Series 15! Three Minifigures had new leg or skirt pieces, while Clumsy Guy came with unique crutches and Tribal Woman cared for a swaddled baby.

Queen As if plucked from a playing card, this royal wears hearts and diamonds on the hem of her unique gown.

- Huge skirt piece covers eight LEGO studs!

- Bar piece printed with flute design

- Goaty goatee beard

- New goat legs piece

Faun This mythical musician is all man in the middle, but mostly goat around the head and the hooves!

- Reflective gold visor.

- Classic LEGO Space logo

Astronaut This off-world explorer travels the galaxy, flying the flag for his love of classic LEGO® Space sets!

- Brand-new fish-head helmet

- Fins rotate like standard arms.

Shark Suit Guy This is the first Minifigure to have fins instead of arms. Luckily, he has no fingernails to bite with those sharp teeth.

LEGO MINIFIGURES

Four sets of collectible Minifigures hit the shelves in 2016: the first Disney Series (see opposite), two regular series, and a special DFB Series marking the Euro 2016 soccer tournament. The latter was named for the Deutsche Fussball-Bund (German Football Association) and featured nothing but soccer players! The regular series, meanwhile, covered every career choice from monarch to banana-man ….

- Red helmet first seen on Series 5 Boxer

Kickboxer This martial artist can swap her head guard for a flowing hair piece. But the gloves always stay on!

- Sticker design is printed on

- Boxing gloves instead of standard hands

Banana Suit Guy This a-peelingly fruity fellow thinks he's the pick of the bunch among costumed LEGO characters.

- Wings attach with neck bracket

- Tail piece fits between torso and legs

Cute Little Devil This mini trick-or-treater's costume features brand-new devilish tail and head gear.

- German National Football Team logo

DFB SERIES

Unusually, all but one of the DFB Series of 16 German national team players came with the same accessory: a soccer ball! The only one who didn't was coach Joachim Löw, who clutched a tactics board instead.

Manuel Neuer This goalkeeper is set apart from his fellow players by his black, long-sleeved shirt and white gloves.

- Flesh-colored printing separates shorts and boots

SERIES 16

Things looked to have taken a darker turn when Series 16 included an Ice Queen, a Cyborg, and a Spooky Boy. But there were also friendly faces, including a Babysitter and even a Little Devil!

- Hood mold first worn by Ice Fisherman Minifigure in 2011

Wildlife Photographer Behind her hood, this naturalist has a second face print without any goggles, ideal for spotting the perfect picture.

- Penguin piece later seen in a THE LEGO BATMAN MOVIE set

LEGO® BRAND STORES

In November 2016, the world's biggest LEGO Store opened in London's Leicester Square. To mark the occasion, 275 individually numbered packs were given away to some of the first customers, each including the shop's mascot minifigure, Lester. The ever-so-British character was later reissued in greater numbers and different packaging but remained available exclusively in the London flagship store.

> ACTUALLY, I COME FROM THE BRICKISH ISLES!

- Rare bowler hat piece

- Umbrella found only in reissue set (40308)

- Union Flag vest print

Lester With his red, white, and blue vest and black bowler hat, this dashing dandy could only be a Brit!

LEGO® STAR WARS™

> **I REBEL.**

After 17 years of sets starring existing characters, 2016 saw the LEGO Group launch its own family of heroes into the *Star Wars* galaxy! The lovable Freemakers appeared in sets and in their own TV show, which ran until 2017. New names from the big screen and from video games also made the jump to minifigure scale during the year.

Goggles clip on to combined helmet/hair piece

Jyn Erso This rogue rebel has a unique helmet and a detailed bodywarmer print underneath her thick fabric poncho.

Shoulder bag helps hold poncho flat

Rank insignia plaque

Identity disk on belt

Orson Krennic The original director of the Death Star is the first *Star Wars* minifigure to wear a white cape.

ROGUE ONE: A STAR WARS STORY

The first *Star Wars* film beyond the Skywalker saga introduced a host of new characters, from rebels Jyn, Bodhi, Baze, and Bistan to Imperial villain Orson Krennic. All were made into minifigures across five fan-pleasing sets.

Choice of helmet or spiky hair piece

Rowan Freemaker The youngest Freemaker uses the Force to build working LEGO starships in his brick-based version of the galaxy.

Kordi Freemaker Rowan's sister pilots the family's salvage ship in StarScavenger (75147), which also includes their older brother, Zander.

Macrobinoculars worn around neck

Same leg print as Zander Freemaker

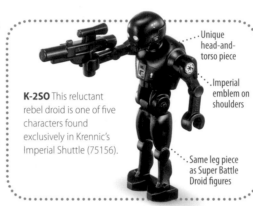

K-2SO This reluctant rebel droid is one of five characters found exclusively in Krennic's Imperial Shuttle (75156).

Unique head-and-torso piece

Imperial emblem on shoulders

Same leg piece as Super Battle Droid figures

Blue breastplate denotes a captain

Brown pants under lightweight armor

THE FREEMAKER ADVENTURES

Animated TV series LEGO® *Star Wars™: The Freemaker Adventures* follows the Freemaker family as they try—and fail—to live a quiet life in the era of the Galactic Empire. Two Freemaker sets were released in 2016.

Shoretrooper What do stormtroopers wear to the beach? In *Rogue One*, they favor this sand-and-sea-colored armor!

Same hair as 2009's Endor Leia, but in a lighter color

Frown can be swapped for a smile

General Leia The fifteenth Leia minifigure was the first to depict her in her role as leader of the Resistance.

Unkar Plutt A "sandwich board" piece over a standard torso creates the Jakku junk dealer's broad head and bulging belly.

Head, shoulders, and belly are all one piece

Bottom of tabard is printed on legs

STAR WARS® BATTLEFRONT™

Since 2007, LEGO *Star Wars* battle packs have featured multiple unnamed troopers for building up minifigure armies. Both battle packs released in 2016 were based on the recently revamped *Star Wars Battlefront* video game.

Blaster burns on armor

Jet Pack Trooper Two of these battle-scarred bullies were among the all-exclusive minifigures in Galactic Empire Battle Pack (75134).

THE FORCE AWAKENS

Sets based on the seventh installment of the Skywalker saga proved just as popular this year as they had in 2015. Key scenes from the planets Jakku and Takodana were recreated, complete with favorite characters.

Eyes magnified by goggles

Wrinkles continue on torso print

Hand-held stud shooter

Maz Kanata This pocket-sized pirate has a unique head piece, combining a cap, goggles, and Kanata's wrinkled features.

DID YOU KNOW?
Minifigure battle packs also feature in the LEGO® Castle, Pharaoh's Quest, and Alien Conquest themes.

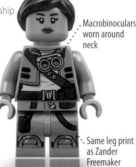

New panther ears head topper.

CINEMATIC UNIVERSE
Following his minifigure debut in 2015, Ant-Man returned in two alternative forms in Super Hero Airport Battle (76051). Black Panther Pursuit (76047) and Doctor Strange's Sanctum Sanctorum (76060) were other highlights from an action-packed year.

Iconic claw necklace

Black Panther For his first minifigure outing, the King of Wakanda teams up with Captain America in one Civil War set.

Printed gray streaks in hair

Doctor Strange
The Sorcerer Supreme and his cloak can both be made to levitate in 2016's only Doctor Strange set!

Powerful Eye of Agamotto amulet

Same figure mold used as a trophy piece in some sets

Ant-Man This one-piece microscale version of Ant-Man has detailed printing to match his Giant Man form (right).

Face printed on large semicircular piece

Giant Man
This brick-built version of Ant-Man maintains the proportions of a minifigure but stands 5 in (14 cm) tall!

Hands made from LEGO® Technic parts

Legs move like a minifigure's

LEGO® MARVEL SUPER HEROES

The biggest film of 2016 was *Captain America: Civil War*, with *Doctor Strange* not far behind. Both inspired new Marvel minifigures, with Black Panther and Stephen Strange both joining the fray for the first time. There were also sets based on animated series *Avengers Assemble* and the world of Spider-Man, plus a new range of compact and comical "Mighty Micros."

Ghost Rider
This hot-headed hero shares his new head mold with a flaming pumpkin from another 2016 Spidey set!

Head piece combines white and transparent parts

Fiery glow shows through holes in jacket

Same hood mold as Wyldstyle from THE LEGO® MOVIE™

Printed web-shooters on wrist

Standard big figure arm pieces

Scarlet Spider This Spidey clone is one of three Super Heroes to wield a new web piece during 2016.

SPIDER-MAN
The largest of three Spidey sets this year was Web Warriors Ultimate Bridge Battle (76057), which saw three Spider-Heroes allied against the Green Goblin. Another fiery friendship also featured in Spider-Man: Ghost Rider Team-Up (76058).

Grand gorget is part of unique torso mold

Thanos The *Avengers Assemble* version of this big figure established the mold for his later movie equivalents.

MIGHTY MICROS
Set apart from other Super Heroes sets, this new subtheme starred short-legged minifigures only. Each hero or villain had a comically exaggerated expression and drove a fun car based on his or her super abilities.

Huge, lopsided grin

Larger facial features than most minifigures.

Thick black outlines on torso print

Exaggerated belt size in relation to tiny legs.

Captain America This compact Cap has simpler graphics than most minifigures for a bold and almost cartoonish look.

Red Skull The Cap's crimson foe looks furious at being brought down to size for the Mighty Micros subtheme!

AVENGERS ASSEMBLE
In 2016, the Avengers went deep underwater and into orbit with Iron Skull Sub Attack (76048) and Avenjet Space Mission (76049). Both introduced new minifigure characters and took their design cues from TV's *Avengers Assemble*.

Classic Captain Marvel emblem

Captain Marvel Carol Danvers comes with two heads in Avenjet Space Mission: one masked and one with her identity revealed.

Long hair hides alternative friendly face print

Wonder Woman The third Diana Prince minifigure is the first based on actor Gal Gadot's live-action version of the character.

Printed defensive bracelets

Unique eagle print on shield

Glow-in-the-dark eyes.

Armor mold first used in Ultra Agents theme

Armored Batman High-tech armor is Batman's only hope when he battles Superman in the Clash of the Heroes set (76044).

LEGO® DC COMICS SUPER HEROES

Classic heroes and villains got very different looks this year thanks to three new Super Heroes subthemes. Sets based on *Batman v Superman: Dawn of Justice* matched their minifigures to the latest movie, while a single huge set stepped back in time to celebrate the style of the 1960s. Finally, the new Mighty Micros line ramped up the comic-book charm.

Robin The Boy Wonder swaps the Batmobile for his own red-and-yellow Robin racer for his Mighty Micros outing.

Cartoonish face print

Highly stylized mask

Simple torso design

MIGHTY MICROS

Big on character but short in stature, these minifigures are no ordinary Super Heroes! Instead, the Mighty Micros come in small, self-contained sets, each featuring one hero, one villain, and two outlandish concept cars.

Over-the-top emblem

Bane This miniaturized muscleman drives a dragster with a spinning silver drill in Mighty Micros: Robin vs. Bane (76062).

DAWN OF JUSTICE

Three sets based on the big-screen sequel to *Man of Steel* pitted Batman against Superman; Batman against a pair of LexCorp henchmen; and Batman, Superman, and Wonder Woman against a new-look, long-haired Lex Luthor!

Building stud on head

Standard minifigure arms

Piggy Ten piggies appear in The Angry Birds Movie sets, all with different faces on the same new body mold.

LEGO® *THE ANGRY BIRDS MOVIE*™

Video game stars the Angry Birds got their own movie in 2016, along with a new LEGO theme! Six sets captured the fun of the film, complete with working catapults!

Face print found in Bird Island Egg Heist (75823)

Red The angriest bird appears in five sets out of six, each time with a different—but always unimpressed—expression.

Wings move like minifigure arms

Smile can be swapped for scowling face on other side

Riddler An enigma wrapped in a bright green bodysuit, this puzzle-loving pest is out to dynamite the classic Batcave!

1960s villains lack the muscle definition of modern foes!

Lighter hair than most Joker minifigures.

Choice of grin or surprised face

The Joker Based on the actor Cesar Romero, this Joker's bristly mustache shows through his white clown makeup!

BATMAN CLASSIC TV SERIES

On its release, the 2,526-piece *Batman* Classic TV Series Batcave (76052) was the biggest ever LEGO® DC Comics Super Heroes set. It included nine colorful minifigures based on the larger-than-life characters from the 1960s TV show.

Unique bear ears hat piece

Flower brought back to life by E.T. in film.

Toy Tag unlocks exclusive battle arena

Finn The *Adventure Time* star is joined by pals Jake the Dog and Lumpy Space Princess in 2016's DIMENSIONS sets.

E.T. The adorable alien film star comes with a pot plant and a buildable telephone for calling his home planet.

LEGO® DIMENSIONS

Even more movie, TV show, and video game characters went through the LEGO DIMENSIONS portal in 2016! Newcomers adding to the play possibilities included the stars of animated series *Adventure Time*, SEGA gaming icon Sonic the Hedgehog, and movie stars from E.T. The Extra-Terrestrial to the Gremlins. Those that came with gold-colored Toy Tags also unlocked new gameplay arenas.

LEGO® MINECRAFT™

Two brick-built Iron Golems and a three-headed Wither were among the foes faced by Steve and Alex in 2016's LEGO Minecraft sets. New molded figures included wither skeletons and peaceful Villagers, while a pair of "Skin Packs" featured a total of eight new minifigures. These packs reflected the wide range of character customization options available to Minecraft players online.

- Barbute helmet print
- Pixelated lava armor print

Knight Skin
The minifigure parts found in Skin Packs are ideal for mixing and matching to create new playable characters.

- Linked arms do not move
- Long torso suggests a knee-length robe

Villager Combined with standard short legs, a new long torso piece makes this monklike figure as tall as a minifigure.

- Printed "no ghosts" shoulder patch
- New sideswept hair piece
- Ghost grenades on bandolier
- Brick-built proton pack on back
- Posable arms for grabbing food

Peter Venkman Ectoplasm oozes over this original Ghostbuster's suit—the result of an encounter with Slimer in the 1984 film.

Jillian Holtzmann Part of a new generation of Ghostbusters in the 2016 film, Holtzy takes the wheel in the updated Ectomobile.

Slimer One of five ghosts found in Firehouse Headquarters, this spudlike spook also appears in a LEGO DIMENSIONS set.

LEGO® GHOSTBUSTERS

The original 1980s Ghostbusters were first made into minifigures for a 2014 LEGO Ideas set. Two years later, they were back in the 4,634-piece Firehouse Headquarters (75827), at the time the third-largest LEGO set ever! Also in 2016, new movie *Ghostbusters: Answer the Call* introduced a fresh team of female ghoul-getters, as seen in the set Ecto-1 & 2 (75828).

- Clever torso design covers none of the letters in the Ford logo

Ford Model A Hot Rod Driver The most casually dressed driver in 2016 wears the Ford logo under his shirt.

LEGO® SPEED CHAMPIONS

Three more makes of car joined the starting grid for the second year of this realistic motorsports theme. Audi, Chevrolet, and Ford lined up with two sets each, while Porsche returned with the largest set of the 2016 wave. A vintage car also joined the collection for the first time, in the shape of a flame-decorated Model A Ford Hot Rod.

- New ponytail piece
- Armor built in to upper torso piece
- Classic LEGO® Pirates hook hand

Nadakhan With two torso pieces and a proud plume of hair, the creepy Sky Pirates chief towers over other minifigures!

- Same hairstyle as Zane, but in gold
- Old-fashioned mechanical design

Echo Zane The ninja meet this rusty replica of Zane in the largest Sky Pirates set, The Lighthouse Siege (70594).

- Mask hides a wide and eager grin

Homemade "purple ninja" costume

Nya The Master of Water goes without a mask in 2016, after years of wearing her Samurai X disguise.

- Water Ninja symbol

Lil' Nelson This adoring young fan of the ninja dons purple robes to ride with Cole in Rock Roader (70589).

- New shoulder armor piece

- Earth Ninja symbol
- Traditional ninja leg wraps

Ghost Cole The Master of Earth has the same ghostly green head piece with dual expressions in two 2016 sets.

LEGO® NINJAGO®

By 2016, Nya was a fully fledged member of the ninja team, bringing their number to six. Together they fought scallywag Sky Pirates, led by the giant genie Nadakhan, and the spirits of their old enemies as summoned by the malevolent Master Yang. Cole was briefly turned into a ghost, while Zane met his "brother"—a clockwork copy of himself!

RARE MINIFIGURES

SOME MINIFIGURES are harder to find than others. But not all are rare for the same reasons. Sometimes, just a handful of a certain minifigure might be made as a very special competition prize. More frequently, larger but still limited runs mark certain events or anniversaries. These are available only while stocks last, at a specific location or with certain purchases. Randomly distributed minifigures, meanwhile, might be found anywhere, but only if you are very lucky. Others were never meant to be rare, only to prove increasingly hard to find as the years go by ....

Comic-Con Deadpool Duck Exclusive minifigures are often given away at the annual San Diego Comic-Con. This 2017 example combines two cult Marvel characters: Deadpool and Howard the Duck!

Toy Fair Iron Man Just 125 people got their hands on this exclusive Marvel minifigure at the 2012 New York Toy Fair. He was given away to promote the new LEGO® Marvel Super Heroes theme.

LEGO Lady Chef Diners at the huge LEGO House attraction in Denmark get a free chef minifigure with their meal! This kitchen queen is the 2020 edition, following an earlier mustachioed version.

LEGO Fan Weekend Minifigure 2009 This smiley fellow was given away in small numbers at a LEGO fan event in 2009. His rare printed torso is what makes him a real catch for collectors.

Mr. Gold Five thousand copies of this gold-colored gent were randomly distributed in LEGO® Minifigures lucky-dip bags in 2013, to add to the excitement of collecting the theme's tenth series.

Kladno Minifigure
Employees at the LEGO Group's Kladno manufacturing complex in Czechia designed this minifigure in 2013. Then 4,000 of them got to take him home as a Christmas treat!

50th Anniversary Minifigure
Only available with limited-edition book *The LEGO® Collector's Guide: Premium Edition*, this 2008 minifigure celebrates the 50th anniversary of the LEGO brick.

De Bouwsteen Minifigure
Just 750 of these redheads were given out by Dutch fan group De Bouwsteen at the 2008 LEGOWorld event. It was produced with special permission from the LEGO Group.

Shadow Leonardo There was no need to shell out for this rare Ninja Turtle in 2012. All 400 were given away as raffle prizes at New York Comic-Con, riding on NYCC-branded skateboards.

LEGO Universe Nexus Astronaut This spaceman was given to fans who preordered the LEGO® Universe game in 2010. He's still waiting for his own preordered oxygen tanks …

Gold C-3PO This dazzling droid is one of just five made from real 14 carat gold. He was minted to mark the 30th anniversary of *Star Wars* in 2007, along with an even rarer solid silver variant.

LEGO® Originals Wooden Minifigure
Standing 8 in (20 cm) tall, this mega minifigure statue is made out of oak from sustainable sources, with ABS plastic hands for gripping brick-built accessories. Launched in 2019, each minifigure is handcrafted and designed to be customized by its owner—using paints, fabrics, or anything else!

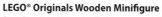

Boba Fett This LEGO® *Star Wars*™ minifigure came in a standard 2003 set. He only became a must-have in later years, when his intricate arm and leg prints turned out to be exclusive to that set!

THE LEGO BATMAN MOVIE

LEGO® Batman got his first theme in 2006, before Batarang-ing on to the big screen in 2015's THE LEGO® MOVIE™. Few minifigures were so deserving of their own film, so it was no surprise that he struggled to share the limelight when the moment arrived! Nevertheless, THE LEGO BATMAN MOVIE sets found room for Bruce Wayne's ego alongside his best friends and foes.

Robin Dick Grayson's eye-popping glasses are part of a new Boy Wonder hair piece made specially for his minifigure.

Worried look can be swapped for a wide grin

Suit based on Batman's "Reggae Man" outfit

Sash continues onto back

Jim Gordon Gotham's top cop wears this ceremonial uniform at his retirement party and in The Scuttler vehicle set (70908).

New not-much-hair piece

Legs and cape first seen in 2016's Batman Classic TV Series Batcave (76052)

Alfred Pennyworth Batman's faithful butler appears in three movie sets but wears this 1960s-style Batsuit in just one of them.

Alternative face shows gritted teeth

Chunky new body armor accessory

GCPD

Barbara Gordon Jim Gordon's daughter follows in her father's footsteps to become Gotham's police commissioner in THE LEGO BATMAN MOVIE.

THE HEROES

Spoiler alert! At the end of THE LEGO BATMAN MOVIE, even the villains join forces with Batman to help him save the day. But for most of the film, his allies are more familiar faces ….

2017

TWO BRICKBUSTER LEGO® films thrilled cinemagoers in 2017, and themes based on THE LEGO® BATMAN MOVIE and THE LEGO® NINJAGO® MOVIE™ kept the excitement building long after the credits had rolled. Also bringing big-screen heroes down to minifigure size were sets inspired by *Star Wars: The Last Jedi*, DC's *Justice League*, Disney's *Pirates of the Caribbean: Dead Men Tell No Tales*, and the latest installments in Marvel's *Infinity Saga*. Meanwhile, in Denmark, the new LEGO® House experience opened its doors to visitors ….

Rocking "The Joker" sign

Joker Manor (70922) The theme's biggest set includes exclusive disco versions of Batman and Robin among its 3,444 pieces.

Rollercoaster encircles whole building

Updated head piece has two expressions

Batman The Caped Crusader's classic look is updated for the movie with a new bright yellow Utility Belt piece.

THE VILLAINS

All of Batman's most famous adversaries appear in the movie, along with some rarely remembered villains from the hero's storied history. That's right: the likes of Polka-Dot Man and Calendar Man are real *Batman* comics characters!

· Unique hair piece

· Skull print on belt

· Mismatched roller skate accessories

Harley Quinn Harley's Smylex-branded top is a reference to the Joker's trademark weapon in the 1989 *Batman* movie.

· Chinless helmet mold first used for collectible Minifigure Hockey Player in 2011

· Mask print makes eyes looks like polka dots, too!

Polka-Dot Man This colorful crook is based on a villain who first faced Batman in Detective Comics in 1962.

· Fabric coattails fit between torso and legs

· Even Joker's trick guns can be dangerous!

The Joker Batman's best frenemy appears in seven movie sets and wears these extra-long coattails in three of them.

· Calendar grid printed on swimming cap piece

· Cape and collar are two separate pieces

Calendar Man This everyday evildoer is dated in more ways than one: he made his comic-book debut in 1958!

· Exclusive flame-print helmet

· Stray tufts of straw ruin Scarecrow's disguise!

Disguised Scarecrow If you like your pizza with extra fear gas, place an order with Scarecrow Special Delivery (70910)!

COLLECTIBLE MINIFIGURES

Twenty LEGO® Minifigures from the movie could only be found in collectible mystery bags. They included six very different versions of Batman, some ultra-obscure and oddball villains, and Dick Grayson wielding a can of Shark Repellent!

· Helmet is a hollow 2x2x2 dome brick

· Unique molded cape part covers shoulders

Red Hood Who is the Red Hood? Lift off this villain's unique red dome helmet and you'll find … another mask!

· One-of-a-kind head piece

· Notepad accessory

Eraser 2B or not 2B? That is the question posed by this pencil-thin pest with a talent for making things disappear!

· Shoes styled like pencil points

· Pink sweatband under cowl

> YOU CAN'T SPELL BALLET WITHOUT EL BAT!

Fairy Batman Is this Batman's most unusual minifigure? Fairy Batman comes with a tutu, a wand, and an exclusive pink Bat-cowl.

· Tutu piece first worn by Ballerina Minifigure in 2016

· Wand and wing molds first used for 2012's Fairy collectible Minifigure

· Printed salad leaves on oversized plate piece

· Silk robe print

· Lobster element new for 2017

Lobster-Lovin' Batman After a long-day's crime fighting, LEGO Batman just loves a microwaved lobster—alone or with new friends!

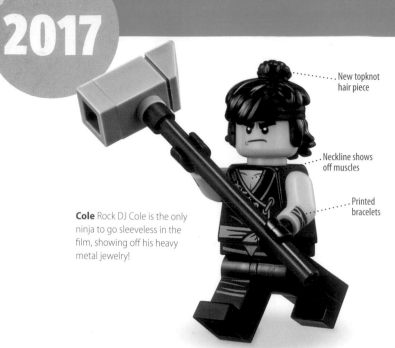

New topknot hair piece

Neckline shows off muscles

Printed bracelets

Cole Rock DJ Cole is the only ninja to go sleeveless in the film, showing off his heavy metal jewelry!

Unique flamelike hair piece

Sticking plaster over left eye

> *THIS HAIR IS GIVING ME SIDEBURNS!*

Kai On film, the Master of Fire has a scar across his right eye. On TV, it is located on the left.

New diamond-print legs

THE LEGO® NINJAGO® MOVIE™

After six years of animated TV adventures, the Wu Crew made the leap to the big screen in September 2017. THE LEGO NINJAGO MOVIE took the team in a new direction, with a comedy adventure that stood apart from the ongoing TV show. And so the movie sets were released as a standalone theme, alongside a range of collectible Minifigures.

Exclusive ponytail piece

Fabric kusazuri armor piece

THE NINJA

All six ninja got makeovers for their movie debut, including new clothes, new hairstyles, and even new faces! But each new look stayed true to the characters' much-loved TV personalities and established elemental powers.

Nya The Water Ninja's movie minifigure has a mole on one cheek. Jay calls it a "mark of eternal beauty."

Scowling face hidden by octopus mask.

Helmet made from two dome-shaped pieces.

Printed jellyfish tendrils on torso.

Stud-shooting "fish-zooka"

Combined shark mask and breathing gear piece

Jelly When it comes to fighting, this aquatic fanatic floats like a jellyfish and stings like … a jellyfish!

Fish and blade make a scale weapon

Breathing gear separate from mask piece

Hammer Head Variants of this big-mouthed bully get up to something fishy in three THE LEGO NINJAGO MOVIE sets.

Flying Jelly Sub (set 70610) Hammer Head takes the controls of this jellyfishlike submarine—complete with swinging "toxic" tentacles.

Four Eyes Octopus officers like this one are the most extensively armed soldiers in Garmadon's Shark Army!

THE SHARK ARMY

Four-armed is not forewarned, as the evil Lord Garmadon is repeatedly foiled by the ninja in THE LEGO NINJAGO MOVIE! He uses insect, bird, and fruit forces against them before finally unleashing his Shark Army!

Transparent red eye elements

COLLECTIBLE MINIFIGURES

THE LEGO NINJAGO MOVIE series of collectible characters featured a total of 20 minifigures. These included several of the ninja in casual clothes, a new Master Wu, and three very different versions of Lord Garmadon.

Hair is part of exclusive hood piece

Lloyd Garmadon All of the Green Ninja's movie minifigures have emerald-colored eyes. In previous sets, they had always been black.

Lopsided hoodie hem printed on leg piece

Tousled hair piece worn only by Jay

Scarf piece new for 2017

Jay Walker A zigzag design on his jacket hints that this might just be the famous Master of Lightning!

Severe new haircut with shaved sides printed on head

Unique backpack piece

Zane A straight smile, parallel eyebrows, and perfectly symmetrical creases in his pants give away this ninja's robotic origins!

Garmadon's movie minifigures are the first to smile!

Torso extender mold first used for Garmadon minifigures in 2012

Flashback Garmadon In his imagination, this is the groovy 1970s dad that Lord Garmadon could have been to Lloyd!

DID YOU KNOW?
Temple of the Ultimate Ultimate Weapon (70617) is the only movie set to feature all six ninja.

Printed dental braces

M:Tron logo on undershirt

Nancy Hot dogs and the classic LEGO® Space theme M:Tron keep this young city-dweller smiling, even when Lord Garmadon attacks!

Hair piece has ponytail at back

Logo of 2002 LEGO theme Galidor

Mother Doomsday This cheery comic book seller is one of 10 ordinary citizens in the 4,867-piece Ninjago City set (70620).

CITIZENS

The everyday inhabitants of Ninjago City appear throughout THE LEGO NINJAGO MOVIE theme. Some of these supporting characters had already been seen in the TV show, but none had been made into real minifigures before!

Blue-and-gold replaces Nya's red-and-black look

Samurai X A printed mask beneath her helmet kept P.I.X.A.L.'s new persona under wraps until the TV show revealed it.

LEGO® NINJAGO®

As the comedy focus of THE LEGO NINJAGO MOVIE created a box-office storm in cinemas, the more character-based original series continued along its own path on TV. Nine sets tied in with the seventh season's "Hands of Time" storyline, introducing the Vermillion Warriors and a new-look Samurai X—a secret identity now passed on from ninja Nya to P.I.X.A.L.!

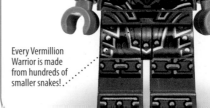

Snake hair first used for Medusa collectible Minifigure in 2013

General Machia This Vermillion Warrior comes with standard legs that can be swapped for a long, brick-built snake tail!

Every Vermillion Warrior is made from hundreds of smaller snakes!

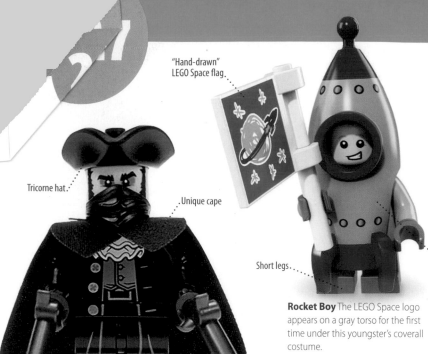

"Hand-drawn" LEGO Space flag

Tricorne hat.

.Unique cape

.Short legs

Rocket Boy The LEGO Space logo appears on a gray torso for the first time under this youngster's coverall costume.

.Exclusive spaceship piece slots over head and torso

.Long black coat print continues on legs

Highwayman This masked man is out to steal one thing only—the hearts of Minifigure collectors everywhere!

LEGO® MINIFIGURES

An air of mystery surrounded Series 17 of the Minifigures theme, as one of its characters was kept under wraps to build up excitement about his identity. The secretive soul turned out to be a dashing Highwayman with a pair of antique pistols. He completed a diverse line-up that included a Roman Gladiator, a Retro Spaceman, a Dance Instructor, and more!

DID YOU KNOW?
Series 17 also included a Butterfly Girl and a man dressed as a giant corncob!

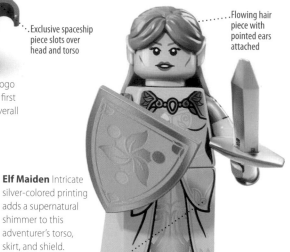

.Flowing hair piece with pointed ears attached

Elf Maiden Intricate silver-colored printing adds a supernatural shimmer to this adventurer's torso, skirt, and shield.

Leaf-shaped dress layers.

Chunky phone made from three pieces.

.Upper arms molded as separate parts

Yuppie This high-tech exec is straight out of the 1980s, with rolled-up suit sleeves and a giant cell phone!

LEGO® NEXO KNIGHTS™

A cloud hovered over Knighton in 2017—the villainous Cloud of Monstrox! The sky-high bad guy used lightning bolts to activate a scary Stone Monster Army and to turn the recently redeemed court jester Jestro into a villain all over again. The NEXO KNIGHTS needed all their app-enabled powers to weather the storm and chip away at their rock-hard foes!

Lightning-tattered clothes.

.Transparent light blue head piece

Electrified Jestro After being struck by lightning, this jester-turned-TV-weatherman is forecasting all hail—as in "All hail Monstrox!"

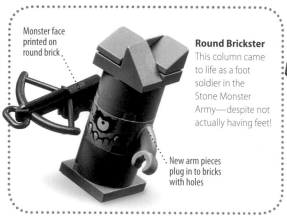

Monster face printed on round brick.

Round Brickster This column came to life as a foot soldier in the Stone Monster Army—despite not actually having feet!

.New arm pieces plug in to bricks with holes

Stone armor piece features unique printing.

Rogul Two of these rocky wraiths appear in 2017 sets, their bodies floating on a vortex of spinning stones!

Roog This slab-handed stone warrior has a younger brother called Reex and an older, four-wheeled monster-truck brother called Rumble!

Black head piece makes hood look spookily empty!.

Lightning-tattered clothes.

Giant fists fit over standard minifigure hands.

"Helmet" adds furrowed brow and pointy ears.

Brand-new lower body part with lightning-effect printing.

General Garg Four Stone Army minifigures wear new gargoyle wings, but only Garg gets to rock them in black!

Printed round tile fits on to unique helmet.

.Spooky shredded cape

Lord Krakenskull As if his helmet wasn't scary enough, this ancient warrior really does have a cracked stone skull underneath!

LEGO® DC COMICS SUPER HEROES

Super Hero team-up movie *Justice League* dominated the DC theme in 2017. Batman, Superman, Cyborg, Aquaman, The Flash, and Wonder Woman all battled Parademons across three exciting sets, with Wonder Woman Diana Prince also starring in a set based on her own blockbuster movie. Prince's minifigure got a cool new cloak, while The Flash and Aquaman got completely new looks.

Wonder Woman Everyone's favorite Amazonian dons a cloak and hood to fight evil Ares in Wonder Woman Warrior Battle (76075).

Hood can be swapped for hair piece

Brighter armor than 2016 variant

Spread-out wings piece

Intricate armor print also seen on green Parademons

Parademon This buggy blue-and-yellow alien comes with a choice of wing pieces (spread or retracted) in Battle of Atlantis (76085).

MIGHTY MICROS

This year's trio of Mighty Micros sets continued the Justice League theme, starring Superman, Batman, and Wonder Woman respectively. As usual, each set also featured a villain and a pair of pocket-sized super-cars.

Back-to-front Superman symbol

Bizarro This muddled-up mimic of the Man of Steel drives a similar car to Superman, only built completely backward!

Extra-large smile and eyes

Simplified Superman torso print

Superman The classic curl hair piece is the only part this compact Son of Krypton shares with other Superman minifigures.

Alternative face shows eyes white with power

Unique hair piece with printed highlights

Aquaman The second Arthur Curry minifigure is the first to be based on the look of movie actor Jason Momoa.

Slightly smaller smile can be seen on the reverse

Detailed armor-panel printing

The Flash This updated speedster has far more printed detail than earlier The Flash minifigures, and a brand-new helmet.

LEGO® DIMENSIONS

The third and final year for this building-and-gaming theme included new Level Packs based on THE LEGO BATMAN MOVIE and '80s adventure film *The Goonies*. Smaller sets added TV stars from *Teen Titans* and *The Powerpuff Girls* to the gameplay, as well as movie minifigures from *Beetlejuice* and *Harry Potter*. Even LEGO CITY's Chase McCain joined in with the fun!

Badge worn on opposite side to earlier Chases

Lighter shirt than 2017 LEGO CITY variant

Chase McCain LEGO CITY's top cop has appeared in several sets and video games, but his DIMENSIONS variant is unique.

Choice of smiling and grumpy face prints

First use for this new hair mold

Beetlejuice The spooky star of his own 1988 movie comes with a brick-built Sandworm monster in matching black and white stripes!

LEGO® DC SUPER HERO GIRLS

Mini dolls got in on the Super Hero action in 2017, with 10 sets based on animated TV series *DC Super Hero Girls*. Wonder Woman, Batgirl, and Harley Quinn all made appearances in the limited-series theme.

Supergirl The hero also known as Kara Danvers attends Super Hero High School (41232) with Lena Luthor and Poison Ivy.

Detachable fabric cape

Thor This mighty minifigure wears a helmet for the first time in 2017, as well as new-look body armor.

Winged helmet found in two sets

Printed armor on left arm

Helmet can be swapped for a flowing hair piece.

Warrior face paint

Exclusive asymmetrical cape

Huge helmet prongs made from rubberized plastic

Hela Thor's power-hungry older sister comes with a brick-built stand so that she can tower over other minifigures!

Valkyrie This hero is exclusive to The Ultimate Battle for Asgard (76084), in which she battles Hela and her Berserkers.

LEGO® MARVEL SUPER HEROES

The smash-hit films *Spider-Man: Homecoming*, *Guardians of the Galaxy Vol. 2*, and *Thor: Ragnarok* all inspired LEGO sets in 2017, with the latter two producing the most new minifigures. The comic-book exploits of the Avengers were also depicted in three sets that introduced new "Power Blast" pieces for even more role-play fun. Finally, the Mighty Micros hit the road again in six small superpower-themed cars.

CINEMATIC UNIVERSE

A total of 25 new minifigures debuted in Marvel movie sets during 2017. And as if that wasn't enough for any fan, there were also special figures of giant Gladiator Hulk and tiny Baby Groot!

Standard minifigure hands can grip giant fists

Arms can bend in any direction

Ms. Marvel Kamala Khan's shape-shifting arms are represented by a single tube piece that can extend in either direction!

DID YOU KNOW?
Ms. Marvel's arms are also used by Elastigirl in a 2018 Disney Pixar *Incredibles 2* set.

Hands can be held in a minifigure's grasp.

Baby Groot Made from a single piece, this tiny Guardian of the Galaxy stands waist-high beside his minifigure pals!

Feet stand on a single LEGO stud

AVENGERS

Comic books *Iron Man*, *She-Hulk*, and *Ms. Marvel* all provided subject matter for must-have sets in 2017. They included the first minifigures of Agent Coulson, She-Hulk herself, and the Kamala Khan incarnation of Ms. Marvel.

Same hair piece mold as Ms. Marvel

Smile can be switched for angry face

Wolverine This mini mutant comes with claspable claw pieces—maybe for styling his square hair and single impressive eyebrow!

Thick sideburns printed on face

Evil eyes printed on otherwise plain black head piece

Helmet appears in two other X-Men sets

X-Men symbol on belt buckle

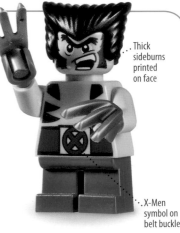

She-Hulk For her debut LEGO appearance, the Hulk's heroic cousin dons an outfit she first wore in the comics during 2004.

Red Hulk The Hulk's crimson counterpart makes his sole set appearance to date in Hulk vs. Red Hulk (76078).

Same head-and-torso mold as 2015 Hulk figure

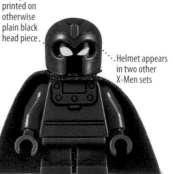

Magneto As a Mighty Micros character, the X-Men's eternal enemy drives a car shaped like a giant cartoon magnet!

MIGHTY MICROS

Made with fewer than 100 pieces each, this year's Marvel Mighty Micros sets pitted Spider-Man against Scorpion, Iron Man against Thanos, and Wolverine against Magneto. All three pairings had short legs but very long histories!

Rose Tico The Aurebesh letters on this Resistance technician's overalls translate as "GLD," for "Ground Logistics Division."

Unique hair piece

Aurebesh script

Same helmet mold as flametrooper

AT-M6 Pilot The pilots controlling the First Order's walkers are never seen in the film, making this minifigure extra-special!

THE LAST JEDI

Spoiler-free sets for Episode VIII included First Order and Resistance ships, as well as a 1,106-piece model BB-8! Nineteen new minifigures appeared in these releases, along with a figure of ball-shaped First Order droid, BB-9E.

Distinctive gray details on armor and helmet

Vice Admiral Holdo
This wise Resistance leader is the first minifigure ever to have lavender-colored hair!

Traditional Gatalentan robe print

Fearsome twisted face print

Supreme Leader Snoke
The phantom menace behind the First Order wears the same gold color as the far friendlier C-3PO!

Blaster found in more than 130 sets

Belt print continues on back

LEGO® STAR WARS™

Another busy year in the galaxy far, far away saw sets based on the original trilogy, the prequels, *The Force Awakens*, *Rebels*, *Rogue One*, and *The Freemaker Adventures*! But the biggest draw was the new Skywalker saga movie, *The Last Jedi*. Anticipation for this was fueled by seven new sets released in September—three months ahead of the film's premiere!

Exclusive blue hair piece

Grand Admiral Thrawn
One of the Empire's top tacticians, Thrawn is the first minifigure representative of the blue-skinned Chiss species.

Admiral's rank plaque

STAR WARS REBELS

Fan-favorite character Thrawn joined the cast of *Rebels* in its third season, having previously starred in best-selling books. A minifigure followed hot on the heels of his animated incarnation, found exclusively in *The Phantom* (75170),

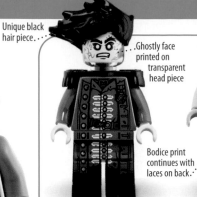

Unique black hair piece

Ghostly face printed on transparent head piece

Long hair piece introduced in 2017

Beads and bandanna are part of hair piece

Captain Jack Sparrow This plucky pirate appeared in every 2011 set, but he now has more intricate details.

Bodice print continues with laces on back

Captain Salazar This spooky sailor has a hair mold that was later repurposed as a torch flame piece!

Carina The daughter of Jack Sparrow's former first mate is a talented astronomer and not, as others claim, a witch!

Floaty shirt and scarf print continues onto legs

LEGO® PIRATES OF THE CARIBBEAN™

Six years after LEGO sets celebrated the first four *Pirates of the Caribbean* movies, a further, huge set was released alongside the fifth film in the series. Measuring 26 in (68 cm) long and featuring 2,294 pieces, *Silent Mary* (71042) captured all the detail of the haunted shipwreck seen in *Dead Men Tell No Tales*. It also came with eight exclusive minifigures.

ROGUE ONE: A STAR WARS STORY

A second wave of sets based on this 2016 film came out in early 2017. It included Battle on Scarif (75171), featuring Jyn in Imperial disguise, and Y-wing Starfighter (75172), boasting two new rebel minifigures.

Fishlike head has a reflective shimmer

Admiral Raddus
An early hero of the Rebellion, this brave officer is the first gray-skinned Mon Calamari minifigure.

Mon Calamari naval uniform

Moroff The first Gigorian minifigure is a hairy rebel-for-hire with a unique "sandwich board" head and chest piece.

Strapped-on gear is part of sandwich board piece

Fur print on legs and hidden torso

LEGO® BRICKHEADZ

Made from around 100 pieces each, LEGO BrickHeadz are highly stylized statuettes designed for display rather than play. In 2017, the theme launched in stores with characters from *Star Wars*, Marvel, Disney, and more.

Lloyd Several exclusive printed pieces are used to give the Green Ninja from THE LEGO NINJAGO MOVIE a blocky BrickHeadz look.

Green eyes are round printed tile pieces

DID YOU KNOW?
This year's LEGO *Star Wars* Advent Calendar (75184) featured BB-8 in a Santa hat!

LEGO® CITY

A previously unknown side of the CITY was revealed in 2017, with seven sets exploring its jungles. Ancient ruins awaited discovery in the undergrowth, along with big cats, crocodiles, and minifigure-eating mega-plants! Meanwhile, at the seaside, a new wave of Coast Guard sets sailed into view, complete with several boats that could really float!

Scar over right eyebrow

Drawstrings for hood, printed on back

Male Jungle Explorer A rope, a radio, packed pockets, and a confident grin are all this outdoor adventurer needs!

JUNGLE EXPLORERS

More than 20 different scientists, archaeologists, engineers, and pilots played a part in the Jungle Explorers' various missions. Together they explored booby-trapped temples, mysterious plane wrecks, and clearings crawling with spiders, snakes, and crocodiles!

Adjustable back legs

Posable head

Tiger This new cat figure was also used for black panthers and distinctively dotted leopards in Jungle Explorers sets.

Rescue Raft Pilot A red life jacket print means this minifigure doesn't always need a separate yellow life jacket piece.

Life jacket print continues on back

Printed spring hook for rope rescues

New face print shared with two 2017 police officers

Badge shows a lifebelt over blue waves

Helicopter Pilot This friendly flyer shares a casual sweater-and-open-jacket look with four other 2017 Coast Guard minifigures.

THIS DOESN'T LOOK LIKE THE CITY TO ME!

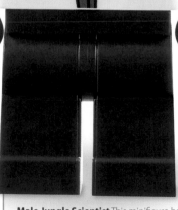

Camouflage colors under lab coat

Test tube samples in pocket

COAST GUARD

Six sets updated the Coast Guard subtheme after four years lost at sea. They included life rafts, rescue planes, surfers, and sharks, as well as the first new Coast Guard headquarters building since 2008.

DID YOU KNOW? The first LEGO ships to really float on water were released way back in 1973!

Male Jungle Scientist This minifigure has smiling and scared face prints, ready for whatever the jungle throws at him!

Face print found in more than 60 sets

Bugatti Chiron Driver The theme's first Bugatti racer wears the famous French company's oval logo on his front and back.

Ferrari Engineer Two automotive experts wear this bold branded top in Ferrari FXX K & Development Center (75882).

Same smiling face as LEGO CITY Rescue Raft Pilot

Mercedes-AMG Petronas Formula One Team Driver This racer is one of six minifigures to wear the iconic Mercedes-Benz three-pointed star symbol in 2017.

The Petronas green car graphic features on the leg of the race suit

Alternative face print shows beads of sweat

Digital tablet tucked into pants

Female Jungle Explorer This well-equipped explorer has a water bottle strapped to her back.

LEGO® SPEED CHAMPIONS

Coming around for a third lap in 2017, the Speed Champions theme added vehicles from Mercedes-Benz and Bugatti to its ever-growing garage of superstar cars. Ferrari was represented by two sets, including a Development Center with a wind tunnel (75882), while McLaren returned with a Bright Orange 720S car. A single Ford set, meanwhile, included two GT cars, a podium, and a trophy.

Common torso print enhanced by LEGO House branding on back.

Printed fabric folds suggest a bigger than average belly!

LEGO® HOUSE

In September 2017, a new 3-acre (12,000-square-meter) attraction opened its doors in the birthplace of the minifigure. Built to resemble a stack of giant LEGO bricks, LEGO House in Billund, Denmark, combines the LEGO Group's story with endless opportunities for play. It is also home to some souvenir minifigures found nowhere else in the world!

Same torso used for more widely available 2018 variant

Slogan reads "Home of the Brick"

Tour Guide Just 80 of these branded minifigures were made for a limited-edition set celebrating the new LEGO House.

Chef This classic cook came as a side order with every meal bought in the LEGO House restaurant during 2017.

Cheerful store employee.

Plain red leg piece first seen in 1978.

VIP Logo Minifigure Amazingly, this is the first ever minifigure to have a plain bright red torso with matching hands!

LEGO® BRAND STORES

Owners of a LEGO VIP Card can gain access to rewards and special offers in brand stores and on LEGO.com. In 2017, cardholders could get their hands on the Exclusive VIP Set (40178), which combined a brick-built replica of a VIP Card with a minifigure-scale LEGO store! It included two new minifigures that were available nowhere else.

Exclusive VIP Set (40178) Just like the real thing, this LEGO store has life-sized minifigure mugs and a giant brick on display.

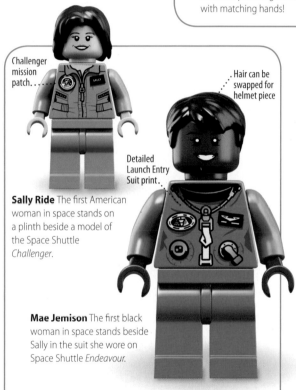

Challenger mission patch.

Hair can be swapped for helmet piece

Detailed Launch Entry Suit print.

Sally Ride The first American woman in space stands on a plinth beside a model of the Space Shuttle *Challenger*.

Mae Jemison The first black woman in space stands beside Sally in the suit she wore on Space Shuttle *Endeavour*.

LEGO® EDUCATION

Designed to encourage role-play and storytelling skills in the classroom, Community Minifigure Set (45022) and Fantasy Minifigure Set (45023) joined the LEGO Education line-up in 2017. Both sets included game cards to trigger ideas and an endlessly customizable range of minifigure parts. With everything from farmers, firefighters, and fishmongers to pixies, prospectors, and pirates, children could mix and match parts to create new characters.

Chain mail armor print

Dungeon keys on belt

Smilin This ironically named imp guards the Goblin Village with a spear twice as tall as he is!

LEGO® ELVES

Goblins came to Elvendale in 2017, adding a new figure style to the mini doll theme. Ten characters all shared the same mold, with different colors and expressive face prints to tell them apart.

One of 12 hairstyles found in the set

Freckled face more often used for minifigure children

Hairdresser and Customer A fabric cape piece is put to use as a hairdresser gown in the Community Minifigures Set.

LEGO® IDEAS

Four fan-inspired sets were released under the LEGO Ideas banner in 2017, but only two included minifigures. The first was the Old Fishing Store (21310), then the largest set in the theme, with 2,049 pieces and four fishing fan minifigures. The second was Women of NASA (21312), in which four real-life space pioneers were honored in minifigure form

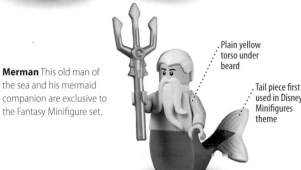

Merman This old man of the sea and his mermaid companion are exclusive to the Fantasy Minifigure set.

Plain yellow torso under beard

Tail piece first used in Disney Minifigures theme

Arms move back and forth

Evil Eye belt buckle

Bieblin This singer/songwriter goblin carries drumsticks and sheet music in his belt.

Nearly Headless Nick The first ever minifigure of Gryffindor Tower's resident ghost is made entirely from white and gray parts.

Carries own head in hand

I'D LOSE MY HEAD IF IT WASN'T ... OH!

15th-century costume

2018

THE LEGO GROUP celebrated two big anniversaries in this year. Not only was it 60 years since the LEGO® brick got its patent, it was also the 40th birthday of the minifigure! To mark these milestones, the collectible range of LEGO® Minifigures threw a costume party dressed, among other things, as LEGO bricks and classic characters. Later in the year, the new Wizarding World theme marked the return of Harry Potter sets—and the debut of medium-height minifigures.

Horace Slughorn Like the 2018 Severus Snape Boggart, Professor Slughorn is found in just one limited-edition "Bricktober" minifigure pack, available as a promotion in select stores.

Chemical flask piece introduced in 2011

LEGO® WIZARDING WORLD™

Seven years after the previous LEGO® Harry Potter™ sets were released, this new theme brought back the boy wizard and his many friends and foes. But that wasn't all—it also added minifigure versions of Newt Scamander and a host of magical characters from prequel films *Fantastic Beasts and Where to Find Them* and *Fantastic Beasts: The Crimes of Grindelwald*.

Unique torso print

The Trolley Witch The fifth version of Hogwarts Express (set 75955) was the first to feature the train's on-board caterer.

Exclusive face print

Same Gryffindor torso print as Hermione

Shocked face on reverse

Lucian Bole This little-known member of the Slytherin Quidditch team appears in just one set, with teammate Marcus Flint.

Hermione Granger Hermione got a fresh look in 2018, including short legs and a brand-new hair piece.

Harry Potter The Boy Who Lived also had short minifigure legs for the first time in Wizarding World releases.

HARRY POTTER

Iconic builds such as Arthur Weasley's Flying Ford Anglia, the Whomping Willow, and Aragog the Acromantula were all revisited in this year's Harry Potter sets, which included a total of 33 brand-new minifigures!

Fur stole continues as part of torso print

Severus Snape Boggart This Boggart is what Snape would look like if he was dressed as Neville Longbottom's grandmother!

Neville's grandma's handbag

Rubeus Hagrid Far more detailed than the first Hagrid figures, the 2018 version towers over Harry and his pals!

Unique torso and arms with standard hands

Jacob Kowalski This minifigure's alternative face print has a chinstrap, for when he wears a helmet instead of hair.

First Newt not to wear an overcoat

Protective padding over suit

Hair mold first seen in LEGO® Friends

Newt Scamander Fantastic Beasts' lead character has ditched his overcoat since he first appeared in a 2016 LEGO Dimensions set.

Queenie Goldstein Tina Goldstein's younger sister comes with a choice of smiling and startled facial expressions.

FANTASTIC BEASTS

Two sets brought Fantastic Beasts to the LEGO Wizarding World in 2018. As well as six all-new minifigures, they included brick-built Erumpent, Occamy, and Thunderbird creatures, plus molded Niffler, Bowtruckle, and Thestral figures.

COLLECTIBLE MINIFIGURES

The Wizarding World launched with a range of 22 collectible Minifigures from both Harry Potter and Fantastic Beasts. Seven came with a new medium-length leg piece, used to depict older versions of the Hogwarts gang.

> AND PRESTO, MY RIGHT ARM IS AN OWL!

Exclusive light brown owl piece

Only Tina wears this hat

Tasty hotdog ready to eat

Wand found in more than 40 sets

Ravenclaw colors on uniform

Tina Goldstein This all-American, hotdog-wielding witch is a more colorful counterpart to her LEGO® Dimensions set variant from 2016.

Cho Chang The first minifigure of Harry's one-time girlfriend wears a fabric skirt piece over her medium-length legs.

Same hair as 2017 Roman Gladiator collectible Minifigure

Unique printed flag piece

Dean Thomas This Quidditch Chaser made his minifigure debut flying the flag for Gryffindor and wearing a unique scarf print.

Combined hat and hair element

Brand-new tied-up beard piece

Printed pattern at the bottom of the bowl

Albus Dumbledore Hogwarts' headmaster carries the magical Pensieve bowl, printed on the inside with a swirling blue pattern.

Hedwig figure first seen in 2010

New legs move like those of a full-height minifigure

Harry Potter Fourth-year Harry's medium-length legs make him one LEGO plate taller than his first-year minifigure on the facing page.

HOGWARTS CASTLE

The biggest set in the Wizarding World theme was the second-largest LEGO set ever released! The 6,020-piece Hogwarts Castle (set 71043) comes with four standard minifigures, plus 24 microfigures in scale with the sprawling building.

Microfigure is all one piece

Ron Weasley Despite standing just four LEGO plates high, this microfigure still captures Ronald's cheeky charm.

Base attaches to a single stud

Microfigure arms and legs cannot be moved.

Voldemort You-Know-Who still cuts a fearsome figure, even when he stands just 0.5 in (12 mm) tall!

LEGO® UNIKITTY

The beloved brick-built princess from THE LEGO® MOVIE™ got her own theme and an animated TV series in 2018. Eight playsets were complemented by 12 collector bags, each featuring a version of UniKitty or her poochlike pal PuppyCorn.

Dinosaur UniKitty A green UniKitty usually means a queasy UniKitty, but this time she is simply wearing dino fancy dress!

Cloud-shaped base plate

LEGO® CITY

The brave inhabitants of LEGO CITY really pushed the boundaries in 2018. While police officers kept order in the mountains, scientists explored an icy Arctic realm and miners dug deep underground. Meanwhile, minifigures in the ever-expanding City Center had fresh opportunities to work and play in brand-new hospitals, hotels, museums, and more!

Branches make carry handles for minifigure hands.

Fierce face can be swapped for worried expression

HE JOINED A SPLINTER GROUP!

Wide-brimmed hat first seen in Swamp Police sets in 2015

Friendly face with laughter lines

Police radio clipped on to vest

WHERE'S STUMPY?

Police Chief The head of the Mountain Police leads his team from a high-tech HQ perched on top of a mountain lion's den!

Same printed pockets as Mine Foreman

Bear claw scratches on belly

Police Motocross Biker
This off-road officer might look a little stern, but she has a friendly smile underneath her biker's helmet.

Disguised Crook Known as Stumpy to his pals, this villain is branching out in a unique tree costume, found in just one set.

MOUNTAIN POLICE

The cops had more than just crooks to contend with in Mountain Police sets! Bears, big cats, and beehives all featured in the subtheme, and officers relied on a new net-shooter gadget to bag the bad guys.

Paw-print design on underpants

Surprised Crook This bare-chested bad guy is only just out of bed when the Mountain Police come calling at his hideout!

Long hair and helmet are all one piece

ID badge for accessing restricted areas

Explosives Engineer This miner makes every excavation go with a bang! She comes with a stick of dynamite in Mining Team (set 60184).

Helmet with lamp new for 2018

Helmet found in just five sets.

Notebook tucked into utility belt

ARCTIC EXPLORERS

LEGO CITY scientists first reached the Arctic in 2014. Four years later, they returned to track down prehistoric animals frozen in the ice. These included a saber-toothed tiger and an enormous woolly mammoth!

Muscle definition shows through vest

Mine Foreman A digital version of this grizzled prospector became a character in the LEGO Legacy mobile game in 2019.

Temperature monitor on belt

New hood piece found in just three sets

Fake-fur hat piece new for 2018

Goggles printed on to head piece

Climbing gear strapped to legs and torso

Arctic Climber This minifigure hasn't turned blue in the cold—he's wearing a full face mask to protect himself from the elements!

Gloves to keep out the cold

Arctic Photographer Seen in two sets, this brave biologist carries a stills camera in one set and a video camera in the other.

Arctic Explorer A cosy hood keeps this Arctic scientist warm, even as she gets chills from digging up ancient polar animals!

Miner The sweat on this minifigure's brow shows just how hard he likes to work. Perhaps that's why he is found in two different sets!

MINERS

Four sets featured engineers and other expert minifigures mining for gold in 2018. Using a mix of heavy machinery and high explosives, the team collect shiny golden nugget pieces designed especially for the subtheme.

CITY-DWELLERS

Large sets such as City Hospital (60204) and Cargo Train (60198) introduced new city workers in 2018. Meanwhile the Outdoor Adventures People Pack (set 60202) included 15 unique characters all having fun on Mount Clutchmore!

Baby figure introduced in 2016.

Baby carrier attaches by a neck bracket

Father and Baby A brand-new baby carrier piece lets this dad go hands free when he goes on a family camping trip.

Same helmet as Arctic Climber.

Rafter This daring watersports enthusiast wears a new style of life jacket, replacing a design that had been in use since 2010.

DID YOU KNOW?
LEGO medics have worn the Star of Life symbol since 1994. It first appeared in Ambulance (set 6666).

Same quiff as NINJAGO's "brown ninja," Dareth

Electric guitar piece introduced in 2014

Rock Star Styled like a 1950s heartthrob, this rock 'n' roller records his hits in a studio above the Downtown Diner.

A single bead of sweat adds to this troubled face

Queasy Rider Builders can choose to give this rollercoaster rider an excited-looking face or one showing the onset of motion sickness!

LEGO® CREATOR EXPERT

After a decade of Modular Buildings in which every minifigure wore the same classic smile, Downtown Diner (set 10260) introduced a range of expressive faces. Elsewhere, Winter Village Fire Station (set 10263) added to the seasonal subtheme, and the 4,124-piece Roller Coaster (set 10261) sent minifigures into a spin!

Helmet can be swapped for gray hair piece

Firefighter A double-breasted uniform with white gloves sets the Winter Village fire crew apart from their LEGO CITY colleagues.

Same shiny buttons as Fire Chief

Fire Chief This senior firefighter has the same face as the LEGO CITY Mine Foreman—plus seven other minifigures to date.

Reassuring smile

Star of Life symbol on jacket

Doctor The first LEGO CITY hospital since 2012 includes four medics wearing white coats over bright-blue scrubs.

Hair and beard are all one piece

A prehistoric tooth serves as a fastener

Caveman What's a wild man like this doing in LEGO CITY? Don't worry—he's just a model on display at the City museum!

Black hat piece in use since 1979

LEGO Trains emblem on high-vis vest

Shiny gold braid and buttons on suit

Bellhop The grin of this smartly dressed gent greets every guest at the five-star hotel in Capital City (set 60200).

Crane Operator Two railway workers wear this olive-green outfit in 2018: the cargo crane operator and her train driver colleague.

2018

THE LEGO® BATMAN MOVIE

The second year of sets based on THE LEGO BATMAN MOVIE featured more of Gotham City's strangest super-villains—alongside more of the Caped Crusader's most curious costumes! The largest new set was The Bat-Space Shuttle (70923), which included a section of the Batcave in which the world's best-dressed detective could choose from three stylish Batsuits arranged on a sliding rail.

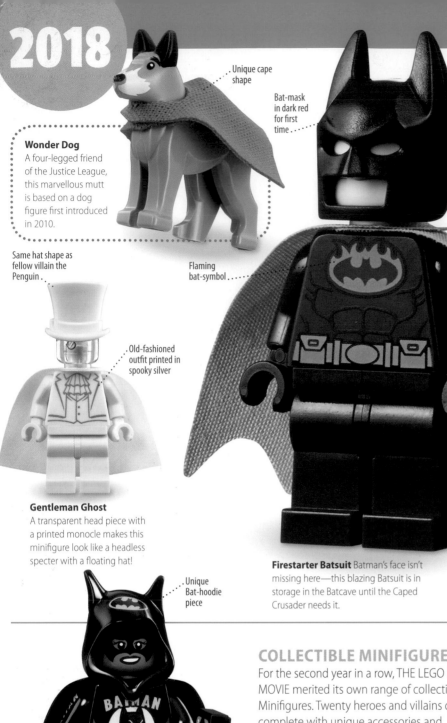

Wonder Dog
A four-legged friend of the Justice League, this marvellous mutt is based on a dog figure first introduced in 2010.

Unique cape shape

Bat-mask in dark red for first time

Same hat shape as fellow villain the Penguin

Old-fashioned outfit printed in spooky silver

Flaming bat-symbol

Gentleman Ghost
A transparent head piece with a printed monocle makes this minifigure look like a headless specter with a floating hat!

Firestarter Batsuit Batman's face isn't missing here—this blazing Batsuit is in storage in the Batcave until the Caped Crusader needs it.

Reggae Man Batsuit
In THE LEGO BATMAN MOVIE, Dick Grayson borrows parts of this outfit to create his colorful Robin costume.

"R" stands for "Reggae," or "Robin"!

Dreadlocks and hat are all part of mask

Specially created dome piece extends bald head

Egg-colored clothing

Egghead Everyone scrambles when this hard-boiled bad guy comes out of his shell. Among other crimes, he is wanted for poaching.

Jor-El Superman's dad wears Kryptonian robes and armor and the same hairstyle as Superman—albeit in an exclusive white variant.

Symbol of the House of El

Printed robe piece

COLLECTIBLE MINIFIGURES

For the second year in a row, THE LEGO BATMAN MOVIE merited its own range of collectible Minifigures. Twenty heroes and villains came complete with unique accessories and display stands emblazoned with the bat-symbol.

Unique Bat-hoodie piece

Leg print reads "#1 BATFAN"

Bat-Merch Batgirl Barbara Gordon, a.k.a. Batgirl, carries Bat-money for buying more Bat-merchandise in this heavily branded outfit.

Swimsuit Batman The skimpiest of all Batsuits sees Bruce Wayne's true identity disguised by just goggles, a cowl, and Bat-emblazoned swimming trunks!

Goggles are part of cowl piece

Belt clock shows same time as head piece

Dolphin-shaped pool toy

Clock King This alarming villain is exclusive to the collectible Minifigures theme. He comes with a pair of clock-hand spears.

Same head mold as Gingerbread Man collectible Minifigure

DID YOU KNOW?
The first Jor-El minifigure came as a free gift from LEGO Stores and LEGO.com in 2013.

226

Lex Luthor Superman's archenemy wears a mechanical super suit of his own making in a rare polybag set.

- Same cape worn by Superman
- Armor extends to Luthor's toes

LEGO® DC SUPER HEROES

Some long-standing DC Comics characters made their minifigure debuts in 2018, alongside other, newer additions to the Justice League. There was still a place for classic heroes and villains, however, with Batman and Lex Luthor among those trying out some surprising new looks. The Mighty Micros subtheme also returned for one more year, giving familiar faces an added cartoon twist.

- Transparent flames built into head piece
- Hands can grip flick-fire Power Blasts

Firestorm This Justice League hero comes with a selection of Power Burst pieces for recreating his flame-throwing abilities.

- Green Lantern Corps symbol over eye

Green Lantern Jessica Cruz This minifigure was exclusive to the LEGO DC Comics Super Heroes DVD *Aquaman: Rage Of Atlantis*.

The Cheetah This feline felon does battle with Wonder Woman, Batman, and Firestorm in Lex Luthor Mech Takedown (set 76097).

- Red hair and cowl are all one piece
- Unique bat-symbol
- Tail piece visible between legs

Batwoman Bruce Wayne's Super Hero cousin makes her first appearance in a LEGO set in Batman: Brother Eye Takedown (set 76111).

Yellow Lantern Batman You will only find this brightly colored Batman with the LEGO *DC Super Heroes Visual Dictionary*, published by DK.

- Yellow uniform protects against Green Lantern powers

MIGHTY MICROS

The third and final year of the Mighty Micros line introduced compact cars for Super Heroes Batman, Nightwing, and Supergirl and for super-villains Harley Quinn, the Joker, and Brainiac.

- Exaggerated features
- Nightwing's bird symbol

Nightwing Like all Mighty Micros minifigures, Nightwing has short legs, even though he is actually the adult Dick Grayson (Robin).

LEGO MINIFIGURES

To celebrate 40 years of LEGO minifigures, the collectible Minifigures theme threw a costume party in 2018. Every set in Series 18 contained a costumed character and came with an exclusive orange base plate for display. Several Minifigures brought gifts along to the party, with three even carrying tile pieces printed to look like tiny LEGO sets!

- One of two facial expressions
- Arms attach directly to brick torso
- Standard brick studs on front

Brick Suit Girl A special torso piece turns this reveler into a LEGO brick! A red version is worn by her pal, Brick Suit Guy.

Cactus Girl This prickly partygoer has arms created just for her and an optional pained expression—in case she pokes herself!

- Cactus arms can be posed at any angle

Flowerpot Girl A special flowerpot piece fits between the standard legs and torso of this positively blooming party guest.

- Choice of sad or happy face
- Huge headdress has green stalk at back

Race Car Guy The number 40 on this racer's car costume is just one more nod to the anniversary of the minifigure!

- Rocket Racers logo from 1999 LEGO® Racers video game
- Wheels of car costume really turn

- Party hat slots into hair piece
- Minifigure design on bow tie

Cake Guy Pink, icing-splattered legs slot inside the cake accessory that this half-baked hero wears as part of his costume.

- Printed torso is a sticker on 1978 version

Police Officer Dressed as one of the very first minifigures from 1978, this partygoer is also carrying the set he appeared in.

LEGO® *STAR WARS*™

The penultimate movie in the Skywalker Saga was still in cinemas at the start of 2018, and *Solo: A Star Wars Story* followed close behind. There were plenty of LEGO sets to represent both, with younger versions of Han Solo and an older Luke Skywalker minifigure in the mix. As ever, sets based on the original trilogy were represented, too.

SOLO: A STAR WARS STORY

Eight sets depicted the young Han Solo's journey from lowly Corellian scrumrat to lovable hyperspace hero. Minifigures in the subtheme included new versions of familiar characters and a host of new friends and enemies.

Printed sideburns

Metallic scarf print flows from torso to legs

Unique helmet design

Cape has hood print on reverse

Han Solo Mudtrooper Young Han's smirking face is the only part of this minifigure not exclusive to just one set.

Fabric collar for warmth

Range Trooper This Imperial specialist is only found in Imperial Conveyex Transport (set 75217), along with an identical colleague.

Lando Calrissian This young version of Lando boasts an exclusive blue cape with a collar and printed black trim.

Aurebesh script on helmet

Orange cape is gray on reverse

Enfys Nest The leader of the Cloud Riders has a plain black head beneath her helmet to preserve her mystique.

Corellian Hound These vicious beasts from Han's homeworld menace minifigures in Moloch's Landspeeder (set 75210) and Han's Landspeeder (set 75209).

Dual-sided face print on head

Qi'Ra Han's childhood friend appears in three Solo sets, each time with a different unique torso print.

Unusual head armor to protect from sunlight

Blaster pistol

Staff used as a club

Moloch This villain's robes are made from a new skirt piece introduced in 2018, and his wormlike head is exclusive.

THE ORIGINAL TRILOGY

Key moments from the start of the Skywalker Saga were revisited in 2018 sets, from Luke's Jedi training with Yoda on Dagobah to Leia and the other rebels' fateful trip to the skies over Bespin.

2003 variant has legs instead of skirt

Princess Leia A new variant of Bespin Leia uses the same skirt mold as Moloch for a very different look.

Alternative face has closed eyes

Luke Skywalker Luke's Dagobah look had not featured in a set since 2004. This update has a double-sided head with determined and restful faces.

Hairy chest

Unique face print

Wuher Tatooine's Mos Eisley Cantina has featured in three sets since 2004, but its owner, Wuher, appears in just one.

- Ceremonial staff

Elite Praetorian Guard
Leader Snoke's personal protectors come in three varieties—with skirt, with legs, and with variant helmets.

- Unique shoulder armor

DID YOU KNOW?
Luke Skywalker minifigures have appeared in more than 60 different sets since 1999.

New hair piece created for old Luke

THE LAST JEDI
Important characters held back from the first wave of Episode VIII sets made their debut in 2018. Among them was the older Luke Skywalker, seen in self-imposed exile in Ahch-To Island Training (set 75200).

Luke Skywalker This Jedi Master minifigure is the first version of Luke to wear a cape and long hair.

Same design seen on Black VIP Card

VIP EXCLUSIVE
Builders who bought the Ultimate Collector Series *Millennium Falcon* (set 75192) in 2017 received a special Black VIP Card and a display stand for it. In 2018, cardholders were treated to an exclusive black minifigure bearing a *Millennium Falcon* design.

LEGO® MARVEL SUPER HEROES

Blockbuster movies *Avengers: Infinity War*, *Black Panther*, and *Ant-Man And The Wasp* all inspired LEGO Marvel Super Heroes sets in 2018. Bringing together members of the Avengers, the Guardians of the Galaxy, and more, the ever-expanding theme also set the pace with one last trio of Mighty Micros sets. This concluded the superbeings in supercars subtheme that had launched in 2016.

Unique tree trunk head piece

I AM LEGO GROOT!

Groot The first Groot minifigure followed tiny Baby Groot figures in 2017 and a giant brick-built figure in 2014.

Bark print on both sides of torso

Cat ears attach to standard head mold

Same face as Bespin Leia under helmet

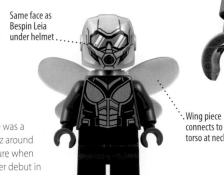

Wasp There was a definite buzz around this minifigure when she made her debut in Quantum Realm Explorers (set 76109).

Wing piece connects to torso at neck

Black Panther Wakanda's champion appeared in two 2018 sets based on his own movie and one *Avengers: Infinity War* set.

MIGHTY MICROS

The last lap for the Mighty Micros included unique cars for Scarlet Spider and Sandman, Star-Lord and Nebula, and Thor and Loki. All six minifigures came with short legs and broad expressions for a cute, cartoonish look.

Star-Lord's signature blaster

Silver cyborg arm

Nebula This blue baddie wields an exclusive tile piece printed to look like Star-Lord's famous mix tape!

Star-Lord Rotate this minifigure's head 180 degrees to reveal the grinning face of Peter Quill underneath his helmet!

Iron Spider-Man Found in just one *Avengers: Infinity War* set, this special web-slinger actually has eight limbs!

Posable robot legs

Flick-fire Power Blast weapon

Owen Grady Intrepid dino trainer Owen comes with two expressions, but the grumpy one best suits his torn-shirt torso print!

- Choice of scared or serious face prints

- Carnotaurus claw marks

LEGO® JURASSIC WORLD™

Hit movie *Jurassic World: Fallen Kingdom* opened in June 2018, exactly 25 years after the original *Jurassic Park* film was released into the wild. Both were celebrated in LEGO form during the year, with seven sets capturing the new movie and one marking an iconic moment from 1993. An exclusive minifigure pack, meanwhile, combined both in one place.

Franklin Webb This computer whiz kid is found in just one *Jurassic World* set: Carnotaurus Gyrosphere Escape (75929).

JURASSIC PARK

Four classic characters were given minifigure makeovers to recreate the iconic kitchen scene in the 25th anniversary set Jurassic Park Velociraptor Chase (75932).

- Fedora found in more than 50 sets

- Face print based on actor Sam Neill

FALLEN KINGDOM

Picking up where 2015's *Jurassic World* sets left off, the *Fallen Kingdom* range presented Owen and his pals with a fresh crop of dino danger! These included a spiky Stygimoloch figure and a colossal Carnotaurus.

- Ideal camouflage colors

- Emergency flare to distract dinosaurs

Ian Malcolm The math genius made his minifigure debut in a "Bricktober" promotional set, the Jurassic World Minifigure Collection (set 5005255), found only in Toys 'R' Us.

Claire Dearing The Dinosaur Protection Group leader wears green in three 2018 set, and gray in one promotional set.

Alan Grant This plucky paleontologist can swap his hat for a tousled hair piece in the Velociraptor Chase set.

- Hairstyle first designed for 2016's Holtzmann Ghostbusters minifigure

Dottie This former go-kart champ now speeds around on roller skates at the drive-in Drifting Diner (41349).

- New helmet piece comes in six colors

Mia All five Friends take up karting in 2018, but only Mia has two different karts in two different sets!

LEGO® FRIENDS

Seven Heartlake City inhabitants got their first mini dolls this year, including diner owner Dottie and carwash king Zack. Meanwhile, the main Friends came in 30 new costumes, including go-karting gear.

- Tinted visor is part of face print

- Armor piece new for 2018

LEGO® NEXO KNIGHTS™

In its third and final year, the NEXO KNIGHTS storyline revolved around the malevolent Monstrox finding new form as a computer virus. As this digital villain villain attacked the Kingdom using his Tech Monsters, the Knights themselves welcomed former apprentice Robin into their ranks as a fully fledged member of the team.

- Horns slot into helmet sides

- New shoulder armor element

Berserker This member of Monstrox's techno army has the same helmet as his comrades—but he wears his backward!

Robin Underwood Previous versions of Robin all had short legs, but in 2018, he stood tall alongside his fellow knights.

- Six Tech Monsters share this face print

- Belt looks like a one-eyed monster

CyberByter Three of these small soldiers appear in 2018 sets, including one named Dennis, who has a stud-shooter right arm.

- Claw parts for arms

- Black skeleton leg parts

Cezar This spiderlike cyber-fiend stands on four legs made out of blaster weapons and robot arm pieces.

LEGO® SPEED CHAMPIONS

Ford, Ferrari, and Porsche were the three big names tearing up the racetrack in this year's Speed Champions releases. Across seven sets, all 14 minifigures were new, with drivers, technicians, race officials, and spectators among their number. As ever, the drivers boasted the highest level of printed detail, with real-world sponsor names and logos recreated in tiny type!

White helmet worn by more than 500 minifigures

Ford Fiesta M-Sport WRC Driver Authentic sponsor logos make this racer's torso and leg prints totally unique.

More than 80 minifigures share this face

Classic Ferrari 250 GTO Driver This speed champion wears 1960s-style racing gear to match her classic car.

Classic Ferrari emblem

Same torso print as Porsche 911 RSR driver

Porsche 911 RSR Technician This crucial member of the Porsche pit crew couldn't be happier to be on the team!

Plain white legs found in more than 300 sets

Bow is part of head piece

Blossom Like each of the minifigures in the theme, the self-proclaimed leader of the Powerpuff Girls has a unique, oversized head mold.

Short minifigure legs

LEGO® POWERPUFF GIRLS™

Minifigures based on Cartoon Network series *The Powerpuff Girls* first appeared in a LEGO Dimensions Team Pack (set 71346) in 2017. They proved so popular that, in 2018, the Girls soared into their own special theme. Just two sets were released, featuring minifigures of heroes Blossom, Bubbles, and Buttercup, alongside the villainous Mojo Jojo and Princess Morbucks.

THE LEGO® NINJAGO® MOVIE™

Just one set in 2018 was themed around this movie, but what a set it was! Made from 3,443 pieces, Ninjago City Docks (set 70657) stood 14 in (37 cm) high and came with 13 minifigures, 11 of which could be found nowhere else. These included the first ever Mystake minifigure and new versions of Cole, Dareth, and Lil' Nelson.

Cardigan print continues on back

Mystake This tea shop owner got a new look for THE LEGO NINJAGO MOVIE, but her trademark cardigan remained.

LEGO® NINJAGO®

The ninja took on two new sets of enemies in 2018. First up were the Sons of Garmadon biker gang, who used powerful Oni Masks to cause chaos in Ninjago City. Then it was the turn of the Dragon Hunters, who made life a misery for the magnificent beasts in the Realm of Oni and Dragons.

One of four collectible Dragon Armor pieces

Dragon Master A rejuvenated Master Wu is well protected in this golden armor, which featured in several 2018 sets.

Iron Baron Four Dragon Hunters share this shoulder armor, but only their top-hatted boss wears it on the right-hand side.

Hair and crown are one piece

Flower print on both sides of cape

Princess Harumi This version of the Sons of Garmadon's secret leader is made up entirely of exclusive parts.

Peg leg first appeared in this color in 2011

Shoulder armor piece first used in NEXO KNIGHTS sets

Ultra Violet This biker wears the Oni Mask of Hatred, one of three special masks found in Sons of Garmadon sets.

New sou'wester hat piece.

Tentacles connect between head and torso.

Captain Jonas Jack and Parker face the possessed form of this usually friendly fisherman in Wrecked Shrimp Boat (70419).

2019

CAN A LEGO® SET be haunted? In 2019, the answer was yes, as the Hidden Side theme launched alongside an Augmented Reality app! Viewing the sets through an app-enabled screen let builders see the spooks that were menacing their minifigures and trap them for virtual rewards. Turning to bigger screens, the year also saw sets based on Netflix smash-hit *Stranger Things*; classic sitcom *Friends*; Marvel's *Avengers: Endgame*; *Star Wars: The Rise of Skywalker*; and, of course, THE LEGO® MOVIE 2™!

LEGO® HIDDEN SIDE

New hat-and-hood piece.

Minifigures are turning into monsters in the spooky town of Newbury! As more and more people are possessed by ghostly forces, it falls to 13-year-old Jack Davids and his best friend Parker to save the town with technology! And with their ghost-catching tech existing as a free real-life app, too, LEGO builders can help the heroes on their Augmented Reality mission . . . .

Exclusive hat-and-hair design

Jack Davids Hidden Side's hero appears in most sets—sometimes in a jacket, sometimes in gloves, but always in his hood!

Bone-shaped keychain on belt

Smartphone accessory shows an approaching ghost!

Parker L. Jackson Newbury newcomer Jack wouldn't last long as a ghost hunter without this street-smart local at his side!

Ripped jeans

Goggles are part of unique hair piece

Monster print on T-shirt

J. B. When not in her lab, this inventor of ghost-catching gear loves to drive the Paranormal Intercept Bus 3000 (70423)!

Mr. Clarke Nonpossessed appearance.

Wild, haunted hair!

Spencer Jack's faithful ghost dog is a single piece made from a spooky mix of white and transparent plastic.

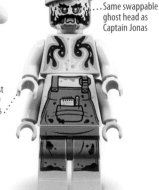

Two-color molding creates wispy effect

Mr. Clarke This teacher has puzzled and petrified looks on his standard head and a gruesome glare on his ghost one!

Detachable wings

Same swappable ghost head as Captain Jonas

Foldaway eyes.

Pop-out giant claws.

Newbury Haunted High School (70425) This huge building's monster face appears from the walls at the flip of a switch!

Extra torso and arms first used in LEGO NINJAGO sets

DID YOU KNOW?
The Hidden Side app has a multiplayer mode that lets three extra people play as ghosts.

Chef Enzo Swap this chef's extra arms and haunted head for his standard face to free him from ghostly control!

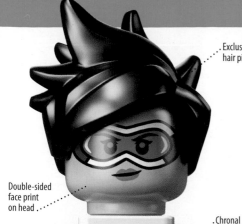

Exclusive new hair piece

Genji A unique helmet piece on a plain silver head captures the cyborg spirit of this former crime clan member.

Printed visor.

Cyborg armor printing continues on back

New hawklike helmet

Tattoo print on right cheek

Adjustable wings built into armor

Pharah This Egyptian aviator wears a winged flying suit based on an armor piece introduced in the NEXO KNIGHTS theme.

Ribbon connects to new hair piece

Double-sided face print on head

Chronal accelerator print

LEGO® OVERWATCH®

Based on the hugely successful video game by Blizzard Entertainment, the LEGO Overwatch theme launched with six sets in January 2019. The futuristic storyline sees a super-intelligent Gorilla called Winston trying to reform the outlawed planetary peace-keeping force called Overwatch. He needs heroes like Tracer, Hanzo, and Pharah on his side to protect the Earth from a dozen different threats!

Rice wine bottle hanging from belt

Hanzo This expert archer faces off against his cyborg brother at the Hanamura dojo in Hanzo vs. Genji (75971).

Face includes printed glasses

Winston A new big figure mold was made for this imposing ape in 2019's largest Overwatch set, Watchpoint: Gibraltar (75975).

Huge hands grip just like a minifigure's

Pixelated eyepatch

Pirate This blocky buccaneer encounters brick-built dolphin, parrot, and turtle pals in his only set appearance to date.

LEGO® MINECRAFT™

LEGO Minecraft was bigger than ever in 2019, with the launch of large, buildable figures of Alex, Steve, and a Skeleton. Minifigure-scale sets were still in demand, however—new characters introduced this year included a Dragon Slayer in The End Battle (21151), a Pirate in Pirate Ship (21152), and a Blacksmith and a Husk in The Creeper Mine (21155).

Tracer The original star of Overwatch featured in the very first set of the theme, where she battled her long-time rival Widowmaker.

LEGO® STRANGER THINGS

In the hit Netflix Original Series *Stranger Things*, a brave band of kids explore the boundaries between their own world and its dark underworld reflection. Epic 2,287-piece LEGO set The Upside Down (75810) recreates both of those realities, with a near-mirror-image set that can be displayed either way up! It comes with seven minifigures of the show's main stars, plus one terrifying monster!

New pudding-bowl hair piece

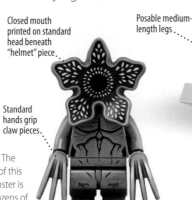

Posable medium-length legs

Enchanted crossbow

Eleven Escapee "El" wears a blonde wig and an old dress when she needs to look like an everyday girl.

Printed waffle piece

Closed mouth printed on standard head beneath "helmet" piece

Standard hands grip claw pieces

Demogorgon The flowerlike face of this nightmare monster is printed with dozens of tiny teeth around an enormous open mouth.

Fabric skirt piece flexes with legs

Same leg mold as Faun collectible Minifigure from 2016

Will Byers A worried face shows that unlucky Will is trapped on the scary side of the Upside Down set!

Dragon Slayer This brand-new character skin minifigure comes with a Minecraft code, which unlocks the same new character look in the online game.

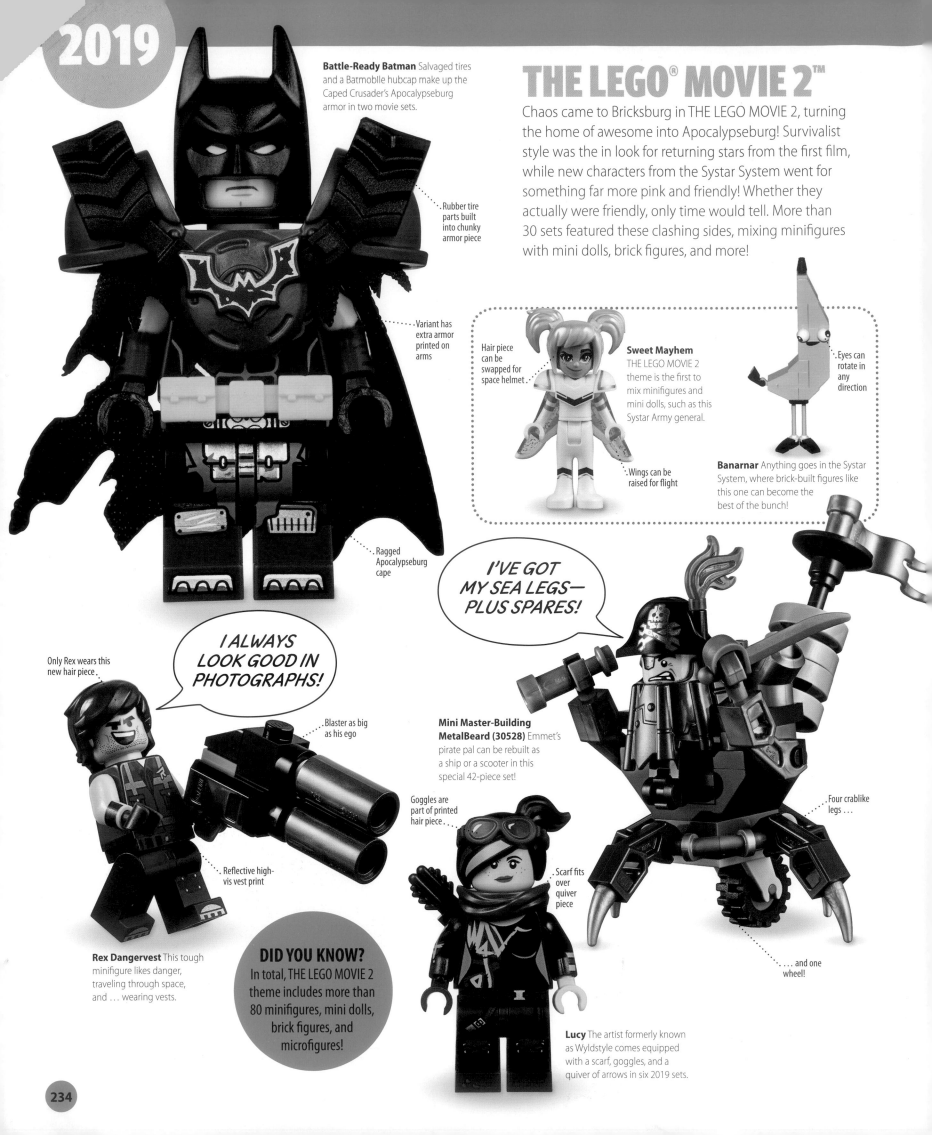

Battle-Ready Batman Salvaged tires and a Batmobile hubcap make up the Caped Crusader's Apocalypseburg armor in two movie sets.

Rubber tire parts built into chunky armor piece

Variant has extra armor printed on arms

Ragged Apocalypseburg cape

THE LEGO® MOVIE 2™

Chaos came to Bricksburg in THE LEGO MOVIE 2, turning the home of awesome into Apocalypseburg! Survivalist style was the in look for returning stars from the first film, while new characters from the Systar System went for something far more pink and friendly! Whether they actually were friendly, only time would tell. More than 30 sets featured these clashing sides, mixing minifigures with mini dolls, brick figures, and more!

Hair piece can be swapped for space helmet

Sweet Mayhem THE LEGO MOVIE 2 theme is the first to mix minifigures and mini dolls, such as this Systar Army general.

Wings can be raised for flight

Eyes can rotate in any direction

Banarnar Anything goes in the Systar System, where brick-built figures like this one can become the best of the bunch!

I'VE GOT MY SEA LEGS— PLUS SPARES!

I ALWAYS LOOK GOOD IN PHOTOGRAPHS!

Only Rex wears this new hair piece

Blaster as big as his ego

Mini Master-Building MetalBeard (30528) Emmet's pirate pal can be rebuilt as a ship or a scooter in this special 42-piece set!

Four crablike legs . . .

Reflective high-vis vest print

Goggles are part of printed hair piece

Scarf fits over quiver piece

. . . and one wheel!

Rex Dangervest This tough minifigure likes danger, traveling through space, and . . . wearing vests.

DID YOU KNOW?
In total, THE LEGO MOVIE 2 theme includes more than 80 minifigures, mini dolls, brick figures, and microfigures!

Lucy The artist formerly known as Wyldstyle comes equipped with a scarf, goggles, and a quiver of arrows in six 2019 sets.

THIS IS WHY WE SEPARATE REDS AND WHITES IN THE SPACE WASH!

Classic minifigure face print

Helmet more durable than original 1970s design

Lenny The first minifigure helmet was reintroduced for the first pink LEGO Space astronaut, who appeared alongside his pals Benny, Jenny, and Kenny.

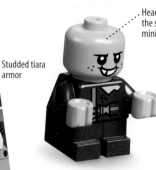

Tail made from road-sweeper brush piece

Rampage Kitty
In Apocalypseburg, UniKitty becomes Warrior Kitty, and an angry Warrior Kitty becomes Rampage Kitty!

Unique printed face brick

Studded tiara armor

Head is half the size of a minifigure's

Warrior face paint

Ragged romper suit

Sewer Babies The epic set Welcome to Apocalypseburg (70840) includes an underground home for these drain-dwelling darlings.

THERE'S NO PLACE LIKE THE SYSTAR SYSTEM.

Exclusive hair piece

Toto the terrier

Dorothy If not in Oz, look to the Systar System for this windswept girl—and her little dog, too!

Printed ruby slippers

COLLECTIBLE MINIFIGURES

A bumper crop of 20 collectible characters made up the lucky-dip series of Minifigures for THE LEGO MOVIE 2. Apocalypseburg inhabitants rubbed shoulders with the strangest Systar System residents, including guest stars from *The Wizard of Oz*!

DID YOU KNOW?
The LEGO MOVIE 2 Minifigures series is the first to include a brick-built figure: super-cute UniKitty.

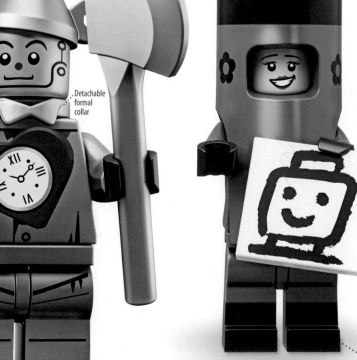

New funnel hat piece

A heart is all the Tin Man ever wanted!

Detachable formal collar

Tin Man This clockwork collectible Minifigure completes a trio of Oz inhabitants alongside the Scarecrow and the Cowardly Lion.

"Sandwich board" costume covers front and back

AARGH! I CAN'T REACH MY MOUTH!

Unique giraffe "mask".

Leaves for lunch

Giraffe Guy Standing head (if not shoulders) above his fellow minifigures is this party animal from the Systar System!

Crayon Girl This creative character from the Systar System has really used her head to draw a fellow minifigure!

Purple feet look like blunt end of crayon

235

Exclusive new hair piece

Sparking snowflake cape

Giant snowflake accessory

Elsa *Frozen* featured in mini doll sets from 2015 onward, but it was 2019 before Elsa was made into a minifigure.

LEGO® MINIFIGURES DISNEY SERIES 2

Stars from across the history of Disney animation lined up together in the second series of Disney collectible Minifigures. Mickey and Minnie Mouse appeared in their earliest black-and-white outfits alongside cheeky chipmunks Chip and Dale, who first hit screens in the 1940s. Characters from the likes of *Frozen* and *The Incredibles 2* added 21st-century sparkle to the 18-Minifigure mix.

DID YOU KNOW?
Frozen's Elsa, Anna, and Olaf also became LEGO® DUPLO® figures in 2019.

I'M SO GLAD IT ISN'T MORE SKIN CREAM!

Magnified eyes printed on hair piece

Smile can be swapped for a scowl

Edna Mode This stylist for super heroes pairs her *Incredibles 2* costume with a bespoke hair piece and high-fashion specs.

Printed snowflake pieces fit inside gift box

Pinstripes printed on front, back, and sides

Gift box pieces first used by Series 18 Minifigures

Jack Skellington The star of *The Nightmare Before Christmas* wears a new bat-shaped bow tie piece and carries a creepy present.

Unique long-hair-and-cowboy-hat piece

Hair piece can be swapped for helmet

Canadian maple leaf on belt buckle

Duke Caboom This dashing daredevil jumps through a ring of brick-built fire in Duke Caboom's Stunt Show (10767)!

Forky This homemade hero can be held by a minifigure or fitted onto a single LEGO stud.

"Drawn on" details are deliberately childlike

Jessie Four exclusive printed parts make this minifigure, including a rodeo shirt torso and cowhide chaps on her legs.

LEGO® TOY STORY 4

The first LEGO Toy Story sets since 2010 introduced updates of Woody, Buzz, and Jessie that used more standard minifigure parts than earlier versions (not counting Buzz's collectible Minifigure from 2016). They also featured fresh faces from the gang's latest adventure, including minifigures of Gabby Gabby and Bunny and special single-piece figures of Ducky and Forky.

Hat is detachable, unlike on earlier Woody figures

Woody Two sets show Woody shooting this smile, while a third gives him a full-on grin and an alarmed look.

Detachable top hat

Acorn accessory

Ruffled fur between ears

Smaller nose than Dale

Two large teeth where Chip has one

Printed spats

Scrooge McDuck Series 2 includes Donald Duck's mega-rich uncle, plus grandnephews Huey, Dewey, and Louie.

Chip Posable medium-length legs allow chipmunk brothers Chip and Dale to run riot.

Dale Both Chip and Dale have unique head molds and mirror-image tail prints on their backs.

LEGO® MARVEL SUPER HEROES

In the year that *Avengers: Endgame* became the most successful movie of all time, seven tie-in sets included more returning Avengers than you could shake an Infinity Gauntlet at. Meanwhile, the *Captain Marvel* movie and Spider-Man (film and comic book) subthemes also contributed some of the year's most unusual and exciting new Marvel Super Heroes minifigures.

White hood piece first worn by Marvel villain Taskmaster.

Sandman The lower half of this shape-shifting villain is made from a LEGO® NEXO KNIGHTS™ stone monster piece.

Face and torso prints seem to drip like wet cement!

Dots on suit represent advanced "Unstable Molecule Fabric".

Spider-Man-2099 This futuristic wall-crawler travels through time to join forces with the original in just one 2019 set.

SPIDER-MAN FAR FROM HOME

Four sets spun off from this big-screen Spidey sequel. Their new minifigures included the web-slinger's best friend, Ned Leeds; a stealth suit Spider-Man; and Peter Parker snacking on a slice of printed pizza!

New spherical helmet piece.

Intricate armor printing continues on back.

Mysterio Alien Ally or enigmatic enemy? With a plain silver head underneath his helmet, this minifigure is giving nothing away!

SPIDER-MAN COMICS

This year's new minifigures from the Multiverse include the ghostly Spider-Woman of Earth-65 and a Spider-Man from 80 years in the future. The scariest version of Sandman so far was also among the updates.

Ghost-Spider This alternative version of Peter's pal Gwen Stacy teams up with Spidey in Spider Mech vs. Venom (76115).

Swimming cap mold introduced in 2012.

Spidey suit visible under clothes

Peter Parker The first Peter Parker minifigure since 2004 has a pulled-back mask piece that can be swapped for hair.

Wavy water effect printed in two shades of blue.

Ears piece adapted from Disney's *Aladdin* Genie Minifigure.

Hydro-Man This rippling rogue towers three times taller than Spidey when built onto his transparent blue brick base.

Alien armor print continues on back

Talos This scheming Skrull sports a new pointy-eared head topper in Captain Marvel and The Skrull Attack (76127).

More high-tech look than 2016 Captain Marvel minifigure

Serious face hidden behind new hair piece

Captain Marvel Carol Danvers' movie minifigure first appeared in a *Captain Marvel* set before joining *Endgame's* all-star line-up.

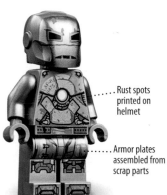

Rust spots printed on helmet

Armor plates assembled from scrap parts

Iron Man Mark 1 Armor This rusty relic appears in a single *Endgame* set, 11 years after its on-screen debut.

AVENGERS MOVIES

More than 20 new minifigures, microfigures, and "big figs" made their debuts in *Avengers: Endgame* sets—including five fresh Iron Man variants! Elsewhere, Captain Marvel battled the first ever Skrull minifigure in her own movie set.

Extra arms can all be posed

Claw piece first made for Wolverine minifigure

Outrider Thanos's alien attack dogs appear in four *Endgame* sets, but this extra-armed variant is exclusive to just one.

Nebula Eleven heroes wear these armored Avengers team suits in Endgame sets—including this former Guardians of the Galaxy villain.

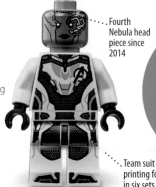

Fourth Nebula head piece since 2014

Team suit printing found in six sets

DID YOU KNOW? There are more than 20 different Iron Man minifigures to collect— plus a microscale version.

Flecks of gray in facial hair

Temperature control unit

Waistband blaster holster

Printed harness for ice abseiling

Boolio The first Ovissian minifigure has a head piece molded from two different colors of plastic, with printed facial features.

Lando Calrissian After appearing in original trilogy and *Solo* sets, Lando got another new look for *The Rise of Skywalker*.

Face print first used in *The Force Awakens* sets

Rey The fourth Rey minifigure swaps her usual gray-and-tan attire for white, but still worn in a criss-cross style.

Holster straps crossed over hips.

Zorii Bliss This spice runner turned Resistance fighter has a plain black head piece beneath her unique gold helmet.

Belt buckle replaces cord tie seen on other Rey torso prints

LEGO® *STAR WARS*™

Lucasfilm and the LEGO Group celebrated 20 years of partnership in 2019. Five LEGO *Star Wars* sets included special anniversary minifigures, while the wider theme focused on the future. New TV shows *Star Wars Resistance* and *The Mandalorian* got their own sets, and—of course—there were plenty of fresh-faced minifigures from ninth saga movie *The Rise of Skywalker*.

THE MOVIES

Five *The Rise of Skywalker* sets came out in October, but the year was also notable for new releases from across the film series. Amazingly, some of these even included characters who had never been minifigures before!

War club

Thermal detonator found in 14 sets

Ushar As one of the fearsome Knights of Ren, Ushar wears unique armor and carries his own choice of weapons.

STAR WARS RESISTANCE

Two 2019 sets are based around this animated series, set between *Return of the Jedi* and *The Force Awakens*. Show and sets alike feature brand-new characters and film favorites such as Leia and Poe.

Unique two-tone hair piece

Kaz Xiono This New Republic racer, stunt pilot, and spy is exclusive to Major Vonreg's TIE Fighter (75240).

New helmet mold

Civilian flight jacket

Major Vonreg First among First Order pilots, this villain's vermillion armor perfectly matches his menacing red-and-black TIE fighter.

Outfit seen in *Rogue One: A Star Wars Story*

Crest of Alderaan on belt buckle

Bail Organa Leia's adoptive father makes his minifigure debut in the Ultimate Collector version of his ship, *Tantive IV* (75244).

Building stud on back of head

D-O A single, specially created droid piece represents BB-8's buddy in two 2019 sets based on *The Rise of Skywalker*.

STAR WARS BATTLEFRONT

In 2017, Iden Versio became the first female lead in a *Star Wars* video game. Two years later, she made her minifigure debut leading three Inferno Squad Agents in a LEGO *Star Wars* battle pack.

Iden Versio This Imperial commander eventually joins the Rebellion, but here she is decked out solely to serve the Emperor!

Inferno Squad stripes on shoulder

Weapon predates blaster pieces

Princess Leia This retro rebel is one of five reissued minifigures from 1999–2003 found exclusively in 20th anniversary sets.

Classic yellow hands and head

Anniversary logo, which features on Leia's back, too

THE MANDALORIAN

In fall 2019, the first ever live-action *Star Wars* TV show was accompanied by a LEGO set featuring four of its characters. AT-ST Raider (75254) included Cara Dune, two Klatoonian Raiders, and the mysterious Mandalorian himself.

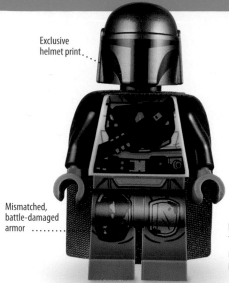

Exclusive helmet print

Mismatched, battle-damaged armor

Din Djarin Boba Fett? Where? The star of *The Mandalorian* may share some similarities, but his minifigure is all new!

Small rebel tattoo under left eye

Cara Dune This blaster for hire teams up with Din Djarin to take down the AT-ST vehicle in the first Mandalorian set.

Low-slung gear belt

DID YOU KNOW?
Din Djarin's new slender fabric cape piece was created specially for him.

CENTRAL PERK

The one with the characters from *Friends* depicts their favorite café hangout as a studio set, complete with lighting rigs. As well as Chandler, Joey, Monica, Phoebe, Rachel, and Ross, it also includes café manager Gunther.

Iconic "Rachel" hairstyle was actually first seen on 2017's Veterinarian Minifigure

Minifigure shield used as tray

Rachel Green
The *Friends* fashionista played by Jennifer Aniston is depicted during her time waiting tables at Central Perk.

Exclusive face print

The LEGO News accessory found in more than 20 sets

Ross Geller The *Friends'* persistent paleontologist has loosened his tie while on a break from thinking about dinosaurs.

LEGO® IDEAS

Famous faces populated three LEGO Ideas sets released this year. First up was modern Stone Age family the Flintstones in set 21316, who rocked up with their neighbors the Rubbles. Then Mickey and Minnie Mouse went back to their roots in the black-and-white Steamboat Willie set (21317). Finally, the six stars of classic comedy series *Friends* shared coffee in Central Perk (21319).

Detachable sailor's hat

STEAMBOAT WILLIE

The name of a 1928 Disney film and the boat in it, *Steamboat Willie* introduced the world to Mickey and Minnie Mouse. The set included vintage versions of both, with variants also appearing as collectible LEGO Minifigures.

Mickey Mouse This star shines bright, wearing the silvery tones in which he first appeared on screen.

Silver shorts are white on collectible variant

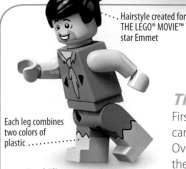

Hairstyle created for THE LEGO® MOVIE™ star Emmet

Each leg combines two colors of plastic

Fred Flintstone Like most minifigures, Fred has no visible nose, but his printed stubble suggests its distinctive shape.

Wilma Flintstone Stone Age style icon Wilma wears a wavy hairstyle first seen on 2011's Ice Skater Minifigure.

Chunky stone necklace printed on front and back

THE FLINTSTONES™

First seen in 1960, this prehistoric cartoon comedy refuses to go extinct. Over the years, it has evolved into films, theme parks, and a LEGO Ideas set featuring four minifigures in the famous Flintstone home.

Legs molded in two colors with printed zigzag detail

Rare white guitar represents Minnie's ukulele

Printed eyelashes distinguish Minnie's head from Mickey's

Minnie Mouse This monochrome mouse carries the sheet music for "Turkey in the Straw," as heard in *Steamboat Willie*.

Sky Police Officer
This deputy drives a truck with working lights and sound effects in Sky Police Diamond Heist (60209).

Combined hat-and-hair piece

New Sky Police uniform print

Sky Police Pilot A new oxygen mask piece helps police pilots breathe at high altitude in four 2019 sets.

SKY POLICE

LEGO CITY crime-fighters scaled new heights in six Sky Police sets using helicopters, planes, drones, and even jet packs! The subtheme also introduced working minifigure parachutes, used in two sets by cops and crooks alike.

Gold Statue
All-gold parts make up this firefighter statue, which is targeted by scheming sky crooks in Drone Chase (60207).

Date on plinth is when the LEGO Group was founded

New goggle-shaped visor piece

Parachute Crook A backpack built on to a new neck bracket piece can connect this minifigure to a fabric parachute.

I ONLY ASKED FOR EYELINER!

Yellow "skin" visible around painted face

Tiger Girl
A paint-splattered artist accompanies this youngster with painted feline features in the Fun Fair People Pack.

Golden rank pins on collar

Fire chief's badge

Utility belt piece first seen in THE LEGO® BATMAN MOVIE sets

Freya McCloud Introduced in LEGO City Adventures, this friendly fire chief was originally exclusive to just one 2019 set.

Ink from leaky pen on top pocket

Harl Hubbs LEGO CITY Adventures' star mechanic appears in the Garage Center set (60232), aimed at younger builders.

LEGO® CITY

The fun of the fair came to LEGO CITY this year, with face-painting, stilt-walking, and more in the People Pack—Fun Fair set (60234). The Sky Police kept an eye on the City from high above, while the latest minifigure astronauts went higher still. Characters from the new animated TV series LEGO® CITY Adventures also appeared in some sets.

Stilt Walker This elevated entertainer follows in the footsteps of an even taller stilt walker from 2014's Fairground Mixer (10244).

Balloon dog accessory introduced in 2018.

Each stilt is three times the height of a standard brick.

New helmet design fits space suit-style visor piece

ONE SMALL STEP IS A GIANT LEAP FOR A MINIFIGURE!

New-look LEGO CITY space logo

Mars Explorer
This astronaut comes with a camera piece, so she could be either winking or focusing on the perfect snapshot!

Cap piece shared with this year's Shower Guy Minifigure

Printed wrinkles in one-size-fits-all suit

Visor protects a hidden smiling face

Lamp body is a LEGO® Technic piece

Spacewalker with Lamp This update on earlier space suits adds orange details—as favored by all of 2019's off-world explorers.

SPACE

Last seen in 2015, the LEGO CITY space program set its sights on the moon and beyond in 2019. Nine sets combined realistic science with near-future innovations, such as the Mars-bound Deep Space Rocket (60228).

Drone Engineer Overalls and a breathing mask equip this scientist to work on drone tech in a sterile environment.

LEGO® DC COMICS SUPER HEROES

The largest ever DC Super Heroes set was released in 2019, celebrating the 30th anniversary of the 1989 movie *Batman*. Boasting 3,306 pieces, 1989 Batmobile (76139) came with three exclusive minifigures, including a new-look Caped Crusader inspired by actor Michael Keaton's costume in the film. Meanwhile, across the theme, other fan-favorite heroes and villains made big impressions in smaller sets.

Brick-built jet pack/ flamethrower

Mask hides angry Human face

Choice of smiling or stern face prints

Bat-symbol is built into cowl

1989 Batman A combined cowl-and-cape piece makes this minifigure the most realistic Batman ever seen in a LEGO set.

Cape is molded with a sideways sweep

Firefly Ant-Man's helmet mold is repurposed in bright yellow to capture the distinctive look of Batman's flying foe.

2019

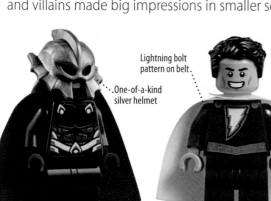

Lightning bolt pattern on belt.

One-of-a-kind silver helmet

Unique print based on dress worn by actor Kim Basinger.

Hair piece appears on more than 70 minifigures in eight colors

Vicki Vale This fearless photojournalist appears alongside Batman and the Joker in 1989 Batmobile.

Ocean Master Exclusive Batman and Aquaman minifigures take on this villain in Batman Batsub and the Underwater Clash (76116).

Shazam! Two new variants of this hero were released in 2019, coinciding with his debut in the DC movie universe.

DID YOU KNOW?
1989 Batmobile features a brick-built minifigure display plinth for all three minifigures.

Icing eyebrows

Gingerbread Woman The fourth cookie-based minifigure since 2013 is the first to be depicted as female.

Cherry buttons

Gingerbread Man A chocolate-brown mustache distinguishes this Gingerbread House inhabitant from his predecessors.

One-off printed skirt piece

LEGO® SPEED CHAMPIONS

Rally and drag racing were added to Speed Champions' growing list of motorsports in 2019, with sets featuring new entrants Mini and Dodge. The 1967 Mini Cooper S Rally and 2018 MINI John Cooper Works Buggy set (75894) included four new minifigures, while 2018 Dodge Challenger SRT Demon and 1970 Dodge Charger R/T (75893) added another three to the theme.

LEGO® SEASONAL

Three large sets celebrated Chinese New Year in 2019. One featured a family of six sharing a New Year's Eve dinner, another featured a mechanical dancing dragon, and the third saw two teams of minifigures compete in a traditional dragon boat race. Later in the year, a 1,477-piece Gingerbread House (10267) joined the Winter Village theme in time for Christmas.

Grazed cheek from a bumpy ride!

2018 Dodge Challenger SRT Demon Driver Dodge's distinctive Demon logo emblazons the front and back of this minifigure.

1967 Mini Cooper S Rally Driver The small symbol above this racer's top pocket represents the mid-1960s Morris Cooper logo.

Same confident face as LEGO CITY's Chase McCain

Demon lettering on legs is repeated on back

Mini Mechanic Two team members wear this outfit to drive and work on the MINI John Cooper Works Buggy.

Oil-smudged face can be swapped for clean look

1970 Dodge Charger R/T Driver The famous Dodge logo is the perfect match for this driver's black-and-red car.

Dragon Dancer Four different minifigures wear this traditional Chinese outfit to welcome the new year in Dragon Dance (41896).

Exclusive dragon design

Same hair as Cole in THE LEGO® NINJAGO® MOVIE™

Dragon Boat Racer Five out of 15 minifigures in Dragon Boat Race (80103) wear this exclusive orange costume.

LEGO® HARRY POTTER™

The LEGO® Wizarding World™ focused on the Harry Potter series in 2019. Seven sets included characters making their minifigure debuts alongside favorite old friends with updated looks. Four new teenage Harry variants used the medium-length legs introduced for 2018's collectible Minifigures line, while the younger Harry, Ron, and Hermione all featured in the first LEGO Harry Potter Advent Calendar (75964).

Same hairstyle as Lloyd in THE LEGO NINJAGO MOVIE

Choice of gritted teeth or smiling face prints

Torso has "POTTER" print on back

Dress print continues all down back

Skirt piece is the height of three standard bricks

Same hood piece worn by Dementors

Lower ax blade is a minifigure ice skate

Black bowler first worn by Businessman LEGO® Minifigure in 2012

Medium-length legs

Brick and plate are the same height as medium legs

Harry Potter Harry's Triwizard Tournament outfit first appeared in a 2005 set but is far more detailed for 2019.

Hermione Granger The first minifigure of Hermione in her Yule Ball gown uses an exclusive printed brick as a skirt.

Face print distinguishes Fleur from Gabrielle

Madame Maxime This half-giant headmistress appears in two 2019 sets, wearing a different extra-long dress in each.

Walden Macnair This hooded Hippogriff hunter wields his ax exclusively in Hagrid's Hut: Buckbeak's Rescue (75947).

Cornelius Fudge The smartest things about the misguided Minister for Magic are his stylish black suit and bowler hat!

Fleur Delacour This young witch and her sister, Gabrielle, wear matching school uniforms in Beauxbatons' Carriage: Arrival at Hogwarts (75958).

Leg piece is longer than her sister's

Hat can be swapped for included hair piece

Character design inspired by villain Dennis Nedry from the first *Jurassic Park* film

Standard backpack accessory

Hoodie hood printed on back of torso

Souvenir Jurassic World T-shirt

Smile can be changed to scared face

Allison Miles This scientist knows how to stay calm, even when facing a triceratops rampage in set 75937!

Badge identifies Allison as a doctor

Danny Nedermeyer Crimes against fashion are just the start for this gaudy, grinning bad guy in *Legend of Isla Nublar*!

Torso print adapted from LEGO CITY Jungle Explorers sets

Sinjin Prescott Danny's right-hand man is on the lookout for treasure on Isla Nublar. Instead, he finds a fearsome Baryonyx!

Hudson Harper Owen saves this young park visitor from mild peril in Dilophosaurus on the Loose (75934).

LEGO® JURASSIC WORLD™

In 2019, LEGO Jurassic World told new stories on the island of Isla Nublar with the latest animated TV series. LEGO *Jurassic World: Legend of Isla Nublar* featured minifigure versions of Owen, Claire, and company, plus a handful of brand-new characters. Four sets pitted the show's most ferocious dinosaurs against these small-screen stars.

LEGO® MINIFIGURES

With Series 19 including the 300th entry in the original LEGO Minifigures line, could there possibly be any more identities to explore? The answer, coming from the 16 characters in this collection, was a resounding "Yes!" Fright Knight, Monkey King, Mummy Queen, Pizza Costume Guy, and Fox Costume Girl were just some of the new names waiting to be found.

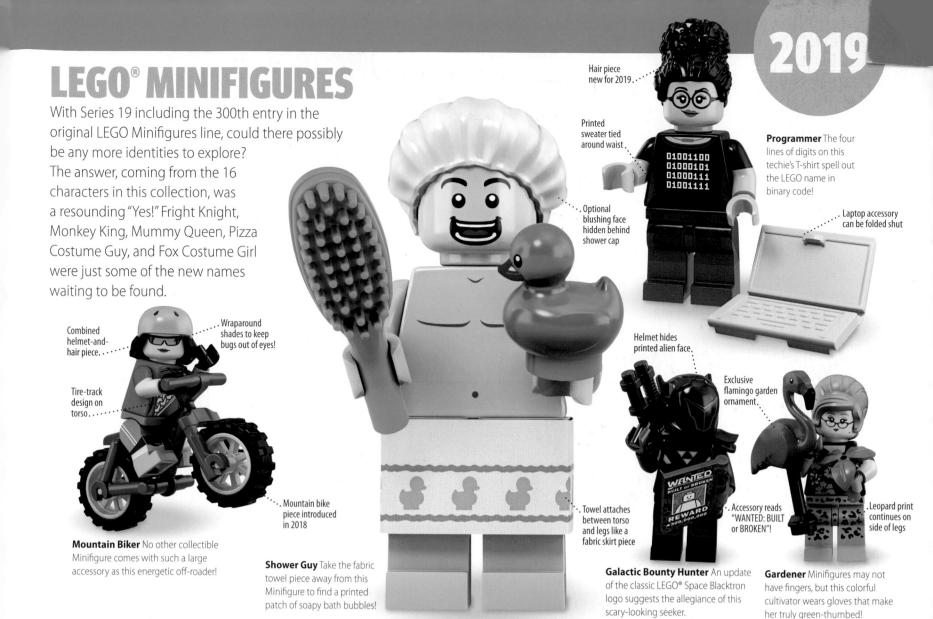

Hair piece new for 2019

Programmer The four lines of digits on this techie's T-shirt spell out the LEGO name in binary code!

Printed sweater tied around waist

01001100
01000101
01000111
01001111

Laptop accessory can be folded shut

Optional blushing face hidden behind shower cap

Combined helmet-and-hair piece

Wraparound shades to keep bugs out of eyes!

Tire-track design on torso

Mountain bike piece introduced in 2018

Helmet hides printed alien face

Exclusive flamingo garden ornament

Towel attaches between torso and legs like a fabric skirt piece

Accessory reads "WANTED: BUILT or BROKEN"!

Leopard print continues on side of legs

Mountain Biker No other collectible Minifigure comes with such a large accessory as this energetic off-roader!

Shower Guy Take the fabric towel piece away from this Minifigure to find a printed patch of soapy bath bubbles!

Galactic Bounty Hunter An update of the classic LEGO® Space Blacktron logo suggests the allegiance of this scary-looking seeker.

Gardener Minifigures may not have fingers, but this colorful cultivator wears gloves that make her truly green-thumbed!

LEGO® NINJAGO®

Fire and ice set the temperature of NINJAGO sets in 2019. First, the Serpentine sorcerer Aspheera lit up the city with her flaming Pyro Viper soldiers. Then the ninja faced the Ice Emperor and his army of Blizzard Samurai in the frozen Never-Realm! New friends helped the team along the way, as did the freshly rediscovered powers of Forbidden Spinjitzu!

New-look Serpentine head design

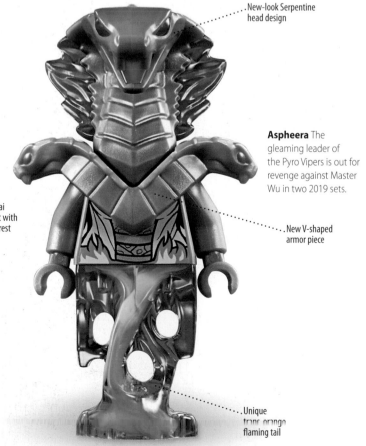

Aspheera The gleaming leader of the Pyro Vipers is out for revenge against Master Wu in two 2019 sets.

New V-shaped armor piece

Unique trans-orange flaming tail

Wolf hood hints at dual identity

Akita This shape-shifter appears in two 2019 sets—once as a minifigure and once as a red and white wolf!

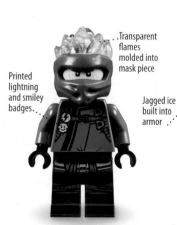

Transparent flames molded into mask piece

Printed lightning and smiley badges

Jay FS All six of the ninja blaze with fearsome Forbidden Spinjitzu powers across a range of Never-Realm sets.

Samurai helmet with icicle crest

Jagged ice built into armor

Ice Emperor The Never-Realm's ruler wasn't always bad. If only he could remember who he used to be!

2020s

The new decade brought with it fresh innovations, including two-headed minifigures, four-legged figures, and even "flying" DC Super Heroes minifigures! New themes based on favorite film series introduced characters from LEGO® Minions and LEGO® Trolls World Tour, while the LEGO® Disney™ storybook sets debuted the micro doll. LEGO heritage was also celebrated with new versions of the much-loved classic astronaut and engine driver minifigures.

Dark red cap most often worn by LEGO City train crew.

THE FUTURE'S SO BRIGHT, I'VE GOT TO WEAR SHADES!

Printed letter tile in use since 1982!

New LEGO Postal Service logo

Air Mail Pilot Aviator sunglasses protect this pilot's eyes when he flies above the clouds in his Mail Plane (60250).

2020

ALONG WITH INTRODUCING all-new figures, 2020 saw many classic minifigures getting updates for the new year. The inhabitants of LEGO® CITY continued to lead busy lives, but now with more characters than ever, and the heroes of Ninjago City stayed true to their ninja training while also embracing video gaming. LEGO® Hidden Side stepped up the spookiness, with themes based on licensed fictional universes adding must-have characters to an ever-growing roster of goodies, baddies, and everything in between.

LEGO CITY

The popularity of animated TV series LEGO® *CITY Adventures* saw more of its minifigure stars make the leap from screen to set during this year. Most were cops or crooks, but there was also Harl Hubbs's car mechanic mate, Tread Octane. Later in the year, a whole new wave of heroes took the plunge in the new Ocean Explorers subtheme.

New breathing mask with headlamps

Classic LEGO® Space-style oxygen tanks

Detachable flippers introduced in 2011.

Diver This scientist and her diving buddy get close to sharks and shipwrecks in the huge Ocean Exploration Ship (60266).

Smart bow tie

Hair tied back for working with food

Hair can be swapped for welding mask.

Steering wheel chain worn around neck

Ice-Cream Vendor The owner of LEGO CITY's first Ice-Cream Truck (60253) takes pride in having the coolest customers.

Tread Octane Tuning Workshop (60258) is where this grease monkey checks the oil in his hot rod— and on his hair!

Seatbelt-style buckle

POLICE

In 2020, more CITY sets than ever before featured named characters. In Police sets, they included LEGO *CITY Adventures* officers Duke DeTain, Sam Grizzled, and Rooky Partnur and crooks Snake Rattler, Vito, and Daisy Kaboom!

Hair can be swapped for flying helmet

Intense expression can be swapped for masked face

Identifying mole stands out in police line-ups.

Striped tie hints at future convict clothes!

Gloves help keep firm grip on helicopter controls.

First CITY minifigure to have this hair piece

Rooky Partnur This fresh-faced law enforcer pilots a police chopper that really flies in Police Helicopter Transport (60244).

Vito Police officer Duke DeTain puts the brakes on this crook when he steals a safe using his sports car.

Ribbon shows awards for service

Ragged prison gear under jacket

Daisy Kaboom With her dyed, orange-tipped hair and personalized car license plate (K4B00M), this crook doesn't care about laying low!

Wheeler CITY Police chief Percival "Wheelie" Wheeler is the first LEGO lawman to speed into action on a skateboard.

Skateboards found in more than 50 sets

Studded belt

LEGO® NINJAGO®

The six ninja faced their greatest ever challenges in 2020! When video game *Prime Empire* took Ninjago City by storm, they were drawn into its digital realm to face Emperor Unagami and his Rat Pack. Then, back in the real world, they visited the seemingly peaceful kingdom of Shintaro—only to uncover the dark influence of the Skull Sorcerer!

Printed stats bar show's Jay's in-game health levels

Weapon handle shaped like video game controller

Digi Jay All six ninja have "Digi" versions in the Prime Empire, complete with stats bars hanging over their heads!

Stats bar connects to shoulder armor

Richie Like the rest of Unagami's Rat Pack, rodent-faced Richie rides a hoverboard and carries in-game bonuses in his belt.

Pixelated potion in belt

Stud shooters built into hoverboard

New visor piece

One armor-clad arm for defense

One bare arm for ease of movement in battle

Armored Cole The Master of Earth and his fellow ninja don gladiator-style gear when they go underground in Shintaro.

Unagami This virtual villain menaces the ninja in three sets—twice on foot and once on his Empire Dragon (71713)!

Mask covers plain black minifigure head

Skull Sorcerer This masked menace guards the powerful Blades of Deliverance in two of the year's biggest NINJAGO sets.

Wings first worn by the Bat Tribe in LEGO® Legends of Chima™

New ponytail piece also available in black

Unique perfectly pointed beard

Circuit-style pathways printed on torso and skirt piece

LEGO® TROLLS WORLD TOUR

Just like the DreamWorks movie on which the theme is based, LEGO Trolls World Tour was all about dancing to your own tune! Its colorful characters all belonged to musical tribes, and each one rocked their own style. The movie stars were based on the must-have Troll Dolls of the 1960s, so they were no strangers to being plastic playthings!

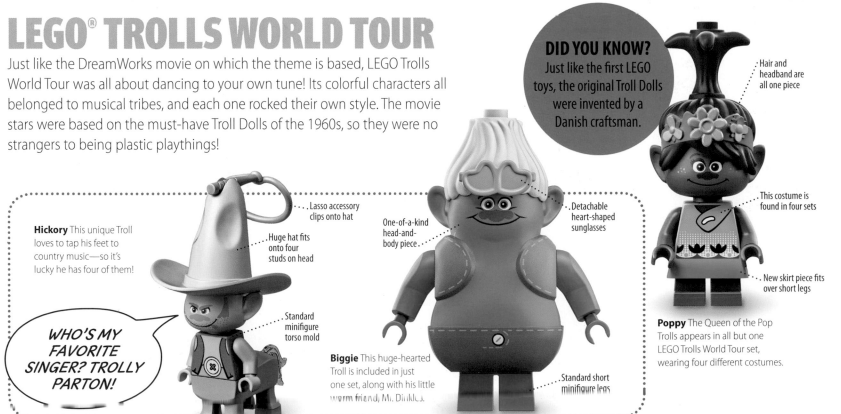

DID YOU KNOW?
Just like the first LEGO toys, the original Troll Dolls were invented by a Danish craftsman.

Hickory This unique Troll loves to tap his feet to country music—so it's lucky he has four of them!

WHO'S MY FAVORITE SINGER? TROLLY PARTON!

Lasso accessory clips onto hat

Huge hat fits onto four studs on head

Standard minifigure torso mold

Unique four-legged lower body

One-of-a-kind head-and-body piece

Biggie This huge-hearted Troll is included in just one set, along with his little worm friend, Mr. Dinkles.

Detachable heart-shaped sunglasses

Standard short minifigure legs

Hair and headband are all one piece

This costume is found in four sets

New skirt piece fits over short legs

Poppy The Queen of the Pop Trolls appears in all but one LEGO Trolls World Tour set, wearing four different costumes.

LEGO HIDDEN SIDE

Back for a second year of split-personality sets and Augmented Reality action, Hidden Side was spookier than ever in 2020! With new haunts, including a creepy castle, a subway station, and a fairground where the clowns were literally bursting with energy, Jack and Parker needed all their smarts (and their smartphones) to stay one step ahead of the specters.

Scott's everyday welding mask

New ghostly part connects both heads to torso

Ordinary mechanic's overalls

I'M NOT POSSESSED! I'VE JUST GOT A ROTTEN COLD!

Unhaunted version of head

Friendly, everyday face

Retro Octan Gas logo

Scott Francis The first minifigure to wear two heads at once also comes with a third, showing his normal appearance!

Hat and hair are one new piece

New double-sided face print on head

Jack Davids The hood is off in 2020, with Jack wearing his baseball cap backward and showing off his hair!

Combined hair-and-headphones piece

Black-and-turquoise diving suit

Parker L. Jackson Jack's best buddy wears headphones in all her 2020 sets but dons diving gear in just one.

No alternative head—this guy is always ghostly!

Nehmaar Reem Newbury's biggest baddie and his scary Shadow-Walkers menace Jack, Parker, and Vaughn in Mystery Castle (70437).

Ghost head can be swapped for standard clown head

New haunted body part fits between legs and torso

Ruffle first worn by 2012's Actor collectible Minifigure

Terry Top This clown looks spooky even when he isn't possessed. He's literally bursting with badness when he *is* possessed!

Standard legs slot into swirling smoke piece

Smiling retro screen piece

Standard minifigure legs.

TeeVee This small-screen sidekick is a close robo-relation of the LEGO Alpha Team communications robot released in 2001.

LEGO® FRIENDS

Chef Lillie made her mini doll debut in 2019, but in 2020, she became a star, hosting a TV show in Baking Competition (41393). In the same set, contestants Stephanie and David wear exclusive aprons.

Stylishly angled toque hat.

Monogrammed chef's whites.

Lillie This brilliant baker's hat-and-hair piece was first made for the collectible Minifigures theme and worn by 2017's Gourmet Chef.

Villainous smirk.

Young Gru Featuring a standard head, torso, and legs, Young Gru is the only true minifigure in the Minions theme.

LEGO® MINIONS

While the LEGO Minions themselves were not technically minifigures, they were led by one in the form of their super-villain human leader, Young Gru. The first two sets released to tie in with the upcoming movie *Minions: The Rise of Gru* celebrated the fun of these mischievous yellow characters—one set with giant brick-built Minion models, and the other with a thrilling motorcycle chase!

Double-height head piece

Kevin Wearing a hard hat and sly expression, Kevin is ready to build amazing inventions with his trusty wrench.

Stuart Though happiest clad in classic overalls, Stuart also wears comfy, striped pajamas. Time for a nap!

Short arms rotate just like a minifigure's.

LEGO® HARRY POTTER™

This year's Wizarding World sets went far beyond Hogwarts—venturing from Privet Drive to The Burrow via the Forbidden Forest! School was still on the schedule, however, with sets depicting both the Room of Requirement and Professor Slughorn's lavish office. As the home of the Slug Club Christmas Party, this latter location also came with eight new smartly dressed minifigures.

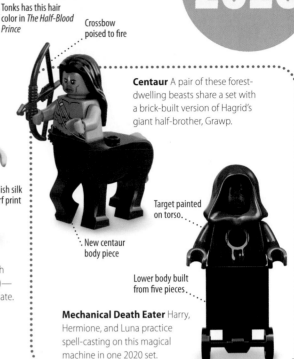

Tonks has this hair color in *The Half-Blood Prince*

Crossbow poised to fire

Centaur A pair of these forest-dwelling beasts share a set with a brick-built version of Hagrid's giant half-brother, Grawp.

New centaur body piece

Stylish silk scarf print

Target painted on torso.

Lower body built from five pieces

Monogram of Slug Club founder Horace Slughorn.

Petunia Dursley Harry's mean aunt makes her minifigure debut alongside an updated version of her equally unpleasant husband, Vernon.

Stern expression

Nymphadora Tonks This Hufflepuff hero battles Death Eaters in The Burrow (75980)—her sole set appearance to date.

Neville Longbottom Of all the minifigures at the Slug Club party, only nonguest Neville has to wear a waiter's uniform.

Spotless white gloves

Dreary fall leaves on blouse

Mechanical Death Eater Harry, Hermione, and Luna practice spell-casting on this magical machine in one 2020 set.

Elemental blade originally designed for LEGO® NINJAGO® sets

SERIES 20

Peapod Costume Girl led the fresh crop of characters in 2020, alongside Sea Rescuer, Drone Boy, and Llama Costume Girl. Not quite so fresh but bordering on funky was the 80s Musician—complete with keytar.

Lime green lipstick completes her look

Apple accessories first seen in LEGO® SCALA™ sets

Space Fan Goggles disguise the stars in her eyes, but this future astronaut wears her space fandom with pride.

Torso print based on a LEGO® Space set from 1979

LEGO® MINIFIGURES

Collectible Minifigures reached another landmark this year, with Series 20 of the main line hitting shops in the spring. The collection included eight female and eight male Minifigures, plus new turtle, toy rabbit, and piñata accessories. At the very start of the year, there was also a LEGO® DC Super Heroes series that showcased characters spanning 80 years of comic-book history.

Blueprint for included rocket accessory

Peapod Costume Girl This fruit-and-veggie-loving Minifigure would like to grow her own food, but she doesn't have a green thumb!

Super Warrlor Inspired by Japanese super hero culture, this martial arts master hides his identity under a unique helmet.

Hair worn in bunches

Transparent wing piece

Printed goggles

DC SUPER HEROES SERIES

All-time icons and lesser-known fan favorites made up this DC comic-book collection. And thanks to a new transparent stand piece, each one could be displayed as if they were flying or leaping into action!

Distinctive dog-eared cowl

Exclusive comic-book piece

IF THE FLASH IS SO FAST, WHY IS HE STILL ON THIS PAGE?

American Eagle symbol

Lasso of Truth

Speed Force accessories fit onto neck bracket.

Transparent "flying" piece

Bat-Mite This bat-fan from the fifth dimension first caused trouble for the Caped Crusader in comics from the 1950s.

Golden wings printed on ankles

Skirt design echoes US flag

Wonder Woman In her classic 1940s outfit, this all-star Amazon flies the flag for the United States—as a skirt!

Energy blast accessories

Bumblebee Teen Titans fans are sure to get a buzz from the first minifigure to depict high-flying scientist Karen Beecher.

The Flash The original speedster, Jay Garrick, can keep up with anything but fashion, so he looks very different from his modern-day counterpart.

I'M MAKING THIS INTO MY WEB PAGE!

LEGO® MARVEL SUPER HEROES

Black Widow went solo with her own film and an updated minifigure in 2020. Meanwhile, Spider-Man teamed up with fellow Web Warriors Spider-Man Noir, a new Spider-Girl, and the supremely silly Spider-Ham. Elsewhere, other members of the Avengers team faced off against heavily armed A.I.M. (Advanced Idea Mechanics) agents, in sets based on the year's new *Marvel's Avengers* video game.

Half-mask shows off confident smile

Spider-Girl High school student Anya Corazon shows off her web-spinning powers in the Spider-Man vs. Doc Ock set (76148).

A.I.M. Agent These high-tech henchmen use Super Hero-stopping gear against Thor, Black Panther, Captain America, and Hawkeye in 2020 sets.

Molded breather covers a printed one

A.I.M.-branded body armor

Unique cartoon pig head piece

Spider-Ham Also known as Peter Porker, the unlikely hero of Earth-8311 hogs all the attention in *Venomosaurus Ambush* (76151).

Fedora hat first seen in LEGO® *Indiana Jones*™ sets

Goggles over spider-web mask

Spider-Man Noir This Peter Parker from an alternative Earth dresses all in black to blend into his world's darkest shadows.

Long black trenchcoat

Hourglass belt buckle

Holsters strapped across each leg

Black Widow The fifth Natasha Romanoff minifigure since 2012 takes on the terrible Taskmaster villain in Black Widow's Helicopter Chase (76162).

Mulan The star of *Mulan's Storybook Adventures* (43174) has a mini doll head piece on a new single-piece body.

Figure stands around three bricks high

Arms do not move

LEGO® DISNEY™

A new chapter of the LEGO Disney story began in 2020. A range of storybook-shaped cases opened to reveal fairytale worlds, plus new micro doll figures to inhabit them! Closing the "books" made them easy to store and carry.

Eyes are larger than 2016's Beast mini doll

The Beast This cursed prince can be transformed using a human mini doll head also included in *Belle's Storybook Adventures* (43177).

Hands cannot hold minifigure accessories

LEGO® STAR WARS™

A new decade of LEGO *Star Wars* began in style, with sets spanning the entire Skywalker saga and beyond. Duel on Mustafar (75269) recreated a famous scene from the prequel movies, while Obi-Wan's Hut (75270) and Luke Skywalker's Landspeeder (75271) revisited the original 1977 film. There were also sets based on 2019's *The Rise of Skywalker* and the TV show *The Mandalorian*.

Brand-new head piece

The Child By far the cutest character in *The Mandalorian*, this Yoda lookalike is doubly adorable in LEGO form.

Helmet design also available in white

Sith Jet Trooper Two of these scarlet flyers are found in the Sith Troopers Battle Pack (75266) and nowhere else.

Exclusive red jet pack piece

Jet trooper symbol

Face print used for Luke since 2015

One of four hairstyles that have been used for Luke

Luke Skywalker The tenth variant of Luke on the planet Tatooine is the first to wear a stylish fabric poncho.

Unique hair-and-visor piece

Energy bow weapon

Grappling gear attached to belt

Jannah This warrior chief from the planet Kef Bir makes her first minifigure appearance in Poe Dameron's X-wing Fighter (75273).

LEGO Trains logo replaces real-world logos used in 1980

40 Years of LEGO Trains (40370) This set recreates a 1980 release and was included with certain purchases in LEGO Stores and online.

Front torso print found in eight 1980 Trains sets

Engine Driver This minifigure is identical to one first seen in 1980, but with even sharper, 21st-century printing on his torso.

Plain blue legs found in more than 750 sets

Helmet can be swapped for a flowing hair piece

Jaguar I-PACE eTROPHY Driver The "e" on this racer's unique outfit shows that she races an all-electric, zero-emissions car.

White-and-pale-blue racing suit

LEGO® EXCLUSIVE

The year 2020 marked the 40th anniversary of the original LEGO® Trains theme. For a limited time, fans could get their hands on a special celebratory build. Later in the year, the spectrum of classic LEGO® Space minifigures came closer to completion when a cheery orange astronaut was exclusively designed for DK's LEGO® *Minifigure: A Visual History*.

First bright orange helmet in this style

Orange Spaceman This DK exclusive follows in the footsteps of red, white, yellow, blue, black, green, and pink LEGO Space explorers.

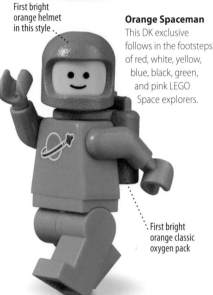

First bright orange classic oxygen pack

LEGO® SPEED CHAMPIONS

The LEGO supercar theme was finely retuned in 2020, with its latest line of vehicles coming out of the workshop wider and more detailed than ever before. The change in scale was notable, but not enough to stop minifigures from taking the wheel. This year's crop included drivers for Jaguar and Lamborghini, both of which were making their debut in the theme.

Face print first used in 2019

Lamborghini badge shown in more detail on back

Lamborghini Huracán Super Trofeo EVO Driver Both of 2020's Lamborghini drivers wear the same black-and-white racing suit.

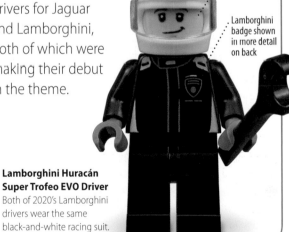

Headband above eyes

Yellow minifigure "skin" visible through mask

Raid Captain This minifigure is distinguished from other Illagers by the Ominous Banner flying above his head.

Unique printed banner piece

Pixelated version of Kai's 2018 robes

Minecraft crossbow new for 2020

Neck bracket used to connect banner

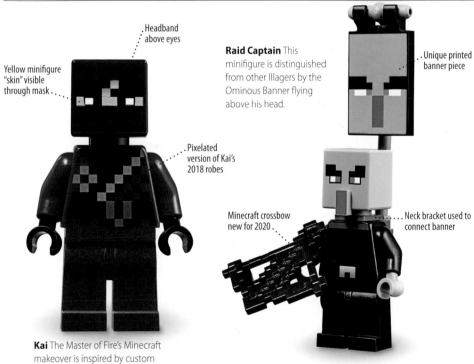

Kai The Master of Fire's Minecraft makeover is inspired by custom character skins made by NINJAGO fans online.

DID YOU KNOW? Minecraft Illagers and Pillagers are hostile—and not to be confused with harmless Villagers!

LEGO® MINECRAFT™

This enduring video game theme clocked in its 50th minifigure-scale set in 2020. Brick-built additions to the ever-expanding world included a cuddly pair of pandas and an enormous Ravager beast, while a Knight and three rampaging Illagers were among the new minifigures. And to top it all off, there was even a special guest appearance from the realm of NINJAGO!

Classic Minecraft shield

Knight This knight in shining armor faces Illagers and an Iron Golem in his sole set appearance to date.

Iron ax accessory

Silver metallic body parts

Index

SOMETHING FISHY IS GOING ON HERE.

WHAT A FIN-TASTIC BOOK!

I'M GETTING REALLY HACKED OFF WITH THIS SILLY HELMET!

ACKNOWLEDGMENTS

Dorling Kindersley would like to thank the following people
and companies for their help in producing this book:

Pamela Afram, Jo Casey, Hannah Dolan, Rahul Ganguly, Emma Grange, Zoe Hedges, Gaurav Joshi,
Lindsay Kent, Lauren Nesworthy, Garima Sharma, Catherine Saunders, Claire Sipi, and Lisa Stock for
editorial assistance; Neha Ahuja, Liam Drane, Ian Ebstein, John Goldsmid, Jon Hall, Guy Harvey,
Mary Lytle, Lisa Robb, Lauren Rosier, Anamica Roy, Clive Savage, Anne Sharples, Rajdeep Singh,
Chitrak Srivastava, Rhys Thomas, and Toby Truphet for design assistance; Edel Schwarz Andersen,
Paul Hansford, Kristian Reimer Hauge, Heidi K. Jensen, Martin Leighton Lindhardt, Jette Orduna,
Elsebeth Søgaard, Randi Sørensen, and Tara Wike at the LEGO Group; Ferrari S.p.A. for inclusion of
their minifigures; MINI for inclusion of their minifigures; James Camplin and Lucy Boughton for
additional consultancy help; Rob Catton and Alastair Cochrane for calculation work; Joseph
Pellegrino for additional photography; Huw Millington and the brickset.com community;
and, lastly, all the wonderful LEGO fans and collectors from across the world who lent us their
minifigures to be photographed: Ann and Andy at minifigforlife.com, Jeremy Allen, Suzanne Allen,
Carl Olof Andersson, Bozó Balázs, Daniel Cooley, Prentice Donnelly, Helen Floodgate, Lluís Gibert,
Tim Goddard, Doug Harefeld, Ben Johnson, Wesley Keen, Giles Kemp, David Kirkham at
minifigsandbricks.co.uk, Simon La Thangue, Richard Lawson, Mark Lee, Brandon Liu, Stefano Maini,
David McClatchey, Neal McClatchey, Huw Millington, Jon Roke, Caroline Savage, Harry Sinclair,
Joseph Venutolo, Sophie Walker, Adam White, and Mark Willis.